THE KING'S

RANGER

The King's Ranger

THOMAS BROWN AND THE

AMERICAN REVOLUTION ON

THE SOUTHERN FRONTIER

EDWARD J. CASHIN

FORDHAM UNIVERSITY PRESS

NEW YORK • 1999

LC 98-56007
ISBN 0-8232-1907-0 (hardcover)
ISBN 0-8232-1908-9 (paperback)

Library of Congress Cataloging-in-Publication Data

Cashin, Edward J., 1927–

    The king's ranger : Thomas Brown and the American Revolution on
the southern frontier / Edward J. Cashin.

      p. cm.

    Originally published: Athens : University of Georgia Press,
© 1989. With new preface.

    Includes bibliographical references (p.   ) and index.

    ISBN 0-8232-1907-0 (hc.)—ISBN 0-8232-1908-9 (pbk.)

    1. Brown, Thomas, 1750–1825.   2. Georgia—History—Revolution,
1775–1783—Biography.   3. United States—History—Revolution,
1775–1783—Biography.   4. American loyalists—Georgia—Biography.
I. Title.

E278.B862C37   1999

973.3′458′092—dc21

[B]   98-56007

          CIP

Maps on pages 60, 176–77, and 198 were drawn by Cartographic Services,
University of Georgia
Text design by Richard Hendel
Printed in the United States of America

To Mary Ann

CONTENTS

MAPS

PREFACE TO THE 1999 EDITION

I welcome the opportunity to introduce Thomas Brown to a new readership. Few participants in the American Revolution had a more dangerous or eventful career, and few figured in such pivotal events as this son of a distinguished Yorkshire family. By following Thomas Brown's adventures, the reader can make sense of the course of the American Revolution on the southern frontier. Given the complexity of the history of that sector, that is no small accomplishment. In fact, the history of the southern phase of the war is so complicated that historians have shied away from it, or have confined themselves to events eastward of the Savannah River. Our school texts dwell on Lexington and Concord, then follow General Washington's heroic efforts to keep his army in the field, and only after Saratoga and the stalemate in the North do they come South, and then it is to describe Cornwallis's long campaign leading to Yorktown. Teachers in their classrooms have no time to do more. As a result, Georgia and the Floridas are peripheral, at best, in our collective memory of the Revolution, and the role of the Indian Nations so murky as not to matter.

The difficulty of enlarging our perspective to include the southern frontier was brought home to me when I met with the producers of a distinguished documentary about the Revolution. I summarized the interpretation in *The King's Ranger*, that the "frontier" was not an empty wilderness, but alive with the people of the Indian Nations. I explained about the origin and unfolding of "the southern strategy," and what happened to the Loyalists after the war. They seemed interested—at least, I think they were—but when I finished, one of them said sadly, "But we have allocated only one of six episodes to the war in the South." They had time only for Cornwallis's campaign through the Carolinas.

The story is complex, but the reward of a careful reading is the intellectual satisfaction one gets when something difficult makes sense. The outline of the main themes is part of the preface to the earlier edition. We need only mention the amazing fact that Thomas Brown took part in all the major engagements and many of the minor skirmishes of the Revolution on the southern frontier, and survived them all. Georgians vilified him after the war as the consummate Tory, as well as for his post-war role in attaching the Creek Nation to the Spanish allegiance. However, he lived as a hero in the Bahamas, and on a grand scale as master of a succession of plantations in the British West Indies, until the bizarre episode on the Island of St. Vincents.

I will take advantage of this opportunity to correct a mistake in the original. I relied on the reminiscences of Thomas Woodward for the account of David Taitt's death as he led a band of Creek Indians to join Thomas Brown in Augusta in 1780. A hint by Kathryn Braund led me to write Dr. Robert J. Morgan, Director of Beaton Institute, University College of Cape Breton, Nova Scotia. Dr. Morgan had done a great deal of research on David Taitt, and provided a summary. When the Spanish attacked West Florida in 1780, Taitt was taken prisoner. He escaped and made his way to London. As compensation for his good service and for his losses, he received land grants in Nova Scotia, where he went in 1784 as the first Provost Marshall of Cape Breton. Taitt, an able surveyor, laid out the town of Sydney. Twice appointed to the colony's executive council, Taitt lived to an honored old age, dying in 1834 at the age of 94. He is buried in St. Paul's Churchyard, Halifax.

I wish to thank Paul Cimbala of the Fordham history faculty for bringing *The King's Ranger* to the attention of Fordham University Press, and Saverio Procario, Director of the Press, for the decision to reissue the book. I am pleased and privileged to thus be again associated with my alma mater, Fordham University.

Augusta State University   EDWARD J. CASHIN

It is impossible to study the American Revolution in Georgia without confronting the name of Thomas Brown at every turn. If one delves into South Carolina and Florida histories, he is there, too. It was equally impossible for men and women of my generation to grow up in Augusta without hearing about the cruel Colonel Brown, the man who hanged thirteen patriots so he could gloat over their suffering. The house where the deed was done was said to be the ancient "White House" on Broad Street. Young boys gave it a wide berth because it was well known that the ghosts of the martyred victims still haunted the place. The villainy of Thomas Brown represented that of the king himself. It was evident to every schoolboy that we had done well to rebel against the likes of Thomas Brown.

An investigation into the American career of Thomas Brown revealed that his story provides a convenient focus for the history of the American Revolution in the South. More significantly, it suggested a new interpretation of that epochal event. That interpretation, which is the theme of the chapters that follow, may be summarized briefly. Thomas Brown came to America in response to Governor James Wright's proclamation opening Georgia's new "Ceded Lands" above the Little River for settlement. The Creek Indians, disgruntled at the cession, went on the warpath and halted further occupation of the new lands. The backcountrymen had reason to believe that the government was partial to the traders and their Indian clients. They were alarmed by the rumor that royal agents were deliberately fomenting an Indian war to put a stop to white encroachment on the hunting grounds. Thomas Brown, the most prominent of the new arrivals, was accused of being a spy and the illegitimate son of Lord North. He defended the king's interests with vigor and was brutally assaulted on August 2, 1775, an event that marked the beginning of the American Revolution in the Georgia backcountry. Brown found allies in neighboring South Carolina and with them formulated a strategy that won the approval of Carolina Governor Lord William

Campbell. They proposed to involve the Indians in a frontier offensive in conjunction with a landing of troops on the coast. The royal governors of Georgia and Florida endorsed this plan, and, for lack of another, it became the obsession of Lord George Germain, the war minister.

Whatever the military merits of the plan, it was hardly calculated to win the hearts and minds of the people of the backcountry, who feared and hated Indians. If the British sided with the savages, they seemed to say, then they were for independence. The prize they sought was the Indian land.

Thomas Brown could not have guessed, when he first proposed the plan, that he would be made superintendent of Indians and charged with the responsibility of carrying out the strategy. To follow Brown on his adventures is to learn much of the complexity of the military, political, and social aspects of the American Revolution.

The account of the unfolding of the British master plan encompasses several subplots: the migration to America, the social upheaval in the backcountry, Indian diplomacy, border warfare, the wrangling between British and military and civil officials, the restoration of Georgia to royal rule, the British evacuation of Georgia, South Carolina, and Florida, the new frontiers of settlement in the Caribbean Islands.

The story of Thomas Brown is the thread that ties together these and other events. Bold to the point of rashness, enterprising, charismatic, sometimes cruel and sometimes gentle, resilient after each adversity, Thomas Brown was, above all, exciting.

The search for information about Thomas Brown proved as interesting as the man himself. Joe Means showed me where Brownsborough was located, a few miles north of Appling in Columbia County. The Georgia patriot and signer of the Constitution William Few claimed Brownsborough as his portion of the spoils of war. Few sold the Brownsborough tract to Juriah Harris, and the now-isolated grave of Juriah Harris marks the spot.

The search benefited from an astounding bit of good luck. While corresponding with a staff person at Oxford's Bodleian Library about another matter, I mentioned my interest in Thomas Brown. The librarian, Joan Leggett, replied that she was a direct descendant of Brown. I am indebted to Mrs. Leggett for some important documents relating to her family history. Subsequently, Joan and her hus-

band, Derek, visited Georgia to view sites connected with her ancestor. She was only partly jesting when she claimed to feel psychic
vibrations as we rode through the woodland that once was Brownsborough.

The search led to Whitby in Yorkshire, England, and to the dis-
covery that Jonas Brown's Newton House was still there, eight miles
southwest of the town. A. A. Berends, keeper of the Whitby Museum,
became interested in Thomas Brown and joined the investigation. He
found a treasure trove of information in a collection of scrapbooks
compiled by a man named Waddington during the nineteenth century. He was also able to find Brown's birthdate in the church register and the location of his boyhood home on a quaint, narrow road
called Grape Lane.

From Whitby the search took us to the far north and the Orkney
Islands. My family suffered hunger pangs on the long train ride, shiv-
ered in the cold of John O'Groats, the northernmost point of the
mainland of Scotland, and were seasick on the bouncy ferry crossing.
Our kindly hostess at a Kirkwall bed and breakfast revived us with
tea and cakes and the warmth of her hospitality, but my family did
not forgive me for a long while. I had written to the archivist at the
Kirkwall Library that I wanted to look at the Balfour Papers for
information about Brown's servants, who were recruited in the
Orkneys, but I neglected to specify the date of my arrival. The archivist had gone on a week's vacation, and no one could find the key to
the archives. The emotion one feels on such an occasion is too pro-
found to be called frustration. Nevertheless, some useful material
was turned up in local histories.

From one extreme to the other, the search brought us to St. Vincent, the lovely island eighty miles west of Barbados, Thomas
Brown's final resting place. Dr. Earle Kirby, a retired veterinarian,
was an excellent guide. He introduced Lester Browne, a direct descendant of Thomas Brown, who was born on the island and edu-
cated in England. We visited Montague House, which has suffered in
its appearance since Thomas Brown built it around 1820 but is still
sturdy and imposing. Not far away is the cemetery plot where the
colonel is buried. In the little church in the nearby village of Georgetown is a plaque to the memory of the colonel and his son the Reverend Thomas A. M. Browne, who was rector of the parish.

Finally, this investigation included research in the inexhaustible
material at the British Museum, the Public Record Office on Chan-

cery Lane, and the new branch at Kew, where portable electronic beepers provide a sharp contrast to the musty old documents they announce.

Heather Lancaster of London is another direct descendant of Thomas Brown, the third we met. She showed us the invaluable Thomas Alexander Browne Collection, named for the colonel's grandson, and gave permission to copy the microfilm of the collection. I am indebted to James E. Derriman for his efficient research into the court records of the King's Bench at the Public Record Office on Chancery Lane.

I want to thank Galen Wilson for his courteous help in my several visits to the William L. Clements Library in Ann Arbor. I should acknowledge the assistance of the staff at the other depositories visited: the William Perkins Library at Duke University, the P. K. Yonge Library at the University of Florida, the St. Augustine Historical Society, the Special Collections Room, University of Georgia Libraries, the South Caroliniana Library at the University of South Carolina in Columbia, the Georgia Department of Archives and History in Atlanta, the New-York Historical Society and the New York Public Library, the Boston Public Library, and the Library of Congress in Washington, D.C.

I am indebted to Phinizy Spalding, Heard Robertson, and Iris Dillard for reading the manuscript and offering suggestions. I appreciate Kaye Keel's cheerful patience in typing the text. I am grateful to the librarians of Reese Library, Augusta College, for their continued assistance in obtaining interlibrary loans and doing bibliographic searches. A. Ray Rowland heads the staff, which includes Mary Ann Cashin, who manages to combine the duties of reference librarian with those of my wife and companion in the long, sometimes taxing, but always interesting search for Thomas Brown.

THE KING'S

RANGER

CHAPTER ONE

FROM YORKSHIRE

TO GEORGIA

Thomas Brown was born on May 27, 1750, in the seaport town of Whitby in Yorkshire's North Riding. His father, Jonas, was a member of a distinguished family, which included Sir Anthony Browne, master of horse to King Henry VIII. A relative claimed the title, though there was some question as to whether Jonas's great-grandfather had been disinherited by Queen Mary for becoming a Protestant.[1] Jonas was a native of Whitby, an ancient fishing town that straddles the River Esk as it enters the North Sea. A description of twentieth-century Whitby would have been as apt in the mid-eighteenth century: "Picturesque in itself with its red roofs and quaint gables, nestling under the cliffs and dominated by the noble ruin of its Abbey on the east, Whitby is as beautiful as any town on the English coast."[2] Beautiful it was and is, but it is fogbound and windswept, too, and can be as cold in July as Georgia in December. The men of Whitby are a hardy lot, and they like it the way it is.

In the year 1739, Jonas Brown married a widow ten years older than himself named Margaret Jackson. Margaret's family, the Newtons, were important in the history of Whitby; her ancestral home was the handsome Tudor mansion called Bagdale Hall. When they were first married, Jonas and Margaret lived on St. Ann's Staith, the street along the dockside of the river. A year later, the couple moved across the river to the east bank and took up more commodious lodgings in a sturdy house on Grape Lane left to him by his aunt, Jane Brown Linskill.[3]

The house was soon filled with children, Jane, Mary, Margaret, Jonas, and Thomas. The Quakers were numerous in Whitby at the time of Thomas's birth. Perhaps the Browns followed that religion for a time. The Quakers do not practice baptism, and there are no baptismal records of the Brown children in the register of old St. Mary's Anglican Parish Church. By 1755, however, the Browns were members of St. Mary's because in that year Thomas was baptized and his date of birth recorded.[4]

As Jonas Brown's family grew, his temporal affairs prospered. By 1747, he owned two ships and put to sea in one of them, the *Marlborough*, a three-hundred-ton Whitby-built "cat," a sturdy, round-bottomed vessel constructed for the carrying trade. His other ship, the *Prince Frederick*, named for the Prince of Wales, was commanded by Thomas Brown, his cousin, or possibly his brother. The relationship would have been close enough to explain Jonas's naming his second son Thomas. Jonas was a shrewd businessman; he acquired the *Hermione*, the *Flora*, the *Carolina*, and the *Resolution*. Three captains employed by Brown were from the Orkney Islands to the north of Scotland's mainland. The captain of the *Flora* was a young mariner from Kirkwall named William Manson. Manson's logs have been preserved; they show that a favored port of call was Charlestown, South Carolina. When Manson transported a cargo of deerskins from Charlestown, he could not have known that he would become a resident in the backcountry of Georgia, where the skins came from. A relative of his, Daniel Manson, settled in Charlestown and became a builder of ships.[5]

With his fortune made and his sense of adventure appeased, Jonas turned his attention to a land industry. Alum was in great demand as an agent for fixing color in textiles, and the great escarpments fronting the North Sea were rich in alum. Jonas bought into a partnership that extracted the mineral from the steep cliffs at Saltwick, just down from Whitby's east cliff. Lionel Charlton, a contemporary, in his *History of Whitby*, published in 1779, gave Brown high praise for his ingenuity. Brown devised a method of conducting water to the alum works and thereby ensured the success of the project.[6]

Thomas Brown's early life must have been oriented to the sea. From his bedroom window, he could look out across the harbor, where the River Esk met the incoming tides. Whitbyites were proud of their new drawbridge, built in 1766, when Thomas was sixteen, which divided the harbor into the upper and lower basins. The thirty-two-foot span of the bridge allowed only the lighter and narrower vessels into the upper harbor. Both harbors were usually crowded because Whitby was a thriving town when Thomas was a youth.

Shipbuilding was the principal industry, and the ancillary occupations of sail making, rope making, and canvas manufacturing employed hundreds of people. Whitby colliers monopolized the coal trade between Newcastle and London. Far more exciting was the search for whales. More and more Whitby cats brought in the valuable oil for processing.[7]

The mouth of the Esk was a gateway to adventure and danger. Two great stone piers jutted out into the unpredictable North Sea, protecting the harbor from the worst of the storms that frequented the rockbound coast. Whitby lifeboat crews were already famous for their ability to rescue sailors whose ships were blown against the rocks on either side of the harbor entrance. Out there lay the destiny of the lads of Whitby. When Thomas Brown was five, his neighbor joined the Royal Navy and sailed off to fame and glory as the discoverer of Australia. Commander James Cook learned his seamanship in Whitby cats. He sailed in the employ of John and Robert Walker, and between voyages he lived in the garret of John Walker's house on Grape Lane, just two doors away from the Browns.[8]

Thomas Brown received a classical education in Lionel Charlton's school upstairs in the Tollbooth, as the town hall was called. Charlton, the historian, would have told Thomas about the Romans who built roads across the desolate moors to Whitby, roads that lasted through time. At the Synod of Whitby in 664 A.D., the English clerics decided to follow the Roman liturgy and calendar rather than the Celtic. The great abbey was the birthplace of English literature. Around the time of the synod, during the rule of the Abbess Hilda, an illiterate cowherd named Caedmon had a vision in which he was given the gift of poetry. He amazed the monks by reciting hymns, one of which, the "Song of Caedmon," survives as the oldest Anglo-Saxon poem. The once magnificent abbey survives, also, although in slowly crumbling ruins.

Sharing the windswept east cliff with the abbey was St. Mary's Church with its cemetery. The nave of the Norman-style church was constructed in 1110; in 1220 the north and south transepts were added. Curiously, because it predated the Protestant Reformation, the sanctuary never had an altar; a simple communion table sufficed. In 1620 the then lord of the manor, in a display of ego rather than good taste, had an elevated pew box constructed directly in front of the sanctuary, effectively blocking the view of the gentry seated in the north and south galleries. It was that way when Thomas Brown at-

tended services with his father; it was still that way in 1987. A series
of steps led up the hill to the church. An incredibly steep cobblestone
road paralleled the steps, which only the foolhardy dared to drive.
Coming down they would hitch horses behind as well as in front of
the coach to break the descent. The more sensible churchgoers took a
longer route down a gentler slope.[9]

Thomas Brown was twenty-one when Commander James Cook
returned to Whitby to visit his friend John Walker. Cook had chosen
a Whitby-built cat, the *Endeavour*, to sail to the South Seas, where he
had discovered and mapped the coasts of New Zealand and Australia. King George III welcomed him on his return in 1771, and all
England sang his praises. On the last day of that year, Cook braved
the cold of Yorkshire's desolate moors and rode to Whitby. Jonas
Brown would have been in the delegation of leading citizens who
went out to meet the hero; he was a friend and neighbor of John
Walker. His sons, Jonas, Jr., and Thomas, were of age; they would
have been there, too.

The entourage entered the town by the Bagdale Road. From the
top of the hill, they could see the deep valley of the Esk and the
huddled red-tiled roofs of the houses that clustered along both banks.
As the riders descended the hill, they passed Bagdale Hall, which had
belonged to Thomas's great-grandfather, Isaac Newton, and in
which his grandmother Adeline had lived. She was dead now in the
year 1771 and so was Thomas's mother, Margaret. The welcoming
party used the new drawbridge to cross to the old section of town on
the east bank where they turned down Grape Lane and left Cook at
John Walker's house, just two doors away from the Browns'. On New
Year's Day 1772, a constant stream of visitors dropped by to pay their
respects. Soon after, Cook left Whitby to prepare for his second voyage to the South Pacific. Upon his return in 1775, he was promoted to
captain. He then departed on a third voyage, and this time he did not
return. He died bravely on a beach in Hawaii in 1779, clubbed by
natives while his own sailors watched helplessly from their long-
boats. Townsfolk never forgot Cook; the statue they raised in his
memory stands on the west cliff, providing a counterpiece to the ancient abbey opposite.[10]

It was about the time of Cook's visit that Thomas Brown went off
to see the world. He transacted business for his father in Nova Scotia,
New England, North and South Carolina, and Barbados. Young

Brown made a point of studying the laws and government of each province. As a result, he made up his mind to settle permanently in America. According to Jonas, Thomas was influenced in his decision by the cordial reception given him by "the most considerable Familys." In 1773 Jonas wrote to Nathaniel Cholmley, member of Parliament from Whitby, and recited his son's good qualities: "I can with propriety inform you that he has had a liberal education which he has greatly improved by travel. I have made it my study to inculcate in him the principles of honour and integrity." Jonas requested a colonial appointment for his son.[11]

Enclosed with Jonas's letter was one from Thomas, written in the formal language of the day. He sent Cholmley a list of positions in Georgia and South Carolina for which he would like to be considered. No appointment was forthcoming, but it is interesting that even before he read about Georgia's newly ceded lands, Thomas Brown had selected Georgia as one of his preferred locations.[12]

The year 1774 was a time of decision for Thomas and, indeed, for Jonas, also. Jonas was in love again. At the age of fifty-five he planned to marry Sarah Williams, a maid of twenty-four, the same age as Thomas. In anticipation of his marriage, he purchased a tract of land from one Tommy Newton in Ugglebarnby, eight miles southwest of Whitby, on the very edge of the bleak moorlands. Except for Newton's crude sheephouse, the site was unimproved.

Centuries earlier a hermit had used a nearby cave for his retreat, and the place was called the Hermitage. A schoolteacher named George Clubb was in charge of the construction of Jonas Brown's mansion house and outbuildings. Clubb also reconstructed a cavelike stone shelter resembling the fabled monk's hermitage and marked it with his own initials. Whitby men had to be careful in their treatment of hermits. At one time in the dimly remembered past the Hermit of Eskdaleside had put a curse on the town for some rudeness; the abbot of the monastery assigned a penance that would cancel the curse. The penance required that every year the men of Whitby were to plant a hedge at Town's End on the west bank. They still enact the ceremony. On the eve of Ascension Day, sticks resembling a hedge or "horngarth" are planted, while a deputy representing the lord of the manor blows a horn and cries, "Out on Ye!" No one seems to care that the penance has little or no relation to the offense. The important thing is to avoid retribution. It was a similar wish to placate the departed that caused George Clubb to construct a proper hermitage.[13]

The site chosen for Newton House was not suited to show it to its best advantage. It sat on a steep hill. A visitor approaching from Whitby down the Sneaton Road would catch only a glimpse of the roof and second story of the house at first; then, as one grew closer, the impressive house would appear. Jonas did not have a title and could not know then that he would inherit one in 1794, but he built as though he were Sir Jonas, lord of the manor. The hill, which inhibited a view of the house from the front, sloped to provide a vista of the moors from the rear. Jonas was more interested in the protective shelter the hill afforded than in its possibilities as a stage setting for his house. The completed mansion was meant to be a wedding present from Jonas to his bride, Sarah. The date for the wedding was set for July 5, 1774.[14]

By then Thomas Brown had decided to become a gentleman planter in America. Shipmasters returning from America brought word of newly ceded lands in Georgia's backcountry, territory opened by proclamation of Georgia Governor James Wright. The land was richer by far than that along the coast. It supported oak and hickory trees, was well watered by creeks that were suitable for mill sites, and, best of all, the region was a thousand miles away from rebellious Boston. If Brown could not go as a government official, he would go as a colonizer, recruiting settlers in Yorkshire and the Orkney Islands. For every head of a family transported, Brown would be entitled to two hundred acres, and fifty more for each family member. According to Governor Wright's notice, an initial payment of five pounds sterling for every hundred acres was required. After the grant was surveyed, another payment was due, not to exceed five shillings per acre.

Jonas posted notices around Whitby and inserted an announcement in *Etherington's York Chronicle* that the *Marlborough*, Jonas's first ship, would sail in June or July and would take passengers "to settle the new ceded valuable lands" in Georgia. Interested parties should apply to Jonas Brown for further information. The same statement was repeated in each weekly issue until the end of July. Whether the voyage was postponed until after Jonas's wedding to Sarah, or whether passengers were slow in their preparations, or whatever the reason, the departure of the *Marlborough* was delayed. The *York Chronicle* for August 12 reported that the ship had sailed that day under Captain George Pressick "with goods and imigrants for Savannah in Georgia."[15]

Similar passages had occurred hundreds of times since the trio of ships sailed into Chesapeake Bay in 1607, and thousands more would follow. For each individual the crossing was a unique and awesome experience. The *Marlborough*'s passenger list included Robert Harrison, innkeeper; David Black, bookbinder; Richard Fenton, canvas weaver, his wife, and two children; Ralph Cook, linen weaver, and his wife; John Tate, carpenter, his wife, and four children; Thomas Oliver, blacksmith, his wife, and two children; Jane Wilson, spinster; James Elliot, husbandman, and his wife; James Berry, linen weaver, and one child; Adam Dryden, gardener; and William Alexander, laborer, his wife, and three children. Twenty-nine in all, they were going "to seek for better employment, to stay there or return." The *Marlborough* sailed out of the protecting piers into the North Sea, and her passengers watched the red-tiled houses and the abbey ruins until they faded from view.[16]

The arrangement these emigrants made with Jonas and Thomas Brown was the same spelled out in greater detail in the announcement for a second transport the following year. Any person who could not pay for transportation would be contracted as a "covenant servant" for three years. Such persons would be furnished with food, lodging, and clothing. Every single man would be allotted fifteen acres of arable land, a new house, corn, cattle, and farming tools and would be supported until his crop was raised.

Every married man would have an additional ten acres for his wife and five more for each child over ten years of age. Each man agreed to cultivate his lands to the best of his ability for his own use and profit and was exempt from any taxes or rents for five years. At the expiration of his contractual time each would pay Thomas Brown one shilling per acre for five years. Thereafter the rent would be two shillings per acre.[17] Thomas Brown would thus become a transplanted lord of the manor, an American country gentleman.

Jonas would have his new mansion and outbuildings in Yorkshire and together with his bride raise a second generation of offspring. Sober, serious Jonas, Jr., would move to Kingston upon Hull, where he would distinguish himself as a magistrate and win a knighthood. The elder Jonas was a devoted father, securing the welfare of his grown children before starting a new brood. The best evidence is that it cost him a small fortune of over £3,000 to establish Thomas's

American colony.[18] It was a generous patrimony, and in a wholly unpredictable way it became the basis for Thomas Brown's postwar prosperity.

Recruiting in the Whitby area was difficult because employment was high. The Browns anticipated the problem and planned to fill the ship's complement with emigrants from the north of Scotland, then in the grip of an agricultural depression. Therefore, the *Marlborough*'s course was northward, around the eastern shoulder of Scotland, beyond the mainland to the fine harbor at Kirkwall in the Orkneys.

The Orkney Islands were and are a unique portion of Great Britain. As far north as Alaska, Canada's Hudson Bay, and the southern cape of Greenland, the Orkneys never really get dark in the summer and experience only a few hours of daylight in winter. The Gulf Stream, so beneficent to the west coast of Scotland, ensures a surprisingly mild climate and plentiful rainfall. The Orkneys confound environmentalists, who insist on the necessity of a forest cover, because the islands are almost completely bereft of trees, yet they contain the most fertile soil to be found in Scotland. At the time of the *Marlborough*'s expedition, an outmoded agricultural system had reduced the population to chronic poverty. From the time the islands were settled by the Vikings, farmers had tilled narrow, scattered strips, called "runrigs." In 1760 an effort was made to consolidate and enlarge the strips, but the resulting "sheads" were hardly an improvement. Only patches of just over an acre each, they were still separated so that a farmer would have to work them one at a time. Crop rotation, so essential to strip farming, was not practiced; no attempt was made to drain rain-soaked fields.

An Orkney historian, George Barry, wrote in 1808 that the migration of young people was caused by the "low state" of agriculture, the smallness of the farms, and "the little respect in which those connected with the cultivation of the soil are held." He characterized the farmers as indolent, wedded to old customs, averse to improvement, but sagacious, honest, faithful in marriage, and mild in temperament. In short, the ordinary Orcadian, male or female, was an entirely unsatisfactory resident of the islands. But "as soon as they remove into another country and mingle with those of their own rank and are under proper regulations, they often distinguish themselves as faithful, active, and skillful in their respective employments."[19]

Thomas Brown offered these individuals, and those from Caithness on the mainland, an opportunity to improve their condition and characters. Brown acquired a partner, James Gordon, in the Orkneys. Gordon was an acquaintance of the William Manson who had sailed under the employ of Jonas Brown. Whether from Manson or someone else, Gordon had learned of Brown's expedition and had pledged over £1,000 to become a partner with the Browns. Gordon seems to have been respected by those with whom he associated in the Orkneys and in America, but he certainly misrepresented his financial situation. He led the Browns to believe that his wealthy relatives would be forthcoming with the promised funds and borrowed money from Jonas Brown to pay for his passage to Georgia. There is evidence of advance planning in Gordon's recruiting of prospective settlers as well as in his own prior departure for Georgia to act as agent for Thomas Brown. He made arrangements with Governor James Wright for the location of the colony, and he purchased or rented LeRoy Hammond's fine house, which was called New Richmond and was located opposite Augusta. After the war, Gordon asked for compensation of £1,629. Jonas Brown, Jr., intervened to explain to the claims commissioners that Gordon had spent Brown's money, not his own. As a result, Gordon received only £117.[20]

James Gordon, as Brown's precursor, found a different Georgia than he had expected from his reading of Governor Wright's enthusiastic proclamations. Although the rebels in Boston were far away in the year 1774, the Creek Indians were altogether too close, and they were on the warpath. In fact, the Georgia backcountry was a tinderbox about to ignite. Gordon had to do a quick study of recent events in Georgia to explain the situation to the immigrants.

The cause of the incendiary condition was a contradictory British policy which attempted to open the backcountry to settlers and at the same time maintain the deerskin trade with the Indians. The principal administrator of the policy was the respected and competent James Wright, governor of Georgia since 1760, knighted by King George III in 1772.[21]

The tension in the backcountry was aggravated by what appeared to be a master stroke by Governor Wright. Wright was intrigued when he learned that the Cherokees were willing to give up a huge tract in north Georgia in return for the cancellation of debts they owed to Augusta traders. The government would sell the land and pay the traders, who would discharge their debts to merchants in Augusta, Charlestown, and London. The newly ceded lands would be settled by those who could pay for them, not by shiftless Crackers. Wright assured the Earl of Hillsborough, "They will of course be something better than the common sort of backcountry people."[22] Wright went to London to get permission to deal with the Cherokees. The ministry approved on the condition that the Creeks would give their consent also.

The journal of David Taitt, deputy of Indian Superintendent John Stuart, reveals the almost brutal pressure applied by the Augusta traders to compel the Creeks to come in for a conference in 1773. The Creeks had a better claim to the region than did the Cherokees and they were not as deeply in debt. They were extremely unwilling to discuss the matter but were told that the trade would be curtailed unless they listened to the governor's talk. So, very reluctantly, they came to Augusta in May 1773.

By now, the Georgia Assembly had entered into the scheme, and that body urged the governor to negotiate for the Oconee as a boundary rather than the Ogeechee. Land-hungry squatters began crossing the Ogeechee in anticipation of the treaty. Others crossed the Little River boundary above Augusta.[23]

William Bartram of Philadelphia, a naturalist like his famous father, John, happened to be in Augusta at the time of the conference. He described the angry reaction of the younger Creek warriors when they learned what was asked of them. They refused to give up any land west of the Ogeechee. A liberal supply of presents by Superintendent John Stuart and the persuasive influence of the older men served to quiet the warriors and save the treaty. Governor Wright had to be satisfied with only 2 million acres, about half of what he hoped for, and nothing beyond the Ogeechee. Two-thirds of the lands in question were between the Savannah and Ogeechee above the Little River; one-third lay in the swamplands and pine barrens of the low country. Even though he got less than he wanted, Wright was delighted with the richness of the northern portion. Bartram related how surveyors and speculators immediately set out from Augusta to spy out the land. Phillip Yonge's map of the region, thenceforth known as the "Ceded Lands," has been called "the finest and most detailed map of a large portion of the pre-revolutionary backcountry in existence."[24]

Wright published a proclamation on June 11, 1773, announcing the sale of the new lands. A copy of this announcement found its way to Whitby and set in motion the adventures of Thomas Brown. Governor Wright inspected the Ceded Lands and ordered a town and fort to be established at the confluence of the Broad and Savannah rivers. He gave the town the name of Dartmouth in honor of the secretary of state. Wright raised a corps of Rangers under Captain Edward Barnard of Augusta, "to keep good order amongst and for the protection of the Inhabitants in the new Ceded Lands."[25] The first task of the Rangers was to expel the numerous squatters.

Unfortunately for Wright's plans and for the peace of Georgia, some of the "mad young people" among the Creeks were determined not to allow the whites to take possession of the territory. On December 25, nine days after the Boston Tea Party, a war party massacred a white family near the headwaters of the Ogeechee on the Ceded Lands.[26]

On January 14, 1774, the Coweta Creeks struck at a stockade fort west of Wrightsborough in the southwest portion of the Ceded Lands. A day-long battle ensued in which seven of twenty whites were killed and five wounded; the Creeks suffered five casualties. Captain Barnard's Rangers and Colonel James Grierson's militia searched the area. On January 25 the Georgia militia was ambushed and routed by a party of Indians. Except for a few men of Captain William Goodgion's company, the militiamen refused to do any more fighting. The report of the incident in the *Georgia Gazette* was tinged with sarcasm: the men went home "with this silly speech in their mouths, that their families were dear to them, that they were in danger, and that they were wanted at home to protect them."[27] Silly or not, the fear of Indians would continue to terrify the frontiersmen and would cause them to stay as close as possible to their families. The Indian attacks did what the Rangers were unable to do; the Ceded Lands were cleared of squatters. The raids also curtailed the settlement promoted by Governor Wright. The "better sort" would be settled below the Little River.

If the hostilities were begun by disgruntled Creeks, they were continued by the Indian-hating settlers, who hoped to put a stop to Indian travel along the Augusta trading road. In March a peace-seeking chief of the Upper Creeks named Mad Turkey came to Augusta as the guest of Captain William Goodgion. Thomas Fee, a blacksmith, offered the chief a drink. When Mad Turkey put the bottle to his lips, the treacherous Fee crushed his skull with a bar of iron. Fee became an immediate hero to the backcountry farmers, if not to the traders. When he was apprehended by Governor Wright's orders and put in

Lands Ceded to His Majesty by the Creek and Cherokee Indians, 1773. (Drawn by Philip Yonge. Original map in the British Public Record Office. The map above was reproduced from a copy in the Hargrett Collection, University of Georgia Libraries.)

confinement at Ninety-Six, South Carolina, a mob broke into the jail and set him free.[28]

The Creek chief Emistisiguo dared to visit Governor Wright in Savannah, avoiding trigger-happy whites along the way. He agreed with the governor that an embargo on trade would compel the Creeks to punish their guilty young people. Wright managed to secure the assent of the other southern governors and ordered a stop to the trade. Those traders who were not in the habit of obeying Wright's regulations disregarded this one also and conducted clandestine bartering in the woods. Wright ordered Barnard's Rangers to end the illicit trade.[29]

Thus, in August 1774, as the *Marlborough* left Whitby with her consignment of passengers bound for Georgia's ballyhooed lands, far from the tumult of Boston, Georgia was wracked by its own peculiar troubles. For the first time since 1763, the royal government of Georgia took the part of the settlers against the usually favored traders and merchants.

So it was that when Savannah's merchants protested the British Intolerable Acts on August 10, 1774, the inhabitants of the backcountry quickly repudiated their stance. Petitions were signed in every backcountry settlement proclaiming loyalty to the king: the town and district of Augusta, St. Paul Parish, Kiokee and Broad River settlements, St. George Parish, Queensborough, the western part of St. George Parish, and the town and township of Wrightsborough. The statement of St. Paul Parish clearly enunciated the backcountry position:

> Because the persons who are most active on this occasion are those whose property lies in or near Savannah and, therefore, are not immediately exposed to the bad effects of an Indian war; whereas, the back settlements of this Province, and our Parish in particular would most certainly be laid waste and depopulated, unless we receive such powerful aid and assistance as none but Great Britain can give. For these and many other reasons, we declare our dissent to all resolutions by which His Majesty's favour and protection might be forfeited.[30]

The signatories to the petitions provide a cast of characters in the drama that was about to unfold. Colonel James Grierson was an Indian trader turned merchant, a respected justice of the peace and colonel of the militia. Captain Edward Barnard had held a position of leadership in Augusta since the war with the French; William Goodgion was Barnard's son-in-law and Grierson's second in militia command. Like Barnard and Grierson, he was a justice of the peace. The Reverend James Seymour was parish priest of St. Paul. He had been specially ordained for the Augusta ministry after a succession of earlier pastors had failed for various reasons. Robert Mackay, a wealthy Scotland-born merchant, had purchased Lachlan McGillivray's White House west of Augusta. John Francis Williams was Mackay's mean-spirited former partner in the trading business. Though they had dissolved their partnership, they were still unhappily related by marriage. Mackay married Mary Malbone Chilcott; Williams was wed to Mary's daughter Catherine.

John Daniel Hammerer was an idealist, who before coming to America had published a plan to civilize the North American Indians by converting them to Christianity. He had some early success in teaching Cherokee children in his school near Carolina's Fort Prince George on the Keowee River. Financial exigency forced him to move his school to the white settlements, first Ninety-Six, then Augusta.[31] Martin Weatherford was a veteran Indian trader, the father of mixed-blood sons, who would risk his life for Thomas Brown in the coming crisis. Two physicians were on the list, Dr. Andrew Johnston and Dr. Francis Begbie, both of whom would be loyal to the king and friends to Thomas Brown. Two Wrightsborough Quakers, Joseph Maddock and Jonathan Sell, were also among the signers.

Others on the list who took up arms against the king were William Candler, Sherwood and William Bugg, John Dooly, John and Zachariah Lamar, and John Howell. For the moment the overriding fear of Indians united future foes in a declaration of loyalty that was also a plea for protection.

St. John Parish, in the low country south of Savannah, was a hotbed of opposition to British policy. A committee chaired by Lyman Hall posted a notice in the *Georgia Gazette* blaming the petitioners for worrying about Indians when "the grand question is whether the Parliament has the right to tax the Americans." In a cruelly accurate thrust the statement ridiculed the St. Paul militia for running at the first sight of Indians.[32]

If Thomas Brown had arrived in the backcountry in August, he would have noted a congenial climate of loyalty to the government. By November, when the *Marlborough* landed, the popular mood had changed. The Indian crisis eased when nine Creek Indians walked

unobserved to the door of Robert Mackay's house in Augusta. Mackay
was entertaining John Stuart's deputy, David Taitt, and the household was sitting down to dinner when they were startled by the sudden appearance of the Creeks. They had come to tell Taitt that they
were ready to talk about peace.[33]

Governor Wright was delighted with the success of his embargo
and prepared for an important conference in October to be held in
the capital city of the province. Georgians of high and low estate
were equally pleased, some because trade would be resumed and
others because they saw an opportunity for more land. The assembly
instructed the governor to negotiate for the strip between the
Ogeechee and Oconee.[34]

Captain Samuel Elbert's Grenadier Company escorted Emistisiguo and seventy Upper Creeks into Savannah with the proper
pomp and ceremony. The Pumpkin King and Chehaw King led fifty
or so Lower Creeks into town. Governor Wright and Superintendent
Stuart initiated the talks on October 18, 1774. To the dismay of the
faction of settlers, the governor did not press for a land cession. The
Indians were told that if they punished their guilty warriors and
surrendered runaway slaves, trade would be restored. The Creeks
were advised to break up their villages on the Oconee and at the
Standing Peach Tree on the Chattahoochee. Wright announced the
terms of the treaty on October 20 and warned whites not to trespass
beyond the Ogeechee. Furthermore, no one was to interfere with any
Indian who traveled the old trails to Augusta. The disappointed settlers held Wright responsible for failing to obtain land, but they
might properly have blamed John Stuart. Stuart objected to any
change in the 1763 boundary and was supported in this policy by
General Thomas Gage.[35]

The best evidence for the adverse effect of the Savannah Treaty is
a petition signed by a number of backcountry farmers and attributed
to a "practitioner of physick" named George Wells. Wells had been
loyal enough in Augusta; his name led all the others in the St. George
Parish protest against the Savannah merchants. Wells had moved to
the backcountry from St. John Parish and reflected the radical ten-
dency of that section as well as a contentious disposition of his own.
(He was accused of leaving St. John after biting off one man's ear and
running away with another's wife.) Wells's petition blamed the Augusta merchants and traders for interfering in the negotiations. It
said that the Indians came to the conference prepared to cede the

Oconee strip. Access to the Oconee would have provided backcountry settlers a valuable outlet for their produce. The merchants engaged in the trade, acting "from self interested views," prevailed upon the governor to preserve the area as a hunting ground for the Indians.[36]

After the October treaty, the settlers became disenchanted with their government. On December 9 a Savannah Whig expressed the opinion that Georgia would soon join the Continental Association and terminate trade with the mother country because "two of the back Parishes which made the most noise are now coming over to us."[37] Indeed, George Wells of Augusta and Button Gwinnett of Sunbury would forge a coalition more radical than the Savannah Whigs might have liked. The "country" faction of radicals would shoulder aside the more conservative Whigs and draft Georgia's first permanent constitution.

It was Thomas Brown's fate that he arrived in Georgia at a time when the mood of the country people had begun to change. Ordinarily sensible individuals were prepared to believe fantastic rumors. One was that the king of England was prepared to engage the Indians in a war against the frontiersmen. Another was that Thomas Brown was really the illegitimate son of Lord North and had come to spy on the colonials.

CHAPTER TWO

SHAPING A SOUTHERN

STRATEGY, 1775

 When Thomas Brown and his party landed in the bustling port town of Savannah, James Gordon was on hand to welcome him. Gordon's fellow Orcadians must have been happy to see a familiar face in this strange new world. Brown, who was once introduced as "honorable, honest, brave, and a Yorkshireman,"[1] found other Yorkshiremen in Savannah, notably the senior James Habersham and his nephew Joseph Clay. Brown engaged Clay to act as agent for freighting the *Marlborough* for its return trip. James Habersham, Jr., formed a friendship with Thomas Brown that endured throughout the war, even though the two took opposing sides. Through Habersham's wife, Hester Wylly, Brown became associated with the Wylly family. Two of Hester's brothers, Alexander and William, would ride with Brown's Rangers.[2]

Governor Sir James Wright was impressed by the twenty-four-year-old Thomas Brown; he referred to him as a "young Gentleman" and soon appointed him to the office of magistrate. Thomas Brown was exactly the "better sort" of person Wright had hoped to attract to Georgia by his advertising campaign in England. Brown and Gordon transacted their business with the governor during the latter part of November. Brown later testified that he received twelve different tracts totaling fifty-six hundred acres soon after his arrival. Most of the land was in the new purchase above the Little River. In spite of the presence of Captain Edward Barnard and his troop of Rangers at Fort James on the Broad River, the Ceded Lands were still dangerously exposed to Indian raids. Therefore, Brown and Gordon restricted their new settlements to St. Paul Parish below the Little River.[3]

Another Orcadian arrived in Savannah shortly after Brown's party in the person of Captain William Manson, former master of the ship *Flora*. Manson knew James Gordon as well as the Browns of Whitby. He acquired lands adjoining Thomas Brown's. These coincidences would indicate some arrangement made before Manson's timely arrival in the *Arundel*. Manson's own testimony, however, suggests that he first thought of becoming a Georgia planter only in 1774, when he found "many of [his] old acquaintances" in Georgia and "was induced to go into the Interior parts of that province to see and judge for [himself]." James Gordon had been in Georgia long enough to act as guide; it is likely that he conducted Brown and Manson on a tour of the backcountry. Manson expressed delight with what he saw; the actuality "far surpassed the Description that had been given me." Back in Savannah, Governor Wright made certain "advantageous proposals," probably regarding deferred payment. Manson's friends, presumably Brown and Gordon, promised to help, so there and then Manson "resolved to become a Settler amongst them." Manson bought a three-hundred-acre tract and arranged for a family to live on it.[4] After this busy period Manson sailed for London.[5] He would secure financial backing from merchants in Newcastle and return with a contingent of servants before the year was out. Then he would meet Thomas Brown under radically different circumstances.

Thomas Brown's immediate concern was the establishing of Brownsborough, his plantation. Located between the forks of Kiokee Creek and watered by Greenbriar Creek, Brownsborough was well situated in the rolling hills of the Georgia piedmont. The Kiokees were already thickly settled; other landowners were Dr. Francis Begbie, who would be Thomas Brown's neighbor in-the Bahamas after the war; Sherwood Bugg, a leading Son of Liberty; Zachariah Lamar, also a patriot; and John Germany, an Indian trader. Another of Brown's neighbors was Daniel Marshall, the great pioneer preacher of the Separate Baptist Church. Marshall settled between the Great and Little Kiokee branches two years before Thomas Brown's arrival. He erected the first Baptist church in Georgia on his property. He and his son Abraham would stand against England in politics just as they opposed the Church of England in doctrine.[6]

Brown set his people to work building his plantation house, cottages for servants, a barn, stables for his fine English horses, a kitchen, and "every other thing necessary to form a complete settlement," as he put it.[7] Brownsborough would be a transplanted English manor worthy of a descendant of Sir Anthony Browne. With James Gordon's help, other scattered parcels of Brown's property were settled. Brown later claimed expenses for building thirty-six farmhouses, but it is not clear how many were at Brownsborough and how many were elsewhere. James Gordon stated that the servants were settled upon "a number of Farms" and "were making extensive and rapid improvements."[8]

Late fall was a good time for the strangers to arrive in Georgia. Winters in Yorkshire's North Riding averaged 38°, and the Orkneys were a few degrees colder. Despite the difference in latitude, therefore, the winter climate was not a problem. If the newcomers had arrived in the summer, they would have risked heat prostration. The contrast between the stark moorlands of Yorkshire and the pine-clad clay hills of the Georgia piedmont was striking. For the Orcadians the transition from their treeless, windswept islands to the towering forests of Georgia's backcountry was even more extreme. They must have marveled at the endless supply of timber for building and firewood. The same forests were rich in deer and turkeys; there was good fishing in the creeks.[9]

Thomas Brown did not record his experiences in establishing the Brownsborough settlement. His first impression of the region must have been similar to those of an anonymous planter who lived thirty miles above Augusta and who wrote extensively about the same part of the Georgia backcountry. Excerpts from his letters were printed in a London publication entitled *American Husbandry* in 1775. To him winter was the "most pleasing season." He had heard some of his neighbors complain of cold winds and frosts, "but to a European constitution they are natural." He had lived in Cadiz, Naples, and the West Indies, places famed for their climates, yet "I much prefer the climate [here] to any in which I have lived before." He hastened to add that he was talking about the country above Augusta, not the Georgia low country.[10]

The land in the backcountry was better than the uncultivated regions of Scotland and northern England, he continued. A rich loam soil overlay the clay and stone underneath. There were some sandy tracts, but they were more fertile than the pine barrens to the south. The "plenty of the finest timber is astonishing to an European upon his first arrival." The oak and pine trees cleared for the first cultivation could be floated downriver and sold. Thus a man could begin an estate without expense. A planter who could use a gun might kill more game in a morning than two families could eat in a week. Game included deer, rabbits, wild hogs, turkeys, ducks, doves, quail, and the like. Fruit was plentiful, especially melons, cucumbers, peaches, pears, apples, and plums. Indian corn was this planter's chief crop, but cabbages, potatoes, and turnips also grew well. He exported his potato crop to markets in the West Indies. Like most other planters, he allowed his cattle to graze in the woods. The only deficiency the gentleman could think of was the want of "society" in the hinterland.[11]

While his people were busy building, Thomas Brown moved into a house in Augusta. The town had outgrown the original forty lots laid out according to James Edward Oglethorpe's instructions of 1736. The main road followed the Indian trail that led from the Fort Moore Bluff parallel to the river. Most of the houses straggled along the road or clustered at its intersection with the Savannah Road. St. Paul's Church, already twenty-five years old, stood near the river a block beyond the Savannah Road. Nearby were the ruins of old Fort Augusta, abandoned since 1768. A long, shallow lagoon cut across the main road half a mile above the fort site. The road then passed Colonel James Grierson's large brick house, fortified by a stockade during the Indian alert of 1774. Another ravine called Hawk's Gully separated Grierson's mansion from William Goodgion's residence. Above Goodgion was Lachlan McGillivray's former trading post owned by Robert Mackay. The main road then forked, with one trail following the river to the Cherokee country and the other thrusting directly westward to the Creeks.[12]

Across the river from Robert Mackay's White House stood LeRoy Hammond's new mansion, which he called Snow Hill. Hammond's other house, New Richmond, lay a mile or so above Snow Hill. When building New Richmond in 1771, Hammond had employed thirty carpenters and plasterers and had spared no expense.[13] This was the house James Gordon acquired as his town residence. Although Creek and Cherokee Indians still visited Augusta, the town was beginning to enjoy some of the amenities of Charlestown and Savannah. Robert Mackay, Jr., described Augusta as "a small town, the houses standing far apart from each other, being few in number, but occupied by very worthy and respectable people."[14] Thomas Brown and James Gordon were welcomed into the society of these worthy and respectable people.

Robert Mackay's correspondence furnishes an insight into Augusta's social life. Brown was with Mackay in Savannah early in January 1775 when the latter reported to his wife that he had lapsed into improper conduct on a Saturday night dinner at the Ugly Club. According to Mackay, "there was not six sober men in all Savannah." One of the carousers was Mackay's roommate, Andrew McLean, whom the Mackays called "Macaroni." Mackay was in Savannah to settle accounts stemming from the death of his business partner, the mean-souled, devious John Francis Williams. Williams had been married to Mackay's stepdaughter Catherine, and no one was happier at news of Williams's death than Catherine. Mary Mackay wrote Robert that their daughter was "so blythe, so gay, so happy." She would have to pretend to mourn a few days because they did not want gossips to say that "she stayed at home till she heard of her Husband's death, then went gadding abroad as soon as the news came."[15] Andrew McLean was as delighted as Katy, and the two married after a discreet lapse of time. McLean was continually in trouble during the war for his Loyalist leanings. Afterward the McLeans would follow Thomas Brown into temporary exile in the Bahamas before they were allowed to return to Augusta.

Robert Mackay returned from his trip to Savannah in a new coach. Coaches and riding chairs were essential means of transportation for Augusta's rising gentry. When his wife's riding chair broke down, LeRoy Hammond ordered a Windsor chaise for two made as soon as possible. He explained, "Mrs. Hammond is confined to Snow Hill until we can get another vehicle of some kind or other."[16] Mary Mackay's circle of friends included the William Glascocks, the John Waltons, the James Griersons, Dr. and Mrs. Andrew Johnston, and James Gordon. On March 22, 1775, Mary Mackay informed her husband that "poor Mr. Gordon was ill" and that Billy Clark would go to New Richmond the next day to make a neighborly call.[17]

Brown visited Savannah in January to dispatch the *Marlborough*. The *Georgia Gazette* of January 11, 1775, which reported the sailing of the *Marlborough*, also mentioned the death of John Francis Williams, which was the reason for Robert Mackay's trip there. William Manson was in Savannah, too, settling his backcountry affairs. These were exciting days in the port city. The assembly was scheduled to meet on January 17. Governor Wright agreed to allow the extralegal Provincial Congress to assemble instead. The delegates from St. Paul were Robert Rae, Robert Hamilton, Edmund Bugg, William Glascock, John Germany, and Leonard Marbury. Hamilton was something of a loudmouth, much like George Wells, but he and the others were men of ability and standing in the community. That all of them would join the Revolution testifies to the radical drift of backcountry politics. Robert Mackay had no sympathy with the proceeding; he thought that the delegates would "break up greater fools than they met."[18] Meanwhile, he and the other merchants lingered in Savannah to find out how their business would be affected. Only five parishes were represented in the Provincial Congress. St. John had already adopted the Association and refused to treat with the parishes that had not. Without St. John the temper of the congress was more moderate than it would have been. Georgia would follow a modified version of the Association. Goods necessary to the Indian trade were exempt, but the importation of other goods from Britain, Ireland, and the West Indies was to stop on March 15. Exports would continue until December 1, 1775. Horse racing and other amusements were discouraged. Every town, district, or parish would elect a committee to enforce the Association. Violators' names would be published so that they would be shunned by the associators.[19]

Although tension increased in Savannah, the backcountry remained calm for a little longer. Thomas Brown's newcomers must have rejoiced in the incomparable weather. The anonymous gentleman whose letters were quoted earlier wrote, "March, April, May and June are a warm spring in which scarce a day offends you; the sky is a clear expanse, clouds rarely to be seen, and the heat nothing offensive; the beauty of our country is then enjoyed every hour of the day—in short, no season in any part of the world can hardly be more agreeable than these months in the back country of Georgia."[20]

The Quaker naturalist William Bartram was even more expansive when he described Augusta in May 1773: "Vegetation in perfection appeared with all her attractive charms, breathing fragrance everywhere." Bartram visited Augusta for the second time in the spring of 1775 and described its location as "the most delightful and eligible of any in Georgia for a city." Bartram was on his way to the Cherokee country with letters of introduction from his friend John Stuart, the Indian superintendent in Charlestown. He followed the river trail, carefully cataloging plants as he went and finally arriving at Fort James on the Broad River. Bartram knew Captain Edward Barnard from his first tour of the backcountry. On this occasion he explored Indian mounds with Dr. Francis Begbie, surgeon to the garrison and Brown's Kiokee neighbor. Within days of Bartram's sojourn Captain

Barnard died of natural causes, ending a long career as one of Augusta's leading citizens. Lieutenant Thomas Waters succeeded to the command. Waters was another whose destiny was to be intertwined with Thomas Brown's.[21]

William Bartram's next stop was Alexander Cameron's residence, Lochaber. Cameron was John Stuart's deputy, second only to Stuart in influence among the Cherokees. The convivial Cameron had recently incurred the displeasure of his chief by acting as foreman of a grand jury in the Ninety-Six District which handed down presentments that Stuart considered disloyal. Cameron's excuse was that he had consumed so much wine (the jurymen were said to have put away one hundred bottles of port) that he did not know what he was signing. Stuart instructed Cameron to be alert to any efforts of disloyal people to alienate the Indians from the king and to prepare them to act if called upon. If the pacifist Bartram carried these instructions among the letters from Stuart which he delivered to Cameron, he was the messenger of war. Stuart's letters would be grist for a devastating rumor campaign by his enemies, and in the rumor of an Indian war would lie the seeds of the eventual British strategy.[22] With Cameron's blessing the gentle Bartram wended his way alone into the mountains. His journal carried no hint of the gathering storm that would engulf the backcountry and ruin the careers of John Stuart and Alexander Cameron.

While William Bartram was collecting his specimens, the news of Lexington and Concord threw the low country into turmoil. "The accounts from the northward have had the worst possible effect," Sir James Wright informed General Gage. Because he was afraid his letters might be intercepted by the radical Whigs in Charlestown, Wright said cryptically, "What is mentioned . . . will by no means do any good." He meant that Gage should not send troops to Savannah. Wright was afraid that the appearance of soldiers would precipitate a war. No one knew Georgia and Georgians better than Sir James, but his decision to decline the offer of soldiers may have been a crucial mistake. Nothing was so dreaded by the liberty faction as the sight of redcoats, with the possible exception of Indians in warpaint.[23]

On May 11 the royal powder magazine in Savannah was broken into. The *Georgia Gazette* for June 21 contained a summons to a meeting at the liberty pole to elect delegates to a provincial congress. The invitation was signed by Noble W. Jones, Archibald Bulloch, John Houstoun, and George Walton. New leaders were emerging, old ones dying; among the latter were Robert Mackay, James Habersham the elder, Edward Barnard, Noble Jones, and Martin Campbell—all died in 1775. On July 4 the second Provincial Congress met and adopted the Continental Association. Georgians were called upon to swear that they would execute any recommendations of the Continental Congress in defense of constitutional liberty. The issue of the *Gazette* that carried this news also noted that Brown's ship, the *Marlborough*, had arrived at Spitshead.[24] The Savannah committee set an example for other local committees on how to enforce the Association. On July 24, one John Hopkins was taken from his home, tarred and feathered, and paraded through the streets. He was accused of behaving disrespectfully toward the committee and of drinking "Damnation to America" in a public tavern. He was told to say "Damnation to all Tories and Success to American Liberty" or be hanged. Hopkins preferred the former option. He later testified that the Reverend Haddon Smith, rector of Christ Church, was targeted for similar treatment. The clergyman sailed on the next ship for England.[25]

On the heels of the news about fighting in New England, the rumor of a British-inspired Indian war spread through Carolina and Georgia. "The Liberty people have now got another pretence for raising men," Governor Wright reported to Lord Dartmouth. "They assert that Mr. Stuart the Superintendent has been endeavouring to raise the Cherokee Indians to come down against them."[26] The rumor that Stuart had instructed Alexander Cameron to start an Indian war reached incredible proportions. Some thirty-four families were reported already massacred. Furthermore, Stuart was acting under orders from the government, transmitted through General Thomas Gage himself. Emotions ran so high in Charlestown that John Stuart had to seek refuge with a friend, John Mullryne, at Thunderbolt near Savannah. Stuart asked ten or so citizens to listen to what he had to say in his own defense. He denied the accusations, but in the conviction of his innocence he went too far. He made his correspondence with Alexander Cameron available to his interrogators.

Joseph Habersham, an admitted "malcontent," found what he thought was the incriminating evidence he was seeking. Cameron had replied to Stuart that in the event of war, Cameron was ready to lead the Indians in support of the government. At another time this statement could hardly be construed as a plot to attack British subjects, but in the inflamed atmosphere of July 1775, that was Habersham's interpretation and he hastened to convey his "proof" to Charlestown.[27] Armed men in canoes chased after Stuart as he was rowed to the safety of a British schooner. "I had a very narrow escape," he told General Gage. From St. Augustine Stuart conducted a debate by correspondence with the Carolina Committee of Intelligence in a fruitless effort to persuade its members that he was not going to launch an Indian war. He might have spared himself the trouble. On September 12, 1775, General Gage informed Stuart that the services of the Indians would be required.[28]

The Carolina Council of Safety was so impressed with Alexander Cameron's potential as an enemy that it tried to hire him away from John Stuart. On June 26 the council instructed Andrew Williamson, a prominent planter of the Ninety-Six District, to pay a visit to Cameron. Williamson was to offer a bribe or a threat, whichever would do the most good. Cameron denied any intention of raising Indians against the province of South Carolina, stating that he would resign first. He spurned Williamson's offer of money. His denials were not believed in Charlestown; the rumor was stronger than the facts.[29]

The Charlestown gentlemen were equally unsuccessful in winning over Thomas Fletchall, colonel of the militia regiment in the backcountry area between the Saluda and Broad rivers. At the council's request Fletchall called his regiment together on July 13 to listen to the terms of the Association. Not one man signed. Major Joseph Robinson then presented a counterassociation pledging support to the newly arrived governor, Lord William Campbell.[30] It was quickly subscribed. Lord William, after expressing astonishment at the "intolerable tyranny and oppression used by the committees in enforcing their mandates," explained to Lord Dartmouth that "several reputable people" from the backcountry had visited him. They proposed "setting on foot" a counterassociation expressing loyalty. Lord William encouraged them, promising protection and reward.[31] Just who these reputable people were is a matter of speculation. Perhaps Colonel Fletchall was among them; he was credited with arousing loyal sentiment. And certainly Thomas Brown was conspicuous in organizing a counterassociation. He had been honored with a magistracy and had taken an oath to uphold the law. He considered the

Association to be illegal and possibly treasonous. Colonel James Grierson of Augusta reported to Governor James Wright:

> It has for some time past been reported that a Colonel Fletcher [sic] of South Carolina has been taking Pains to Spirit up the back Inhabitants in favor of Government, and that in Consequence a Number of them have entered into a Certain Association or resolution in Opposition to those of the other part of that Province and I think it is alledged that Messrs. Brown and Thompson, two Young Gentlemen who came lately into this Country, has approved of and Joined therein, and also made themselves busy in persuading the Inhabitants to come in to them.[32]

By taking the initiative and assuming the leadership of the loyal faction, Thomas Brown became a marked man in the Georgia backcountry. Responsibility was part of his heritage as a member of a distinguished family, and during the exciting month of July 1775 he discovered a talent for oratory. He refused to recognize the authority of the Georgia Provincial Congress or of its standing committee, the Council of Safety. According to James Grierson, Brown's efforts to organize a loyal association "irritated the People about this place." The report spread rapidly that the bold young gentleman was actually the illegitimate son of Lord North, sent to Georgia to reduce the people to slavery.[33] An important convert to the royal cause was Captain Moses Kirkland of the Carolina Rangers. Major James Mayson and Kirkland had led the Rangers in seizing gunpowder stored at Fort Charlotte and had taken it to Ninety-Six. Kirkland warned Fletchall that the gunpowder would be used to force people to sign the Association. He invited Fletchall to take possession of the powder. Fletchall was unwilling to do anything so bold, but he did not prevent Joseph Robinson and the Cunningham brothers, Robert and Patrick, from acting. At the head of two hundred men they arrived at Ninety-Six on July 17 and seized the powder. For good measure they charged Major Mayson with robbing the king's fort and put him in the Ninety-six jail.[34] If Lord William had chosen this moment to go into the country, he might have found the support he needed to regain control of Charlestown.

Instead, the Charlestown Council of Safety took the initiative, sending two of its more ardent patriots into the backcountry. On July 23 it was resolved that William Henry Drayton and the Reverend

William Tennent would go into the "interior parts" and convince the people of the necessity of uniting "in order to preserve themselves and their children from slavery."[35]

On August 2 Drayton and Tennent left Charlestown. On that same day Thomas Brown was made an object lesson by the Sons of Liberty. James Gordon was at Brownsborough, and Brown was staying at New Richmond, Gordon's residence. Nearly one hundred Liberty Boys called upon several gentlemen to force them to swear to uphold the Association. Brown's friend William Thomson fled to the comparative safety of Alexander Cameron's residence at the Cherokee town of Keowee. Cameron wrote to Andrew McLean that Thomson had arrived but was ill with a fever "from fatigue and uneasiness of mind." He said that Thomson had told him that McLean had "been obliged to push the same day that he and Mr. Brown were attacked." Cameron inquired about the safety of Robert Mackay, James Grierson, Dr. Andrew Johnston, Parson James Seymour, John Daniel Hammerer, and "all our friends." This was a perilous time for those friends.[36]

According to Cameron, the leader of the mob was "that heroic patriot" Captain Robert Hamilton. Thomas Graham and Chesley Bostick were other instigators. In a letter to his father, Brown did not identify the individuals who visited him at New Richmond to demand that he sign the Association. He began the confrontation warily, asking to be excused from joining. The committeemen demanded to know Brown's reasons for refusing to take the oath of the Association. Brown said that he did not want to take up arms against the country that had given him being, but on the other hand he did not want to fight those among whom he intended to spend the rest of his days. They replied that the oath required neither alternative. Brown admitted that the obligation to take up arms was not expressly mentioned, but it was implied. The Association required obedience to any measure ordained by Congress; the use of arms was a distinct possibility. Furthermore, Brown had recently taken the oath of allegiance as magistrate and could not take another oath in opposition to it.[37]

This dramatic debate on the front porch of the big house at New Richmond had counterparts elsewhere. Few were so well chronicled or so dramatic, however, as that between the lone young gentleman from Yorkshire and the hundred or so Sons of Liberty. The crowd began to grow impatient. Their spokesmen told Brown plainly that he could not remain neutral; if he was not with them, he was against them. Brown replied that they could not deprive him of the privilege of thinking what he thought. He then went inside his house. The committeemen, frustrated so far, threatened to destroy his property. At that point, Brown put his pistols in his pockets, stepped onto the porch again, and demanded to know what the crowd intended to do. They told him plainly that they intended to drag him to Augusta and force him to subscribe to the Articles of Association. Brown said that if they were for public liberty, they ought to be for private liberty and allow him to live in peace. At that, about fifty of the visitors left the premises.

The rest, however, grew more agitated and moved toward Brown in a threatening manner. Brown warned that the first person to touch him must be ready to "abide by the consequences." Six or eight drew their swords and rushed at him. Brown's first pistol misfired, but with the second he shot "their Ringleader" through the foot. Brown later identified the ringleader as Chesley Bostick. The two would see more of each other as the war progressed. When the liberty men grabbed his pistols, Brown drew his sword: "I parried off their repeated lunges and kept them at Bay for some time," his narrative continued. But a "cowardly miscreant" came up behind him and hit him in the head with a rifle butt, fracturing his skull. Brown was carried off toward Augusta in a semiconscious state; his house was ransacked. He told his father that he was tied to a tree and burning pieces of lightwood were thrust under his feet. In a later description of the episode, Brown was more graphic. His hair was stripped off with knives, he was scalped in three or four places, and his legs were tarred and burned so badly that he lost two toes and could not walk properly for several months.[38]

Brown's testimony is borne out by references to him by Whigs. Veterans of the Revolution would remember him as "Burntfoot Brown." The committee's report of the affair in the *Georgia Gazette* is couched in cruel sarcasm: "The said Thomas Brown is now a little remarkable, wears his hair very short and a handkerchief around his head in order that his intellect . . . may not be affected." John Wilson, secretary of the committee, added details that Brown was unable or unwilling to describe. Brown was exhibited in a cart from the head of town down to Martin Weatherford's house on the east side of Augusta. Martin Weatherford was not ready to side openly with Brown in this early phase of the war, but in time he would declare for the king, fight alongside Thomas Brown, and with him emigrate to the Bahamas. It was probably Weatherford who secured a physician. Brown said that the doctor was an acquaintance; it may have been Dr. Andrew Johnston. The next morning, according to John Wilson's report, Brown recanted. He reportedly said that William Thomson had misled him. He would do all in his power to "discountenance" Fletchall's faction. At this, Brown was discharged "and complimented with a chair." Wilson's account concluded by saying that Brown subsequently joined Fletchall and thereby violated his honor. Therefore, the Augusta Committee decreed that he was not to be considered a gentleman.[39] What Brown thought of the committeemen can only be imagined.

Brown did not mention anything about recanting in his various accounts of his ordeal. It is entirely possible that he could not remember; he told his father that he was "insensible" for two days. There is no doubt that his skull was fractured; he suffered headaches for the rest of his life. He left Augusta with the connivance of a friendly guard, probably Martin Weatherford, and made his way to Moses Kirkland's camp at Ninety-Six. One who watched him come in wrote a comment in his journal that summed up everything that had happened to Thomas Brown: "They burnt his feet, tarred, feathered and cut off his hair. After that he got so he was able to sit on horseback, he came to our poast [sic]."[40] Brown must have been a sight to compel attention from all, sympathy from many.

According to his own account Brown raised three hundred men with the intention of going to Augusta and punishing his tormentors. Nothing came of this early threat except the rumor that Brown was marching on Augusta. James Wilson, secretary of the Augusta committee whose notice in the *Gazette* had been so disdainful of Brown, now adopted a different tone. On behalf of the apprehensive committee, he appealed to Colonel James Grierson to call out the militia to defend against the expected invasion. Grierson was not in sympathy with the liberty party and referred the request to Governor Wright. The Augusta committee then turned to the de facto source of power in Georgia, the Council of Safety in Savannah. Captain Samuel Elbert's grenadier company and some of the light infantry were sent hurrying to Augusta at public expense. Governor Wright noted sadly that they left Savannah "without any application or authority from me."[41]

Thomas Brown found two whom he counted as allies, men "of great influence in that Quarter," Moses Kirkland and Robert Cunningham. Andrew Pickens, who rose to prominence during the war, was of the opinion that Kirkland and Cunningham were disappointed that James Mayson received a colonel's commission from the Carolina Council and they did not. Pickens thought that Cunningham was the best man and should have been selected: "If Cunningham had been appointed colonel at that time, we would not have had so violent an opposition to our cause in this country."[42] More than a touch of pique must have motivated Kirkland and Cunningham, and more than personal attachment bound their followers to them. Certain it was that whatever they felt paled by comparison to the fury that drove Thomas Brown. Brown's appearance upon the Carolina scene added a new dimension to the hostility the up-country people exhibited toward the representatives of Charlestown. Brown and his new friends made recruitment their first order of business. Brown claimed that four thousand men signed a pledge not to take up arms against the king. He was often casual about numbers, and four thousand is best construed as a measure of his activity and expectations.

The Charlestown Whigs, William Henry Drayton and William Tennent, arrived in the backcountry during the height of the Loyalists' anti-Association campaign. Drayton's first encounter with Brown and Cunningham occurred on August 15 near the Enoree River. Drayton referred to Brown as "he that was tarred and feathered at Augusta" and "a Scotchman." Brown had obtained John Dalrymple's pamphlet from Governor Lord William Campbell, which he proceeded to read aloud to the crowd that had gathered. Americans were warned that allegiance to Congress could only mean war. Drayton resorted to ridicule in response and noted that all Cunningham and Brown could do was "grin horribly."[43]

The second meeting took place a few days later at Colonel Thomas Fletchall's place on Bullock's Creek. "We have at length visited the great and mighty nabob Fletchall," reported Tennent, and "found him surrounded by his court, viz.; Cunningham, Brown and Robinson, who watch all his motions and have him under great command." Drayton won the first trick by persuading Fletchall to assemble his men. Fletchall's "high council" was furious; "much venom appears in Cunningham's countenance and conversation," Drayton wrote. Major Joseph Robinson's looks were against him, Drayton thought, but neither Robinson nor Cunningham spoke much. Brown did the talking and, according to Drayton, "his bitterness and violence are intolerable." Brown almost provoked Drayton into losing his temper by saying that the town emissaries "did not mean well to the King." Drayton indignantly denied the charge, and Fletchall prevented further trouble by sending everyone to bed. Thomas Brown, with his bandaged head and burned feet, made a powerful impression on the two men from Charlestown. According to Drayton, Brown was "as dangerous a man as any in this Colony." And Tennent warned, "Brown will bring them to blood if he can."[44]

Brown and his friends won the second trick by spreading the word to Fletchall's men to stay home. Only a few showed up to be harangued by both sides. Brown made a statement which Drayton regarded as incriminating, saying that when the king's troops arrived he would join them and he hoped his listeners would too. The Reverend William Tennent's favorite theme to his backcountry listeners was that the other faction was trying to get the Indians to join them in a "hellish plot" to massacre the associators. Drayton's tactic was even more effective. He sent word to Charlestown to cut off trade with nonassociators. Brown's side could only appeal to loyalty to the king and a desire for peace.[45]

Drayton and Tennent went to Augusta by separate ways and met at LeRoy Hammond's house, Snow Hill. Tennent brought the alarming news he had heard along the way that there was to be a rally of the king's friends twenty miles above Augusta. Tennent was certain that they intended some sort of mischief, probably in cooperation with Indians. Drayton was convinced that Kirkland was raising men for an attack on Augusta and called out the Georgia and Carolina militia. Drayton reported by the council at Charlestown that he had ordered Major Andrew Williamson to the river crossing thirty miles above Augusta, Colonel William Thomson's Rangers to the ridge forty miles to the east, and Colonel Richard Richardson to the Enoree to check any movement by Fletchall. Drayton drew upon his plenipotentiary powers to issue a proclamation that anyone who joined Kirkland would be regarded as a public enemy. Drayton's army then moved off to attack Kirkland, Cunningham, and Brown.[46]

Drayton's force consisted of 120 Carolinians and 84 Georgians. Dragging four cannon, they marched from Snow Hill on a Wednesday and arrived at Ninety-Six on Friday evening. Drayton was jubilant at the combined effect of his proclamation, his little army, and his cannon. Kirkland's followers deserted him, and Kirkland was reported to be willing to leave the province, but Drayton sent word that he must stand trial for his bad conduct.[47]

Thomas Brown's version of the threat that called forth Drayton's military maneuvers was quite different. The force Kirkland assembled and which was "so magnified by Drayton consisted of four men whom Colonel Kirkland kept about his person to prevent his being butchered by Drayton's orders." Brown confided to Lord William Campbell that Kirkland left the country "on the errand well known to your Lordship." The remark was significant. It indicated that a strategy had been developed, that Brown and Kirkland were parties to it, and that the governor was involved.

At the time Drayton's men were camped at Ninety-Six, Moses Kirkland was safely aboard a British man-of-war in Charlestown Harbor. Kirkland's young son was with him, disguised as a girl because Kirkland had heard that his enemies planned to seize his son as a hostage. Kirkland went to St. Augustine, where he secured the cooperation of John Stuart and from there sailed to Virginia. His intention was to proceed to Boston to put his plan before General Thomas Gage.[48]

Kirkland's errand soon became a cause célèbre when he was captured and locked up in a Philadelphia prison. General George Washington personally informed Congress that Kirkland was "a dangerous fellow." He sent along the papers taken from Kirkland, including some of a "very interesting nature" from John Stuart in which Stuart suggested that the war between the Choctaws and Creeks should be ended so that the Creeks would be free to act. He was opposed to an indiscriminate attack by Indians but would dispose them to join in "any concerted plan" to assist "their well disposed neighbors," the loyal inhabitants. Washington told General Philip Schuyler that Stuart's dispatches proved that the British ministry intended to use Indians against the Americans.[49]

There was irony in the plan hatched by Brown and Kirkland. They had borrowed upon the rumor the Whigs used as propaganda. Let John Stuart unleash his Indians on the frontier while British troops landed on the coast. That was the essence of the rumor and of the plan. The royal governors of South Carolina, Georgia, and Florida would be early converts to the strategy. In time it became the obsession of General Sir Henry Clinton and Lord George Germain, the war minister for the colonies.

With Kirkland away on his errand, Brown and Robert Cunningham raised a number of men to oppose Drayton. Brown told Lord William that they had already assembled 2,200 men when Colonel Fletchall arrived with 250 more and assumed command of the camp. William Drayton estimated that there were only 1,200 to 1,400 men under Fletchall. Drayton boasted about the good order in his own command of 1,100. Both Drayton and Brown testified that their men were eager to attack the other army, but no blood was shed. Instead, Drayton persuaded Fletchall to sign a treaty on September 16, 1775, pledging that neither party would give aid and comfort to any British troops, nor would they dispute the authority of Congress.[50]

A disgusted Thomas Brown explained to Lord William Campbell how Drayton manipulated Fletchall. Drayton requested an interview with Fletchall, Cunningham, and Brown. Brown and Cunningham were considered by their men to be too valuable to risk sending into the enemy camp, but they had no objection to Fletchall attending "with some Officers of inconsiderable Consequence as Messengers." So Fletchall took along six men, most of them "as ignorant and illiterate as himself," in Brown's opinion. Brown drafted a set of instructions for them demanding the freeing of prisoners, the end of trade restrictions against nonassociators, the dissolution of unconstitutional bodies, and the disarming of their troops. In short, Brown called for a surrender by the other party. Unfortunately for his cause, Brown's instructions were not even read. Fletchall, as Brown put it, "had such frequent recourse to the bottle as to soon render himself *non compos*." Drayton drew up his own set of articles and had the uncomprehending Fletchall sign them.[51]

Fletchall's men were furious at what they regarded as a betrayal and were willing to follow Cunningham and Brown into battle. The two leaders decided, however, that war was a matter for Lord William to decide. The men were sent home, prepared to be rallied again. Before that could happen British redcoats were needed; without them "we are of opinion twould be an experiment rather too hazardous."[52]

Lord William's reply to Thomas Brown was so complimentary and so warmly personal that Brown cherished it the rest of his life and handed it down to his children. "The behaviour of Mr. Cunningham and you merits much more than I can express," wrote the governor, "and I trust will meet with both thanks and reward from

that Sovereign, whose just Rights you have so warmly and disin-
terestedly defended and from that Country whose Laws you have
with so much true patriotism endeavoured to support." He approved
of Brown's good judgment in not risking lives prematurely. As an
indication of his high regard for Brown, the governor asked him for
a list of those who deserved commissions. Any other information
Brown would like to convey should be entrusted to Lady Campbell
because the governor had been forced to seek refuge on board the
armed ship *Cherokee*.[53]

The triumphant Drayton broadcast dispatches to consolidate his
victory. The Charlestown council was asked to seize the governor
and hold him hostage. Drayton had the curious notion that such an
action would "convince every person of the rectitude of our designs."
In a high-handed manner Drayton ordered Alexander Cameron out
of the Cherokee country and sent word to Robert Cunningham that
he must agree to the terms of the recent treaty or be treated as an
outlaw.[54]

Robert Cunningham replied by letter that Drayton should be
ashamed of himself for taking advantage of men who were frightened
out of their wits by men shouting and wearing liberty caps and by
cannon firing. As for himself, Cunningham had no intention of signing that "false and disgraceful" document.[55]

When Drayton's expedition marched off from Snow Hill, the Reverend Tennent did not leave for Charlestown immediately. Instead,
he dallied around Augusta, visiting prominent citizens. Alarms and
rumors made Augusta a nervous place that summer. Tennent went to
unusual lengths in describing the fortifications that guarded "every
valuable house" in town. Three-inch planks were set in grooves of
upright posts forming walls ten to twelve feet high. Some houses had
large pentagonal flankers at each corner that could contain up to
forty men. The flankers were two-storied structures; on the second
level three-pounder cannons were mounted. The flankers were used
as offices and storehouses in times of peace.

On September 5 Tennent made it a point to pay a courtesy call on
the widow of Augusta's former first citizen, Edward Barnard. Perhaps because he was well received by Mrs. Barnard, other doors
were opened to him. He was entertained by William Goodgion, Barnard's son-in-law, who was not in sympathy with Tennent's cause
and who would one day declare for the king. Tennent also called on
John Walton at his plantation several miles south of town. It could

not have been a mere coincidence that George Walton was there. Walton was a member of Georgia's Council of Safety and therefore the most influential Georgian Tennent met on his tour. A pleasant buggy ride back to town very nearly resulted in tragedy. The reins broke and the horse ran out of control. The wheel caught a log and the two occupants were thrown out violently. Walton was so badly bruised that Tennent had him carried back to the house, where he was subjected to a letting of blood. Fortunately for Georgia, George Walton was not killed by either the accident or the cure.[56]

When Thomas Brown went to Charlestown to convey a message to the governor, he was arrested by orders of the Council of Safety and questioned at length. Brown refused to answer, warning that any action against him would be a violation of the council's own treaty and "wou'd be attended with the most fatal consequence in the back country." The council made several "illiberal" remarks about Brown's correspondence with the governor and told him to quit the province immediately.[57]

Lord William Campbell forwarded Brown's account of his adventures to Lord Dartmouth with the remark that Brown was a "young Gentleman of some fortune from the North of England," who had been treated with "diabolical cruelty by the Rebels" and had since been "extremely active and spirited" in the king's interests. Campbell managed to get a message through to Brown, instructing him to go to Savannah and from there to St. Augustine to confer on a plan of action. Meanwhile, Brown was to consider himself in the employ of the government.[58]

Violence flared up in the backcountry when Robert Cunningham was arrested by orders of the council. His brother Patrick retaliated by seizing a supply of ammunition which William Henry Drayton was sending to placate the Cherokees. Ironically, Patrick Cunningham and his followers believed that Drayton intended to set the Indians upon the nonassociators. Members of the Provincial Congress, shocked that anyone would impute such unworthy designs to them, used the same arguments in their defense that John Stuart had used in his and concluded, "The Congress in a body, and also, individually, declare in the most solemn manner, before Almighty God, that they do not believe any order was ever issued or any idea was ever entertained . . . to cause the Indians to commence hostilities upon the frontiers, or any part thereof."[59]

Patrick Cunningham was joined by Major Joseph Robinson, and

their numbers swelled to two thousand men. Majors Andrew Williamson and James Mayson were commissioned by the council to put down the uprising, but because they had only five hundred men they thought it prudent to barricade themselves in the fort at Ninety-Six. There they were besieged and some shooting ensued before a truce was arranged.

This second treaty of Ninety-Six, signed on November 22, 1775, provided for a safe-conduct out of the fort for Williamson and Mayson's men. Major Robinson would withdraw his troops beyond the Saluda, and no one of the opposite party would be molested. The signers for the Council of Safety were Andrew Williamson, James Mayson, Andrew Pickens, and John Bowie. For the governor and king were Joseph Robinson, Patrick Cunningham, and Richard Pearis. Despite the clear terms of the treaty, the leaders of the king's friends were hunted down by Colonel Richard Richardson with a large Whig force from North Carolina under his command. They found the unheroic Thomas Fletchall cowering in a cave and sent him down to Charlestown with a number of his partisans. Joseph Robinson and Patrick Cunningham remained at large.[60]

Brown and Robert Cunningham had been careful to restrain their followers until Governor William Campbell gave the word. The governor was greatly annoyed at the premature rising. He blamed its failure on "the want of a leader of either consequence or knowledge enough to direct their enterprises." So Patrick Cunningham and Joseph Robinson were found wanting. The sieve of war was sifting men. Fletchall was disgraced; Moses Kirkland lacked character, as revealed by his cringing behavior while a prisoner of Congress. Robert Cunningham was the popular hero, but he did not enjoy the governor's confidence. He was not aware of the plan to bring down the Indians in conjunction with troops and was shocked when he learned about it later. Thomas Brown, only twenty-five years of age and one year arrived in America, had emerged as a leader. He was respected by the multitude and accepted by those in authority. He was convinced that, with Robert Cunningham a prisoner and Kirkland away, the responsibility for rescuing the backcountry for the king devolved upon him.[61]

Among the troops who hunted down the Loyalists was a detachment under LeRoy Hammond. Marching with Hammond was a young Orcadian, a former servant of Thomas Brown, sixteen-year-old Baikia Harvey, who had joined the Revolution. "Mr. Gordon was very good to me, but Mr. Brown us'd me very ill," he informed his godfather in the Orkneys. He had run away and joined Richardson's expedition. He was astonished at the sheer number of men under arms; his wild guess was that there were eight thousand. He was even more impressed with their shooting skill: "They can hit the bigness of a Dollar betwixt two and three hundred yards distance," he exclaimed. Boys no older than he carried their own guns alongside their fathers, "and all their Cry is Liberty or Death." He testified that he saw Liberty Boys capture more than two hundred Tories. "They have taken all their arms from them and put the head men in gaile [sic] so that they will never be able to make war against them any more." LeRoy Hammond probably became acquainted with young Harvey on the march, and when they returned, Hammond arranged with James Gordon to "buy the boy's time," that is, to pay off his obligation to Brown. The youngster was delighted with the new arrangement: "He and his Lady uses me very well," he said of Hammond, "I rides with my master and loves them both."[62]

Thomas Brown's interlude in Savannah coincided with the arrival of the second contingent of indentured servants on the *Marlborough*, Thomas Walker, captain, on December 15, 1775. The contractual arrangements between these servants and the Browns, as with the earlier group, were spelled out in detail in the English newspapers. On July 28, 1775, a notice in *Etherington's York Chronicle* announced that the *Marlborough* would depart from Whitby on August 10, 1775. Eighteen people took passage, among them Isaac Herbert, who was listed as agent and attorney for Jonas Brown and was "going to superintend a plantation." Herbert was a rarity among Brown's servants in that he remained loyal to his master during the war and was allowed to remain in Georgia after the war. A storekeeper during the war, he was a successful Augusta merchant afterward.[63]

As in 1774, most of the recruits came from northern Scotland, Caithness, and the Orkney Islands. Of the fifty-three Scots, twenty-five were men, sixteen women, and the rest children. Most were farmers who gave as reasons for leaving that they could not pay the high rent or that their land had been turned into pasturage for sheep. The tradespeople, weavers, wrights, and fishermen came to America for an age-old reason—to better their fortunes. Whole families came; for example, there were eight Calders and six Millers. One Robert Gorson, age fifty and servant to a farmer, was singled out by the customs officials as "a very bad character." That only one man was so described probably indicates that the rest of the people who sailed from Kirkwall on September 15, 1775, were respectable enough.[64]

The newcomers had been assured by the printed circulars that their Georgia homes were a thousand miles from Boston and their province had "no connection or concern with the trouble now subsiding with Great Britain." The *Marlborough*'s passengers soon learned that the trouble was not subsiding and that Georgia was no longer immune to it. When they disembarked at Savannah on December 12, 1775, they must have been astonished to find that Thomas Brown, their master, was still crippled from his torture and under sentence of banishment from Georgia.[65]

The same issue of the *Georgia Gazette* that carried the notice of the December 12 arrival of the *Marlborough* also announced the landing of William Manson and his one hundred settlers from the *Georgia Packet* on December 19, 1775. The crossing had taken fourteen weeks. At one time, half the passengers were down with fever. Four children died of smallpox. Dr. Thomas Taylor, a member of Manson's party, described Brown's travails in a letter to a friend who knew the Browns in Whitby. The letter, dated December 26, stated that Thomas Brown was under orders to leave the province within ten days. Dr. Taylor went on to say that Governor Wright had been reduced to a "mere cypher" and everything was done by a committee composed of "Barbers, Taylors, Cordwainers, etc. whose insolence and pertness would raise any Englishmen's indignation."[66]

It was fortunate for Manson that he happened to know the president of the Council of Safety. George Walton had acted as a witness for Manson in registering his land grants the previous year. Manson appealed to Walton to rescue four of his men from a South Carolina recruiting officer. The Council of Safety took his part and ordered the officer to release the men or pay the expenses Manson had incurred in transporting them to America. The officer complied. One of these men, John Douglass, would appear on the council's list of "dangerous persons" before the year was out. For a while longer Manson was able to go about the business of settling his land in the backcountry. A Quaker, he planted his little colony near the Quaker township of Wrightsborough. He wrote to his mother that he had decided to name his settlement Friendsborough. He assured her that he was far removed from the disturbances in the low country and there was no cause for her to worry. He noted that James Gordon was in good health and so were his people.[67]

Dr. Thomas Taylor conducted about half of Manson's party to their settlement. Their experience must have paralleled that of the new arrivals from the *Marlborough*. They spent eight nights on the road, camping out of doors in frost and snow on five of the nights. The landscape was sandy and swampy for the first hundred miles, then it began to improve in richness and diversity. Near Wrightsborough the pleasant hills and dales were covered with pine, oak, and hickory. The area was well settled. Dr. Taylor found most of his new neighbors "amazingly ignorant of the true state of affairs." Not one in fifty had heard of Lord North's conciliatory efforts. They believed that the ministry had "vowed death and destruction to the whole continent."[68] For a while longer the settlements at Brownsborough and Friendsborough would be maintained, but they were on borrowed time. Both Gordon and Manson were regarded with suspicion by the fire-eaters among the liberty faction. In July 1776 Robert Hamilton applied to the Council of Safety to "take possession of Mr. Gordon's Fort." At the same time he objected to Manson's having certain goods, probably because he believed that they were imported in violation of the Association.[69] By July, the newcomers, like the old, had to choose between independence and the king.

CHAPTER THREE

TESTING THE PLAN,

1776

 Governor James Wright was exiled from his own province soon after Thomas Brown left Savannah. The arrival of four British ships at the mouth of the Savannah River on January 18, 1776, so alarmed the Council of Safety that it placed the governor under house arrest. Wright, however, managed to take refuge aboard the HMS *Scarborough* on February 11.[1]

There was high excitement in Savannah when the British men-of-war made their way upriver and freed some twenty rice-laden vessels that had been detained by order of the Council of Safety. On the night of March 2 British troops boarded the vessels and set them adrift, but the liberty men floated a fireship among the rice boats, burning three or four. About fifteen, including the *Georgia Packet* with William Manson's cargo of rice, ran the gauntlet of gunfire from the Savannah side and made their way to the sea. Unfortunately for Manson, the rice was confiscated by the Royal Navy to provision the British troops in Boston.[2]

Fear of the British warships drove the Provincial Congress from Savannah to Augusta. The collapse of royal government was the occasion for the promulgation on April 15, 1776, of a new state constitution, a short and simple document known as "Rules and Regulations." It provided for an elected legislature, which appointed the president. The president acted as chairman of the Council of Safety, the de facto government while the legislature was not in session. Archibald Bulloch was elected on May 1, 1776, to serve as the state's first president. Thus Georgia was ready to assume its sovereign status when delegates George Walton, Lyman Hall, and Button Gwinnett declared it to be so in Congress assembled on July 4, 1776.[3]

The HMS *Hinchinbrook* stopped in Savannah on January 18 on its way to St. Augustine. Lord William Campbell was among the passengers, and Thomas Brown very likely took passage on the same ship. Lord William introduced the young Yorkshireman to Florida's crusty Governor Patrick Tonyn, a man of action and a former comrade in arms of General Henry Clinton. Recognizing a kindred spirit in Thomas Brown, Tonyn became Brown's patron and most zealous booster during the tumultuous ten years ahead.[4]

Soon after his arrival in Florida, Brown unfolded the plan he and Kirkland had concocted with the approval of Lord William Campbell. The plan had as its object the restoration of royal rule in Georgia and South Carolina by employing Indian allies on the frontier in conjunction with British troops along the coast. Essential to the plan was that the Indians be accompanied by white Loyalists who knew backcountry people well enough to distinguish between friends and enemies. Tonyn was completely won over. "Nothing could have been more easy," he would later say. The Indians were ready for action, and proper leadership would prevent indiscriminate attacks on friendly people. "There is no mystery in it, no difficulty," Tonyn informed his friend General Clinton. John Stuart was present, and, according to Tonyn, "he adopted the measure with spirit when the plan was read to us by Mr. Brown."[5]

Tonyn did not know, because Stuart did not choose to tell him, that Stuart had already been authorized to employ Indians against the rebels. General Thomas Gage had written to Stuart on September 12, 1775, to say that the rebels were using Indians against the British in Massachusetts and therefore Stuart was free "to make them take Arms against His Majesty's Enemies, and to distress them all in their power, . . . no time should be lost to distress a set of People so wantonly rebellious."[6]

In fairness to Stuart, he had spent the better part of the year protesting against allegations that he intended to bring the Indians down on the frontier. Indeed, he had grave doubts about whether the Indians could be properly restrained when the war lust was upon them. Furthermore, his family was still detained in Charlestown as hostages against his good behavior. So on February 15, 1776, John Stuart went off with mixed feelings to Cape Fear, North Carolina, to confer with General Henry Clinton, whose southern expedition had reached that point on its way to Charlestown.

On February 24 Governor Tonyn asked Thomas Brown to put his

plan in writing. Brown did so that same day in two long letters addressed to Tonyn and Stuart. The substance of his message was that the Carolina backcountry was a rich agricultural region and most of the inhabitants were well disposed toward the king's government. The well-organized liberty faction, however, established committees that were supported by three hundred Rangers under Colonel William Thomson. Leaders of the government party were ferreted out by the committees and arrested on suspicion. The loyal faction was further hampered by a lack of ammunition.

With Kirkland and Robert Cunningham under arrest, Brown was perhaps the best-known leader among the king's friends still at large. Therefore, Brown proposed to transport twenty horseloads of gunpowder to his friends. He needed Stuart's cooperation because his intended route was round about Georgia through the Creek Indian country. A party of Indians, under the direction of one of Stuart's deputies, David Taitt or Alexander Cameron, would escort Brown's train through the Ceded Lands of Georgia into Carolina. Brown would send messengers ahead to inform his friends that the Indians would do them no harm but would assist them against their enemies. Brown argued that if the British did not employ the Indians, the other side would. He had heard that George Galphin, appointed Indian commissioner by the Continental Congress and a man of legendary influence among the Creeks, had summoned them to a conference in Augusta in April.

Of all Brown's decisions, the one to enter the Indian country was the boldest. There is no evidence that he had ever seen an Indian before he reached St. Augustine, yet he plunged into the unknown on an adventure that would reshape his career. The timing of Brown's venture was crucial. He thought he could rally three thousand men in conjunction with the landing of Clinton's regulars on the coast. The army could easily be supplied by the large herds of cattle in the interior. Brown argued that the provincial troops which Governor Tonyn proposed to enlist might well be employed in the cattle-rustling business. Thomas Brown did not realize at the time that he might be commanding Tonyn's Rangers, or maybe he did.

A prime target for the cattle raiders, Brown suggested, was the large herds owned by George Galphin, the rebel Indian commissioner, at his trading post on the Ogeechee. Robert Rae, Samuel Elbert, and Thomas Graham were other cattle barons named by Brown. It was no coincidence that they were "violent partisans" or

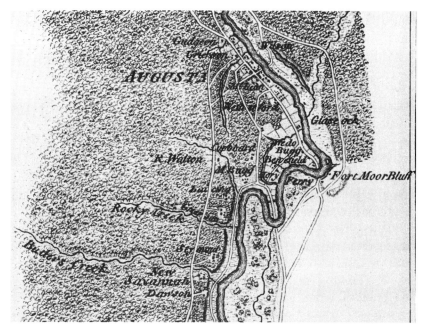

Augusta Area, 1779. Detail of "Sketch of the Northern Frontiers of Georgia" (Drawn by Archibald Campbell. The map above was reproduced from a copy in the Hargrett Collection, University of Georgia Libraries.)

that Thomas Graham had been among Brown's assailants on August 2, 1775.

According to Brown, Fort Charlotte, South Carolina, was the only stronghold of any consequence in the interior, and it was highly vulnerable to a siege. On the Georgia side above Fort Charlotte was Fort Dartmouth on the Broad River, which was still garrisoned by the twenty-five Rangers formerly commanded by the late Edward Barnard and now by Thomas Waters. Brown was not certain of the loyalty of Captain Waters because Waters had surrendered the fort to a band of Liberty Boys. The Georgia Council of Safety then ordered them to give the fort back to the Rangers, so the fort was once more under Waters's command.

Other than these two backcountry posts, the town of Augusta was defenseless, or to use Brown's expression, Augusta was "very accessible to the Creek Indians to whom it lays quite exposed." There were about a hundred houses in Augusta, several of them stockaded (as the Reverend Tennent had described the previous September). The fall of Augusta would "distress the rebels beyond measure," Brown believed, and would open the Savannah River to the friends of the royal government.[7]

Governor Tonyn cannot be blamed for thinking that he had initiated a coordinated plan of action as Thomas Brown prepared to lead his caravan into the forests and John Stuart took passage to confer with General Henry Clinton at Cape Fear. In fact, Tonyn was ready to carry out Brown's plan himself: "I have no doubt at all if I do not restore Sir James Wright to his government, I shall at least draw the Georgia troops from opposing your army." Tonyn reminded Clinton that he held the rank of lieutenant colonel and would like to be made brigadier general. With 120 men of the Fourteenth Regiment, 30 of the Sixteenth Regiment, and two companies or more of Brown's recruits from the backcountry, Tonyn could invade Georgia as soon as Stuart had the Indians ready.

Tonyn was especially complimentary to Thomas Brown in his letter to Clinton. Although new to Tonyn's acquaintance, Brown was "very deserving, confidential and of noble sentiments." In addition, he was "a very active spirited, sensible young man." Lord William Campbell was with Clinton at Cape Fear, and he added his endorsement of Brown. Clinton replied to Tonyn that the strong recommendations of Tonyn and Campbell induced him to permit Brown to raise two or more companies of riflemen. He was to assemble them at St. Augustine and to hold himself in readiness to join Clinton on the first notice. He offered Brown a captain's commission for this service.[8]

Tonyn relayed Clinton's letter to Brown, but without waiting for Brown's reply Tonyn explained that Brown did not mean to be captain of the rifle companies. Those companies were to serve under Tonyn's direction. Brown's role was more important—to raise eight or nine hundred troops in the backcountry; "with these he designs to join the Indians [which] the Superintendent may be able to put into motion." Tonyn sent Clinton a copy of Brown's letter of February 24 and added, "Nobody is acquainted with this design as yet but Brown."[9] If John Stuart had seemed to favor Brown's plan at first, he had second thoughts about it.

The problem with Brown's plan, as Stuart pondered it, was that it threatened Stuart's sole management of Indian affairs. If whites were to be sent along with Indians, Stuart wanted to command them. He cautioned General Clinton against sending orders to the Indians through anyone but himself. (Thomas Brown was among the Indians at the time.) He asked Lord George Germain to "support his consequence in the eyes of the Indians and prevent his being clashed with in the Management of them."[10] His request was granted, at least to the extent of a colonel's commission. Governor Tonyn said bluntly that Stuart was jealous. Moreover, he was old and infirm and "stands in need of a strong spur." Tonyn might have added that Stuart's residence in far-off Pensacola would make communications difficult and cooperation nearly impossible. For his part, Clinton did not quash the idea of a combined attack from frontier and sea, he simply postponed it. Stuart sent word to his deputies to wait for orders, or as Tonyn phrased it, to "strike no stroke until they heard further from him."[11]

The surprising feature in the plan adopted by Tonyn is that the governor should have been swayed so completely by Thomas Brown, the rawest of novices in Indian affairs, and should have scorned the cautionary warnings of Stuart, the professional. Of course, Brown's plan carried the considerable weight of Lord William Campbell's endorsement, but Lord William knew less about Indians than did Brown. Thomas Brown was a quick learner, however. He entered the Creek country in late March or early April and stayed there for the remainder of the year, forming close personal attachments with the tribal chieftains that were possible only as the result of prolonged association.

Brown's route to the interior was to the west of the great Okefenokee Swamp, through Seminole country and into the Lower Creek towns along the Flint and Chattahoochee rivers. An entire new world opened before the young Yorkshireman. There were fourteen villages usually designated as the Lower Creek towns. Above them and west of the Chattahoochee were the twenty-four towns of the Upper Creeks. The Upper and Lower Creeks rarely acted in concert; in fact, the Lower Creeks seldom agreed among themselves on matters of policy. The one overriding influence on all the towns was their dependence upon the whites for trading goods. John Stuart and the colonial governors had given priority to trade over other considerations, and therefore most of the Creeks were favorably disposed toward the English.[12]

The one man who could spoil Brown's plan was George Galphin. Galphin had lived among the Creeks as a representative of Brown, Rae and Company, had taken a Creek wife, and fathered her children. After he retired from the forests, he maintained an open house for his Indian friends at his plantation at Silver Bluff, on the Carolina side of the Savannah River below Augusta. He also kept a trading post at Old Town on the Ogeechee River and cooperated with John Rae in the establishment of Queensborough. Backcountry Georgians never wholly trusted Galphin. To their way of thinking, a friend of the Indians was no friend of theirs. One of Brown's correspondents in Augusta confided to him that Galphin was rumored to be a secret agent of the king: "The common report is that all his effects will be seized and sold at public vendue." Whether the Georgians appreciated it or not, Galphin was crucial to their cause.[13]

Thomas Brown quickly discovered how formidable a rival Galphin was. The lower towns were buzzing with debate about Galphin's invitation to a congress in Augusta. Brown attempted to dissuade the Indians from going but with limited success. Creeks from Coweta, Hitchita, and Cussita took the old trail to Augusta. Brown's unwitting allies were the violently disposed people of the backcountry. According to Galphin, a plot had been laid to murder all the Creeks who came in to Augusta and thereby start a war between Indians and whites. In fact, one Coweta brave was killed by a party of whites led by the notorious Indian-hater Thomas Fee.[14]

Galphin tried to put the best face on it when the talks began on May 16. He was sorry about the murder of the Coweta, but he understood that the Indian had stolen a horse from the man who did the deed. The Chavulky Warrior of the Cowetas delivered a long talk in which he said that David Taitt, Stuart's deputy, had tried to prevent his coming to Augusta, but he came anyway. Galphin had always supplied him with the goods he needed. Taitt told him that Galphin was now poor and had nothing to give. The Warrior then replied, "I only want to have the honor of seeing Mr. Galphin and to shake him by the hand." After he finished his "good talk" he asked that a separate piece of paper be used to record the rest of what he had to say. It was not the custom of Indians to kill people for stealing a horse. His people must have satisfaction. He was one who gave away the land (in 1763) for the "Virginia people" to live in, who have now grown so numerous. Ten white people had fired on two of his people and killed one, "and as we are all met here like brothers I hope that they will fire upon the person who was guilty of the murder that he may suffer." Finally, when he gave up the land, it was for white people to live peacefully upon it, and now they had built two forts. What was the purpose of the forts?

Galphin said that the forts were erected because Taitt had spread rumors of an Indian attack. The back settlers wanted places of refuge for their women and children. The guilty man would have to be taken to Savannah for trial, but he had not yet been caught. In fact, he was never caught. The failure to punish the culprits cost Galphin and Georgia dearly. The Cowetas transferred their allegiance to David Taitt and Thomas Brown.[15]

Galphin could not offer presents in the traditional manner, nor could he reopen the trade. "We are now just like a parcel of carpenters set to work to build a house without one single tool," Galphin complained. It was a hard task to keep the Creeks friendly when both the British and the backcountry Georgians were trying to incite them. "They have every temptation to break with us and yet I think I could keep them peaceable, if it was not for the people on the ceded land," Galphin told one of the North Carolina Indian commissioners. He enclosed a petition gotten up by George Wells and signed by persons calling themselves inhabitants of St. George, St. Paul, and the Ceded Lands in the province of Georgia. The statement complained about the Indian traffic along the trails leading to Augusta and accused the Indians of robbing and murdering white people along the way. The petition, addressed to the new commanding general of the southern department, Charles Lee, suggested that the time was right "to exterminate and rout those savages out of their nation." If the general would send a sufficient armed force the petitioners were ready to hazard their lives and fortunes to join in "so desirable a purpose."[16] These Georgians would have an opportunity for heroism sooner than they liked.

While the Georgians were plotting to destroy the Creeks, Thomas Brown was learning how to live with them. When he arrived at the Chiaha town on the Flint River with his impressive train of ammunition, the Indians were delighted. They assumed that the powder was for them. They were aware that John Stuart's brother Henry was on his way from Pensacola to the Cherokees with a similar caravan; they had long expected a supply of powder. They could not know that Brown intended to distribute the powder to white people in Carolina. Thomas Brown was bold but not foolhardy. He did not reveal his intentions immediately. Instead, he said that the powder was at the disposal of the deputy, David Taitt. Brown then waited for Taitt to come down from the Upper Creek country to join him. Taitt made good use of the occasion. He summoned the Lower Creek chiefs to meet him at the Chiaha town, promised to send to Pensacola for powder for them, explained the need for an escort for Brown's train, and finally urged the Creeks to ignore George Galphin. Taitt planned to lead a group of Upper Creeks into Carolina while Brown and the Lower Creeks went by another route. Brown would send word to his Carolina friends that help was on the way. He confidently expected a thousand or so Loyalists to join him.[17]

Before Brown could leave the Chiaha town, dispatches from Stuart arrived ordering Taitt to cancel the operation. Brown was bitterly disappointed. He and Taitt would await orders "with the utmost impatience." Nor was he consoled by General Clinton's offer, relayed through Governor Tonyn, of a captain's commission. Brown expressed sardonic thanks for the general's kindness but declined. He explained that with Cunningham and Kirkland arrested "no leader of consequence" was left in South Carolina. If he accepted the rank of captain, he would fall so low in the estimation of the backcountry Loyalists that his usefulness would be at an end. What Brown did not say explicitly was that Joseph Robinson held the rank of major and Brown could not permit Robinson to outrank him. Governor Tonyn would later explain to General Sir William Howe that he commissioned Brown a provincial lieutenant colonel so "that he might have a rank superior, to a Major Robinson of South Carolina." The commission, dated June 1, 1776, gave Brown control of the backcountry underground.

There is no indication that Brown was to command a corps of Rangers at the time of his commission. The concept of a provincial corps of Rangers evolved from Tonyn's need to round up cattle on the Georgia borderlands and the need, implicit in Brown's plan, for white men to ride with the Indians and regulate their behavior. Brown began recruiting Rangers from among the traders and packhorsemen in the Indian country.[18] Brown later described the men who joined him as possessing "a perfect knowledge of the language, customs, manners and disposition of the different tribes of Creeks and Cherokees . . . expert woodsmen capable of swimming any river in the province . . . the best guides in the southern district."[19]

According to a trader, the men with Brown were mostly "runaways" from Carolina. It was correctly supposed that their purpose was to pilot an army to the frontiers of Georgia. George Galphin complained that Brown and Taitt gave "ammunition to every fellow that asks for it." Reports of Brown's activities were noised along the backcountry grapevine. LeRoy Hammond relayed word to Andrew Williamson, who in turn informed William Henry Drayton that Brown and a party of his men were at a "great ball play" in the Creek nation. Brown's men attempted to seize an uncooperative trader named Adam Tapley even though it was a rule among the Creeks that a trader carrying goods was inviolate. The Indians rescued Tapley and broke Brown's sword. They then brought Tapley to Taitt, who knew the rules better than his brash associate. Drayton was told that Brown had gone off in disgust to Florida.[20] The report was wrong; Brown remained among the Creeks, learning valuable lessons in diplomacy and patience. Much of the trouble he and Taitt experienced was caused by the Indians returning from Augusta. Galphin had tried to appease the Cowetas with a hundred kegs of rum. The Coweta town was dangerous and unpredictable while the rum lasted. Taitt persuaded Emistisiguo and a large party of Upper Creeks to go with Brown to the Oconee and offer protection to well-disposed persons who might come into the Indian country from Carolina. But Handsome Fellow of the Cowetas called a meeting of the Upper Creeks to tell them what he had heard at Augusta, and Brown and Emistisiguo could collect only twelve Indians to go with them to the Oconee.[21]

While Brown waited for orders to lead the Creeks against the frontiers of Georgia and Carolina, Governor Tonyn commissioned other officers who were to serve under Brown in the East Florida Rangers. The governor's expense account of June 24 shows that Rangers were active on St. Marys frontier by that date. At year's end six units were operating under Lieutenants Williams, Moore, York, Phillips, Jefferson, and Hall. It may have been unusual for the Rangers to begin duty without their commanding officer, but this was an unusual war. The governor admitted as much in a dispatch to Lord George Germain. He very nearly apologized when describing the Rangers' success in rustling Georgia cattle: "This, my Lord, is not a very honourable method of making war, but my Lord, it is the only one left for supplying the town and Garrison with fresh provisions. . . . Besides, my Lord, the love of Plunder engages many daring Fellows, instead of joining with, to oppose the Rebels."[22]

Neither Tonyn nor Thomas Brown had given up the idea of carrying ammunition to their friends in the Carolina backcountry. In July Brown began his belated expedition with fifty horseloads of ammunition and an escort of Lower Creeks. It was his bad luck that the Cherokees went on the warpath just then. To the Georgians, Brown's movement seemed to be part of a coordinated plan. General Charles Lee received a letter from Savannah, dated July 11, 1776, informing him of the murder of four families on the frontier and stating that "these Indians are to be joined by six hundred Creeks and a number of the King's men who are to march down and cut the settlements all off." Refugees from Georgia's Ceded Lands were convinced that the Creeks intended to join the Cherokees. The Cherokee attacks seemed to confirm the truth of the plan discovered in the intercepted letters of John Stuart's deputy, Henry Stuart.[23]

Henry Stuart had been sent on his mission in October 1775 by his brother John. He was to deliver ammunition to the Cherokees so that they would be better able to cooperate with the king's troops if called upon. Stuart's journey was long, from Pensacola through the Chickasaw country, and then a tedious fifty-five days to Toquah in the Overhill Cherokee country. Henry Stuart wrote to his brother on May 7 to tell him that he had delivered twenty-one horseloads of ammunition. That was not enough for the Cherokees, and there would be none left for the back settlers of Carolina. "Three of the people here who were with Major Robinson" wanted to know what help they could expect from John Stuart. They said that a great many were ready to assemble if they were assured of assistance. Later Captain John York came in with several Carolina Loyalists to say that "the friends of government were very numerous but wanted arms and ammunition." Captain York enlisted in Brown's Florida Rangers before the year was out.[24]

Dismayed to find that the Cherokees were on the verge of war, Henry Stuart and Alexander Cameron tried vainly to dissuade them. The Georgians and Carolinians, however, were convinced that Stuart's mission, like Brown's, was to launch the long-rumored Indian war. One of Stuart's letters was intercepted and tampered with, and the doctored document was forwarded to Congress with a note to the effect that it was proof that the "detestable villain" John Stuart was actually doing what he had been accused of doing for over a year.[25] The dispatches and the eruption of the Cherokee war were reflected in one of the complaints against the king which was included in the Declaration of Independence: "He has endeavored to bring on the inhabitants of our frontiers, the merciless Indian savages."

The Carolinians made effective use of their evidence of British intrigue to win back some of the Loyalists of 1775 who were repelled by the British employment of Indians. Robert Cunningham was the most important convert. He was freed from imprisonment and "much caressed in town," to the discomfort of some of his former foes in the country.[26]

The British plan to bring down Indians in concert with a landing of troops was already widely known as the result of the documents taken from Moses Kirkland and read before Congress. The arrival of a British fleet off Charlestown on June 28, 1776, seemed to be proof that the plan was being followed. The moderate Henry Laurens told his son John that the joint attacks confirmed the perfidy of Stuart and his agents. When John Rutledge asked the Carolina General Assembly to ratify the Continental Declaration of Independence, he stated that the coincidence of the Indian uprising and the British naval attack "convinces us of what, indeed, we had before little reason to doubt, of the indiscriminate atrocity and unrelenting tyranny of the hand that directs the British war."[27]

General Charles Lee reached Charlestown in time to reap the glory of warding off the naval attack by Sir Peter Parker and General Henry

Clinton. The failure of the warships to penetrate the town's defenses was a bitter blow to Carolina Loyalists. Lord William Campbell was a disappointed spectator aboard the HMS *Bristol*. Before he sailed north with the fleet, he managed to send two messengers into the backcountry to encourage his friends to keep up their spirits. Evan McLaurin and Robert Phillips, described by Lord William as "two very worthy and trusty men," were his emissaries. Phillips, like York, would become a Ranger officer; McLaurin later served as major in the South Carolina Royalists.[28]

General Charles Lee's next objective was the Indian frontier. He called upon Virginia to send men to march against the mountain Cherokees while the Carolinians attacked the lower towns. Colonel Andrew Williamson was raised to the rank of general and entrusted with the mission. The implacable William Henry Drayton sent instructions "to make smooth work as you go—that is, you cut up every Indian corn field and burn every Indian town—and that every Indian taken shall be the slave and property of the taker; that the nation be extirpated, and the lands become the property of the public." Williamson conducted his mission with such dispatch that within a month he was able to report to Drayton: "I have now burnt down every town and destroyed all the corn from the Cherokee line to the middle settlements." Because the Cherokee town of Chote was in Georgia, Williamson asked the Georgians to attack that town. The backcountry people who signed George Wells's petition had, like Drayton, also talked about extirpating the Indians, but when their opportunity came, they did not volunteer. George Galphin said that Captain Leonard Marbury "could not get one of these people to go with him that wants to declare war." Williamson's Carolinians had to do the job.[29] The Cherokee rampage caused Thomas Brown to turn back to the Creek country. Then, too, he had heard of the petition in favor of a Creek war. His Indians did not want to be caught too far from their homes.[30]

If George Galphin was aware of Brown's activity, the inhabitants of Augusta must have been. Brown's friends were in peril there. Andrew McLean was forced to testify before the Savannah Council of Safety that he had not corresponded with Alexander Cameron. McLean did not feel obliged to tell the council that John Stuart had prevailed upon him to open a branch of his trading house in Pensacola. It was at this time that Colonel Robert Hamilton, leader of the Liberty Boys, who had treated Brown so badly, demanded permission to seize James Gordon's fortified house and take possession of stores belonging to William Manson. Others, including Isaac Herbert, the Reverend James Seymour, Colonel James Grierson, William Goodgion, and Martin Weatherford, maintained a low profile and anxiously hoped for the arrival of British troops. An informant, either James Gordon or Isaac Herbert, wrote to tell Brown that his plantations had been plundered a second time and his servants taken away. "Your cattle and mine have long fattened these lawless villains, the English horses you so much valued are now drawing the baggage wagons in Augusta and the chief part of your white servants are compelled to bear arms in the Battalion." Brown's correspondent expressed scorn for "the shirtless Crackers" who enlisted in the battalion. Chesley Bostick, the erstwhile Liberty Boy who had been shot and wounded by Brown at the New Richmond confrontation, now had the rank of captain. His first important assignment was command of Fort Barrington on the Altamaha, renamed Fort Howe. Other backcountrymen enlisted in the regiment of light horse under Leonard Marbury.[31]

General Charles Lee was in a condition approaching euphoria after the British sea assault on Charlestown failed in July and the militia of both Carolinas devastated the Cherokee country in August. He allowed himself to be persuaded by the Georgians to launch an invasion of Florida to put an end to cattle rustling and to intimidate the Creeks. Lee committed himself to the plan before he realized how little the Georgians could contribute. "They will propose anything, and after they have proposed it, discover that they are incapable of performing," he wrote to a subordinate. Three-fourths of the invading army of two thousand were Continentals from the Carolinas and Virginia under the immediate command of General Robert Howe. The pomp and ceremony that attended the army's departure from Savannah on August 19 were the high-water mark of the campaign. The rest was disaster. Lee was the only officer with enough prestige to resolve conflicts between Carolinians, Virginians, and Georgians regarding rank and priorities. But Lee was called north at the crucial moment, and he took an escort of North Carolina and Virginia troops with him. The main body of the invaders reached Sunbury but could go no farther. The swamps and the September sun proved to be deadlier than the enemy, and in late September South Carolina recalled her troops.[32]

Lachlan McIntosh, raised to the rank of brigadier by act of Congress on September 16, was left with the responsibility of guarding the frontier. The general confided to his brother William that "people of wild extravagant imagination may talk of conquests and extenting [sic] our territory," but he intended to stay on the defensive. He gave orders to the light horse to station themselves in a semicircle of forts from the Broad River, down the Ogeechee, and across the Altamaha. They were supposed to patrol the intervening gaps in the defensive line. The plan was sound on paper. Actually, McIntosh was never quite sure where his troopers were. Chronic malcontents such as George Wells made life miserable for McIntosh by complaining that the light horsemen were loitering about the settlements rather than patrolling the frontier. McIntosh was convinced that the faction led by Button Gwinnett and George Wells encouraged insubordination among backcountrymen who were opposed to military discipline in the first place.[33]

In Governor Tonyn's opinion, the rebel invasion failed at least partly because Brown's Indians were ready to fall upon the frontier. The Georgians were well aware that Brown was lurking about. George Galphin vainly tried to persuade Leonard Marbury's light horse to dash out and seize Brown. In fact, Brown visited the Upper Creek towns after his return from the Cherokee country. Two hundred Indians volunteered to follow him in an attack on Georgia. George Galphin knew about the danger and so must the backcountrymen who were on the march toward Florida. Perhaps Tonyn was right; news about menacing Indians was unsettling to men whose first concern was their homes and families.[34]

At the outset of the invasion Tonyn sent desperate messages asking John Stuart and David Taitt to enlist the help of the Creeks. Instead, Stuart invited the Creeks to come down to Pensacola for a conference. The lack of coordination may have been owing to a failure of communication, but it was typical of the disjointed British strategy. First, the Cherokee uprising had taken place against John Stuart's wishes. Then, during the Georgia invasion, Tonyn tried to enlist the Creeks but Stuart lured them away from the threatened borderland.[35]

Actually, John Stuart was doing his best to carry out his part of the plan. His October congress drew more than five hundred Indians to Pensacola. He scored a major diplomatic triumph by settling the war between the Choctaws and Creeks, thereby freeing the Creeks to turn their attention to the Georgians. Stuart informed Lord George Germain that he had secured the consent of the Upper Creeks to escort a military expedition carrying arms and ammunition to Carolina. He hoped that the Lower Creeks would go to Governor Tonyn's assistance.[36] While Stuart was engaged in his talks with the Creeks, he received word from William McIntosh, his deputy, that the Georgians were invading the Creek country. The Creeks immediately left Pensacola to defend their towns. Although the report proved to be false, Stuart was pleased with "the spirit of the nation."[37]

Thomas Brown's diplomatic skills were put to the test when Stuart summoned the Lower Creeks to Pensacola at the moment when Brown was trying to recruit them for service in East Florida. The situation required careful handling of the Indians, but more skill was required in dealing with John Stuart. Brown was well aware that Stuart did not like Tonyn's interference in Indian affairs, and Brown was Tonyn's alter ego among the Indians. Brown arrived in the Chiaha town to learn that the head men were about to leave for Pensacola.

He wrote to Stuart and in the most polite circumlocution explained that Stuart's meeting was interfering with his plans. The Indians had agreed to a man to go with him but only after they went to see Stuart. He planned to store some of his ammunition at the Chiaha town and the rest at Tuckabatchee, an Upper Creek town. He would employ his time recruiting white men for the king's service. He awaited Stuart's orders and was prepared to proceed whenever and wherever Stuart directed. Brown completed his letter at the Euchee town. In a more urgent tone, he added that he had just heard that the rebels were on the march toward Florida. He requested an immediate attack on some part of the Georgia backcountry to draw the invaders back from the coast. All the assistance possible should be sent to St. Augustine. He intended to wait for Stuart's orders at Tuckabatchee. Interestingly, he referred to the North Carolina General Robert Howe as "a quondam intimate acquaintance of mine." Perhaps they had met during Brown's earlier tour of the colonies. Brown expected half-breed Tom Gray to bring a talk from General Charles Lee and had asked the Chiahas and Cussitas to seize him.[38]

Two Georgia traders told George Galphin that Brown personally tried to arrest Tom Gray in the Cussita town, but the Cussitas defended Gray. The episode found its way into the correspondence of

Georgia's highest-ranking military men. General Lachlan McIntosh wrote to General Robert Howe that Tom Gray "was obliged to run away from his own town in the middle of the first night he arrived there to save his life."[39]

If the Georgia traders are to be believed, Brown was unable to travel to the Upper Creeks or anywhere else that October. When the informants left the Creek country, Brown was suffering from a boil as big as a man's fist, which prevented him from mounting a horse. While he recuperated in the Chiaha town, the Chiahas went off on a hunting trip. Near Fort Barrington on the Altamaha they encountered a party of Georgia Rangers. Four Rangers were killed and two wounded. A mild panic swept the Georgia borderlands. The attack was the first real test of the effectiveness of General Lachlan McIntosh's defensive strategy. McIntosh ordered Major Leonard Marbury to bring the light horse down from the backcountry. McIntosh waited for fourteen days on the Altamaha, but Marbury never came. Apparently, he could not persuade his officers to leave their homes unguarded. Captains James McFarland, Benjamin Few, Drury Cade, and Lieutenant William Bugg were arrested for disobedience.[40]

Frustrated by his subordinates, McIntosh was nearly out of patience with the Creeks. He advised General Robert Howe, his superior, that he could see no reason for sparing them any longer. Nevertheless, McIntosh made one last try at diplomacy. Tom Gray, who had fled the Creek country in October, was sent back in December with another talk. In it McIntosh introduced himself as one of the old people who had come over with "Squire Oglethorpe." He loved his brothers the Creeks and hoped that he could prevent his own warriors from destroying the Creek towns in the same way the Carolinians had those of the Cherokees. The Creeks answered by staging another raid along the Altamaha. Again, four Georgia Rangers were killed, their bodies were pinned with arrows, and all were scalped. McIntosh understood that his talk had failed and was convinced that Georgia faced an all-out Indian war.[41]

Governor Tonyn expected Thomas Brown to return to Florida in November with an escort of Indians. On November 9 Brown wrote to Tonyn to say that he was waiting for the Creeks to return from Pensacola, after which he hoped to start for St. Augustine. He warned that if the Indians were not employed soon, the whole nation would be "thrown into the utmost disorder and confusion."[42] During December Brown encouraged small war parties to take up the hatchet, but it is impossible to say to what extent he was responsible for the Altamaha raid in which four Georgia light horsemen were killed. Stuart, Tonyn, and Brown, and indeed their superior, Lord George Germain in London, all were anxious for the assistance of the Indians. British policy was responsible for Indian warfare.

CHAPTER FOUR

FRONTIER WAR,

1777–1778

 Thomas Brown's plan depended on the willingness of the Creeks and Cherokees to fight alongside the Loyalists. Georgia's counterplan, though it was never clearly articulated, was to flush the British instigators of Indians out of Florida and by diplomacy to persuade the Indians to remain neutral. The better part of two years, 1777 and 1778, was spent in border warfare. The Georgians attempted ambitious invasions, and the "Florida Scout," as Brown's Rangers were called, frustrated the invaders by elusive swamp fighting and far-ranging raids.

When Indians offered their help, Governor Tonyn was forced to organize a campaign to use them. On January 12 he sent a message to Perryman, a Creek chief whose war party was scouting along the St. Marys in company with a unit of Rangers commanded by Captain Samson Williams. Tonyn begged Perryman to be patient: "You may depend on the proper steps being taken as soon as possible."[1] In Brown's absence, Tonyn directed the Ranger officers separately to supervise the Indians and guide the regulars.

The Ranger officers were men of standing in the backcountry, even if some of their men were not. Ranger Captains Sam Williams and James Moore had been active on the frontiers since late June. Captain John York was one of the Carolina Loyalists briefly imprisoned with Fletchall. Before he came to Florida, he traveled to the Cherokee country to inquire from Henry Stuart what help his friends might expect from that quarter. Captain Robert Phillips was one of the two emissaries Lord William Campbell sent into the backcountry after the abortive siege of Charlestown.

Tonyn's main difficulty in launching the operation was the reluctance of the chief military officer to cooperate. Colonel Augustine Prevost did not care to engage in a cattle-rustling expedition. Prevost was a fifty-four-year-old Swiss-born career soldier who was transferred to the newly organized Sixtieth Royal American Regiment in 1756 and was wounded in the Battle of Quebec. After serving in the West Indies, he was given command of the First Battalion in 1765. In 1775 he was sent to Europe to raise the Third and Fourth battalions, and in 1776 he was given command of the troops in Florida. His two brothers and one son were in the Royal Americans. The historian of the corps remarked that there were so many legitimate and illegitimate members of that family in the corps that the Royal Americans was known as the Prevost Regiment.[2]

As usual, the principals put their arguments in writing, at least partly to convince Whitehall of the soundness of their positions. Tonyn's letters revealed exasperation. A supply of meat was urgently needed in St. Augustine. The Rangers were able to round up cattle, but troops were needed to chase the rebels away from the Satilla River and to guard against an attack from Fort Howe. Prevost should not be concerned about the behavior of the Indians: "I will venture to say that in general for resolution and courage they are equal to any troops who will oppose them."[3] Prevost finally agreed to make the march even though he considered the enterprise ill-advised and unmilitary.

To Tonyn's relief and satisfaction, Thomas Brown arrived in St. Augustine in time to take charge of the Rangers and Indians. Although he had been among the Creeks for almost a year, he was allowed no time to enjoy the amenities of St. Augustine. Tonyn wrote to the Creek warriors that Brown would lead them: "He is my particular friend . . . and as he is a person of rank by birth and family and as a warrior has also the rank of lieutenant colonel, you can depend upon his abilities and knowledge to conduct you with good sense and good judgment." Tonyn cautioned Brown to take his orders from Lieutenant Colonel Lewis V. Fuser. Harmony between the provincials and regulars was essential; therefore, Tonyn was counting on Brown's tact and discretion. Brown was also to encourage any loyal subjects he encountered and reconcile the rebellious ones.[4] How Brown was supposed to do that, Tonyn did not say.

Lachlan McIntosh had extended his defense perimeter after the Chiaha attack on Fort Howe. A new fort named McIntosh was erected on the Satilla and garrisoned by forty-eight Carolina Rangers and

THE AREA OF OPERATION OF THE KING'S RANGERS, 1775–1785

TENNESSEE

OVERHILL CHEROKEE

MIDDLE CHEROKEE

LOWER CHEROKEE

NORTH CAROLINA

Tennessee River

Broad River

Catawba River

Saluda River

Ninety-Six

ALABAMA

Coosa River

Talapoosa R

UPPER CREEKS

Okchai
Okfuskee

Little Tallassee

Tukabatchee

Fushatchee

LOWER CREEKS

Coweta
Cusseta
Ousitche
Oconee
Chiaha

GEORGIA

Brownsborough

Augusta

Ogeechee River

Oconee River

SOUTH CAROLINA

Santee R

Savannah River

Charlestown

Ocmulgee River

Alabama R.

Chattahoochee R.

Flint River

Savannah

Altamaha River

Satilla River

Pensacola

Okefenokee Swamp

St. Marys R.

ATLANTIC OCEAN

Nassau River

FLORIDA

Alligator Creek
Thomas Creek

St. Augustine

Apalachicola R.

N

0   50   100 Miles
0   50   100 Kilometers

GULF OF MEXICO

St. Johns River

Present state boundaries are shown for reference.

twenty-two soldiers of the First Georgia Battalion under the command of Colonel Richard Winn. The stockade was built of split pine logs, surrounded by a ditch. Earth from the ditch covered the bottom of the stockade to a height of four feet. The excavations were not complete and the ground surrounding the fort had not been entirely cleared when Thomas Brown and a single companion came upon it on the Sunday evening of February 16, 1777. Brown crept up to the fort with the intention of capturing a sentry, but none came out that night.

Brown returned to his camp a mile away, where Captain James Moore's Rangers and fifty Indians were waiting. They quickly surrounded Fort McIntosh. The Cowkeeper, a Seminole chieftain, and his Indians with five Rangers lay in ambush on the road leading to the fort. Chief Hycutt and his warriors hid in the swamp behind it. Brown and twelve Rangers concealed themselves in a creekbed just forty paces from the fort. Another chief, Philoutougi, and his band were stationed along a branch that fed the creek.

Brown's purpose was to take prisoners and through them discover the strength of the garrison, but he could not restrain the Indians. When three woodcutters emerged from the gates in the morning, the Cowkeeper gave a war whoop and opened fire. The garrison was alerted, and sporadic shooting continued for several hours. According to a dispatch smuggled through the British besiegers, Winn reported that a white man who called himself Colonel Brown demanded a surrender. Winn said that he was given the alternative "no mercy." Brown later reported that "from the Panic with which they were struck by the hooping of the Indians they imagined they would receive no quarter from them." To his credit, Winn's reply was soldierly: "Sir, we have considered your proposition but are bound in honor not to comply." He then bid defiance to the attackers, and the battle continued. Winn reported four casualties and added, "Our men are in high spirits and fight like soldiers."[5]

The rider who carried Winn's brave message reached General McIntosh in Savannah on Wednesday, February 19. McIntosh ordered all the men he could collect, about seventy, to march immediately to Fort McIntosh. He wrote General Howe that he believed an invasion of Georgia had begun. He would need help from South Carolina because "it is next to impossible to get any of our light horse from the Westward, let the Exigence be ever so great." McIntosh then ordered Colonel John Screven to reinforce Fort Howe, the next likely target. He told Screven that Fort McIntosh was besieged by Colonel Brown and added by way of explanation, "little Brown." The inference is that Brown was short of stature but also that he was known already by both McIntosh and Screven.[6]

Lieutenant Colonel Lewis V. Fuser with his regulars arrived before Fort McIntosh at 11 A.M. on Tuesday, February 18. Fuser ordered the drums beaten for a parley. Ranger Captain James Moore took the white flag of truce, and Thomas Brown, dressed in a red coat, walked to the gate and asked for an officer to come out to talk terms. Colonel Winn agreed. The British regulars were drawn up in line as the Americans came out. Brown was careful to warn the Indians not to open fire. Colonel Winn and Lieutenant Colonel Fuser signed the articles of capitulation, but the fourth article was separately signed by Brown: "I promise upon my honour, that no hurt shall happen to them by the Savages," it read. Brown commented privately to Governor Tonyn, "Poor fellows, they generally associate the ideas of Indians with fire and faggot."[7]

The sixty-eight prisoners were paroled and allowed to find their way to Fort Howe. When they began to straggle in on the morning of the nineteenth, Captain Chesley Bostick, commanding Fort Howe, sent a rider to inform General McIntosh of the bad news. The general was reluctant to believe that Fort McIntosh had fallen, and he hoped that the parolees were deserters. He ordered Bostick to maintain his post "to the last."[8]

Thomas Brown was bitterly disappointed that Fuser had failed to give the Indians and Rangers the credit they deserved. The Indians behaved like men and were treated like children. Brown reported to Tonyn, "He has told them repeatedly in an imperious tone to go about their business—not an Indian has been asked to his table—the Rangers insulted with the Epithet of plunderers . . . the Colonel's haughtiness or rather insolence has almost ruined the plan for supplying the Garrison." It was with difficulty that Brown would prevail upon the Rangers to hunt cattle.[9]

General McIntosh personally led the remaining troops of the First Battalion to the Altamaha. He later informed General George Washington that he lost twelve men in a skirmish and was wounded himself, but he prevented the enemy from crossing the Altamaha.[10]

The attack on Fort McIntosh caused consternation in Savannah. The cattle round-up was interpreted as an enemy invasion. The implementation of the new Georgia constitution was delayed by a

month, and the Council of Safety granted President Archibald Bulloch emergency powers. Bulloch died before he could exercise them,
and Button Gwinnett was elected to his place. Gwinnett had aspired
to be Georgia's first brigadier general and took seriously his responsibility as commander in chief of the state militia. He was determined
to invade Florida and capture St. Augustine, but Major General
Robert Howe considered the idea foolhardy in the extreme. Howe
sent Colonel Thomas Sumter with a regiment of Carolina horse to
Fort Howe and a battalion of Carolina foot soldiers to Sunbury but
otherwise declined to participate in what he believed to be a fore-
doomed enterprise.[11]

Whatever chance the Georgians had of success depended on close
cooperation between Gwinnett's state forces and Lachlan McIntosh's
Continentals. Gwinnett ordered the arrest of Lachlan's brother
George for treason at the outset of the expedition. The charges, based
on a friendly reference to George McIntosh in one of Tonyn's letters,
were not sustained, but Gwinnett and his faction were convinced that
none of the McIntoshes could be trusted. Therefore, the president's
communiqués to the general were few and even those tended to be
curt to the point of rudeness.[12]

The bifurcated expedition reached Sunbury in mid-April and
completely broke down over protocol. President Gwinnett insisted on
his right to call a council of war to determine overall strategy. McIntosh and his officers concluded that "a Continental General was altogether useless in this state if he had not a right to call Councils of
War, Court Martials and other orders respecting his own Brigade."[13]
McIntosh would not yield the point.

The Georgia Council of Safety resolved the contretemps by recall-
ing Gwinnett and McIntosh and ordering Colonel Samuel Elbert to
go on with the invasion. McIntosh defended his record before the new
House of Assembly on May 1, 1777. He denounced the "oppressions,
Slanders and falsehoods" of his enemies and said that the purpose of
the expedition was merely to gratify the "dangerous ambition" of
Button Gwinnett. Gwinnett challenged McIntosh to a duel. George
Wells, the sometime "practitioner of physick," organizer of petitions,
and fulminator against the Continental light horse, was Gwinnett's
second. Major Joseph Habersham represented McIntosh. The principals met at Governor Wright's plantation outside Savannah. They
faced each other at deadly close range and fired point-blank. Both
men were wounded in the leg. George Wells was not a skillful enough

physician to prevent gangrene from taking Gwinnett's life three days later. Georgia was torn asunder by the factional turmoil that ensued.[14]

The McIntosh-Gwinnett furor eclipsed Elbert's activities in Florida. On May 1 Elbert embarked his Continentals of the First and Second Georgia battalions at Sunbury and proceeded down the inland waterway. Elbert planned to rendezvous with Colonel John Baker's mounted Georgia militia twelve miles above the St. Johns River. Baker's command crossed the St. Marys and reached the meeting place on May 12. Instead of Elbert, Baker met Thomas Brown.[15]

Brown had left the regulars, now commanded by Colonel Prevost's brother Major James Mark Prevost, at a place called Cowford on the St. Johns. He took his Rangers and Indians upriver by boat and reconnoitered the country above the St. Johns. Brown found Baker's camp and, as before at Fort McIntosh, set an ambush to capture a prisoner and obtain information. But Baker's patrols were on the alert and fired at one of the Indians. Having lost the element of surprise, Brown returned to his boats and prepared to bring his information to Major Prevost. First, Brown ordered fifteen Indians to drive off the Georgians' horses and promised to wait for them. The Indians managed to steal the horses but were overtaken by sixty of Baker's troopers. Baker recovered his horses, but he could not persuade his men to stand and fight the Indians. Brown was amazed and pleased that his fifteen Indians chased sixty Georgians for over a mile. A young Chiaha brave was killed, but he was the only casualty.[16]

Brown was glad to find that Major Prevost was willing to intercept Baker's force. His Rangers had been continually on the move for five days "without an hour's sleep during the whole time," but they were cheerful at the prospect of a fight. The regulars, Rangers, and Indians quickly found the trail of the retreating Georgians. Brown left the slow-moving foot soldiers behind. The plan was for him to engage the enemy while Prevost came up. Brown managed to get around the enemy and post his men on the road along which he expected Baker to march. At 9 A.M. on May 17 the unsuspecting Georgians rode into an ambush near Thomas Creek. When they were fifty yards away, the Rangers opened fire. Baker ordered his men to dismount and return fire. The Rangers and Indians in the woods attacked Baker on his flank. The Georgians mounted and retreated in confusion. To their "utmost consternation," they ran into Prevost's redcoats advancing in three columns along the road. The speed of their horses saved them. The Rangers' mounts were too fatigued for a long pursuit. Brown informed Governor Tonyn that he had Colonel Baker's baggage and papers with a plan of Elbert's campaign.[17]

According to Major Patrick Murray, one of Prevost's officers, about forty Georgians surrendered. All but sixteen were put to death by the Indians. Murray reported that Major Prevost had difficulty in saving that many from the fury of the Indians. Governor Tonyn provided an explanation, if not an excuse. The Chiaha brave who was killed in the horse-stealing skirmish had been scalped, his body mangled, and all his "features" cut off. This atrocity "greatly exasperated" the Indians and accounted for their ferocity. Thomas Brown must have had second thoughts about his ability to control the conduct of his red allies when their blood lust was up.[18]

A few stragglers managed to reach Colonel Elbert and his three hundred Continentals stranded on Amelia Island. Their transports had not been able to cut through the shallow narrows between the island and the mainland. Elbert informed General McIntosh that he intended to retreat to the Georgia border at the St. Marys and make a stand there.[19]

Governor Tonyn understandably was pleased at the defense of his frontier. His success might have been greater if his ship, the *Rebecca*, had not been blown out to sea on its way to attack Elbert's naval escort at Amelia Island. The *Rebecca* had a brisk running fight with an American brigantine, and by the time the ship returned to the St. Johns, the Georgians had departed from Amelia. Tonyn had special praise for Major James Mark Prevost, probably because Thomas Brown had good things to say about Prevost in his report. Prevost's tact in dealing with the Rangers and Indians contrasted sharply with Lieutenant Colonel Fuser's rudeness. Tonyn found new accolades for his protégé: "Mr. Brown's sufferings from the Rebels render him in an uncommon degree worthy of the Attention of Government, much more, my Lord, does his indefatigable and undaunted spirit ever intent upon and strenuously exerted for his Majesty's service."[20]

A sour note was struck by Augustine Prevost, raised to the rank of brigadier general on April 1, 1777. He gave full credit for the British victory in the fracas at Thomas Creek to his brother. He blamed the Rangers for their failure to chase after and catch the rebels. When

Governor Tonyn inquired whether funds from the military chest might be used to defray the cost of the late expedition, Prevost demurred. As he saw it, "the Indians had their plunder, the rangers the cattle, the Soldiers nothing but the trouble."[21]

It was clear that Prevost did not share the enthusiasm for the grand strategy that possessed Tonyn and Brown. After the Battle of Thomas Creek, Prevost grumbled to Sir William Howe that "little dependence can be placed on the Indians." He did not care much for the Rangers either. They observed no regulations, according to Prevost, and went wherever they pleased. Prevost's complaints notwithstanding, the British high command had become infatuated with Brown's plan, and Prevost would have to go along, like it or not.[22]

General Sir William Howe was prompted by one of the plan's chief sponsors, Lord William Campbell, to send orders to John Stuart to organize the men who would lead the Indians. There were a number of loyal Carolinians among the Creeks at the beginning of the year. Stuart was to assign the men to companies under trustworthy leaders, who would have the difficult responsibility of distinguishing between loyal and disloyal inhabitants in the backcountry.[23] From the beginning, the weakness of the plan had been how to get the Indians to fight certain whites while restraining them from assaulting others. On the other side, Georgians such as General McIntosh and George Galphin, who wanted to maintain peaceful relations with the Indians, had the equally difficult task of controlling their Indian haters. Backcountrymen did not distinguish between Galphin's friends and John Stuart's allies. In the year 1777 the Indian haters led by George Wells were in the ascendancy in Georgia politics.

John Stuart was as lukewarm in his support of the plan in 1777 as he had been from the beginning. He complained to Lord George Germain that the Creeks were discouraged because of the defeat of the Cherokees. Besides, the plan called for troops to march with the Indians, and he saw no troops at hand. Stuart did what he could; he sent his staunchest ally, Emistisiguo, to help the Cherokees, who were worried about another invasion by the Carolinians. Stuart's deputies could not find "persons of abilities who can be confided in" in the Indian country. Evan McLaurin, sent into the Carolina backcountry by Lord William Campbell, was one of those Stuart had been counting on, but he was flushed out of the Indian country by the Georgians. Thomas Brown warned David Taitt to expel "bad men" like Thomas Gough and the same Adam Tapley he had tried to arrest the year before. Taitt regretted that he could not send Brown the help he wanted in Florida, and he appealed to Stuart to hurry the long-expected troops.[24]

In June Stuart, who had long used the excuse that Indians would not be of service without troops, informed Lord George Germain not to send troops because the Indian country was bereft of provisions. Such advice would scuttle the plan. Instead, Germain ordered Governor Tonyn to employ the men under his command to "second the Indians in their enterprises." Germain was determined to rescue the province of Georgia. In June Tonyn learned belatedly that his military rival, Prevost, had been made brigadier general and that the command of East and West Florida troops devolved upon Prevost.[25]

The practical effect of the promotion was that the plan to send troops into the Indian country now depended upon two men who did not believe in it, Prevost and Stuart. Tonyn endured the slight to his ambition (made worse to a proud Englishman because Prevost was a "foreigner"), but he drew the line at surrendering command of his special corps, Brown's Rangers. Tonyn and Prevost feuded with each other for the better part of a year over control of the Rangers. Prevost grumbled that Tonyn never treated him with the confidence or candor his rank deserved. "Wild schemes I believe he has sometimes entertained of conquering Georgia," said Prevost. He suspected that Tonyn wanted to reap all the glory.[26]

John Stuart's latest reason for inactivity was that Prevost was slow to approve the offensive operations which Stuart finally arranged. In September David Taitt obtained the agreement of the Lower Creeks to attack Georgia. They were ready to march under the supervision of Assistant Deputy William McIntosh. Two hundred white traders were formed into a volunteer company to fight alongside the Indians. Nothing was wanting but Prevost's approbation, Stuart wrote to Germain.[27]

The Georgians expected an Indian attack. George Wells, now a militia colonel and member of the legislature, was loud in his demands that Georgia strike the first blow, but George Galphin was responsible for frustrating Stuart's war plans and thwarting "those damned villains" like George Wells "that wants a Creek war." Galphin's tactic was to invite the Creeks to another conference and thereby create a schism in the nation. Because the old trail to Augusta had become too dangerous for red travelers, this meeting was held at Galphin's Old Town plantation on the Ogeechee. Handsome Fellow of the Okfuskees led the Galphin faction as he had the year before. When Emistisiguo remonstrated against going, Handsome Fellow threatened to kill him. The Cussita King led a large delegation from his town to meet Galphin. The Cowetas would not go; they were engaged in a feud with the backcountry Georgians. Their hostility was nurtured by Stuart's new assistant deputy, Alexander McGillivray, the mixed-blood son of Lachlan McGillivray, who ranked with George Galphin as a giant in the Indian trade and in influence among the tribes. The two were on opposite sides now, and their followers were divided.

On June 17, 1777, some four hundred Creek warriors met George Galphin, Robert Rae, and the Georgia Indian commissioners at Old Town on the Ogeechee. Handsome Fellow and the Cussita King talked fondly of their old trading path to Augusta and how much they would like to reopen it. They needed a great quantity of presents to take back with them to show that Galphin was not poor and that they again could be supplied from Augusta. Galphin had enough rum to keep the Okfuskees and Cussitas drunk for a month. He had some guns and ammunition that had been obtained from the French, but there were few goods for the visitors to take away. Galphin invited them to go to Philadelphia, where they would be astonished at the quantity of goods the Continental Congress possessed. Handsome Fellow was not interested in far-off Philadelphia, but he would like to see Charlestown. And so under Galphin's promise of protection, the Indians went visiting and were made much of by the Carolina governor and officials.[28]

David Taitt informed Thomas Brown that he hoped to spoil Galphin's party by dispatching Coweta warriors on the frontier. Perhaps this was the signal for which Brown was waiting. With Governor Tonyn's approval, if not that of the cautious Prevost (who complained that he did not know where the Rangers were or what they were doing), Brown scattered his Rangers to all parts of Georgia's exposed frontiers. Governor Tonyn informed Stuart that they were scouting parties whose primary purpose was observation and intelligence. Inevitably, there was skirmishing, too. One band of Rangers penetrated to within five miles of Savannah and another was reported to have passed through the town of Augusta. Brown's party moved up the Georgia coast and occupied St. Simons Island, the site of Oglethorpe's Fort Frederica.[29]

The Rangers, or Florida Scout as the Georgians called them, were loose on the Georgia frontiers at the same time as the Coweta war parties. It is impossible to tell how much cooperation existed between Tories and Indians. Governor Tonyn would later say that if it were not for the Rangers, "I could hardly have employed the Indians to lay waste Georgia, butchering indiscriminately men, women and children, which would have been the case had they acted by themselves." The Cowetas skirmished with Captain Elijah Clarke's Wilkes County militia and burned a fort on the Ogeechee, killing the wife and daughter of one Samuel Dilkes, regarded by the Indians as a trespasser on their lands. Another band of Indians ambushed a patrol of Georgia Continentals and killed Captain Thomas Dooly.[30]

The Georgia government was severely tested in its first year under a new constitution. The Executive Council Minutes of August 5, 1777, noted that "a number of Indians and Florida Scout have posted themselves upon Ogeechee in order to distress the people of this state." They were "daily committing outrages upon the persons and property of the people of the said State." The council directed Georgia Governor John Adam Treutlen to call out the Effingham County militia to search for the enemy. General McIntosh was asked to send fifty of his soldiers to guard Effingham.[31]

With the frontier people aroused to new hostility against Indians, Handsome Fellow and his touring party could not have returned to Georgia at a worse time. The late Thomas Dooly's brother, Captain John Dooly of the Continental Regiment of Horse, intercepted the Indians at Galphin's house at Silver Bluff and brought them to Augusta as prisoners. Governor John Rutledge and the Carolinians, who had so carefully cultivated the friendship of the visitors, were outraged at Dooly in particular and Georgia in general. The Georgia government had posted a reward for the arrest of William Henry Drayton for proposing the annexation of Georgia by South Carolina. Rutledge ordered Carolina troops to rescue the Indian prisoners, but George Galphin managed the crisis with his usual adroitness. He persuaded Dooly to release the Indians to Lieutenant Colonel Robert Rae, Galphin's fellow Indian commissioner. Rae escorted the Creeks to the Ogeechee, but not without incident. Brown's Rangers intercepted the party and killed Captain John Gerard. According to Governor Rutledge, Galphin had learned that his life was in danger, and Rutledge assumed that the Rangers mistook Gerard for Galphin.

Governor Tonyn interpreted the episode differently. Two Rangers tried to take Gerard prisoner to gain information, but Gerard drew his pistol, and a Ranger shot him.[32]

Whether true or not, the Georgians believed that the Rangers meant to kill Galphin. Colonel Samuel Elbert ordered Colonel John Baker to collect his regiment and intercept the party of Rangers that had waylaid Captain Gerard. Baker's men refused to turn out for several reasons, as reported by Elbert to General McIntosh: the inhabitants of the backcountry were cooped up in frontier forts and were starving; the light horse was mutinous and would not march "downwards" until they were paid; the men under him were unwell. Elbert had talked to Handsome Fellow's party in Augusta and urged them to assassinate Taitt, Cameron, and William McIntosh in revenge for the plot against Galphin.[33] Nothing came of it because their ally Handsome Fellow died of natural causes before he reached Okfuskee town.

For General Lachlan McIntosh and his friends, the situation was bleak. The ruling faction would not forgive McIntosh for the fatal duel with Button Gwinnett. According to Governor Treutlen, Gwinnett "lost his life in endeavoring to maintain the civil power in opposition to the cunning and subterfuge of designing men," namely McIntosh and his friends. McIntosh's enemies circulated a petition to Congress asking for the removal of the general from the state. It was said that Colonel John Baker forced his entire regiment to sign the petition. John Wereat informed Georgia's congressional delegate, George Walton, that the state was in the hands of a cabal consisting of Governor Treutlen, George Wells, Lyman Hall, Benjamin Andrew, and a few others, who conspired against the general, his relatives, and friends. Some people were moving to Carolina, others to Florida. "It is probable that by the conduct of those who misrule the state, we shall in a short time, be joined to Carolina or Florida," Wereat wrote. "God avert the latter, the former would be infinitely preferable to our present situation, when neither liberty or property are secure."[34] Walton used his influence with General George Washington to have McIntosh transferred to the North. To the harassed McIntosh, Valley Forge must have seemed an improvement. General Robert Howe assumed command and had to resist the demands of George Wells and others to launch a war against the Creeks.

It was at this time, in the early fall, that John Stuart's reluctant offensive was to be launched. George Wells was accused of wanting a war merely to get plunder, but Wells and his faction were not altogether wrong in expecting an Indian war. If Stuart's plans had worked, a major attack would have devastated the Georgia frontier and, presumably, General Prevost would have attacked from below. But George Galphin again thwarted John Stuart. Galphin succeeded in convincing Handsome Fellow's warriors that Stuart and Emistisiguo had sent the Coweta raiding parties against Georgia so that the Georgians would attack Handsome Fellow's band. After Handsome Fellow's death, his people felt obliged to get revenge.[35]

The pro-Galphin Okfuskees attempted to kill Tautt and Cameron as well as Emistisiguo, but the youthful Alexander McGillivray managed to save the lives of his friends. The Cussitas planned to kill William McIntosh, but the Cowetas and Chiahas protected him. The British deputies and traders had to leave the Indian country for a while in fear of their lives.[36] The year's maneuvering therefore resulted in a stunning victory for George Galphin. At least temporarily, Galphin had done by diplomacy what George Wells wanted to do by war, except that Wells would have taken the Indians' land. If Galphin had not negated the British plan, at least he had postponed it.

As the year 1777 ended, both sides tried to regroup. Neither the Americans nor the British could improve upon their original strategy. The Georgians were as determined as ever to invade Florida, and the British talked seriously about carrying out Brown's plan, which, by 1778, had become Lord George Germain's plan. The Carolina Loyalists grew impatient for the arrival of troops and began to filter down to Florida. Loyal Georgians were forced to leave the state, and their lands were confiscated. The longer the delay in sending troops, the fewer Loyalists there would be to greet their deliverers.

The Indians continued to quarrel about where their best interest lay. In November some of Galphin's allies returned to Old Town to receive congratulations and supplies. Galphin had plenty of the former but less and less of the latter. The ever-encroaching Georgians managed to spoil Galphin's best talks.

Stuart had the advantage of an apparently inexhaustible larder at Pensacola. Stuart's expenses were £19,000 in 1776, £37,729 in 1777, and £54,224 in 1778. One historian of the Revolution believes that if Stuart had not died when he did (on March 21, 1779) his prodigality might have ruined his career.[37] Stuart and Galphin both used trade embargoes to win back the Indians, but the Creeks soon realized that Galphin's embargo was born of a shortage of supplies.

The Creeks, including the fickle Okfuskees and Cussitas, soon begged Stuart to send back the deputies and traders, and by March, Tait and William McIntosh were once again in the Creek country. Alexander McGillivray, protected by his Creek parentage, had not left. Stuart never managed to mount a major Indian offensive, but he did encourage small war parties to make sporadic raids. The implacable Cowetas continued to annoy the Georgia frontier.[38]

The Continental Congress responded to the pleadings of Georgia's delegates by authorizing yet another invasion of Florida. General George Washington left the matter in the hands of Robert Howe, raised to the rank of major general in October 1777. Howe disliked the idea of an invasion of Florida as much as General Augustine Prevost was opposed to an invasion of Georgia. Howe blamed the war clamor on backcountry people who were motivated by an inveterate hatred of Indians. "The zealots for this war may think I overrate their [Indians'] strength, but I warn them, I do not," he argued.[39] Howe succeeded in worrying Washington, if not the Georgians. Washington replied to Howe that he had no idea that the Indians were so numerous, "and it therefore behooves us more to cultivate their friendship." The high command on both sides desired the allegiance of the Indians. An important difference was that on the American side, the backcountry Georgians wanted the Indians' land more than their allegiance. The Georgia governor made a gesture at cultivating the goodwill of the Indians by appointing half-breed Tom Gray a captain and permitting him to raise a company of Indians to join in the invasion of Florida.[40]

While the Americans planned their third Florida campaign, the dispossessed governors of South Carolina and Georgia begged Germain to remember the plan first outlined by Brown. If Carolina were attacked "in front," they should "possess themselves of the backcountry through Georgia." With the backcountry and coast under control, there was no middle ground for the rebels to hide in. They urged Germain to order an invasion before the winter of 1778. Germain sent their letter to Sir William Howe.[41]

Germain wrote to Sir Henry Clinton on March 8, 1778, to tell him that he was appointed Howe's successor as commander of the royal forces in America and that he should turn his attention to Georgia.

Two thousand men would be sufficient to take and keep Savannah. At the proper time General Prevost should be ordered to attack the southern frontier "with the Florida Rangers and a party of Indians." In concert "Mr. Stuart brings down a large body of Indians toward Augusta." Then backcountry Loyalists would be recruited to cooperate with a major offensive against Charlestown. Thomas Brown's plan had never been articulated so succinctly or with so much authority.[42]

The British ministry added a new dimension to Brown's plan. Clinton was to act as a member of a three-man commission with Lord Carlisle and William Eden. The three were styled "the British Commissioners for Restoring Peace in America." As an experiment in reconciliation, civil government would be restored in Georgia at the earliest possible moment. The peace plan was based on the premise that enough of the people were loyal to make the civil government work. The commander selected for the Georgia experiment was Lieutenant Colonel Archibald Campbell. In addition to his military role, Campbell was given a commission to act as civil governor of Georgia and of South Carolina as well, if events fell out propitiously. It was assumed that the appointment would be temporary, and Governor Sir James Wright prepared to regain his vacated chair in Savannah.[43] Lieutenant Colonel Thomas Brown would have taken satisfaction if he had known the attention his plan was getting in high places. But in Florida, he and and his Rangers were the center of controversy.

During the winter of 1777–78 Brown was stationed at Fort Tonyn on the St. Marys, Florida's front line of defense. His Rangers controlled the area below the Altamaha and kept St. Augustine supplied with provisions. The Rangers' raids drove the Georgians to distraction but failed to impress General Augustine Prevost. He reported to Howe on February 12, 1778, that there were now four companies of Rangers but that they were of little service. They were "without almost any control or regulation." Brown never criticized his Rangers, except indirectly. He informed Governor Tonyn on February 19 that his men were "improving in discipline."[44] Tonyn attempted to counter Prevost's criticism of the Rangers by writing a defense of the corps. He explained that Thomas Brown was a gentleman of education and fortune. He showed "a most exemplary and daring spirit" by going into the Indian country and engaging the Indians in the king's service. Brown commanded the Indians and Rangers at the capture of Fort McIntosh. He attacked the rebels above the St. Johns and had them beaten when Major Prevost arrived. General Prevost had never complimented Brown on these engagements or conveyed Howe's message of congratulations to him. Brown was hurt by the general's attitude, but "Honour is his great Pursuit," and no ill usage could distract him from the king's service. Had it not been for the Rangers, Florida would not have had three thousand head of cattle, Tonyn would not have dared employ Indians in battle, and the regulars could not have found their way in the woods.[45]

On March 12, 1778, Brown added to his laurels. With a hundred Rangers and ten Indians he swam across the quarter-mile-wide Altamaha. It was with the "utmost difficulty" that the Rangers kept their powder dry. They crept up to Fort Howe during the night. At daybreak they stormed the entrenchments with the loss of one killed, Lieutenant True Drew, and four wounded. Two of the fort's defenders were killed, four wounded, and twenty-three taken prisoner. The artillery was destroyed and the fort burned. In his report Brown singled out Ranger Andrew Johnston, son of Dr. Lewis Johnston, as the first man to mount the enemy's works. Brown was a fighter and did not need a reason to attack an enemy position, but he supplied Tonyn with an excuse. Fort Howe was an obstacle to the Rangers' foraging. "I flatter myself the Garrison and Province will be better supplied with cattle."[46]

General Prevost was not impressed. "I never considered the destruction of that post as an object of any consequence," he wrote to Howe. In his opinion, the rash act was one more reason why he should have command over "that truly independent Corps of Rangers." Tonyn presented his rebuttal on April 4. If Prevost were not so backward in supporting the Rangers, a road might be opened to the back settlements now that Fort Howe was destroyed. Tonyn regretted that both Prevosts had fallen in with the anti-Tonyn faction: "Their prejudices against and jealousies of Lt. Col. Brown is highly ungenerous and hurtful." Prevost's answer followed immediately. The nub of the problem was Brown's rank. Was he entitled to outrank majors in the regular army? Neither of the Prevosts could abide the idea of young Brown giving orders to army majors, particularly to Major James Mark Prevost.[47]

The storming of Fort Howe was of more consequence than Prevost admitted or understood. It meant that Brown could send his Rangers into Carolina to take a census of loyal inhabitants. The day of deliverance was at hand. Moses Kirkland, briefly reunited with Brown as Stuart's deputy to the Seminoles, went off for the second time to explain the plan to Sir Henry Clinton. On the Georgia side, General Robert Howe was convinced that the Fort Howe attack was a signal for an uprising of Loyalists and that the uprising was a prelude to invasion.[48]

Brown was ready with his intelligence report on April 10. He had established contact with his old ally Robert Cunningham, who assured Brown that twenty-five hundred men between the forks of the Saluda and Broad rivers were ready to accompany him "on any service whenever orders are sent." There were another thousand on the Congaree and the Ridge, sixteen hundred on the Pedee and Enoree, and twelve hundred on the Green River. Corn had been stored for two years in preparation for the uprising. Brown took the opportunity in his letter to Prevost to promote himself: "To most of these loyalists I am known and with all their principals personally acquainted."[49]

Brown was directly responsible for the movement of Loyalists to Florida. He had kept up a correspondence with his friends since his exile, and when Governor Tonyn needed more Rangers, Brown wrote to his contacts in the Ninety-Six District.[50] The trek of the first contingent under leaders named Murphy and Gregory thoroughly alarmed the Georgia Whigs. Georgia Governor John Houstoun informed Congress on April 16 that between five and six hundred marched through the back parts of Georgia on their way to Florida, stealing horses, arms, and ammunition as they went, and "I am sorry to say, were joined by some in this state." The Executive Council attempted to quiet the fears of backcountry Georgians by meeting in Augusta. The council's resolution to meet was dated April 13. On April 16 Thomas Brown informed Governor Tonyn that the influential backcountry members would cause the seat of government to be transferred to Augusta. Evidently Brown's intelligence system was working well.[51] The commotion made by the first passage prevented other Loyalists from following their example. Captain John York of the Rangers discouraged a large body of Loyalists from crossing into Georgia because the Georgia militia had been alerted.[52]

Some of the newcomers joined Brown's Rangers, but most of them were formed into a new provincial regiment styled the South Carolina Royalists. Governor Tonyn, in a conciliatory gesture, agreed to put them under the direct command of General Prevost, who assigned them to his brother the major to learn something of military discipline. The general's opinion of Rangers began to improve rapidly thereafter. Despite the expectations of both Prevosts, General Clinton gave command of the South Carolina Royalists to Lord William Campbell's former secretary, Colonel Alexander Innes. Joseph Robinson, Thomas Brown's associate in the Fletchall-Drayton affair, was made lieutenant colonel, and Evan McLaurin, emissary of Lord William Campbell and later of John Stuart, was named major. Some of Brown's officers, John York for one, were assigned to the new corps.[53]

Although Governor Tonyn conceded the new corps to General Prevost, he continued to resist yielding control of Brown's Rangers until the Georgia invasion was actually under way. Brown's outpost on the St. Marys stood directly in the path of the invaders. Tonyn asked Prevost to send help to Brown. Prevost said that he would send no officer to be commanded by Brown: "Mr. Brown might stay at [the] St. Mary's and when the rebels had drove him and the Rangers from thence they would find the King's Troops at [the] St. John's." Furthermore, Brown's Rangers would not be given provisions from Prevost's stores, even though the Rangers had helped stock those stores. Tonyn was beaten; regretfully and for the time being only, he asked Brown to yield command of the frontier forces to Major Beamsley Glazier of the Sixtieth Regiment. He hoped Brown would "wave every punctilio" and assured him that it would not reflect upon his honor to serve under a regular officer.[54]

Brown, without leaving his post, offered his resignation. He never intended to sacrifice His Majesty's service to punctilio, he said, but he would not serve under "every subaltern." The request implied a severe censure upon his conduct as an officer and a gentleman. Besides, Brown reminded Tonyn, the king had approved the independent status of the Rangers. Tonyn sent Brown's letter of resignation to Sir William Howe with a lengthy recital of Brown's virtues, explaining that when he first became acquainted with Brown, he felt for his suffering and admired his spirit. He had appointed him to command the Rangers because he was the best qualified. If he were allowed to resign, "I know not another person who is fit for supplying his place." Clinton, who had replaced Howe, replied to Tonyn that he agreed with Howe that Prevost must be the supreme military commander in Florida and therefore should take charge of Brown's

Rangers.[55] Before that order reached Florida, the invasion of 1778 had reached its climax.

The first contact between the invaders and the Rangers is chronicled in the journal of John Fauchereau Grimké of South Carolina, who served with Colonel Charles Pinckney's South Carolina Continentals. General Robert Howe commanded the six hundred Carolina and five hundred Georgia Continentals. The Georgia militia marched as a separate force under Governor John Houstoun, while the South Carolina militia lagged far behind under General Andrew Williamson. The campaign suffered from the same lack of coordination that crippled the abortive Gwinnett-McIntosh invasion. Grimké noted that General Howe was not acquainted with the governor's plans and intentions.[56]

On June 18, 1778, the Carolinians heard that Lieutenant Colonel Brown had three hundred men at Fort Tonyn on the St. Marys. The South Carolina Royalists and some regulars were halfway between the St. Marys and St. Johns. On June 28 the Continentals crossed the St. Marys. Three horsemen rode up to observe the crossing; they were pursued but escaped into a swamp. Grimké recorded that it was commonly believed that one of the riders was "Col. Brown himself who commands the Corps of Rangers in East Florida." The report was confirmed several days later. When the Americans reached Fort Tonyn and found that Brown had burned it, the army was "much disappointed," Grimké noted.[57]

If Thomas Brown was an observer of the crossing, he was not an idle one. He knew that nothing worried the men of the backcountry more than a threat to their homes. Therefore, he sent Captain James Moore, who had once walked with Brown to the gates of Fort McIntosh, on a roundabout raid. With seventy-six Rangers and some Indians, Moore was supposed to rendezvous with a body of backcountry Loyalists and attack the invaders from the rear. If the strategy had worked, Thomas Brown—and therefore Governor Tonyn—would have reaped the glory which General Prevost was concerned about. Some of Moore's men deserted, however, and disclosed his location. Moore was ambushed, wounded, and captured, then shot to death. Such actions invited reprisals.[58]

After taking all the baggage he could carry and burning Fort Tonyn, Brown and his men could have retreated with honor. Brown, however, was determined to contest every mile of the Americans'

advance. He and his Rangers hid in a swamp and subsisted on pal-
metto roots. Major James Mark Prevost took a position about seventeen miles south of Brown at a bridge over Alligator Creek. Prevost
sent a detachment to rescue the Rangers, but Brown declined to be
rescued. "I was determined to harrass and annoy the Rebels as much
as was in our power," Brown explained to Governor Tonyn. General
Augustine Prevost would add Brown's refusal to retreat to the list of
reasons why the Rangers should come under his control.

Brown collected his scattered command and began to withdraw
when General James Screven advanced with one hundred mounted
militia. Captain Patrick Murray of Prevost's Royal Americans recorded in his memoirs a graphic description of what followed. About
noon on June 30, 1778, the British regulars were cleaning their arms
and bathing in Alligator Creek. The Grenadiers were finishing a
breastwork across the road. There were swamps on both sides of the
road.

A Ranger sergeant rode in to report to Major Prevost that Colonel
Brown and his corps were coming into camp, but no one was prepared for the manner in which they came. The first Rangers filed
across the bridge in good order, but the rear guard dashed in pell-
mell, the Americans in hot pursuit, brandishing sabers and rifles and
shouting, "Down with the Tories!" While the drummer beat "The
Grenadiers' March" and the British regulars ran for their muskets,
Rangers jumped into the breastworks and filed out into the swamps,
or, in Murray's words, they "were seen flying" into the swamps in
front of the camp. The regulars replaced the Rangers in the ditch
after Ranger Captain Smith and Lieutenant Johnson were mortally
wounded defending the position. With the regulars keeping up a
brisk fire from the road, Brown led two companies through the
swamp and around the flank of the attackers. American Lieutenant
Colonel Elijah Clarke was wounded in the leg and barely escaped
capture. This was the first personal encounter between Thomas
Brown and Elijah Clarke, but it would not be the last. Caught between the Rangers on the flank and regulars in the front and injured,
Screven ordered a retreat, taking his wounded with him. Back at the
American camp on the St. Marys, it was reported that Brown had
tried to surround the Americans and Screven had escaped from the
trap.[59]

Major Prevost did not allow a pursuit of the Georgians. The next
morning, Prevost, Brown, and Murray, with a company of South

Carolina Royalists under Captain John York, advanced ten miles and surprised an enemy crew repairing a bridge. Captain York gave them a chase but could not catch them. That was the last action in the campaign of 1778. The invaders, wracked by dissension and disease, turned back. Instead of punishing the retreating army, General Prevost recalled his troops. Prevost gave his brother credit for the victory at Alligator Bridge, but Tonyn reported that only "a few of the King's troops assisted the Rangers." There is no doubt that Brown had become a hero to the people of East Florida. A 1784 memorial by the inhabitants recited how the rebels who had advanced below the St. Marys "were beat back and frustrated in their designs, chiefly by the spirited exertions of the militia embodied by Governor Tonyn . . . under the conduct and command of that active and enterprising officer, Lieutenant Colonel Brown." Adding to Brown's public stature was his appointment to the Governor's Council. He took his seat in December 1778 but had few opportunities to do much sitting.[60]

General Prevost must have been pleased with his small victory over Governor Tonyn when Clinton made it clear that the East Florida Rangers were to come under his control. Yet he was far from satisfied. Brown's rank was the problem. In the Alligator Creek engagement, Brown as lieutenant colonel did not feel obliged to take orders from Major James Mark Prevost. The only regular lieutenant colonel serving in East Florida was Lewis V. Fuser, and he was too infirm to be given the task of supervising the Rangers. General Prevost grumbled that he was now obliged to provision the Rangers, who were of no service except to plunder. He demanded to know if Brown's rank was legal and valid, "as it appears rather hard that old officers should be commanded by a young man entirely unacquainted with military matters, though otherwise zealous and deserving." If Brown was entitled to his rank, then Prevost wanted his majors promoted to lieutenant colonels. The promotion of James Mark Prevost had already been approved, and Prevost gained his other point when Clinton ruled that provincial officers would rank below the youngest regular officer in the rank immediately beneath them.[61]

General Prevost had to change his low opinion of plundering expeditions when his provisions diminished. In November Prevost sent his brother into Georgia to collect cattle. Lieutenant Colonel Fuser was now well enough to lead a separate force, which was to threaten Sunbury and thereby serve as a diversion. Brown and his Rangers, now clearly under command of Fuser, the ailing senior officer, again initiated the fighting as they had done at Fort McIntosh, Thomas Creek, and Alligator Bridge.

Hearing that General Screven and Colonel John White were approaching on the road between Midway and Sunbury, Fuser ordered Brown to reconnoiter and harass the Americans. Brown picked thirty-two of his best men and went to meet the enemy. Brown's men concealed themselves in a thicket beside the road. Screven and White halted their command at that very place. Brown listened as attentively as did the Americans to the usual prebattle harangues delivered by Screven and White. With an instinct for the dramatic moment, Brown waited until the speeches were finished, then ordered his men to fire. The surprise was complete. Screven fell in the first volley, and after a confused melee the Americans retreated. Later there was controversy about the manner of Screven's death. It was said that a Ranger shot him after he was already disabled to avenge the murder of Ranger Captain James Moore. In his own account of the battle, however, Brown said that the wounded Screven was brought back to Lieutenant Colonel Prevost's camp and treated "with tenderness and humanity" but did not recover from his wounds. Brown paid him a tribute: "He had the character of a brave, worthy man."[62]

The Georgia historian Hugh M'Call is the authority for the account of the action following the Rangers' engagement of the enemy. Lieutenant Colonel Mark Prevost came up to support the Rangers, and the regulars joined battle with the Americans. Prevost's horse was felled by a cannon shot, but he remounted and completed the victory. Afterward, he burned the Midway Meeting House and began a leisurely retreat, bringing out of Georgia what he had come for, two thousand head of cattle.[63]

Fuser's role in the expedition was to distract the Americans. He accomplished that purpose so well that the Georgians were convinced that he was the vanguard of an expected invasion. When Fuser demanded that Lieutenant Colonel John McIntosh surrender Fort Morris at Sunbury, McIntosh gave the celebrated response, "Come and take it." Fuser decided he had created enough of a diversion and retreated. The Georgians, understandably, believed that McIntosh's brave words had turned back the invasion.[64]

The real invasion was about to begin, however. The plan was to be carried out at last. It will be recalled that Lord George Germain wrote to General Sir Henry Clinton that at the proper time he should order General Prevost to attack the southern frontiers "while Mr. Stuart brings down a large body of Indians towards Augusta." By November the British invasion force was ready to sail from New York; the proper time had arrived. Never before had coordination between Stuart and the military been more crucial. Unfortunately for the British, relations between Governor Tonyn at St. Augustine and John Stuart in Pensacola were severely strained.

When the 1778 Georgia invasion was first launched, Governor Tonyn sent a desperate plea to Perryman, the half-breed who had led his band to Florida in 1777, to come again. At the same time he urged Deputies William McIntosh and David Taitt to bring down more Indians. Perryman arrived in St. Augustine with word that many Creeks were prepared to come but that McIntosh and Taitt had delivered "peace talks" and invited the head men to visit Stuart in Pensacola. Tonyn wrote Stuart that the summons to Pensacola could not have come at a worse time: "I assure you sir, this is not a time to hesitate." Stuart's emissaries, David Holmes and Timothy Barnard, finally reached East Florida with a contingent of Indians long after the invaders had returned to Georgia. Tonyn did not bother to conceal his scorn in a letter of September 8 to Stuart. The party that arrived with Holmes and Barnard on August 29 was "inconsiderable" and eight weeks late. Both men were nephews of George Galphin, and Tonyn believed that they were deliberately late. Tonyn wondered if Stuart really expected him to send a message to Pensacola, which was six hundred miles away, to get permission to treat with Indians who were one hundred miles away.[65]

Lord George Germain sided with Tonyn in the dispute. He wrote Stuart on December 2, ordering him to dismiss McIntosh and Taitt for giving peace talks just when Indians were needed in East Florida: "I cannot suppose they acted by any orders from you." At the same time, Germain reminded Stuart of the importance of performing his part in the plan. He hoped Stuart would go with the first party of Indians to Augusta and meet the king's troops there.[66]

John Stuart's letter crossed Germain's. Stuart was as angry at Tonyn as Tonyn was at him. He did not like Tonyn's "preemptory and pressing demands" of McIntosh and Taitt. He had called a general meeting, and "at that very juncture, it pleased Governor Tonyn" to invite Perryman to East Florida. Tonyn's interference had "not failed to create me an infinite deal of trouble." He wanted Tonyn "restrained." Stuart enclosed a letter from Prevost, which also blamed Tonyn. Mistakes were made, Prevost said, "when officers step out of their own departments and assume the direction of another without deigning to communicate with the officer placed by the King at the head of it." Prevost was grinding his own ax, of course.[67]

In his letter of December 4, Stuart showed no awareness that he was supposed to have the Indians ready for the great offensive. David Taitt would later testify that Stuart first learned that the invasion from New York was under way in the latter part of January in a letter from Governor Tonyn of December 16.[68] Stuart should have been ready earlier. Governor Tonyn's letter of September 8, which Stuart enclosed to Germain on December 4, alerted Stuart to Clinton's instructions to attack the southern provinces in the fall. The letter stated that great assistance would be expected from Stuart's department. Several factors were at work against the British plan. Stuart was ill during November and December. George Galphin introduced confusion into the Indian country with another of his conferences in November. It could be argued that the man chiefly at fault for not giving Stuart his orders in due time was General Augustine Prevost. Prevost had the professional soldier's disdain for Indian warfare and never showed any enthusiasm for the plan advocated by his rival Tonyn. And John Stuart knew Indians too well to believe that they could be held in check when the lust of battle was upon them so he temporized and the plan was undercut at the moment it should have been implemented. The troops would be sent, but the Indians would not act in concert with them.

CHAPTER FIVE

THE PLAN UNFOLDS,

1779

 When Moses Kirkland laid the plan for a coordinated attack by sea and frontier before General Sir Henry Clinton in New York on October 13, 1778, it was an exercise in redundance. Clinton already knew about it. In fact, the plan was known to George Washington, the Continental Congress, and all the Whig authorities in Georgia and Carolina as the result of Kirkland's arrest and the publication of his dispatches in 1776. Clinton had had Brown's plan explained to him personally by John Stuart at Cape Fear and mailed to him by his friend Governor Tonyn. Tonyn, Governor James Wright, and Lord William Campbell, before the latter's death in 1778, had not let him forget the plan. Lord George Germain had outlined the plan to Clinton in his letter of appointment to the rank of commander in chief on March 8, 1778. Kirkland's visit did more to promote Kirkland than the plan. It reminded Clinton that Kirkland was one of the original planners and returned him to the center of action. At the time, Kirkland was John Stuart's deputy stationed in St. Augustine and therefore was in a position to facilitate communication between the military and the Indians. He had every reason to hope for a higher post when Georgia and South Carolina were restored to the king. The unfolding of the plan began well when Clinton invited Kirkland to join the expedition as assistant deputy quartermaster general.[1]

The officer selected by Clinton to carry out the military part of the plan was a thirty-nine-year-old Scot, Lieutenant Colonel Archibald Campbell. He had been a prisoner of war until he was exchanged for Lieutenant Colonel Ethan Allen in May 1778 and was therefore available for the mission. Campbell was described on one hand as "courteous, humane, polished in his manners" and on the other as "vain, arrogant and cruel." The expedition acquired added significance when the peace commissioners, of which Clinton was one, bestowed civil as well as military powers upon Campbell. He was to restore civilian rule in Georgia and South Carolina also, if possible.[2]

On October 20 Clinton ordered General Prevost to march to the St. Marys with all available troops to be ready to join Campbell and take command of the expedition, but Prevost did not receive the dispatch until November 27. Therefore, the November expedition to Midway and the threat to Sunbury were, in fact, a joint cattle round-up and not an abortive invasion, as some Georgia historians have asserted.[3]

On December 28 Campbell's force of three thousand British, Hessians, and Loyalists landed and overwhelmed General Robert Howe's defenders of Savannah. Among those captured were George Walton, colonel of the Georgia militia, who was badly wounded, and George Wells, champion of the backcountry. Campbell issued a proclamation, affixing the name of Hyde Parker, commodore of the expedition, before his because he was keenly sensitive that his own rank of lieutenant colonel was not commensurate with the importance of the occasion. All who wanted to return to the allegiance of the king were invited to do so; deserters would be pardoned; all well-disposed persons would be protected; and no taxes would be imposed upon the province. Finally, "God and the World" were called upon to witness that those who remained opposed to the reestablishment of royal government would be answerable for the miseries that would befall them.[4]

Campbell poured out his private pique in his journal: "Why the temporary rank of a Brigadier General was refused to a Lieutenant Colonel of four years standing, who had been selected as a fit officer to be entrusted with the command of eight battalions of infantry on a service of the first importance to the nation . . . is a question that can only be solved by those who had the power of granting it."[5] On January 12 Campbell prepared to vacate his quarters, "deemed the best in the Metropolis," in favor of General Augustine Prevost.

On the march to Savannah, Prevost's force of 900 men captured Fort Morris with its contingent of 220 men. Prevost had high praise for his troops and for their "cheerfulness under the most severe fatigues." He was proud of his officers, who subsisted on the same fare as the men and endured the same hardships.[6]

On January 15 Campbell yielded command to Prevost. He confided to his journal that he did not like this "supercession," but it was his duty to obey orders. He was free in his comments to Peace Commissioner William Eden: "Prevost seems a worthy man, but too old and inactive for this service. He will do in garrison and I shall gallop with the light troops." Campbell did not share Prevost's good opinion of the Florida troops. They were "900 rag tag and Bobtails." Some citizens of Savannah complained that Prevost's men from the southward "had more the appearance of a plundering party."[7]

As Campbell prepared for his gallop to Augusta, where, according to the plan, he would rendezvous with the backcountry Loyalists and the Indians, he dispatched a message to Lord George Germain. "I need not inform Your Lordship, how much I prize the hope of being the first British Officer to rend a Stripe and a Star from the flag of Congress. If I am successful it will rest with my Sovereign to decide its Merits and Consequences."[8]

On January 22, 1779, Campbell began his march from Ebenezer. Leading the advance were Brown's Florida Rangers. The Carolina Royalists, under Lieutenant Colonel Joseph Robinson, closed the rear. The colonel of the Royalists, Alexander Innes, had not yet taken command of his corps. He had come to Georgia with Campbell and immediately returned to London with dispatches. Campbell's first impression of the Rangers was that they were "a mere rabble of undisciplined Freebooters." Moreover, he objected to Prevost's interference with respect to the Rangers almost as much as Prevost had resented Tonyn's. The Georgians were rallying at the Burke County jail, where several Loyalists were held hostage. Prevost ordered Brown to rescue them. Brown received the order on January 26 when he reached Briar Creek, and he set off immediately on a path that veered off the Augusta Road.[9]

Campbell recorded in his journal that he disapproved of the order because either Brown would be beaten or the rebels would retire too far into the backcountry before Campbell could get behind them. In fact, the Americans were ready for Brown. The Burke County militia was rallied by Lieutenant Colonel James Ingram, adjutant to General Benjamin Lincoln, Robert Howe's successor as commander of the Southern Department. Ingram believed that Prevost and Brown had joined Campbell and the entire force of 3,000 was on the way to Augusta. He said that he had 250 men who behaved like regulars camped at the jail. Militia Colonels John Twiggs and Benjamin Few

Note the position of the King's Rangers in the British defense line to the right of the city. (Preparation supervised by Ranger Alexander C. Wylly. Courtesy University of Georgia Libraries.)

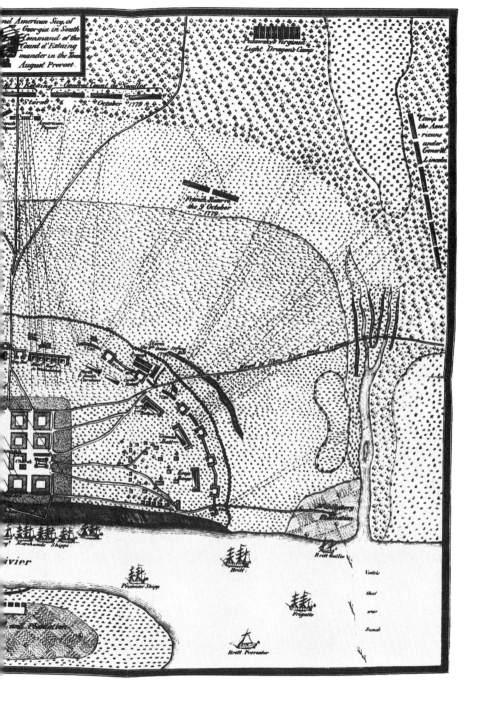

nd American Siege of
Georgia in South
Command of the
Count d'Estaing
mander in the Town
August Prevost

were there, as was Lieutenant Colonel William Few. Brown boldly attacked the log house that served as a fort but was beaten off. The Georgia historian Hugh M'Call wrote that Brown was reinforced by a party of Carolina Loyalists, probably Robinson's, and renewed the attack after dark. At least five Rangers were killed and Brown's arm was shattered. During the next day the Rangers rejoined Campbell, who noted that they were "seemingly much jaded and not a little disconcerted with their repulse."[10]

Lieutenant Colonel Campbell's fears were realized when the Burke County Whigs joined forces with Colonel Samuel Elbert's retreating army. Campbell laid a careful plan to surround the Americans at McBean Creek, but two Florida Rangers blundered into the enemy camp and gave the game away. Campbell's opinion of the Rangers did not improve as a result. The British breakfasted on beef and pork stew left by the Americans.[11]

Campbell's march led past Silver Bluff. There was irony in the juxtaposition of the man who was carrying out the British plan and the man who did more than anyone else to disrupt the strategy. Campbell reflected the uncertainty felt by many Georgians regarding the allegiance of George Galphin. He sent a message to Galphin inviting him to persuade the Indians to remain neutral. Campbell, of course, did not really want the Indians to remain quiet because he expected to meet them in Augusta. The British scouts sent to spy on Galphin intercepted a message which Campbell interpreted as encouraging the Creeks to war. Campbell decided to hold ninety of Galphin's slaves as hostage against Galphin's good behavior.[12]

Actually Campbell accomplished more than he realized. Galphin was about to resume trade with the Creeks at his post at Old Town on the Ogeechee during that January. A month earlier ten head men, including Opeitley Mico of Tallasee and the Cussita King, had called on Galphin and asked him to reopen the trading path. Galphin had long favored the resumption of trade but was hampered by a chronic shortage of supplies and the open hostility of the Georgians toward Indians. "The people upon the frontiers threatened to kill me and the Indians too if I supplied them," he wrote to Henry Laurens. Galphin was convinced that the settlers, not John Stuart, were responsible for bringing down continual raids upon the frontier. The message that annoyed Campbell was Galphin's warning to the Creeks not to come to the Ogeechee just then but to wait until he could meet them and ensure their safety. Campbell caught the first messenger, but a second one got through. Campbell noted that he received "a penitential" letter from Galphin, who promised to cooperate in the future.[13]

On January 30, Campbell used his artillery to blast the Americans out of Fort Henderson on Spirit Creek. Early on the morning of the thirty-first, as the British prepared for their entry into Augusta, the scouts brought Captain William Manson into camp. It must have been an emotional moment for Brown and Manson to be reunited after three years. Brown had been recovering from a fractured skull in December 1775; in January 1779 it was a fractured arm. Daniel Manson, a Charlestown shipbuilder and a distant relative, was also with Campbell, and William's brother Thomas may have been present. With so many to testify to his good character, it is strange that Campbell's secretary, John Wilson, put him down as "at best a dubious character." In this war everyone was suspect. Manson told Campbell that the Americans had an ambush prepared at the Cupboard, a swamp just below Augusta. The report was true, but Elbert withdrew that same morning without a fight, and Manson led the British into Augusta without incident.[14]

At last the Augusta Loyalists could display their true feelings. The Reverend James Seymour described how many of the rebellious inhabitants crossed into Carolina, but "the Loyalists remained at Home to receive their friends." Surely Thomas Brown was counted among these friends. His partner, Gordon, was there to greet him. Gordon had been forced to leave the frontier plantations because of the Indian raids. He had hired a substitute to enlist in the militia and achieved modest success in the mercantile trade. Martin Weatherford, who had risked the wrath of the Liberty Boys and taken the tortured Brown into his home, was there. So was Andrew McLean, the "Little Macaroni" who had courted and won the widow Katy, daughter of Robert and Mary Mackay. Isaac Herbert, now a storekeeper, was a friendly face. Colonel James Grierson and Lieutenant Colonel William Goodgion were old acquaintances, and of course, his father's master mariner, William Manson, could resume an interrupted friendship. Brown was in the unique position of introducing Lieutenant Colonel Campbell to the loyal Augustans. The result, as Parson Seymour explained, was that "a few of us, whose Characters Col. Campbell had been previously informed of, were treated with the greatest marks of Attention by himself and officers."[15]

While in Augusta, Campbell used James Grierson's stockaded house as his headquarters. Brown and his officers were quartered in

St. Paul's Church. The Rangers were given the duty of guarding against attack from the woods to the south of town. A detachment of Rangers under Captain Moses Wheatley was sent to guard Brown's plantation at Brownsborough. Brown's fractured arm limited his activity. Lieutenant Colonel Joseph Robinson's Carolina Royalists shared the responsibility for patrolling the hinterland. Captain Robert Phillips, one of Brown's veterans now with the Royalists, and Captain John Hamilton went into Wilkes County expecting to meet Colonel James Boyd's contingent of Loyalists from Carolina. Hamilton got into a skirmish at Carr's Fort, and a hundred of Brown's Rangers with some light infantry were dispatched to help him. The Rangers were especially useful in their old business of foraging. The unfortunate George Galphin lost seventy horses and numerous cattle to the Rangers.[16]

Ranger Captain Wheatley earned Campbell's displeasure by his "extreme inattention." Wheatley was surprised by a detachment of Captain Leonard Marbury's light horse, and seventeen of his men were captured. Captain Phillips made up for it by defeating the same party and taking ten prisoners. The raiders from the Carolina side hurt their own cause by perpetrating a particularly brutal act. An unnamed rebel major, a prisoner of war, had asked for protection for his family. Campbell did the gentlemanly thing and assigned a trusted sergeant named MacAlister to guard the major's house. MacAlister was killed by an American raiding party, and his body was hacked to pieces. According to Campbell, the British troops "were greatly exasperated by this shameful Act" and later avenged MacAlister at Briar Creek.[17]

During the first week of British occupation of Augusta, the plan seemed to be working out as expected. Campbell had every reason to believe that Indians from the west and Loyalists from the east were on the way to join him. In fact, both were. Campbell counted eleven hundred men who came in to take the oath of allegiance to the king. They were formed into twenty militia companies, each within its own district. The inhabitants of Wilkes County were aware that Indians were approaching and humbly asked for protection. Campbell rather grandly guaranteed their security in an address circulated through the backcountry. How the Indians were to distinguish between yesterday's enemies and today's friends was an intrinsic dilemma in the British plan. Campbell took care to dispatch a message to his

Creek allies to caution them not to wage war against people on the Georgia side of the Savannah River.[18]

Meanwhile, Campbell had flatboats made under the supervision of boat builder Daniel Manson in preparation for a daring night attack on General Andrew Williamson's outpost on Fort Moore's Bluff. Spies acquainted him with exact knowledge of the terrain. Thomas Brown knew the territory as well as most inhabitants; his intelligence must have been of use to Campbell. During their brief acquaintance, Campbell's opinion of Brown rose considerably; he overcame his disapproval of the attack on the Burke County jail to commend Brown in a letter of March 4 to Clinton: "The Personal Gallantry of this officer did him the highest honor."[19]

Campbell's foray did not come off, partly because his respected second in command, Colonel James Maitland, was against it and partly because four escaping slaves roused the Carolinians on Moore's Bluff at the very hour of the intended surprise. Maitland's caution was well founded. Williamson's eight hundred troops were joined by sixteen hundred reinforcements, twelve hundred of them North Carolinians under General John Ashe. Campbell believed that there were thirty-eight hundred men on the opposite shore. Without waiting any longer for Boyd's loyal Carolinians, Campbell abandoned Augusta early on the morning of February 14, 1779. He could boast that they went away with more ammunition and provisions than they had when the expedition began.[20]

That boast was scant comfort to the loyal Augustans when they awoke to find their guardians gone without a by-your-leave. The Reverend Seymour commented that the "two weeks of sunshine" were over. Without notice, the British army "left the poor Loyalists exposed to the Fury of the Rebel Army. . . . Our Feelings at first on that Occasion cannot be easily described. We expected to be plundered of everything we had, and even that our Lives were in Danger."[21] Fortunately, South Carolina's General Andrew Williamson was a humane conqueror. He did not permit plundering or reprisals. Ten of the leading Loyalists, including Seymour, were made prisoners but were treated well.

The Florida Rangers flanked Campbell's retreating column, which reached Boggy Gut, twenty-five miles below Augusta, in one long day's march. On the following day, February 15, Campbell heard that Colonel Boyd's Carolina Loyalists had been defeated at Kettle

Creek the day before as they were on their march to join him. Colonels Andrew Pickens and John Dooly and Lieutenant Colonel Elijah Clarke led the victorious Carolina and Georgia militia. Campbell quickly secured both banks of Briar Creek and sent the Florida Rangers and Carolina Loyalists to Wrightsborough to meet the survivors of the fight at Kettle Creek. On February 18, 270 of Boyd's people were escorted into Campbell's camp on Briar Creek. Campbell praised their loyalty and zeal and provided for their needs. The refugees were formed into another regiment of Carolina Royalists under their own officers.[22] The southward march was resumed. On February 20, Lieutenant Colonel James Mark Prevost met Campbell at Hudson's Ferry and informed him that he was to take command of the advanced troops. Campbell showed Prevost his map of the countryside and demonstrated how the rebels might be trapped if they followed as far as the mouth of Briar Creek. The Florida Rangers remained with Prevost, and the Carolina Royalists under Robinson were sent down to guard a river crossing at Tuckasaw King.[23]

Campbell decided that he had done as much as he could in Georgia and prepared to leave. On March 4 he named Lieutenant Colonel James Mark Prevost the acting governor of Georgia until Governor James Wright arrived from England. Before sailing on March 11, he received the welcome news that the younger Prevost had followed Campbell's advice and had won a complete victory over North Carolina General John Ashe at Briar Creek on March 3, 1779. Presumably, Brown's Rangers participated in the action. It was noted that as the Seventy-first Regiment charged the rebels one of the Highlanders called out, "Now my Boys, remember poor Macalister."[24]

Meanwhile, Lord George Germain could not control his anxiety about the working out of the plan. He assumed that Campbell would gather "very considerable numbers" at Augusta and penetrate into Carolina. Clinton would send "timely reinforcements" before General Washington could do anything. On March 13, 1779, Germain wrote to General Prevost expressing surprise that he had not heard about the Indians. He understood that John Stuart had the Indians ready to cooperate whenever they were needed. He could only hope that they were on the way to Augusta to meet Campbell.[25]

On the same day Indians were also on Augustine Prevost's mind. From his camp in Ebenezer, he wrote to the Creek chiefs warning

them not to wage war on Georgians or on women and children anywhere. The rebel men in arms in Carolina, however, were eligible
targets. The Indians could distinguish friendly Loyalists because
they would wear a red cross in their hats as well as a pine brush.[26] It
is not recorded whether the Loyalists who were fortunate enough to
hear about this method of identification felt more secure.

The Americans were equally anxious as to the whereabouts of the
Indians. It was assumed that no white person of any age or sex would
be safe in an Indian war. That certainty was an effective rallying
force for the backcountry militia. General Andrew Williamson sent
Colonels Andrew Pickens and LeRoy Hammond of South Carolina
and Colonel John Dooly of Georgia to prevent a junction between the
Indians and British.[27]

David Taitt, already under a cloud because of the failure of the
Indians to come to Governor Tonyn's assistance the year before, had
to bear the brunt of the impossible task that fell to him. In spite of
Germain's orders to be ready to move, John Stuart was too absorbed
in his own problems, too distant in Pensacola, and too ill to carry out
his responsibilities. Stuart informed Taitt on February 1 that he was
to collect the Upper Creeks and march to Augusta to meet Lieutenant
Colonel Campbell. The entire month was spent organizing the attack
force. On the march Taitt received Campbell's orders warning the
Indians not to attack Georgians. With increasing misgivings, Taitt
and twenty-five white traders led the more than four hundred Creeks
to the Ogeechee. On March 25 Prevost's letter reached Taitt. The
ludicrous scheme to distinguish friends from enemies further dis-
heartened Taitt. Most of the white men he encountered claimed to
have Campbell's protection. Adding to the confusion, Taitt received
intelligence that the Carolina mounted militia was advancing to meet
him. This message was brought by an unnamed British colonel who
urged the Indians to be careful. Taitt burned an abandoned fort and
turned the Indians loose to raid Carolina. Taitt, Alexander McGillivray, and a few Upper Creeks joined the British in Savannah, as did
William McIntosh with about fifty Lower Creeks.[28]

LeRoy Hammond's large contingent of mounted militia ran into
one of the scattered parties of Indians near Rocky Comfort Creek on
March 22, killed eight, and took six prisoners, including three white
men. Hammond returned in triumph to Williamson's camp on the
Savannah River, the scalps of those killed tied to a pole and carried
"after the manner of an Ensign."[29]

Colonel Andrew Pickens routed another band of Creeks the day after Hammond's victory. The comparatively large number of rebel troops thoroughly discouraged the Indians from continuing into Carolina, except for one party under the exceptional leadership of Emistisiguo, which crossed the Savannah and caused alarms along the Carolina frontier. Lieutenant Colonel James Mark Prevost, controlling the area below Briar Creek, made an effort to expel the Carolina raiders from Georgia, but his detachment of Carolina Loyalists was defeated in a nighttime engagement by Lieutenant Colonel Ely Kershaw of Carolina and Colonel John Twiggs of the Georgia militia.[30]

Alexander Cameron made an effort to recruit Cherokees to join Campbell, but they set off on March 30, much too late to be of any assistance to Campbell's mission. The best summation of the way the plan was carried out was expressed by Germain: "No part of this plan was executed as it was expected it would have been."[31] Germain would have liked to put the blame on John Stuart, who was already in trouble for running up exorbitant expenses. In high exasperation, Germain wrote to Stuart informing him that he had just learned from Campbell that from his arrival in Georgia until his departure "he had not seen nor heard of an Indian." If he had been joined by a considerable body of them while at Augusta, he would have opened the way to communication with the loyal inhabitants of the Carolina backcountry. Germain cited the "repeated orders" to Stuart to keep the Indians in readiness for cooperation with Campbell and Stuart's assurances that war parties were continually out upon the frontier. Death protected Stuart from playing the scapegoat. Alexander Cameron informed Germain that Colonel Stuart died on Sunday, March 21, after an illness of several months. Cameron and Charles Stuart volunteered to handle Indian affairs until a successor was appointed.[32]

The American side was jubilant over the failure of the British strategy. A South Carolina newspaper reported that the British had been disappointed in their expectation that large numbers would join them. Credit was given to the "vigilance and activity" of General Andrew Williamson.[33]

General Benjamin Lincoln kept Congress and General Washington posted on the flow of events. On February 27 he told John Jay that his success had blasted the "hopes and expectations of the disaffected." Washington expressed immense relief that the Indians had failed to support Campbell properly; he hoped that it would be "a fresh proof to the disaffected . . . that they are leaning upon a broken reed."[34]

Although the plan had not worked as hoped, the British strategists did not lose faith in it. After all, half a state was better than none. Lower Georgia was restored to the crown and the exiled royal officials returned to resume civil government. Georgia was unique among its sisters in that it was the only state to regain colonial status under the conciliatory provisions of the Carlisle Commission. The port of Savannah offered a convenient base of operations for a larger British force from the North. The plan would not be abandoned; mistakes made in the first campaign would be corrected.

The first step was to find a replacement for John Stuart. One condition was that the new superintendent must be active enough to move out into the Indian country. Stuart had run up enormous expenses by continually inviting the Indians to Pensacola instead of going to them himself. Stuart's inactivity put too much responsibility in the hands of his deputies, and Germain had lost confidence in deputies after the failure of the Upper and Lower Creeks to support Governor Tonyn in 1778.

It must have occurred to General Prevost, and certainly to Governor Tonyn, that the earliest proponent of the plan would be the proper one to execute it. Prevost had apparently forgotten his earlier jealousies for he endorsed Brown's appointment in a letter to Clinton on April 16, 1779: "His knowledge of the Indians, his Patience and Temper, His activity and zeal to animate them and Bravery to Head them whenever wanted for the King's Service, induce me to Recommend him to your Excellency as a very Proper Person to Succeed to that Employment." Governor Tonyn followed on May 1 with an equally strong endorsement of Brown. Clinton had temporarily appointed Alexander Cameron to Stuart's position on April 29. He explained to Prevost that he was aware of Brown's merits and would keep him in mind for future promotions.[35]

Tonyn replied that he just had received word from Germain that the Florida Rangers were no longer attached to him but to the army under Clinton's command. He hoped that Clinton would keep the Rangers in service. He emphasized Brown's "great and distinguished merit and unexampled zeal and activity for His Majesty's service." Tonyn wrote to Prevost to say that Florida would not pay for the Rangers' subsistence after June 24; he hoped that the terms under which they enlisted would be honored. A year before, Prevost would have been glad to get rid of the Rangers. Since then he had discovered the value of a roving body of mounted men. He asked Clinton to honor the dates of the original Ranger commissions (Brown's was dated from June 1, 1776) and again praised Brown for "his knowledge of the Country and his connections with many of the inhabitants which would be invaluable in future campaigns." In addition, Brown was "a very deserving and spirited gentleman."[36]

In London, Lord Germain made a Solomon-like decision. He would split Stuart's superintendency into two districts and give Brown the eastern and Cameron the western. In his letter of notification to Brown, dated June 25, 1779, Germain cited the testimonials he had received attesting to Brown's knowledge, zeal, and integrity. He made it clear that he expected Brown to carry out the old plan: "The King's Service now requires that the procuring, sending out or leading Parties of the Indians to co-operate with His Majesty's Forces or otherwise to annoy the Enemy should be the principal object of your attention." He added the standard caution against wanton cruelty.[37]

The new arrangement in Indian administration was curious in one respect. Alexander Cameron had spent years among the Cherokees and fathered mixed-blood children. He believed that no one else was held in such high regard by these Indians and was disappointed that Brown was named superintendent of the Cherokees and Creeks while he was relegated to the western Indians. He told Clinton that the Cherokees would go over to the rebels when they heard he was not to be their agent. Instead of attracting sympathy, Cameron drew down a reprimand from Lord George Germain. It was "highly improper" of Cameron to tell the Cherokees that he would have nothing more to do with them. He should have recommended Colonel Brown to them and promised his cooperation. Brown was one of the last to hear about his appointment because the ship carrying the dispatches was lost to the enemy.[38]

The management of Indian affairs suffered during the hiatus in the superintendency. Brown and his Rangers were caught up in the military game of checkmate, played out by Prevost and Lincoln. It began when a group of Georgia refugees petitioned Lincoln to provide protection for a provisional Whig government in Augusta. Lincoln began the ponderous business of moving his army upriver, leaving General William Moultrie to guard against a direct British crossing at Purysburg. Lincoln intended to cross the river at Augusta, take some strong ground, and prevent any future junction of the "unfriendly and the savages." In short, Lincoln meant to render it impossible for the British to carry out their plan. He also meant to "give a new existence to the State of Georgia" by helping to establish a government in Augusta.[39] Lincoln was pestered by South Carolina Governor John Rutledge, who argued for a scorched-earth policy in Georgia. Rutledge sent orders to General Andrew Williamson that he was to "destroy all the cattle, horses, provisions and carriages they meet with in Georgia." Lincoln countermanded the order and threatened to resign if Rutledge continued to interfere.

After Lincoln began his march on April 20, 1779, General Prevost made an uncharacteristically bold move. Intending simply to draw Lincoln out of the backcountry, he crossed the river on April 29 and brushed past Moultrie's guard. There was so little opposition that he might have taken Charlestown, but he was as poorly prepared to capture the town as the people of Charlestown were to defend it.

Frantic calls were issued by Governor John Rutledge for General Lincoln to hasten to the rescue of the principal town in the state. Moultrie wrote Lincoln that the Charlestonians were "frightened out of their wits." Lincoln hated to give up his plan to secure the backcountry. He compromised by crossing the Savannah River at Augusta and hurrying down the Georgia side as far as Jarrett's Ferry, where he crossed into Carolina on May 6.[40]

Brown's Rangers were in the vanguard of Prevost's invasion force which threatened Charlestown. Prevost, now with the rank of major general, demanded the surrender of the town on May 12. Local authorities made a counteroffer, proposing neutrality for the rest of the war. Prevost could not wait around to parlay because Lincoln was rapidly approaching. He retired to James and Johns islands with easy access to supplies by sea. On June 20 the inconclusive Battle of Stono was fought, after which Prevost withdrew from island to island toward Savannah.[41]

While still at Beaufort, Prevost learned that many backcountrymen had broken their oaths and were plundering the lower settlements. He sent a Hessian regiment to Georgia ahead of his main force under the escort of Brown's Rangers. Prevost left the Seventy-first Regiment at Beaufort, South Carolina, and followed the Hessians to Savannah. The Rangers were assigned the exposed and unhealthy post at Ebenezer.[42]

Whig journals criticized Prevost's foray into Carolina because of the "infamous banditti and horse thieves" with him. The culprits were not Brown's Rangers but the mounted volunteers who rode with Daniel McGirth, a Carolina Loyalist increasingly notorious for his plundering excursions. Specifically praised were Colonel Thomas Brown, Colonel Maitland, and a few other officers "who did not come divested of politeness and humanity." The hundred or so Indians who had come in with David Taitt and William McIntosh accompanied Prevost's expedition. Prevost, always uneasy about using Indians, insisted that they behave like regular troops. According to the *Royal Georgia Gazette*, the Indians "behaved well." They took prisoners and instead of mistreating them, delivered them to Colonel Brown at Ebenezer. Then they went to Savannah to receive the thanks of General Prevost before returning to their country. But Prevost was not done with Indians. David Holmes brought in 140 Creeks and 35 white men to offer their services. Because of the hiatus in the superintendency, no one knew what to do with them. Governor James Wright, who had taken up his interrupted administration the previous July, complained about the confusion in the Indian Department.[43]

The man who was supposed to be in charge of that office still did not know it. In fact, half a year elapsed between Thomas Brown's appointment and his receipt of his orders. Meanwhile, Brown was busy reorganizing his corps. His first choice of a name, the King's Georgia Rangers, was disallowed, probably because Major James Wright, Jr., the governor's son, was authorized to raise a mounted unit called the Georgia Loyalists. Brown adopted the name King's Carolina Rangers. When Brown assumed command of Wright's Corps for the march on Augusta in 1780 the name Carolina was dropped and Brown's men were called simply the King's Rangers. General Prevost endorsed a higher pay scale for the unit, and, adding to the incentive to join, new uniforms were issued to the Rangers. Handsome green jackets with crimson collars and cuffs distinguished the riders, whose sole identification before had been a red cockade.[44] Brown described his Rangers as mostly South Carolinians who had a "perfect knowledge" of the Indians and the Indian country. They could swim any river in the province and were the best guides he could want. Many of them had served with him in Florida. Brown probably persuaded some of the thirty-five white men who accompanied David Holmes and his party of Indians to join his outfit. The crusty old Swiss Prevost adopted a new tone when he spoke of the Rangers. "What officers and men there are now, of the New Rangers," he reported to Clinton at the end of July, "have a very decent appearance and behave well." He had a poorer opinion of Major Wright's recruits, who were "mostly deserters and prisoners." Young Wright would get in trouble for his indiscriminate recruiting.[45]

Although Augustine Prevost's Carolina expedition was a success in its intended purpose of drawing Lincoln's army out of the backcountry, General Clinton was not pleased. He scolded Prevost for invading Carolina without permission.[46] But Prevost's action accomplished the purpose of delaying the formation of a Whig government in Augusta.

Not until July 24 was a state Supreme Executive Council organized with John Wereat as president. General Lachlan McIntosh was sent back to Georgia by General Washington along with sixty Virginia Continentals. General Lincoln hoped that McIntosh could "keep the Indians in awe" and foster the reestablishment of civil rule.[47] It boded ill for McIntosh and for peace in the backcountry that George Wells, the inveterate enemy of the McIntoshes, had been released from a British prison ship and elected colonel of Richmond County's lower battalion. Wells was angry at the Wereat council for ignoring the constitution of 1777 and claiming emergency powers. He accused the council of coddling Tories. To make matters worse, General McIntosh had the bad judgment to lodge at the home of Andrew McLean, the known but tolerated Tory. Wells's ire was fueled when Wereat directed McIntosh to relieve Wells of his militia command. Wells called for new elections, and his radical friends rallied behind him.[48]

The sudden appearance of a French fleet off Tybee Island put an end to the Whig bickering and the British complacency. On September 3 Governor Wright wrote Lord George Germain, "No man could have thought or believed that a French Fleet of 25 Sail of the Line, with at least 9 Frigates, and a number of other Vessels, would have come on the coast of Georgia in the month of September, and Landed from 4 to 5000 troops to besiege the town of Savannah, but My Lord amazing as this is, it is certainly Fact."[49] The amazing apparition of Count Henri d'Estaing was not accidental. George Washington and South Carolina Governor John Rutledge had appealed to the French admiral for help. D'Estaing decided that he could afford a two-week diversion on his way to catch the easterly winds to France, so he visited Georgia. His success would have interfered seriously with the implementation of the British plan. Savannah in British hands provided an open door for an invasion force from New York. D'Estaing attempted to close that door.[50]

Prevost, who was as surprised as Governor Wright, called in Brown's Rangers from Ebenezer, Delancey's New York Brigade from Sunbury, and the New Jersey Volunteers from the Ogeechee and waited impatiently for Maitland's Seventy-first Regiment from Beaufort. When d'Estaing demanded that Prevost surrender on September 15, Prevost asked for a twenty-four-hour truce. During that period of grace Maitland came in. The British forces were outnumbered badly when Lincoln's troops joined the French, but they had the advantage of a tight semicircle of defenses. The experience of fighting behind formal works was a new one for Brown and his men. The association with regulars was an opportunity for education in skills the Rangers had not acquired. If they knew how to form a battle line and make a bayonet charge, as they did the following September, they very likely learned the tactic during the siege of Savannah. One of Brown's new recruits, Captain Alexander C. Wylly, was responsible for a remarkably fine map of the battlefield, showing the King's Rangers anchoring the extreme right of the line near the river.[51]

The grand assault of October 9, 1779, was personally led by d'Estaing and Lincoln and aimed at the Spring Hill redoubt along the Augusta Road, not far from the Rangers' position. Lieutenant Thomas Tawse of the Seventy-first, in command of the South Carolina provincials, bore the brunt of the attack. Tawse himself was killed. Hessian Lieutenant Colonel Fredrich von Porbeck was field officer on the right wing. He heard d'Estaing shout, "Advance, my brave grenadiers, kill the wretches." He saw d'Estaing suffer wounds to his left arm and chest and take cover behind a tombstone. Major Beamsley Glazier's Grenadier Battalion of the Royal Americans moved forward with their bayonets fixed to support von Porbeck. The allied attack wavered and broke.[52]

There were heroes enough on both sides. The victory was celebrated by the British press in England, Scotland, and America. King George III ordered salutes fired from the Tower of London and in St. James Park. Prevost and Maitland became famous. On the part of the allies, d'Estaing was respected for his bravery. So was the Count Casimir Pulaski, who was killed when he advanced too far ahead of his men. Sergeant William Jasper was a hero already for replacing the flag on a shattered staff at Fort Moultrie in 1776; he died attempting to plant a flag on the British works. An unsung hero was Baikia Harvey, the young man from the Orkney Islands who had run away from Thomas Brown in 1775. In attacking the British fortifications defended by his former master, he fought quite literally for his freedom and died in that cause.[53]

After the siege of Savannah, the Whigs resumed their factional fighting in Augusta. Meanwhile, the interregnum in the British Indian Department dragged on. Alexander Cameron, acting under Clinton's temporary appointment, urged the Creeks and Cherokees to fall on the backs of the rebels at Savannah. A band of Cherokees responded but too late to be of service. Prevost wrote to Clinton on November 6 that he had heard nothing of the Indians, "their services always mercenary and precarious." Even though Thomas Brown had not been notified officially, Prevost considered the appointment a sure thing because on November 7 he informed Clinton that Brown was willing to surrender his command of the Rangers when he assumed the office of superintendent. Prevost recommended his son Captain George Prevost of the Royal Americans as a replacement for Brown.[54] The request was not acted upon, and it is hard to believe that Brown was willing to go along with it. If the Indians were to be effective in war, Brown's Rangers would have to ride with them. Given Augustine Prevost's distrust of Indians, the Rangers under George Prevost would serve a different purpose.

Finally, on the last day of the year, Brown wrote to Lord George Germain that he had just learned of his appointment by way of Pensacola. The original dispatches had been lost when the ship carrying them was captured. Brown reported that the Indians were dissatisfied at the confusion in administration since Stuart's death, and he hoped to conciliate them at a congress in Savannah, which he would call with General Prevost's consent.[55]

General Clinton expected great things from Brown. The plan had been tested; the time had come to make it work. The might of Britain would be directed to the southern country. The army would land, Loyalists would rise, and Thomas Brown would have the Indians ready to cooperate on the frontiers. This time, Germain and Clinton were determined to make it work.

CHAPTER SIX

THE PLAN AS

THE SOUTHERN

STRATEGY, 1780

 Thomas Brown lost no time in organizing his department. He would keep John Stuart's personnel but cut expenses. A deputy, David Taitt, would be assigned to the Creeks, with commissaries Alexander McGillivray for the Upper Creeks and William McIntosh for the Lower Creeks. He would assign one commissary to the Cherokee mountain towns and one to the valley towns. Each commissary would employ an interpreter, a packhorseman, and a guide. In addition, each would have two "conductors" and three packhorsemen, presumably for escorting the Indians on their raids. Brown realized that his assignment was different from Stuart's. The sedentary Stuart had devoted his efforts to preventing the Indians from joining the enemy. Brown had to bring them into action. A clerk and an interpreter would be stationed as storekeeper in Savannah and at St. Augustine because of the frequent traffic of Indians to those places. Brown's first problem was what to do with three hundred Cherokees who were in Savannah that winter. He had the responsibility to feed and entertain them.[1]

Sir Henry Clinton's mighty armada suddenly intruded into Thomas Brown's new jurisdiction at the end of January. Clinton's invasion force consisted of four flank battalions, twelve regiments and corps, a detachment of artillery, 250 cavalry, and ample provisions. Thanks to Augustine Prevost's defense of Savannah, Clinton had an easy entry into the South. General Benjamin Lincoln had retired to Charlestown, and Clinton determined to make that city his objective. The plan suffered from Clinton's inability to do two things at once. He would take Charlestown first and the backcountry later.[2]

Clinton conferred with Brown soon after landing and advised him to cancel his planned congress in Savannah. He would rather have Brown wait until troops were ready to move into the backcountry and then summon the Indians. Brown should cooperate with Brigadier General James Paterson, who would command the expedition to Augusta. Brown saw Paterson on February 15 and informed him that the Indians were already alerted. He needed only one month's notice to have them at Augusta to meet the king's troops. Paterson asked Brown to call the Indians to Augusta in mid-April. Brown was at last in a position to execute the plan he had first discussed in 1775 even though it was to be a disjointed version of the original strategy. He would employ the Cherokees camped near Savannah, and he was convinced that the Creeks would be eager to cooperate. He wrote to Lord George Germain: "It is their earnest request that a streight [sic] path and communication may be opened . . . by way of Augusta." He recommended that a post be established in Augusta where it would be contiguous to the Creeks, Cherokees, and Carolina loyalists. Brown repeated to Germain the same arguments he had used in 1776. More than twenty-five hundred men to whom he had administered the oath of allegiance by order of Lord William Campbell were ready to take the field. They waited only for arms and ammunition.[3]

General Augustine Prevost had serious misgivings about the operation even before Brown and Paterson met. Prevost had no objection to Paterson taking fifteen hundred men from his command, but "little or nothing remains in any of our publick stores that cou'd be of service in the defence of this place or to assist in fitting out the expedition under Gen'l Patterson." Four days later, Prevost complained that Paterson's march would leave him "to struggle against almost unsurmountable obstacles" in Savannah and St. Augustine.[4]

Governor James Wright harbored no such misgivings. Like Thomas Brown he wanted to recover the Georgia backcountry because of the stores of corn and supply of livestock as well as the strategic advantages. Wright was a staunch advocate of the importance of an Augusta garrison.[5]

On February 11 Clinton's forces began landing on Johns Island near Charlestown. The South Carolina Assembly, again in a state of panic, voted dictatorial powers to Governor John Rutledge. For his part, Clinton decided that taking Charlestown would be a bigger chore than he had thought. Lincoln had collected all available troops for its defense, leaving only a skeleton troop in the Augusta area under Andrew Williamson, and John Rutledge would soon summon those men. Clinton explained to Prevost, "I find it therefore necessary to reverse my plan of operations in the backcountry for the present." He directed Paterson to join him instead of advancing upon Augusta. The plan thus suffered another postponement.[6]

Clinton asked Colonel Alexander Innes to go to Savannah on a sensitive matter touching on the Indians and Thomas Brown. Innes was "to reconcile Col. Brown to remaining behind with the Indians . . . to keep them in good humor." As soon as Charlestown fell, he would get back with Brown regarding the Indians. He hoped that Brown would explain to the Indians the reasons for the sudden change of plans. Innes was instructed to bring back a few Indians with him so that they would be awed by the size of the king's army.[7]

Brown was a good soldier and did the best he could. He sent word to the Creeks to disregard his previous instructions. Keeping the Cherokees in good humor was more difficult. An outbreak of smallpox in Savannah terrified the Indians, whose nation had suffered from that disease before. They told Brown that they would be ready at any time to face the enemy but not the pox. Brown, with General Prevost's concurrence, let them return to their mountains. Brown notified Lord George Germain of Clinton's change of plans and urged his lordship not to forget the importance of Augusta.[8]

If Brown could not criticize Clinton, Prevost and Wright could and did. The general worried that Savannah would be defenseless, and the governor expressed the same sentiments with much more pathos. Wright especially regretted the abandonment of the backcountry. Clinton tried to reassure both men by saying that the enemy was bottled up in Charlestown and not likely to bother Savannah and that he would take up the Augusta campaign as soon as Charlestown fell. Contrary to Clinton's prediction, a body of rebel raiders appeared on the Ogeechee. A detachment of New York Volunteers rode out from Savannah into an ambush and had to be rescued by another party, including the King's Rangers. The raiders retreated but not before plundering Governor Wright's plantations. That sent Wright into another impassioned plea for help. "In short Sir," he wrote to Clinton, "this Province is or will be broke up and totally ruined if something is not speedily done." The best suggestion he could make was that another mounted troop be raised, but he admitted that Clinton and Paterson had made horses scarce: "Every brute that could scarce walk was carried away." Despite misgivings, Prevost decided to employ Daniel McGirth's unsavory band of irregulars along the Ogeechee as a temporary expedient. Loyal inhabitants soon complained that McGirth's gang were worse plunderers than the rebels. Prevost asked Brown to recruit officers and men to mount two troops as soon as official sanction was received. Governor Wright was convinced that "nothing can save this province but a Post at Augusta."[9]

Meanwhile, Thomas Brown revealed a grasp of the continental scope of his jurisdiction. While waiting, perhaps impatiently, for orders to move into the backcountry, he influenced British affairs elsewhere. On April 11, 1780, he informed Germain that his deputies McGillivray and McIntosh were leading six to eight hundred Creeks to Pensacola in response to Major General John Campbell's call for help against the Spaniards.[10] Brown also opened a line of communication with the British Fort Detroit with the object of coordinating the activities of the northern and southern Indians.[11]

The surrender of Charlestown on May 12 changed the complexion of the war. Resistance throughout Georgia and South Carolina collapsed. Amid the general rejoicing on the British side, Clinton decided to return to his former strategy, the execution of the plan. He explained to Governor Wright that he had been prevented from sending a considerable force to Augusta by the demands of the Charlestown campaign, but now he wanted Colonel Brown to march to the frontier "as Expeditiously as possible." Clinton ordered Lieutenant Colonel Alured Clarke to relieve Augustine Prevost of command in Savannah and to dispatch Brown to Augusta, in cooperation with the British forces on the Carolina side under Lieutenant Colonel Nisbet Balfour.[12] For months, Prevost had begged to be allowed to return to England so no one was happier than he that the fall of Charlestown won his release. Lieutenant Colonel James Mark Prevost had departed on the ship that brought Governor Wright the previous July. Mark Prevost's promising career was cut short by a fever. He died in Jamaica within the year of his departure from Georgia.[13]

Thomas Brown would have to become accustomed to working with a new set of British officers, notably Alured Clarke in Savannah, Nisbet Balfour, and later John Harris Cruger at Ninety-Six. More important, he would have a new commander in the Southern Department. Clinton announced that he would return to New York, leaving Major General Lord Charles Cornwallis in charge. Cornwallis was disturbingly vague about the plan and had the professional soldier's disdain for Indians and dislike of rangers. Before leaving Savannah, Brown joined other officers in writing a farewell message to Augustine Prevost which must have touched the heart of that old soldier, who was more accustomed to criticism than to praise. Prevost was thanked for his fairness and for his consideration of the men under his command. The address was signed by Lieutenant Colonel John Harris Cruger, First Battalion, Delancey's Brigade; Lieutenant Colonel Isaac Allen, Third Battalion, New Jersey Volunteers; Major Thomas Bowden, Second Battalion, Delancey's Brigade; Major James Wright, Jr., Georgia Loyalists; and Lieutenant Colonel Thomas Brown, King's Rangers.[14]

Brown had difficulty finding enough horses and wagons to begin his expedition. Before his departure, he sent off an express to the chiefs of the pro-Galphin faction and asked them to meet him in Augusta. He was convinced that they would remain in the British interests for the rest of the war. He estimated that 360 Creeks were "now upon Service" on the frontiers of Georgia and South Carolina. Since his residence in Augusta might interfere with the routine business of his department, he named Charles Shaw, a former deputy of John Stuart, to act as deputy superintendent in Savannah.

Brown probably began his march on the last day of May. He crossed the Savannah River at Ebenezer and went up the Carolina side, a route that took him to George Galphin's home at Silver Bluff. Brown paused long enough to charge Galphin with high treason. The struggle was over for George Galphin. He had fought valiantly to keep the Indians out of this war. Thomas Brown had waged an equally long campaign to involve them. Brown promised the dissident chiefs that they would once again be welcomed in Augusta, a promise Galphin could not make. Before he could be tried or punished for his actions, if indeed a trial was contemplated, George Galphin died at his home at Silver Bluff on December 1, 1780.[15]

While at Galphin's, Brown was agreeably surprised to receive a visit from his prewar friend LeRoy Hammond. Hammond was prepared to surrender his command on General Clinton's terms. Brown sent his second in command, Major James Wright, Jr., to Hammond's regimental muster field to accept the submission of the regiment. On the march from Silver Bluff to Augusta other militiamen offered to switch sides but Brown sent them home.[16]

There was an important difference about Augusta the second time Thomas Brown rode into town. For almost five months the Whig amateurs in government had enjoyed self-rule. They would not relinquish that privilege lightly. On January 23, 1780, the Georgia Assembly enacted an ordinance for "the more speedy and effectually settling and strengthening this State." Two hundred acres were promised to any head of family who settled in Georgia, five hundred to anyone building a sawmill or gristmill, and up to six thousand for the construction of ironworks. The act provided a five-man commission for Augusta and charged it with the responsibility of implementing James Edward Oglethorpe's original gridiron plan for the orderly expansion of the town. A new town, Washington, was authorized for frontier Wilkes County. The legislation provided for the growth of the backcountry and was surprisingly mature for these beginners in government. There was symbolism, perhaps inadvertent, in the assembly's agenda for the backcountry. Brownsborough had been the place fixed for holding elections in Richmond County since 1777. It was now bypassed in favor of Augusta.[17]

During the Whig interlude, George Wells enjoyed the political ascendancy he had agitated for since 1774. He was one of the members of the Augusta Commission, as was George Walton, and he was president of the Executive Council. His fellow member of Button Gwinnett's Liberty Club of 1777, Richard Howley, was governor. Friends of Lachlan McIntosh did not fare well under the 1780 regime. John Wereat expected to be expelled from the assembly because of his ties to McIntosh. He referred to Howley, Walton, and Wells as "the triumvirate that rules this poor state" and feared new plans of prosecution.[18] Walton and Howley were elected delegates to Congress, and on February 5 the Executive Council directed Howley to proceed to Philadelphia. George Wells became the acting governor. His characteristic feistiness was revealed in the council's decision not to dissolve the government if the British overran Georgia but to retire to Heard's Fort in Wilkes County and if necessary to the mountains in north Georgia. If Wells had envisioned himself as the peripatetic embodiment of the state of Georgia, he did not live to achieve that glory. He forced young Major James Jackson into a quarrel and challenged him to a duel. The reason is not known, but Jackson was from John

Wereat's town in England, lived with Wereat for a time, and Wells hated Wereat. That could have been cause enough for the irascible Wells.

Wells, who had watched Button Gwinnett fall to Lachlan McIntosh, was himself killed by Jackson on February 16, 1780. Stephen Heard was elected in his stead. On May 23 the Executive Council ordered the governor to retire to some place of safety.[19]

Before he left Charlestown for New York on June 8, 1780, General Clinton issued a series of dispatches offering pardon to all who would declare allegiance to the king by June 20. The deadline imposed difficulties for the officers, like Brown, who were on the march into the backcountry. Before the arrival of Lieutenant Colonel Nisbet Balfour at Ninety-Six, Richard Pearis received the surrender of Whigs in that district, including Andrew Williamson and Andrew Pickens. Williamson was suspected by other Whigs, including Pickens, of having already gone over to the British interests. Williamson faithfully observed his oath and cooperated with the British, but there is no evidence that he had previously been a traitor to the American cause.[20] Moses Kirkland returned to the Ninety-Six District with a commission from Clinton to raise a regiment of militia.

From Heard's Fort in Wilkes County Stephen Heard dispatched a messenger to ask Brown about the terms of surrender. Brown sent his comrade William Manson with the answer that those who surrendered would be treated as prisoners on parole. They would have to yield their arms and would then be under the king's protection. Manson had been in trouble with the Augusta Whigs almost continually. Brown's arrival spared him from exile and rewarded him with a moment in history. Manson received the submission of John Dooly's regiment consisting of four to six hundred men and sent 210 stand of arms to Augusta, then carried news of the pacification of the Ceded Lands to Governor Wright in Savannah. Wright asked him to convey the same message to Lord Cornwallis in Charlestown.[21] Meanwhile, Brown accepted the surrender of Benjamin Garden's and Robert Middleton's South Carolina regiments. All were paroled and sent home with no other punishment or penalty. But Brown made it clear that he would hang "without favour or distinction" any person who should disturb the peace.[22]

It was a time for celebration for Brown's friends. James Gordon returned to Augusta from his plantation upriver near Fort Charlotte. Grierson and Goodgion resumed their militia commands. Isaac Herbert's store was at Brown's disposal. The Reverend Seymour recovered possession of his church, which had been used as a hospital by the Whigs for sick troopers. "I was happy once again to have an opportunity of performing Divine Services in my ruinous church," he wrote to his superiors. Brown soon realized that he, too, needed a hospital; Seymour let him have the parsonage and retired to his farm outside Augusta. Andrew McLean put out his British flag. The recriminations against known Whigs were few. Martin Weatherford threatened to pummel John Wereat. Wereat's response, according to George Walton, was to cower in a ditch.[23] If that was all he suffered, Wereat was better treated under the administration of Tory Thomas Brown than he had been under that of Whig George Wells.

Brown's immediate problem was not the enemy but his own superiors. Young Major Wright had sent recruiters into Charlestown and allegedly carried off several prisoners whom he enlisted in his corps. Cornwallis called it kidnapping and was determined to bring Wright before a court-martial. He ordered Balfour in explicit language to recall Wright and his corps to Savannah immediately. Brown was suspected of having enlisted former rebels, and his Rangers were to return to Savannah, too. "I insist on his being put on the same restrictions as Major Wright"; neither could recruit in South Carolina. Cornwallis intended to take the Rangers away from Brown: "The Colonel may stay to manage the Indian business, but not to keep any military command." Even in that capacity, Brown was not to take any initiative. He was instructed to keep the Indians in good humor "but in no account employ them in any operation of war."[24]

Seldom has a military commander given such positive orders with such negative results. Thomas Brown's retention of his post in Augusta was evidence of his skills in diplomacy. Brown realized that the war was not over, even if Cornwallis thought otherwise. He had been given the Indian superintendency with the understanding that he would use the Indians in cooperation with the troops and regulate their behavior. Before he learned of Cornwallis's displeasure, he wrote to suggest that the Cherokees might be called upon to drive off the Virginia and North Carolina "banditti" who were trespassing on their lands.[25]

The key influence on Cornwallis was the arrogant Lieutenant Colonel Nisbet Balfour, installed temporarily at Ninety-Six. Balfour shared Cornwallis's opinion that most of Clinton's directives were misguided. Major Patrick Ferguson of the Seventy-first Regiment, whom Clinton had placed in charge of the loyal militia in the back-country, was "ridiculous," according to Balfour. Brown's command at Augusta was "made of very sad stuff." Young Major Wright should go home to his father. Brown's and Wright's recruiting in South Carolina, authorized by Prevost and approved by Clinton, should stop. Balfour toyed with the notion of disregarding the paroles (given under Clinton's orders) by Brown and Pearis.[26]

Brown made it his first order of business to confront Balfour. He took 250 of his Rangers along with him to Ninety-Six. Brown was able to convince the critical Balfour of the necessity of disman-tling Fort Rutledge on the upper Savannah River, which was a stand-ing insult to the Cherokees, and of constructing a works in Augusta. Captain Joseph Smith led a company of Rangers to take posses-sion of the military stores at Fort Rutledge. Brown's old friend and rescuer Martin Weatherford accompanied the Rangers as wagon-master.[27]

Brown's visit to Ninety-Six did not guarantee his command at Au-gusta. Brown and Wright, Jr., had to make their own cases with the general. Major Wright expressed "infinite concern" that he had in-curred Cornwallis's displeasure. He explained that he had General Clinton's permission to recruit in Carolina and denied enlisting pris-oners. His father, the governor, wrote separately to say that Corn-wallis must have been misinformed. He emphasized the good job that Brown and young Wright had done in restoring peace to the back-country and hoped they would not be transferred.[28]

Brown's own letter to Cornwallis was essentially a defense of the plan he had lived with and fought for. It must have been frustrating to educate each new superior officer, especially when Brown had the support of Sir Henry Clinton and Lord George Germain. Even while Cornwallis was making up his mind whether or not to remove Brown and the Rangers from Augusta, Germain was under the impression that the plan was being followed. He wrote to Brown on June 5, 1780, instructing him to prevail upon the Cherokees to meet Cornwallis on his march through Carolina. It was understood that the King's Rangers would ride with the Cherokees. In his letter to Cornwallis of July 16, Brown reminded his lordship that the Rangers were mostly Carolinians, many of them with experience in the Indian country. They knew the Indians' language and were personally acquainted with the chiefs. If Indians were to be used in warfare, the Rangers were best suited to regulate their behavior. With such men, Brown "could be answerable of the peace and security of the frontiers." He doubted whether other troops, who were strangers to the Indians, could be as effective.[29]

Brown explained why he could be more useful in the backcountry than on the coast. As he put it, "modesty forbids me not to mention" his past exploits. He related how the Whigs spread the rumor that he was the illegitimate son of Lord North sent to poison the minds of the people. He described his brutal treatment at the hands of the Liberty Boys. He took credit for rallying the Loyalists of the Carolina interior, without mentioning Cunningham, Robinson, or Kirkland. He told of retiring to Charlestown in an attempt to meet with Lord William Campbell, then of his flight to Savannah and to Florida. He described how he and his Rangers secured provisions for St. Augustine and held the frontier seventy miles in advance of any other troops. At Governor Tonyn's request, he sent his men into the interior to bring down other recruits who formed the battalion now commanded by Colonel Innes. He helped turn back the rebel invasion of Florida and wounded and captured General Screven. During all the Florida and Georgia campaigns he had never received a reprimand or rebuke from a superior. On the contrary, he had received the thanks of General Howe, Lord Dartmouth, Lord George Germain, Sir Henry Clinton, and Governor Tonyn.

Then Brown reviewed his brief tenure as Indian superintendent, pointing out that he had turned out a larger number of Creeks for the assistance of West Florida than ever Stuart or even Sir William Johnson in New York had raised. He stressed that his ability to lead the Indians would be impaired if he lost command of the Rangers. Finally, he had invited the Creeks and Cherokees to visit him in Augusta and expected them after the August celebration of the harvest called the "busk." Brown's letter, devoid of modesty and laced with exaggerations, gives a good insight into his character as well as his record. He might easily have played one general against another. He could have referred to Germain's instructions to lead the Indians actively; he might have reminded Cornwallis of Clinton's orders to march with his Rangers to Augusta. He could have claimed authorization from General Prevost and Lieutenant Colonel Alured Clarke to recruit men for his regiment. His letter was remarkably devoid of such self-justification. It was a nice touch to send his dispatch by Ranger Captain Andrew Johnston, who had been the first to storm Fort McIntosh in 1778. The ranger's father, Lewis, was now a mem-

ber of Sir James Wright's council. If Cornwallis was impressed by the
social bearing and political connection of the Ranger, so much the
better.[30]

Cornwallis replied in a stuffy tone that he did not have to give
reasons for his actions. But he yielded the point to say that he had
heard that Brown and Wright "were practicing all the tricks of recruiting to the great terror and disgust of the inhabitants." Nor did
he think highly of the Creeks' performance at Pensacola. He understood that they had deserted just when they were needed most. (Actually Major General John Campbell had sent the Indians away before
the Spanish attack.) Cornwallis unbent to the point of telling Brown
that he had given no offense and that his zeal for king and country
was never doubted. Nevertheless, Cornwallis wanted Brown out of
Augusta, and in a separate letter to Alured Clarke in Savannah, he
repeated his orders for Isaac Allen's Corps to march to Augusta.[31]

If Brown had not persuaded Cornwallis, he had impressed the
general's alter ego, Nisbet Balfour. Balfour convinced Cornwallis
that Allen's regiment was needed to police the Savannah River above
Augusta. Therefore, Cornwallis instructed Balfour's successor at
Ninety-Six, Lieutenant Colonel John Harris Cruger, to use his discretion about when Brown should leave Augusta. During August rebel
activity in the backcountry increased and Cornwallis gradually gave
up his lofty principle of making an example of Brown for alleged
improper recruiting. Cornwallis needed all the recruits he could get.
Finally, on August 31, he told Cruger flatly, "I consent to your keeping the Florida Rangers as long as you please at Augusta." At the
same time Cruger was authorized to take whatever action was necessary to restore order in the backcountry: "I give my sanction to any
act of rigour you may think necessary," Cornwallis wrote. Cruger
would act upon the suggestion.[32]

Freed from the threat of losing his post, Brown could devote his
attention to pacifying the countryside. His task was complicated by
the Disqualifying Act, enacted by the loyal Georgia Assembly and
signed into law on July 1, 1780. It barred 159 leading rebels from
office and denied them the right to bear arms. These rebels could be
obliged to post bond for good behavior. Penalties ranged from fines
or imprisonment to impressment in the Royal Navy.[33]

Enforcement of the Disqualifying Act was the responsibility of the
military commanders in areas with no civil establishment. Just how
to enforce the law was a perplexing problem for Thomas Brown. If

he were as vindictive and cruel as legend depicts him, he would have arrested such leading rebels as John Wereat and hanged some of those who had fractured his skull and burned his feet, such as Chesley Bostick. Brown was a soldier subject to authority. His orders were to protect former rebels who had laid down their arms and sworn allegiance to the king. Therefore, Wereat and Bostick walked the streets of Augusta undisturbed, living proof that Brown placed duty over vengeance.

The real danger to the restored peace was in Wilkes County, the former Ceded Lands, where more than five hundred men were on parole. Brown suggested to Cruger at Ninety-Six that the former officers, at least, ought to be removed from the area. In a letter to the commanders of the various posts, Cornwallis went beyond Clinton's instructions of June 5. According to historian Hugh M'Call, Cornwallis ordered "that every militia man who has borne arms with us and afterward joined the enemy shall be immediately hanged." M'Call recorded that the morning after Cornwallis's dispatch was received, five prisoners were hanged by Brown. If so, this was the first such incident, and it can be ascribed more to obedience than to vengeance.[34]

Cornwallis required active cooperation of those who had taken the oath of allegiance; passive neutrality was not enough. Georgia Whigs regarded this as a change in the terms of their original surrender, which justified their taking up arms again. Elijah Clarke, who had never surrendered in the first place, attempted to rally the discontented. He began his campaign in South Carolina's Ninety-Six District, recruiting men and foraging for supplies as he moved toward Georgia.

Thomas Brown's friend Colonel Alexander Innes had taken over command of the South Carolina Royalists from Lieutenant Colonel Joseph Robinson and was stationed on the Enoree River. On August 7 Innes located Clarke near Wofford Ironworks and engaged in an ineffectual skirmish. Clarke was reinforced by parties of North Carolinians and was ready for Innes's second attack on August 17 at Musgrove's Mill. The British were beaten off with heavy casualties; both Clarke and Innes were wounded.[35]

Clarke's injuries did not deter him from his Georgia campaign. The magnet that drew him was the storehouse of Indian supplies. Then, too, the Indians were gathering in Augusta at the invitation of the superintendent; in the minds of Clarke's followers, this war was against Indians. Backcountry Georgians had overcome their initial timidity about fighting the Indians, and they must have resented Brown's turning back the clock of history by removing squatters between the Ogeechee and Oconee and by opening the old trading road. Clarke's men might have lacked a sense of history, but they could recognize an opportunity to rescue Georgia from the Indians.

There was a convenient confusion in the American high command. While Clarke and Innes were maneuvering near Musgrove's Mill on August 16, Cornwallis routed Horatio Gates's army at Camden. Gates, successor to Benjamin Lincoln, never had much of a grasp of the situation in the Southern Department. After Camden he completely lost control of events. Gates apparently had no inkling of Clarke's invasion of Georgia until a month after it happened.[36]

Clarke was disappointed in his intention of rallying one thousand men, with which he planned to take Ninety-Six as well as Augusta. Lieutenant Colonel James M'Call could muster fewer than a hundred men in South Carolina. Clarke sent word to the Georgians under parole that he expected them to meet him at Soap Creek in Wilkes County. Joshua Burnett was one of those who received Clarke's summons. According to Burnett, Clarke threatened "to put every one of them to death" if they did not appear at the rendezvous.[37] The choice that the parolees faced was whether to join Clarke and risk being hanged by Brown or to remain quiet and risk being shot by Clarke. The Georgia backcountry was no longer a sanctuary for neutrals, as the Quakers of Wrightsborough soon discovered.

If Thomas Brown was unaware of Clarke's approach, Clarke was equally ignorant about the number of Indians who had joined Brown. Except for a mischance, there would have been far more Indians in Augusta than Clarke could have handled. Approximately a thousand Creeks answered Brown's summons and began the journey to Augusta. Faithful David Taitt marched with them. The large party had crossed the Chattahoochee and reached the forks of Upatoi Creek when Taitt became violently ill and was said to be "deranged." Their devotion to him was so great that most of the Indians returned with Taitt to Coweta town, where he died and was buried. Little Prince of the Tuckabatchees and about 250 Creeks continued the journey to Augusta. Taitt had served John Stuart loyally and well. When Brown, the novice, superseded him, he accepted the new administration with good grace and, in fact, gave his life to the service.

If Taitt had lived, Elijah Clarke's raid might well have had a different outcome.[38]

According to Joshua Burnett, six hundred men rode to the outskirts of Augusta with Elijah Clarke. They surprised and captured a British officer and forced him to reveal the disposition of Brown's forces. The Creek Indians were camped outside Augusta, probably at a place called Indian Springs along the Creek trading path. Between the Indians and Augusta was Robert Mackay's house with the Indian supplies and defended by Captain Andrew Johnston's company of Rangers. Brown's Rangers and some men from the New Jersey Volunteers were stationed at Grierson's fortified house on the west side of town and at the church in the town itself. Clarke showed that he had learned something of military strategy at Kettle Creek and Musgrove's Mill. He divided his command. Major Samuel Taylor attacked the Indian camp while Lieutenant Colonel James M'Call circled around to enter Augusta from the east. Clarke himself followed the Savannah Road to the center of town.[39]

The battle began on the morning of September 14, when Taylor's men surprised the Indian camp. There was no time for Colonel Grierson to call out the loyal militia. Brown led his Rangers to the sound of firing and joined forces with the retreating Indians. By then Clarke had gotten in behind him and captured Fort Grierson and its garrison. Clarke advanced quickly to the Mackay house. Captain Johnston was killed defending the house, and his men were made prisoners. There was a poignant moment when Andrew McLean brought the news of the first day's encounter to Savannah. Andrew Johnston's father, Dr. Lewis Johnston, was with Governor Wright. When McLean was asked if anyone was killed he answered, "Captain Johnston." According to Dr. Johnston's daughter-in-law, it "was a shock too great for the father's tender feelings, and he of course immediately returned home."[40]

Just as Clarke's raiders gained possession of the Mackay house, Brown's Rangers and the Indians appeared on the quick march down the Creek road to its junction with the main road leading to Augusta. Between the house and the road the Mackays and McLeans cultivated a garden. The slight elevation was called Garden Hill, and it was here that the battle was joined.[41]

Brown, like Clarke, displayed a grasp of military tactics. He formed a line of battle, his Rangers with bayonets fixed on the right and the Indians with their rifles on the left. Two pieces of artillery flanked Brown's line, one on each side. The firing of the cannon was the signal for the charge. Andrew McLean reported that the rebels were beaten back with considerable loss and Brown gained possession of the house and outbuildings. Brown later informed Cornwallis that the two brass one-pounders were "extremely useful in our engagement with the Rebels, particularly in dislodging them from the houses they occupied."[42] Some of Clarke's men circled through a thicket and captured one of the cannons. Brown retained the other piece. Clarke kept up a sporadic fire on the British position until early afternoon, when his men began to drift away to sample some of the plunder.

The Mackay house was constructed of stone and reasonably strong. Brown had the floorboards placed over the windows and cut loopholes for firing. Earthworks were dug around the house for the Indians. Before the fighting was renewed on the morning of the fifteenth, Brown sent his second dispatch to John Harris Cruger in Ninety-Six. Cruger first heard about Brown's plight from Sir Patrick Houstoun, whose brother John served on the other side as Georgia's governor. Houstoun would draw praise from Cruger for accompanying him on his rescue operations. Ranger Captain Joseph Smith managed to get through the American lines to carry the second message to Cruger. The note was a calm statement of the situation rather than a desperate appeal for help. Brown believed that the rebel force numbered six hundred, though they claimed to have thirteen hundred. In any case, Brown was not strong enough to drive the enemy out of town.[43]

Early on the same morning, fifty Cherokees crossed the river in canoes and climbed the riverbank to join the Rangers. Clarke closed off the river approach by stationing his men along the bank. He then brought up two cannon, a four-pounder and a six-pounder, from Fort Grierson. The Georgians dug earthworks virtually encircling the British position. Clarke then opened a heavy rifle fire. Thomas Brown himself was a casualty; a rifle shot penetrated both thighs. He refused to remove his boots until the pain from his swollen legs became unbearable.

Clarke's only experienced artillerist was Captain William Martin. He managed to set up the captured cannon and began a barrage that did a great deal of damage to the Mackay house before a Ranger's bullet ended Martin's life. The second day's fighting left dead and wounded men strewn across Garden Hill. That evening Clarke sent a messenger, under a flag of truce, requiring Brown's surrender. Although wounded and without provisions for a siege, Brown did not behave like a beaten man. He warned Clarke and his followers that their taking up arms would bring retaliation. He would not surrender; he would do his duty to the last extremity. Clarke sent an answer in kind, saying that Brown would be held responsible for what might happen. Clarke intended to continue the fight at the risk of all of his men. Brown replied that if Clarke had nothing further to say, hostilities would commence with the return of the flag of truce. An angry burst of firing broke out from the American lines, and sporadic shooting continued during the night and swelled again at daybreak. When the morning fog lifted, the attackers drew back from their position, leaving a skirmish line to prevent Brown's people from access to the river.[44]

The suffering of the wounded inside the Mackay house and outbuildings was aggravated by the lack of food or water. Raw pumpkins provided some nourishment, and the more desperate were reduced to drinking their own urine. Brown's resolution was steeled by the hope that his appeal for help had reached John Harris Cruger at Ninety-Six. Indeed, on the fifteenth, Cruger had been told by "two persons of credit and veracity," probably Captain Smith and Sir Patrick Houstoun, that Brown was besieged. Cruger delayed long enough to collect a hundred militiamen to hold the fort under command of Colonel Moses Kirkland. At 9 A.M. on September 16 Cruger marched with his battalion of Delancey's New York Brigade, Lieutenant Colonel Isaac Allen's New Jersey Volunteers, and Innes's South Carolina Royalists.[45]

Clarke's spies brought him news of Cruger's approach on the seventeenth, the fourth day of the siege. By then Clarke's numbers were depleted because some Burke County men had left to visit their families, and others, according to Hugh M'Call, "actuated by the hope of obtaining plunder rather than by motives of zeal in the cause of their country, had decamped, laden with goods."[46] Cruger's troops were seen advancing down Martintown Road on the Carolina side of the river at eight o'clock on the morning of September 18. Clarke could not prevent his men from making a quick retreat, although he managed to maintain a firing line for about an hour. Cruger's scouts crossed over and conferred with Brown. The Rangers and Indians then kept up a covering fire while Cruger's main force gained the

Georgia riverbank. They waded across the rapids and climbed Hawk's Gully. As Cruger approached the Mackay house from the east, Brown ordered the Rangers to sally out. Clarke's remaining force then fled. The Rangers recaptured the artillery and returned with prisoners. The Indians pursued the Georgians, and, out of Brown's sight, they resorted to the savage warfare dreaded by back-country people. Colonel James Grierson marched into town with some of Cruger's troops and took prisoners along the way.

The fate of the prisoners was foreordained. Those who had broken their parole were hanged. That was official policy, and no one on the British side questioned it. The account of the siege printed in Savannah on September 23 made it clear that stern measures were forthcoming: "Matters are now in such a train that the seeds of Rebellion will be rooted out of Georgia, the blow now given being pursued with vigour." A few days later, Governor Wright addressed the Commons House of the Assembly. The attack on Augusta, he said, proves that "vigourous measures are still necessary to crush the Rebellion in the back parts of this Province." Cornwallis wrote to Germain that he hoped that Cruger would be able to suppress the insurrection without any assistance from him. Cruger left no doubt that he had assumed command in Augusta and that he intended to teach the guilty a lesson: "I am now sending out patrols of horse to pick up the traiterous rebels of the neighborhood." He confided to Nisbet Balfour that he expected that the rebel prisoners "will be roughly handled, some very probably suspended for their good deeds." One of Cruger's officers wrote to a friend, "We have now got a method that will put an end to the rebellion in a short time—by hanging every man that has taken protection and is found acting against us." As for Cornwallis, he believed that the Indians were the injured party. They "were on a peaceable and friendly visit to Lt. Col. Brown who had directions to give them presents and to exhort them to remain quiet at home and take no part in the present troubles in this country."[47]

Considering the extent of the British outrage, it is surprising that only thirteen of the prisoners were hanged. Governor Wright hoped that the hangings "will have a very Good Effect." Whether Cornwallis or Cruger was responsible for the hangings, Georgians blamed Thomas Brown. Hugh M'Call wrote that Brown had Captain Ashby and twelve of the wounded hanged on the staircase of the Mackay house "so that he might have the satisfaction of seeing the victims of his vengeance expire." The British account accused Clarke's men of committing atrocities: "The scenes of villainy and rapine that mark the progress of the banditti are beyond describing."[48]

The retreating Elijah Clarke sent an appeal for help to his friends in the mountains. He related how Tories and Indians under Cruger and Brown had followed him into the upper settlements of Georgia and how the Indians fell upon Clarke's sick and wounded, scalping and torturing women and children, including several Tory families by mistake. "It is too painful for me to dwell on this gloomy subject," said Clarke, "my own family being lost in the general calamity." Clarke was blamed by his own men for bringing the retribution down upon the settlements. Andrew Pickens, still observing his parole, asked the mountaineers not to allow any other small parties to make attacks similar to Clarke's for fear of drawing more punishment upon their friends. Clarke was wrong about Brown following him (Brown's wound incapacitated him), but he was right about Cruger. Cruger reported to Cornwallis that he pursued Clarke to the Broad River and that he had burned the houses of "the most notorious villains" and driven off their cattle. About a hundred of Clarke's followers gave themselves up, and he sent twenty-three of the "worst characters" to Charlestown. Cruger called up two hundred loyal militia to police the countryside.[49]

There were instances of brutality in the countryside as the Rangers and loyal militia rode about looking for members of Clarke's band. Governor-in-exile Stephen Heard named James Grierson, Andrew Moore, and Thomas Waters as the men most active in searching the backcountry. Another was James Ingram, onetime aide to Benjamin Lincoln and a foe of Thomas Brown at the 1779 skirmish at the Burke County jail. After the fall of Charlestown, he cast his lot with the British.[50]

Hugh M'Call is the authority for the statement that those who were suspected of having helped Clarke were hanged without trial and that aged relatives of the raiders were herded into filthy prisons. Grierson was accused of dragging a seventy-eight-year-old man named Alexander into Augusta behind a cart. M'Call credits Ranger Captain Alexander C. Wylly with saving the life of John Jones, who resisted capture. Apparently, Andrew McLean interceded with Brown to spare the life of Charles Hammond, father of Samuel Hammond, a Whig who released himself from parole. There is no doubt that there was a punitive roundup of the disaffected. The degree of cruelty was a matter of debate. Whigs were convinced of the worst. John Rutledge addressed the South Carolina delegates and used Brown's conduct at Augusta to justify the hanging of Tory prisoners after the Battle of Kings Mountain: "It is said (and I believe it) that of the Prisoners whom Brown took at Augusta, he gave up four to the Indians who killed em,—cut off their Heads and kicked their bodies about the Streets and that he (Brown) hung upwards of 30 prisoners."[51]

Thomas Brown vehemently denied these allegations when they found their way into David Ramsay's history of the war. He wrote to Ramsay in 1786 that he had "never deviated from the line of conduct the laws of war and humanity prescribed," and he specifically denied having caused or even seen any Indian barbarities. Despite his denials, Brown's reputation was ruined in Georgia as long as the Revolution was remembered. In 1887 historian Charles Colcock Jones, Jr., called Brown a "devil incarnate, as brave as Apollyon and as Insatiate as Molock," who presided over "outrages and bloody orgies."[52] By delving into private motivations and delectations, in spite of Brown's denials, Jones indulged in the extravagant rhetoric of his day at the expense of his obligations to history. The best refutation of the characterization of Brown as fiend is the testimony of his career. He was too protective of his honor as an officer and a gentleman to have abandoned the conventional rules of war. The British never questioned his conduct. Even among his contemporaries in the Continental army, there were those, like "Lighthorse Harry" Lee, who admired Brown as a gallant officer.

The first Battle of Augusta had an immediate and tangible impact on the wider war in that it led directly to the October 7, 1780, Battle of Kings Mountain, the turning point of the Revolution in the South. Major Patrick Ferguson had recruited a large body of Loyalists in the Carolina backcountry. With them he attempted to intercept Clarke's raiders as they retreated to the mountains. Cornwallis explained what happened in a letter to Clinton: "Major Ferguson was tempted to stay near the mountains longer than he intended, in hopes of cutting off Col. Clarke on his return from Georgia. He was not aware that the enemy was so near him, and in endeavoring to execute my orders of passing the Catawbaw and joining me at Charlottetown he was attacked by a very superior force and totally defeated at King's Mountain." Found among Ferguson's papers was a dispatch from

Cornwallis dated September 23, 1780, with news that Cruger had arrived in time to save Brown in Augusta.[53]

Although Clarke was criticized by some of his fellow Whigs, his raid roused the countryside. Small bands of North and South Carolinians took to the field. The victorious Whigs at Kings Mountain were like Highland clans, each under its own chief. Three days before Kings Mountain the mountain men wrote to the distracted General Horatio Gates that they were at Gilbertown waiting for Elijah Clarke. They had fifteen hundred good men and asked Gates to send a general officer to take command. The letter was signed by Benjamin Cleaveland, Isaac Shelby, John Sevier, Andrew Hampton, William Campbell, and Joseph Winston. Gates had no time to act on the request before the battle occurred. Indeed, he did not hear about Clarke's attack on Augusta until October 10, when he wrote to the president of Congress that Clarke had defeated Brown at Augusta and retired with three hundred horses loaded with plunder. He had not heard from Clarke and assumed that he was busy securing his prisoners in the mountains.[54]

Francis Marion was terrorizing the region between the Santee and Pedee rivers until Banastre Tarleton chased him into the swamp. The dashing Tarleton was then sent after Thomas Sumter, whom Cornwallis called "so daring and troublesome a Man," and defeated him at a place called Blackstocks. Georgians under Benjamin Few and John Twiggs as well as those under Elijah Clarke operated independently in the area between the Tyger and Pacolet rivers.[55]

The defeat of Ferguson and the new spirit of insurgency were enough to discourage the loyal subjects in the Carolina backcountry. Lieutenant Colonel Cruger, after his return from Georgia to Ninety-Six, reported to Cornwallis that people were ready to give up as soon as a rebel army appeared.[56]

Cornwallis was aware of Robert Cunningham's prestige among the backcountry Loyalists and in a gesture that was more symbolic than practical created for him the position of brigadier general of militia and hoped he could inspire new enthusiasm among the dispirited. Moses Kirkland regarded Cunningham's promotion as a personal affront. He resigned his commission and moved to Augusta.[57]

British control of the Georgia backcountry after Kings Mountain was tenuous at best. Lieutenant Governor John Graham was sent into the Ceded Lands to investigate the situation there. Graham reported that 255 men were loyal and formed a militia regiment under Colonel Thomas Waters. Twice as many others were disaffected. Of these, 140 had left with Clarke, 42 were sent down to Charlestown as prisoners by Graham, 21 were held hostage for the good behavior of others, and 49 were "notorious active rebels laying out."[58]

Governor Wright was alarmed by Graham's survey. In addition to the notorious rebels laying out, there were another forty in Augusta as prisoners, which Wright confessed "we really don't know what to do with." Brown's Rangers were stretched thin in an attempt to patrol the Ceded Lands as far as the Broad River.[59]

The most important consequence of Kings Mountain was that Cornwallis decided to bring down the Indians upon the Carolina frontier. Thus Cornwallis became a tardy convert to Indian warfare and to the plan for using them. Circumstances were different from those in 1775 when the plan was first developed, but the strategy was the same—to employ the Indians to prevent the disloyal from retreating into a backcountry sanctuary. In November 1780 Cornwallis used the Cherokees to attack the mountain settlements in North Carolina and force the victors of Kings Mountain to withdraw from South Carolina. The Indians could penetrate into frontier fastnesses where regular troops could not go. Thomas Brown reported to Cornwallis that he had conveyed orders to the Cherokee chiefs in Augusta "to harrass the Mountaineers and divert their attention from the Loyalists in North and South Carolina to their own immediate concerns." Brown's deputies would prevent any wanton outrages.[60]

Cornwallis's decision to resort to Indian warfare enhanced Thomas Brown's importance in overall British strategy. Indeed, as 1780 drew to an end, Brown presided over a virtual empire. Creeks responsible to him were vital to the defense of Pensacola. Cherokees were on the warpath in North Carolina. Brown boasted to Cornwallis that he had opened communications with Detroit and Quebec in the North as well as Pensacola in the South. If his lordship wanted to send dispatches to any of those places, Brown would be glad to oblige. His Indians were as proficient in intercepting rebel correspondence as in delivering British messages. Brown enclosed a letter from Patrick Henry, governor of Virginia, intended for the Spanish governor at New Orleans. He had instructed the Indians to obstruct navigation on the Ohio as well as the Mississippi rivers, and the Cherokees had taken prisoners who were traveling by river to New Orleans and brought them to Augusta. For the women and children the long trek must have been a terrible experience. There was more than brag in Brown's letter. Brown's expense account for the year 1780 proves that he paid the Cherokees for an expedition to Quebec. A memorial to Brown's wilderness domain is a remarkably detailed map of the southeastern region of North America drawn for Brown by the master cartographer Joseph Purcell.[61]

If Thomas Brown happened to be in a philosophical mood as the year drew to a close, he might have pondered the changes in his fortunes the year brought. At the age of thirty, he was at the height of his American career. He had returned in triumph to the scene of his worst humiliation. He was the authority in civil as well as military affairs. Although he would not prosecute his former enemies out of vengeance, he did not hesitate to carry out Cornwallis's orders to hang those who broke their paroles.

He enjoyed the confidence of Lord George Germain and Sir Henry Clinton. He had endured Cornwallis's fit of peevishness about recruiting irregularities and had overcome the general's opposition to Indian warfare. He won the respect of his fellow officers by his brave stand in the Mackay house; the loyalty of his Rangers was proven beyond dispute. The victory over Clarke had won him the privilege of constructing a proper fortification, which he tactfully named Fort Cornwallis; he hoped it would provide security against any future raids.

With James Gordon's help, and with slave labor, he began to cultivate his plantation at Brownsborough again. His dream of living out his life as a Georgia planter seemed once more a possibility.

CHAPTER SEVEN

THE PLAN FAILS,

1781

 The resort to Indian warfare in North Carolina in 1780 was reminiscent of earlier British employment of Indians on the Georgia frontier during the invasions of Florida. In its immediate objective, the strategy was successful, but in the larger sense it failed because of a lack of coordination between the British military and the Indian offensives. It failed, too, because of a more fundamental flaw. The backcountry people, however loyal to the king, were reluctant to ally themselves with Indians. If the British won, the Indians would keep their land. If the British lost, the settlers could claim the land as the spoils of victory. Thomas Brown's efforts to chase the trespassers off the Indian hunting grounds endeared him to the Indians but not to the settlers.

The plan failed also because the backcountrymen were learning to fight for their homes and were becoming more proficient in Indian warfare. During the winter of 1780–81 Colonels John Sevier and Arthur Campbell at the head of North Carolina and Virginia militia destroyed more than a thousand Cherokee houses and fifty thousand bushels of corn. In January General Nathanael Greene, desperately short of men, instructed the mountain leaders to make peace with the Cherokees and join his army. But the Cherokees were not beaten yet, and they went on the warpath again in February. The mountaineers retaliated with an even fiercer campaign. Thomas Brown complained that the white people were more savage than any Indians he knew: "Thirteen villages destroyed! Men, women and children thrown into flames, impaled alive or butchered in cold blood!"[1]

Some of the Cherokee chiefs asked for peace in late April 1781. They declared that the "bad situation" their nation was in was not their fault; it was "due to the designs of Colonel Brown." Chief Tassel said that he would have no more to do with Brown or his talks because Brown "brought all the troubles upon us."[2]

The situation on the western frontier was equally bad for the British. A superior Spanish force besieged Pensacola in March and April, and Major General John Campbell surrendered on May 8, 1781. Alexander Cameron decided to join Thomas Brown in Augusta and administer Indian affairs jointly. With Pensacola in Spanish hands, Augusta was the most important link between the British and the western tribes.[3]

That connection became increasingly tenuous as British control of the Georgia backcountry deteriorated rapidly in 1781. General Nathanael Greene gave Whig partisans reasons to hope. He assured Georgia Colonel Benjamin Few that help was forthcoming. General Daniel Morgan would "give support to your actions and spirit up the people in that quarter."[4]

Morgan intended to go all the way to Georgia and expected to gather up Georgia refugees as he went. Cornwallis sent the dashing Banastre Tarleton to head off Morgan. The result was the Battle of Cowpens. "I have given him a devil of a whipping," reported the jubilant Morgan.[5] The American victory emboldened the Whigs in the Georgia backcountry, just as Greene had hoped, but Morgan got no closer to Georgia than Cowpens. Greene needed all the men he could muster to meet Cornwallis. As Cornwallis pursued Greene into North Carolina, Governor James Wright worried about what would happen to Georgia: "If Lord Cornwallis Penetrates far into No. Carolina I shall expect a Rebel Army will come in behind him and throw us into the utmost confusion and danger."[6]

Meanwhile, Thomas Brown completed his fieldworks in Augusta. Pastor James Seymour yielded possession of his church. He explained to his superiors that "the Burying Ground is now made a strong fortification . . . the Society may expect a Letter from Col. Brown soon apologizing for that measure." Engineer John Douglass, whom Brown respected and admired, was mainly responsible for the construction of the fort. Their careers were fated to be intertwined.[7] Brown hoped that the security of the fort would cause the loyal militia to behave more reliably while he and his Rangers patrolled the countryside.

Particularly troublesome was a rebel party under Captain James McKay that haunted the swamps along the Savannah River and plun-

dered riverboats bound for Augusta. With his link with Savannah
jeopardized, Brown ordered Ranger Lieutenant Kemp with a party
of Rangers and militia to search for the raiders. A guide named Willie
was employed to conduct Kemp to McKay's camp. Willie managed to
alert McKay, and Kemp's troopers rode into an ambush. The militia
fled without a fight, and the Rangers surrendered. McKay asked
Kemp to join them. The Ranger refused and was stripped and shot.
The same thing happened to each of the other Rangers except one,
who pretended to join McKay but escaped at his first chance and told
Brown about the fate of his comrades.[8]

Brown sent Captain Alexander C. Wylly with forty Rangers and
thirty Indians in search of McKay's band. Wylly learned that McKay
had joined forces with a large contingent of South Carolinians under
Colonel William Harden and sent for Brown, who covered the sixty-
mile distance in two days with some two hundred Rangers and Indians. About a hundred militiamen joined them on the march. Brown
encamped at Wiggan's plantation some thirty miles from Black
Swamp. Hugh M'Call's account of the episode is critical of Brown for
sleeping in the plantation house instead of among his men. M'Call
characterized Brown as "always imprudent." Brown did live an exciting life and was sometimes imprudent. In this instance, however,
sleeping in the house was not what was questionable, especially since
Brown was still recuperating from the serious wound he had received
at the Mackay House. Brown's deputy in Savannah, Charles Shaw,
informed Lord George Germain that Brown was suffering from excessive fatigue as well as from the effects of his wound. Therefore,
sleeping in a house was not imprudent. Chasing after a numerically
superior force and camping within striking distance of them was another matter. Harden attacked shortly after midnight and terrified
the loyal militia posted on the left side of the camp. Brown reported
that the militia "fled into camp in the greatest disorder and confusion
imaginable." The Rangers formed into line and repulsed the Carolinians.[9]

The next morning at eight o'clock Harden reappeared, this time
on the right side of the camp. His men dismounted and engaged in a
rifle exchange with the British. The remaining loyal militia then fled;
some joined the other side. Brown ordered his Rangers and Indians
to mount and charge. This time Harden's men scattered, many seeking refuge in the swamps. "They were principally indebted to the
speed of their horses for their escape," Brown told Balfour.[10]

Then occurred one of the cruelty stories associated with Brown as long as the Revolution was remembered. The Whig version says that Brown turned Willie the guide over to the Indians, who ripped him open with knives in Brown's presence. It relates that Mrs. McKay, a widow, learned that her son, a youth of seventeen, was one of Brown's prisoners. She brought food and wine to Brown and pleaded for her son's life. According to Hugh M'Call, Brown "received her refreshments but turned a deaf ear to her entreaties." Her son and some others were hanged and delivered to the Indians.[11]

After the war, Brown attempted to set the record straight. He informed Charleston historian David Ramsay, who first published the above account, that Rannal McKay had a reputation as a bad character. While Brown was on his march to Augusta in 1780, McKay took the parole, and his mother promised to make him observe it. Young McKay later joined James McKay's band. When Willie led Kemp's Rangers into ambush, Rannal McKay was one of those who tortured the Rangers before they were put to death. Young McKay confessed his complicity, and Brown hanged him without compunction. He also hanged eleven others who were involved. A different fate awaited Willie. An Indian who had been a close friend of Kemp's dispatched him with a tomahawk. Brown said that this was the only such incident ever committed by an Indian under his command. Creeks, Chickasaws, and Cherokees were with Brown in the fight against Harden. Among the dead were Dog King and the Far Off King, both of the Cussetas.[12]

Brown's men searched houses within thirty miles of Wiggan's plantation and managed to recover some of the plundered stores. "Wherever he found any goods concealed," Shaw reported, "he destroyed the settlement." By such stern measures he hoped to put a stop to plundering. Brown asked Balfour to post a small force near the mouth of Briar Creek or the river would never be safe. Balfour congratulated Brown for defeating Harden and promised more supplies for the Indians but no additional manpower. Brown would have to guard the river himself.[13]

While Brown was engaged with Harden on the lower Savannah River, rebel parties infiltrated the region above Augusta. According to an increasingly distraught Governor Wright, a party of sixty or so rebels entered the Ceded Lands (Wilkes County) and murdered eleven persons in their homes, some in their beds. The village of Wrightsborough was plundered. Brown sent Grierson with a hundred militiamen to Wrightsborough and another hundred under Major Henry Williams to the Broad River in a vain effort to catch the raiders. Grierson returned to Augusta with prisoners accused of helping the enemy. Brown informed Governor Wright that he had heard that Elijah Clarke, Benjamin Few, and John Twiggs were preparing an incursion into Georgia. He was concerned that the people who harbored the first invaders might do so again. Brown wanted to keep the militia in the field but could not because they needed their pay. Lieutenant Colonel John Harris Cruger had his own problems with Andrew Pickens's partisans in the Ninety-Six District and could give no help. In Governor Wright's words, the province was reduced to "a precarious and dangerous situation."[14]

Lord George Germain, unaware of the actual conditions in the backcountry, still hoped to use Indians offensively. He informed Brown that he expected war parties from Canada to attack the rebel frontiers, and he asked Brown to direct the Cherokees to cooperate with them. The object was to prevent frontiersmen from joining Greene's army. The Cherokees had exhausted themselves in the winter campaign against the mountain settlements, but Brown was able to tell Germain that the Upper Creeks under the faithful Emistisiguo had set off to harass the "rebel banditti" of Long Island, Watauga, and Holsten.[15]

On March 15, 1781, Cornwallis caught up with Greene at Guilford Courthouse, North Carolina. The British won the field but were so exhausted that Cornwallis withdrew to Wilmington, then marched north into Virginia, leaving the defense of South Carolina and Georgia with the attenuated occupation army under Lord Francis Rawdon. Governor Wright complained that "the very great Distance Lord Cornwallis and his Army are at gives every opportunity to the Disaffected to Collect and Murder, Plunder, etc., in a most cruel and shocking manner."[16] The *Royal Georgia Gazette* in Savannah elaborated on the crisis: "A set of the most barbarous wretches that ever infected any country, amounting some say to 200, others 250, lately crossed the Savannah from the northward, surprized and murdered several Loyalists at Wrightsborough and on the Ceded Lands, stripping their families of the necessities of life."[17]

Reverend James Seymour was one of those who brought the distressing news to Savannah. He had to abandon his farm outside Augusta in fear of his life. After he left in late April, his family was robbed of everything of value. He thought that Brown's new fort,

Fort Cornwallis, was sufficiently strong for its own defense, but the rebels controlled the countryside.[18] The rebel raiders felt justified in committing any manner of outrage in retaliation for the treatment of their families and properties by the British. Each side blamed the other for atrocities. The Quakers of Wrightsborough paid a price for remaining neutral, and more of them were forced to seek refuge in Savannah.

Although the rebel raiders appeared to spring up from some mysterious dragon seed, the long arm of Nathanael Greene actually directed events. As early as February 19, 1781, Andrew Pickens argued with Greene about marching so far away from home. His men had reached Guilford Courthouse in northern North Carolina and complained that there were enough Virginians and North Carolinians to defend that part of the country. They could be more effective against the British posts in the South Carolina and Georgia backcountry. The Georgians, in particular, were beginning to desert. Pickens was aware that irregulars such as James McKay were operating along the lower Savannah. Unfortunately, as Pickens acknowledged, McKay and his men were "bent chiefly to plunder," so friends as well as foes suffered. Pickens suggested that Major James Jackson be permitted to return to Georgia to bring order into the Whig resistance there. Three weeks later, Pickens asked permission to go back himself: "I look on it I am capable of doing more good there than here." Greene agreed and ordered Pickens to return to his district with the South Carolina and Georgia troops.[19]

On his march southward Pickens met up with Elijah Clarke, who had fought and defeated a British detachment in the Long Canes region. Pickens was sorry to inform Greene that the British commander, Major James Dunlap, was shot after he had surrendered. Pickens offered a reward for the arrest of the assailant. Greene was pleased about Clarke's victory but dismayed about "the inhuman attack upon Major Dunlap." By then, Greene had decided to follow Pickens into South Carolina. Cornwallis would have to give up his invasion of Virginia or risk losing his backposts in South Carolina and Georgia.[20]

Greene ordered Lieutenant Colonel Henry Lee to precede the rest of the army with three companies of cavalry, three companies of light infantry, and Major Pinkerthan Eaton's North Carolina infantry. He cautioned the impetuous "Lighthorse Harry" to remember that he commanded mortal men, and "their Powers may not keep pace with your ambitions." Greene reported to General Washington that he had ordered Pickens to lay siege to Augusta and Ninety-Six.[21]

Thus there was more of a coordinated plan behind the invasion of Georgia than the British perceived. The scattered bands of raiders gathered at a rendezvous on the Little River on April 16, 1781. Colonel Elijah Clarke was recuperating from an attack of smallpox, and Lieutenant Colonel Micajah Williamson assumed command. Majors James Jackson and Samuel Hammond were there with their men. They advanced to the very outskirts of Augusta to begin a siege. Their men knew that the legendary "Burntfoot Brown" would not give up easily. But they were hampered by the absence of artillery and a lack of supplies. James Jackson made his presence felt by giving speeches to encourage the men to maintain their position; help was on the way.

Thomas Brown hoped that his friends would reach Augusta first. On May 1, 1781, he reported to Colonel von Porbeck, the Hessian commander of the Savannah garrison, that Jackson was hovering about with eighty mounted militia on the Carolina side while four to five hundred cavalry besieged Augusta on the Georgia side. The public stores were at the late George Galphin's stockade at Silver Bluff. Brown detached a company of Rangers under Captain Samuel Roworth to guard the supplies. He had managed to bring what he needed by night from Silver Bluff to Augusta and so was well provided with ammunition.[22]

Brown did not remain idly in his fort while the Whigs closed in. He sent John Douglass on a daring raid with a detachment of royal militia. Brown later testified that Douglass surprised a group of rebels guarding horses. The guards were bayoneted, and Douglass captured four hundred horses. What Brown did with four hundred horses is not clear. Ranger officers were sent out to seek help from the Indians. Captain Alexander Wylly went among the Cherokees with instructions to bring that nation into action, but the Cherokees were discouraged by the incursions of the mountain militia of Virginia and North Carolina.[23] Brown hoped to receive assistance from the Creeks also, but most of them were away on the Pensacola campaign.

Von Porbeck had 500 troops in Savannah and about 350 militia in the surrounding country. Governor Wright and his council implored him to send a hundred regulars to Augusta. The answer was no. Von Porbeck said that his own garrison was too weak to afford any help to Brown. The frustrated Wright complained to Lord George Germain about allowing a "foreigner" to have charge of the military in Georgia.[24]

The best Wright could do was to ask Major Philip Dill to collect loyal militia in St. George and St. Matthew parishes and relieve Brown. Dill was intercepted by Captains Isaac Shelby and Paddy Carr at Walker's Bridge on Briar Creek and forced to retreat. Shelby and Carr then ambushed a party of Rangers and Indians at the Widow Bugg's plantation at New Savannah. Prisoners were executed. Loyalists learned that a "Georgia parole" meant death.[25]

In early May, Augusta was the focus of attention. Pickens wrote Greene from LeRoy Hammond's Snow Hill that he had arrived opposite Augusta but lacked arms and ammunition. Elijah Clarke was well enough by May 15 to resume command of the Georgia militia outside the town. Meanwhile, Greene's army fought Lord Rawdon's at Hobkirk Hill. Although Rawdon had the better of it, he decided to withdraw from Camden and ordered Cruger at Ninety-Six to abandon his post and join Brown in Augusta. The message never reached Cruger, but Pickens expected Cruger and expressed an inability to oppose him. It was in this context that Greene sent Lee to join Pickens. The sensitive problem of command was circumvented by Greene's orders for Lee to "cooperate" with Brigadier General Pickens. Lee was technically in command as the representative of Greene. While Greene moved upon Ninety-Six, Lee covered the seventy-five miles to Augusta in three days; his infantry and dragoons alternated on horseback. Greene congratulated his lieutenant: "For rapid marches you exceed Lord Cornwallis and everybody else."[26]

Lee decided to concentrate first on Fort Galphin. With his weary troopers and with Samuel Hammond's and William Harden's regiments from Pickens's command, he reached Silver Bluff on May 21, a day "sultry beyond measure." Lee counted on Ranger Captain Samuel Roworth being unaware of the presence of regulars. Lee ordered the militia to attack, then feign retreat to draw the Rangers out of the fort. The ruse worked and Captain Michael Rudolph quickly overcame the South Carolina loyal militia in the fort. The prize was incredibly rich—guns, ammunition, blankets, tools, and medicine— precisely those items the Americans needed but lacked. Without the stores captured at Fort Galphin the subsequent Battle of Augusta could not have been fought. Pickens, who had been a beggar for supplies, was now in a position to send provisions to General Greene.[27]

Lee was so jubilant that he told Greene he could take Savannah in ten days. He sent Captain Joseph Eggleston to join Clarke on the hill outside Augusta. Following Lee's orders, Eggleston carried a flag to Brown to inform him of the arrival of Greene's army and to call upon him to surrender. Lee felt insulted when Brown declined to reply. On the evening of May 22 Lee joined Pickens and Clarke on the hill above Augusta. Lee had his first look at Fort Cornwallis; he thought it was "judiciously constructed, well finished and secure from storm."[28] The fort stood near the river on the western edge of Oglethorpe's original town. The thirty-year-old church was situated between the fort and the river; none of the accounts of the battle mentions the church, however, so Brown might have dismantled it to provide lumber for the platforms inside the breastworks. A long, narrow lagoon, mapped in 1779 by Archibald Campbell, flowed westerly along the south side of town and emptied into the river at a distance of half a mile from Fort Cornwallis. The main street crossed the lagoon gully on a bridge. On the west side of the gully stood Colonel James Grierson's fortified house. Lee and Pickens decided to attack Grierson first. Lee's cavalry was in position to intercept Brown if he tried to come to Grierson's relief.

If Brown was trapped, his behavior belied it. On May 19, before Lee's arrival, Brown led a sally out of the fort and scattered the Georgia and Carolina militia. Alexander McLean carried an optimistic report to Savannah, claiming that the Rangers killed upward of ninety and took at least eighty horses. Brown planned another attack for the night of May 20, but Colonel James Grierson sent a note asking Brown to postpone the surprise. The Americans were infiltrating the gully between the two forts in an effort to cut communications between Brown and Grierson and so Grierson planned to keep a strong force in the gully that night. Grierson sent something which he considered to be especially valuable to Brown with the request that it be kept with Brown's papers "till we get over our present troubles."[29]

The American assault on Fort Grierson was launched on May 22. Major Samuel Hammond led the attack. Every second man was equipped with an ax. The Carolinians swarmed across the shallow gully and began to cut away the stockade. Realizing that resistance was futile, Grierson and his men escaped over the side of the fort nearest the river and ran along the riverbank toward Fort Cornwallis with the attackers in hot pursuit.

Brown came out of his fort and covered Grierson's escape with a cannonade. Lee's artillery returned fire. Martin Weatherford later remembered Grierson, Major Henry Williams, and the other militia crowding through the gate of Fort Cornwallis. For Williams, it was a family reunion. His father, Captain Samuel Williams, was a veteran in the King's Rangers; his two brothers, Edward and William, were with Brown as militiamen. Dr. Thomas Taylor, William Manson's associate, was surgeon to the royal militia. He escaped to Fort Cornwallis, as did Lieutenant Colonel William Goodgion. Richard Pearis was there, too, as were Thomas Waters, David Douglass, and James Ingram. Brown had requisitioned all the slaves he could find in Augusta to work on bolstering the fort's defenses.[30] In addition, there were Cherokee, Creek, and Chickasaw warriors in the fort; some had their families with them.

A casualty of the first day's fighting was Major Eaton, who had led his North Carolina light infantry in pursuit of Grierson's militia. Most of the fallen were Grierson's men, slain as they retreated. A captured officer asked Lee for permission to go into Fort Cornwallis and obtain medicine for his fellow prisoners. Lee agreed and sent a flag to Brown with the message that it was being done at the request of the prisoners. Brown returned the medicine with a polite note saying that he had not replied to previous flags because of past altercations with the person he assumed to be in command, Clarke. Lee noted that he and Pickens were gratified to produce a renewal of communication; they still hoped to avert a bloody struggle to the death. Lee did not mention in his memoirs how Clarke might have felt about the rebuff. Lee regarded Brown as a fellow officer and therefore a gentleman; the siege went slowly, he noted, "so vigilant and resolute was the active and sagacious officer" on the other side. Lee's opinion of Clarke's militia was not so flattering. "They excell the goths and the vandals in their schemes of plunder, murder and iniquity," he wrote to Greene, "all this under pretense of supporting the virtuous cause of America." Greene agreed with Lee and tried to temper the ferocity of his followers. "The idea of exterminating the Tories is not less barbarous than unpolitical," he warned Pickens, "and if persisted it will keep this Country in the greatest confusion and distress."[31]

During the first week of the siege the Americans dug an entrenchment from the riverbank across the western front of the fort and another along the eastern side. The trenches would provide protection for workers to build a wooden siege tower. Lee had seen one designed by Carolina Colonel Hezekiah Maham at the siege of Fort Watson. The tower was constructed of notched logs to a height of thirty feet; the interior was filled with dirt and stone. There was room for riflemen to fire between the logs and a platform that would support a six-pounder cannon, larger than anything in Brown's arsenal. The builders were partially shielded by an abandoned wooden house between the tower and the fort.

Brown did what he could to distract the besiegers from their project. On the night of May 28 Brown and his Rangers and Indians launched a surprise attack on the militia in the west entrenchments. Lee's infantry under Captain Samuel Handy rallied and regained the works at bayonet point. Thereafter Lee placed his own troops in the trenches and put them on shifts through the night.

On the twenty-ninth Brown sallied out again, and again there was fierce hand-to-hand combat in the trenches. On this night Captain Michael Rudolph's cavalry used the bayonet to drive the Rangers back to the fort. Brown came out a third time on the thirtieth. This time he attacked both the front and rear works. Handy's Marylanders bore the brunt of it in the hardest fight of all. On May 31 Lee and Pickens sent a flag by Captain Joseph Armstrong and offered Brown an opportunity to surrender. Brown replied that it was his duty and inclination to defend his position to the last extremity.[32]

By June 1, it was very nearly the last extremity. Brown had failed to halt the constant digging of approach trenches and gave up the effort. Tarleton Brown, one of Harden's officers who occupied the siege works, remembered that he and his men rolled up cowhides and put them on the embankments and fired between them at the fort. The Rangers inside were expert marksmen, however. The man standing next to Tarleton Brown was shot in the head as he aimed his rifle.[33] On June 1 the tower was finished. Brown built a platform in the southwest angle of his fort, mounted two cannons, and directed the fire on the tower. Black pioneers within the fort filled bags with sand and piled them upon the platform to protect the cannoneers and riflemen. The front of the tower was covered with cowhides to shield Lee's sharpshooters inside.

On June 2 the six-pounder was mounted on the tower. It commanded most of the interior of Brown's fort. Before noon, the two British cannons were knocked out of action. The interior of the fort was exposed except for the lateral earthworks, which Brown constructed within the fort, and the deep trench along the west wall of the fort. Pickens related the good news to Greene, praising the militia for being more dependable than ever before. He explained that the tower stood 150 yards from the fort and redoubts were being prepared only 50 yards in front of Brown's ditch. He hoped that the siege would end in a few days so his men could plant a crop that season.[34]

Brown sent a Scots sergeant who pretended to be a deserter with instructions to burn down the tower if he had a chance. Lee was almost fooled but guessed that his wily antagonist must be up to mischief and had the spy placed under guard.

During the night of June 2, Brown's men burned the houses nearest the fort but left two standing. Lee knew that there must be a reason why the two were not destroyed, but he could not know that Brown's workers had dug a tunnel under one of the houses and placed a huge amount of explosives in the tunnel. Brown gambled on the success of this last strategy. If the Americans occupied the vacant house, he would blow it up. Therefore, when Lee and Pickens sent another summons to surrender on June 3 and expressed a willingness to discuss terms, Brown's answer was the same as before.

Lee and Pickens decided to launch a grand assault on Fort Cornwallis on June 4. Ironically, that was, as all Britons knew, the king's birthday. Pickens's militia was sent to reconnoiter the empty houses to ascertain whether they might take shelter there for the final battle. Then they withdrew. Within the fort, Brown had heard the movement of troops and his spies had seen the Americans enter the buildings. At 3 A.M. a violent explosion rent the house, and Lee had the answer to his puzzle. The house had been a trap.

The American assault columns were drawn up at 9 A.M. on June 4 when Lee and Pickens tried yet again to negotiate with Brown. This time they asked that Brown send his prisoners out of the fort and remove them from danger. If he won the engagement he could have them back again. According to Hugh M'Call and Joseph Johnson, Brown had paraded his prisoners on the parapets of the fort; one of them was the aged Alexander. Both accounts are vague about when this exhibition of prisoners occurred, but they mention it as another example of Brown's villainy. Lee's version, which is the most detailed and which M'Call follows faithfully except for the prisoners incident, did not mention the alleged mistreatment. Joseph Johnson, whose history was based on veterans' reminiscences, added an intriguing story. He wrote that Brown prevailed upon a lady "who was neither old nor ugly" to arrange to meet Lee. The lady and the colonel got along so well that Brown's capitulation was arranged.[35] Perhaps there was a friendly lady in Augusta, but it is doubtful that her services were needed.

Brown replied that he could take care of his own prisoners, but he sent his flag with word that he was willing to discuss the American offer of June 3. Brown suggested the same terms Clinton had granted Lincoln at the surrender of Charlestown. The exchange of flags had one advantage for Brown which Lee noted. It saved him the embarrassment of surrendering on the king's birthday.

On June 5, Lee and Pickens replied to Brown's terms with the statement that "our sympathy for the unfortunate and gallant of our profession has induced us to grant the honorable terms which we herewith transmit." Since the message was dated June 5, and 8 A.M. on the same day was designated as the hour for surrender, the last arrangements must have taken place in the early hours of the morning. Officers would be sent to Savannah on parole; the rank and file were prisoners of war. Brown's sick and wounded would be cared for by British surgeons. Brown asked that his Indians be allowed to go to Savannah with him. The American reply was noncommittal on that point. Brown wanted the honor of marching his garrison out of the fort with shouldered arms and drums beating. Again, the victors were generous. "The judicious and gallant defence made by the garrison entitles them to every mark of military respect," they replied.[36]

When the British garrison marched out and piled their arms, Brown was not with them. He was conducted to Lee's quarters by Captain Joseph Armstrong. He told Lee that the Scot sergeant was no deserter but a good soldier acting under orders. Lee released the sergeant, who "with joy rejoined his commander."[37]

If Lee and Pickens played by the rules of war, they could not persuade their troops to do so. Lee realized the danger Brown was in and made Captain Armstrong responsible for his safety. If Brown were killed, Lee wrote, "the laurels acquired by the arms of America would have been stained by the murder of a gallant soldier who had committed himself to his enemy on their plighted faith." Armstrong's task was difficult. He later confessed that he had never encountered such personal danger as when he guarded Thomas Brown. Every person who approached seemed ready to kill his prisoners. Tarleton Brown recalled without compunction that he and his companions followed Armstrong's party downriver, hoping to get a chance to kill Brown.[38]

Lee left Augusta on June 6 and the next day wrote to Brown stating that General Greene had approved the arrangements and would rely on Brown's personal honor for carrying out the terms of his parole as well as those of his officers. General Pickens had been instructed to provide transportation for the officers' personal effects.[39]

As soon as Lee left Augusta, Colonel James Grierson was killed while a prisoner in his own house. Major Henry Williams was wounded in a separate attack. Dr. Thomas Taylor blamed Lee for not providing protection for Grierson. He visited Grierson, "that gallant unfortunate man," on the morning he was murdered. "Upon my carrying him a drink of water some of the miscreants about bestow'd on us both the most bitter curses," Taylor wrote. Grierson knew that his life was in danger and asked Taylor to appeal through Brown to Lee. Taylor said that Brown's intercession was in vain. "Patriots at home may exclaim and with some Justice on the Impropriety of employing Indians, but their cruelties in this part of the continent have been exceeded in number at least four-fold by those of the Rebels. Putting a man to Death in cold blood is very prettily nicknamed giving a Georgia parole."[40]

Georgia veterans remembered the death of Grierson. Micajah Brooks said that "he was shot in the upper part of a log house in a place something like a balcony by a Whig whose name was James Alexander . . . said James Alexander was in disguise." Samuel Beckaem added the information that Major Henry Williams was with Grierson and that he was shot by Andrew Shulus. Williams was brought to Savannah, where he recovered from his wound. Beckaem justified the attack on Grierson because Alexander's aged father was one of the hostages Grierson brought in to Augusta after the Whig raid in February, and Grierson left "an aged Mother, Sisters and brothers . . . to starve."[41]

Although the ordinary soldier believed that Grierson got what he deserved, Pickens was displeased and Greene was furious. He called it "an insult to the Arms of the United States and an outrage upon the rights of humanity." He offered a reward of one hundred guineas for the arrest of the guilty parties.[42] No arrests were made, and the reward went unclaimed.

Governor Wright informed Balfour that "Poor Grierson was Basely

Murdered." He hoped that "this worthy Man's Death will not Pass without due Notice." Wright was concerned about Brown's life. He would believe that he was safe only when he saw him. Lieutenant Colonel Beamsley Glazier, one of the heroes of the siege of Savannah, threatened to hang six of the Charlestown prisoners in St. Augustine if Brown were harmed. Alured Clarke, now a brigadier general, brought a detachment from St. Augustine to Savannah, intending to go to Brown's assistance, but was too late. So was a force of one hundred men from the King's American Regiment dispatched from Charlestown by Lord Rawdon. Rawdon admitted that he should have sent them to Augusta instead of to Savannah.[43]

Grierson's murder invited retaliations by the British. A furor was raised that summer when the British hanged South Carolina Colonel Isaac Hayne, who had attempted to kidnap the paroled Andrew Williamson. General Nathanael Greene protested to Lieutenant Colonel Balfour, who replied that Hayne was executed according to Cornwallis's standing order regarding rebels who broke their paroles and took up arms. Balfour reminded Greene that Grierson and Dunlap had fallen "by the hands of licensed and protected murderers."[44] Hayne's execution was protested by the Duke of Richmond in a speech in the House of Lords on January 31, 1782, in which he stated that Carolina Loyalists had denounced the deed. This speech led Colonel Thomas Fletchall, Lieutenant Colonel Joseph Robinson, Major Evan McLaurin, and eight others to deliver an address to the king on behalf of the loyal inhabitants of the Carolina frontier. The signers were refugees in Charlestown at the time. They approved Hayne's execution and said that similar measures should have been taken long before. The timid policy toward rebels simply encouraged rebellion. Affixed to the document were the names of more than three hundred loyal persons who had been killed after they had surrendered.[45]

While the loyal Georgians attempted to make the best of a bad situation in Savannah, the Whigs exploited their success in the backcountry. Although Nathanael Greene failed in his efforts to force Lieutenant Colonel John Harris Cruger to surrender Ninety-Six, that last backcountry post was abandoned by Lord Francis Rawdon in June 1781. Nathanael Greene sent Joseph Clay to Augusta with instructions to establish a constitutional government as quickly as possible. Until the middle of July Greene's main purpose was to restore order in Georgia. When he received news that the emperor of Austria and the empress of Russia had offered to mediate the war between

England and America, Greene changed his policy. A negotiated peace might mean a settlement on the basis of *uti possidetis,* with each side retaining the territory occupied. Clay was told to arrange for regular elections: "A legislature is necessary to give you political existence, not only in America, but in Europe much more than here."[46] With a republican government in Augusta, peace negotiators in Paris could argue for the independence of Georgia even though Savannah remained in British hands.

Greene did what he could to give Georgia de facto existence. He made James Jackson lieutenant colonel of a regular Georgia Legion. John Twiggs, the senior militia colonel, was appointed brigadier general. On August 16, 1781, elections were held according to the constitution of 1777. The newly elected delegates to the assembly chose Nathan Brownson as governor. Brownson congratulated General Greene on the success of his efforts to restore civil government in Georgia.[47] Thus the campaign waged by Greene against Thomas Brown had more than local ramifications. The future of Georgia was at stake.

Governor James Wright saw it more clearly than anyone else on the British side. He warned Balfour that Augusta was "the Key to this Province and if the Rebels are possessed of this place they have the command of the whole country." The rebels established their government there after Lieutenant Colonel Campbell gave it up in 1779, and they were gathering to do the same again. Wright was particularly annoyed because Balfour paid so little attention to Georgia. The effect of abandoning the post at Ninety-Six was "trifling," Wright said, when compared to abandoning Augusta. Wright's duty to His Majesty's service, to the loyal inhabitants, to the king, and to himself all united to compel him to demand the recapture of Augusta.[48]

Balfour managed to put off Wright's dramatic demand with a subtle suggestion that Wright and the other proponents of the southern strategy had been wrong all along. "With your Excellency, I regret the loss of the Backcountry, especially Ninety-Six and Augusta and the more so as the manner of it was a general Revolt of the Inhabitants."[49] In other words, the alleged loyalty of the backcountry was a fiction. Wright was not persuaded; he estimated that there were still seventy-eight hundred inhabitants in the Georgia backcountry, and most of them were loyal but would make their peace with the rebels if no help was sent. "If you saw and knew the consequences of not taking post at Augusta, you would strain a point to do it," Wright argued. "Possibly Georgia may be considered as of little consequence, but be assured if America is recovered it will be one of the first Colonies on the Continent."[50] Nathanael Greene, on the other side, hoped to make Georgia one of the foremost states on the continent.

Wright appealed to General Clinton in New York, explaining that his requests to Balfour had gone unheeded and that "this Province is broke up, Ruined and in a manner Lost for want of a little assistance." He complained to Lord George Germain, "your Lordship Sees the Consequences of not protecting and holding these two Provinces, I always dreaded it from the Moment Lord Cornwallis went into Virginia . . . God knows what will become of us." At last, Wright gave up his campaign "as I find it in Vain to write," he reported to William Knox, Germain's secretary; "I believe I shall trouble none of your generals any more."[51] Wright believed that Georgia was lost when Augusta fell, even though the low country remained under British control.

Governor Wright's expense account provides an insight into the plight of the refugees from the backcountry. The militia officers who surrendered with Brown were supported by the government. Among them were Lieutenant Colonel William Goodgion, who considered himself lucky to be alive. After the surrender of Fort Cornwallis, he had been told to prepare for death, for he would be shot at any moment. For five days he was kept in suspense, then reprieved and sent down to Savannah.[52] With him was the dangerously wounded Major Henry Williams, Major William Johnston, who "came almost naked to Savannah," Captains James Weatherford, Nathaniel Young, and Ashton, volunteers David Douglass, James Ingram, and James Stewart, and messengers Martin Weatherford and Alexander McLean, who had risked their lives carrying dispatches from Augusta. Reverend James Seymour was given money to take care of James Grierson's two children. Andrew McLean, the onetime "Macaroni," had lost everything and had to be supported at public expense. Goodgion and Seymour were put on the governor's committee charged with the care of refugees.[53]

Meanwhile, Thomas Brown was a prisoner on parole; though quiet, he was not passive. The rules of war required that he refrain from military activity until he could be exchanged for an American officer of equal rank. Instead of waiting idly in Savannah, Brown went to Charlestown in hopes of expediting his exchange. The British commander there, General Alexander Leslie, was responsible for arranging a wholesale swap of prisoners with General Greene. Brown wanted to make sure he was on the list.

In Charlestown, Brown was greeted by his two associates from the Orkney Islands, William Manson and James Gordon. During that July and August, Brown began a lifelong acquaintance with Lord Francis Rawdon, later Earl of Moira. Rawdon might have blamed himself for the loss of Augusta. His orders to Cruger to abandon Ninety-Six and join Brown had been intercepted. After the two-week battle was joined, Rawdon should have sent reinforcements, but the regiment he finally sent to Georgia went to Savannah and not Augusta. Thomas Brown did not blame his superiors for their failure to come to his assistance. In a letter to Lord George Germain, Brown assumed the responsibility. Augusta was lost because he could not rally his Indian allies. The Cherokees had not recovered from the punishment they had received from the fierce attacks of the North Carolinians. Most of the Creeks were off on the Pensacola campaign. They came at Brown's call, but the distance was too great. Some fifteen hundred Creek warriors were reported to have reached the Ogeechee River, forty miles west of Augusta, on the day Brown surrendered. If he had known that, Brown would not have surrendered his post.[54]

With Augusta and Pensacola in enemy hands, the British had no avenue of supply to their Indian allies. The new Whig government in Georgia, wisely coached by General Greene, attempted to take advantage of its opportunity. Governor Nathan Brownson sent out a conciliatory talk: "We asked you only to stand still and look on and not to be persuaded by Brown's lying talk to engage against us."[55]

The Raven led a contingent of loyal Cherokees to Savannah to see Thomas Brown. When Brown had not returned from Charlestown by September 1, the chief left a "talk" for "our father Col. Brown." The northern Indians had the king's warriors to support them, but the Cherokees were forced to fight alone. The Raven acknowledged that when he had seen Brown in Augusta the previous year, he was "under his displeasure" because of his bad conduct earlier. Since then he had done what his father desired him to do. He hoped to be restored to Brown's affection.[56]

The appearance of Indians in Savannah gave the desperate Governor Wright another straw to grasp. Wright sent a message across town to General Alured Clarke to request that he authorize Colonel Brown to employ Indians against the Georgia frontiers since no help was forthcoming from the military. Clarke was willing to do that much and so informed Brown. The fact that Brown was in a position to act militarily indicates that he must have been exchanged by October 1781. Brown alerted the Creeks to be ready, but a major obstacle was a lack of money. His personal credit was ruined, and he needed supplies for the Indians. He wrote to General Clinton that both Wright and Tonyn wanted him to call out the Indians and he had no means of supplying them. He warned that "an impolitic frugality or ill-timed parsimony" might prove injurious to the king's service.[57]

Despite the vicissitudes of war, Brown's credit was good at Whitehall. Lord George Germain instructed the British commander in Charlestown, Major General Alexander Leslie, to pay Brown's expenses. His lordship was not sure exactly what services the Indians were performing at the time, but "it is wise to keep them in good humour and to use the most likely means of preserving their friendship." Supplies were on the way for Colonel Brown. Brown's expense account reveals that Leslie advanced him the relatively generous sum of £10,740 compared to the £5,754 total he had received previously.[58]

In addition to seeking help from the Indians, Governor Wright raised three troops of horses at the expense of the province. The Augusta refugees formed one of them. They called themselves the Volunteers of Augusta and improvised a dashing song to be sung to the tune of "The Lilies of France."

> Come join, my brave lads, come all from afar,
> We're all volunteers, all ready for war;
> Our service is free, for honour we fight,
> Regardless of hardships by day or by night.
> Chorus: Then all draw your swords, and
>   constantly sing,
>   Success to our Troop, our country and
>   King.
> The Rebels they murder,—Revenge is the word,
> Let each lad return with blood on his sword;
> See Grierson's pale ghost point afresh to his wound,
> We'll conquer, my boys, or fall dead on the ground.

Then brandish your swords, and
constantly sing,
Success to our Troop, our Country and
King.
They've plunder'd our houses, attempted our lives,
Drove off from their homes our children and wives;
Such plundering miscreants or mercy can crave,
Such murdering villains, no mercy shall have.
Then chop with your swords, and
constantly sing,
Success to our Troop, our Country and
King.
Then think not of plunder, but ruin on the foe,
Pursue then, my boys, with blow after blow;
Till in their own blood we see them all welter,
Or behind the blue Mountains retreat for a shelter.
Then chop with your swords, and
constantly sing,
Success to our Troop, our Country
and King.
When back through Augusta, our horses shall prance,
We'll dismount at the Captain's, and there have
a dance;
We'll toss off full bumpers of favourite grog,
Be merry all night, in the morning drink knog.
Success to our Troop, our Country and
King.[59]

Captain James Ingram was the commanding officer of the troop. He once had fought against Thomas Brown at Burke County jail; now they rode together.

The second company was led by Captain William Martin Johnston and the third by Captain John Lightenstone. Johnston was the son of Dr. Lewis Johnston and the brother of the late Ranger Captain Andrew Johnston. He had served with the New York Volunteers in Lieutenant Colonel Archibald Campbell's campaign and had fought in the defense of Savannah. Captain Lightenstone was his father-in-law. Their story was told by Elizabeth Lichtenstein Johnston in her *Recollections of a Georgia Loyalist*. She was the wife of Captain Johnston and daughter of Captain Lightenstone (who had changed his name from Lichtenstein). Elizabeth, only seventeen in 1781, was delighted that her husband would be near her in Savannah. She discovered, however, that every third night his company had to patrol the countryside, so frequent were the alarms. Johnston's company was stationed on the Ogeechee to guard that approach to Savannah.[60]

In addition to the three mounted companies, the King's Rangers were reassembled. Thomas Brown welcomed another Wylly into his corps. Alexander C. Wylly had been one of his most reliable captains. His brother William returned from England in 1780 and practiced law for ten months, then formed a company attached to the royal artillery. In October and November 1781 he raised another company from among the refugees and joined the King's Rangers. His fortunes would be linked to those of Thomas Brown far into the future even to the remote island of St. Vincent.[61] The father of the Ranger brothers, Alexander, was the Speaker of the Royal Assembly and the prewar partner of Dr. Lewis Johnston. Thus it was appropriate that Captains Johnston and Wylly should be partners in the defense of Savannah.

On November 2 Johnston was surprised by Whig Colonel James Jackson's Georgia Legion with James McKay's mounted militia. According to Hugh M'Call, Johnston was in the act of handing his sword to Jackson when the notorious Tory-hater Captain Paddy Carr killed one of Johnston's men. Johnston then called upon his men to sell their lives dearly. They retreated into a house and beat off their attackers. M'Call blamed McKay and his band for quitting the fight and going off in search of plunder. During the afternoon of the same day Lieutenant Colonel George Campbell led his King's American Regiment to the relief of Johnston. With him were the King's Rangers under Captain William Wylly.[62]

At the same time a detachment of his Rangers was fighting Jackson in the Ogeechee swamps, Brown himself was chasing after plunderers on Hilton Head Island. At least General Nathanael Greene thought he was. Greene protested to the British commander in Charlestown that a party under Colonel Brown was burning houses on Hilton Head.[63] Greene was usually well informed (he knew the identity of the Loyalists in the Ogeechee skirmish) so he was probably right about Brown being on the Hilton Head raid.

Georgia's new general, John Twiggs, advanced his militia to Burke County in support of Jackson's Legion. Thomas Brown relied upon the time-tested strategy to make Twiggs retreat. His commissaries led war parties of Creeks to the backcountry frontiers, and Twiggs hastily returned to defend Augusta.[64]

Twiggs managed to chase the Creeks back across the Oconee. A party of his stragglers was intercepted by Tory irregulars under Benjamin Brantley. Executive Council member Myrick Davies was taken prisoner and later killed. Governor Nathan Brownson notified General Greene of the unfortunate incident: "In this Gentleman the State has suffered a great loss, he was truly a patriot . . . his Assassination, will I doubt not increase the horrors of war, already to[o] Horrible in this part of the Continent." Greene replied that he was going to send a Continental general officer to take command of the forces in Georgia. General Anthony Wayne would bring organization and discipline to the final effort to free Georgia from British control.[65]

On December 5, 1781, Brown wrote an end-of-the-year report to his superior, General Leslie. In spite of the loss of the Georgia and Carolina backcountry and of Cornwallis's army at Yorktown, and, he might have added, of the failure of the southern strategy, the Indians remained steady in their attachment to the British. The Cherokees had suffered greatly from the loss of their hunting grounds and from their continual skirmishes with the mountaineers. Brown was forced to supply clothing as well as ammunition to them by a roundabout six-hundred-mile-route. He intended to send two to three hundred packhorses to the Cherokees. He had to supply the Creeks with goods they had formerly purchased from Augusta or Pensacola.

The Upper Creeks were actively opposing the Spaniards in Pensacola and Mobile in the South and were harassing rebel settlements on the Ohio River in the North. Far from being beaten or discouraged, Brown was ready to go on the offensive. The Spanish garrison at Pensacola had been reduced by sickness to five hundred men. Creek Indians prevented their being supplied from the countryside, and they had to rely on jerked beef from Mexico. He thought the Spaniards might easily be dislodged. If the Spanish forces attacked East Florida, as Governor Tonyn thought they would, Brown had five hundred Indians ready to march to his assistance.[66]

There was a pleasant moment for Brown and his circle that December when Dr. Thomas Taylor married Bellamy Johnston, daughter of Dr. Andrew Johnston, formerly of Augusta. Lewis Johnston, member of the Royal Council and a former surgeon in the Royal

Navy, was Andrew Johnston's brother and would have been at the wedding. So would his son Captain William M. Johnston and his young wife Elizabeth. We can imagine that the Reverend James Seymour, William Goodgion, Sir Patrick Houstoun, Andrew McLean, and the other backcountry expatriates were there, too. Taylor wrote to John Wesley saying that he and his bride would like to stay in Georgia. He believed, however, that poor generalship had lost the war. The southern provinces could be held with half the force that lay idle in New York. In Georgia the loyal people in the countryside had no choice but to submit to the rebels: "Indeed, we may truely [sic] say, 'The Glory is departed.'"[67]

CHAPTER EIGHT

THE LAST CAMPAIGN,

1782

A reshuffle in the Indian Department was caused by the death of Alexander Cameron on December 29, 1781, in Savannah. Lieutenant Governor John Graham applied for the position even before Cameron breathed his last. Governor Wright endorsed Graham's candidacy, as did the members of his council. General Alexander Leslie in Charlestown agreed to make a temporary appointment pending approval from Whitehall. The principal reason for Graham's nomination apparently was that he had suffered great financial losses in the course of the war.[1]

Graham's reasons did not seem valid to Thomas Brown, who argued that the Indian country should be administered as a whole and offered to supervise the western part without additional pay. Nor did it satisfy Farquhar Bethune, Cameron's deputy, who had lived among the Choctaws. He did not mind telling Lord George Germain that management of the Indians should go to one who knew the Indians "rather than as an emolument to a private citizen." Bethune admitted that he would have welcomed an appointment, but he had "no friends to recommend me."[2]

There were new faces on the other side also as the year began. On January 9, General Greene congratulated Georgia's Governor John Martin upon his election and told him, "General Wayne marches tomorrow." Greene expressed displeasure at the Georgians' excessive plundering. Governor Martin's situation was desperate. The Creeks were active in the upper part of Wilkes County. The state could not equip Colonel Jackson's legion properly and reduced the number of dragoons from one hundred to forty. Farmers refused to accept certificates in payment for provisions for the troops. British control of the ports of Savannah and Charlestown caused a critical shortage of salt.[3]

Martin, like Brownson before him, tried valiantly to detach the Indians from the British cause. In one of his first official acts, Martin sent a talk to the Creeks explaining that the British made war on the Americans so as to enslave them "the same as the negroes." If successful, the king would next make slaves of the Indians. The good friends of the Americans, the Spanish, had taken Mobile and Pensacola and would soon capture St. Augustine. The reason the Spaniards had not offered to help the Indians was that the Creeks insisted on harboring "Brown's liars." Martin ordered out half the militia and sent them downriver to meet General Wayne. Martin cautioned Wayne that, though as good as any, "they will never stand the bayonet."[4]

Wayne established his camp at the Three Sisters Ferry on the Savannah and surveyed the situation confronting him. He estimated that 900 regular troops were in Savannah. He informed Greene that Colonel Brown with 50 dragoons and 250 infantry were at Gibbons Plantation foraging for provisions. "They shall not continue that practice with impunity," he promised.[5]

Thomas Brown had 474 men under his command according to his own statement in February 1782. There had evidently been some recent reorganization in General Alured Clarke's sector because we hear no more of Lieutenant Colonel George Campbell and the King's American Regiment. Thomas Brown bore the brunt of the foraging and fighting outside Savannah.[6]

At the urging of Greene, Wayne persuaded the vindictive Georgians to grant pardons to Loyalists. As a result, Governor John Martin issued two proclamations on February 20, 1782, from the temporary seat of government at Ebenezer. One was written in German and addressed specifically to the Hessians. Each man who would leave the British service was promised two hundred acres with a cow and two swine. The other announcement promised full pardon and protection to Loyalists who surrendered to Wayne before March 15.[7]

The policy produced immediate results. On February 22, Wayne informed Greene that two prominent Loyalists had given themselves up. Sir Patrick Houstoun, who had carried Brown's appeal for help to John Harris Cruger at Ninety-Six during the first siege of Augusta, was one. The other was Major David Douglass of the Volunteers of Augusta. In addition, a number of Hessians had already come in.[8]

The desertion of Douglass stung the pride of the Volunteers of Augusta. James Weatherford with seven other members of the troop made a daring raid on Augusta. They found Douglass at William Glascock's house. After taking them and another Continental officer prisoners, they did the gentlemanly thing and released them on parole. The *Royal Georgia Gazette* observed that this treatment was quite different from the "Georgia parole" meted out by the likes of Paddy Carr. The raiders meant to do the same to Governor John Martin, who lived only a mile from Glascock, but Martin was away from home. Weatherford's troops returned with horses, booty, and a new verse to add to their song.[9]

Wayne made a mild apology to Greene for letting Weatherford's party slip through. Except for such small reconnoitering expeditions, he explained, the British were confined to their lines in Savannah. "We are bullying the enemy at their lines with Jackson's little legion and a few Crackers and other species of tories who have lately surrendered themselves and joined our arms."[10]

Life was not pleasant for those, like Douglass, who changed their allegiance. Governor Martin informed Wayne that attempts had been made on Douglass's life. Martin had to offer Douglass his personal protection. He went on to say that a citizen had been deliberately murdered in the streets by "one of our back inhabitants" out of revenge. "If every man is to be a judge in his own cause," wrote Martin, "there will shortly be no safety in this country."[11]

General Greene suggested another expedient for recruiting troops in Georgia, one that might have changed the course of race relations if it had been adopted. He recommended the employment of black men in the militia. Governor Martin, a Connecticut native, was receptive to the idea. "The raising of a body of blacks I am sure would answer every purpose intended," he replied. But he had been in Georgia long enough to know that those who fought for land envisioned plantations and that in their minds plantations and slavery were inseparable. Martin was willing to present the subject to the assembly, but he correctly predicted, "I am afraid it will not go down with the people here."[12]

As the Georgia Whigs made desperate efforts to keep an army in the field, General Alured Clarke remained inactive with a much larger force. Dr. Thomas Taylor expressed the impatience which most Savannah Loyalists must have felt: "Here in Georgia Col. Clarke with 1,000 regular troops and 500 or 600 refugee militia besides inhabitants and Indians and seamen is blocked up by General

Wayne with about 300 men." Even good soldier Thomas Brown complained to Lord George Germain of the inactivity of the British commander in Savannah.[13] Because of Wayne's close siege, Brown found
it increasingly difficult to supply the Indians. The Cherokees lost all
their towns east of the mountains to a force of Carolinians and Georgians under Andrew Pickens. While Wayne invested Savannah in April, Elijah Clarke crossed the Oconee and routed a large war party of
Creeks.[14]

Brown's plan had been reduced to the final absurdity. Indians who
were supposed to cooperate with the king's troops in the liberation of
the Loyalists and the suppression of the rebels could not break
through the rebel lines to join the British in Savannah. A party of
three hundred Creeks with the veteran commissary Joseph Cornell
bound for Savannah blundered into Wayne's camp. Wayne gave
them a conciliatory speech and let them go. He was convinced that
the enemy had intended to move out in force when the Creeks
reached Savannah and that he had scotched that plan. The difference between Elijah Clarke's and Anthony Wayne's attitude toward
Creeks was striking. The Indians had not met anyone on the American side who preferred talk to fighting since the death of George
Galphin in 1781. When Georgia Governor Martin offered to smoke
the peace pipe, many of the chiefs were ready to join him.[15]

Wayne was correct in assuming that there was a plan to effect a
junction between the Indians and Thomas Brown. Brown expected a
contingent of Upper Creeks to join him under the leadership of his
staunchest ally, Emistisiguo. He posted Captain Donald Cameron
with a company of Rangers and some Choctaw Indians at a crossing
on the Altamaha. On April 12 Major Francis Moore of Wayne's army
attempted to drive Cameron back to Savannah. Both sides claimed
victory, but the Americans lost their leader. Wayne informed Greene
that Moore was "a brave, Judicious, worthy Officer." In a separate
engagement, Jackson's dragoons defeated a party of Loyalists and
killed Major Philip Dill.[16]

Wayne tightened his grip on Savannah in April, moving to within
six miles of the town. A British deserter told Wayne about a storehouse Brown used on the St. Marys. Wayne sent the notorious Captain Paddy Carr to destroy it. According to Major John Habersham,
Carr's men then deserted so they could plunder the Darien neighborhood. Habersham himself encountered a party of Indians on their
way to Savannah. Habersham pretended to be Brown and led the

unsuspecting visitors into a trap. He told Wayne how his dragoons tied an Indian to a tree in an effort to gain information, shot him, and cut him to pieces. As Habersham patrolled the southern approach to Savannah, Colonel James Jackson intercepted a foraging party of Choctaws who attempted to bring cattle to Savannah from Carolina. Nathanael Greene approved of Wayne's siege tactics but warned against being too bold. The enemy was not yet defeated.[17]

Thomas Brown, still expecting Emistisiguo's band, dispatched Captain James Ingram and the Volunteers of Augusta to the Ogeechee with a hundred militia. Ingram encountered Jackson's Legion at the Ogeechee Ferry on May 19. Ingram forced Jackson to take up a defensive position and joined Brown, who was on his way to the Ogeechee with 80 Rangers and 260 infantry. Brown knew that Wayne was near and determined to take possession of a strategic causeway leading back to Savannah across a swamp. Wayne had the same idea, and the advance parties of each force met on the causeway.

Brown's Rangers were driven back, but his infantry stood firm and repulsed the Americans. The next morning, as Wayne waited to resume the engagement, Brown returned to Savannah by the White Bluff Road. As battles go, the encounter between Brown and Wayne was almost insignificant. Much was made of it, however. General Greene congratulated Wayne: "You have disgraced one of the best officers the enemy have, and I am in hopes this stroke will keep up the spirit of desertion among them." Greene's comment was a nice compliment to Brown.[18]

The affair was memorialized in doggerel in a Philadelphia newspaper:

> The old Tory rout
> Had spread round about
> That our brave Wayne with five hundred
> Were taken or slain
> Upon Georgia's plain.
> But Tories, you've cursedly blundered
> The case was, one Brown
> Had marched out of town
> Well armed and prepared for a tramp;
> But Wayne was aware
> Prepared for the snare

And drove Brown into a swamp
Some ran and some fell
As Wayne's bayonets tell
Our hero charging with glory
Mars victory gave
To Americans brave
Charles Thompson proclaims it—ye Tory.[19]

Brown, however, thought he had won a complete victory. Many years later he recalled how he made Jackson "scamper."[20]

Wayne intercepted a letter from General Alured Clarke to Brown and learned that Lord North had resigned on March 30. Realizing that peace was at hand, Wayne hoped to take Savannah first. "Do let us dig the caitiffs out," he urged Greene, "it will give an éclat to our arms to effect a business in which the armament of our great and good ally failed." Wayne would do what d'Estaing could not.[21]

It was not over yet, and Wayne was almost undone by overconfidence. He did not expect trouble from the rear. On the night of June 23, Emistisiguo surprised him and drove the Americans out of their camp. Wayne's horse was shot from under him as he rallied his men. Shouting "death or victory," Wayne formed his infantry and led a bayonet charge in which Emistisiguo was killed and his warriors routed. Only twelve prisoners were taken, and they were shot. The rest of the Creeks made their way to Savannah.[22]

Emistisiguo was a faithful friend of Thomas Brown as he had been of John Stuart. He responded to every call at the final cost of his life. Brown paid tribute to his ally in a letter to the new British commander in America, Sir Guy Carleton. The chief had led his warriors on a march of five hundred miles through enemy country without being discovered. The "brave, gallant Emistisiguo" surprised and routed the rebels, and most of his followers completed their mission.[23] Georgia had already been lost when the chief gave his life in a pathetic punctuation mark, putting an end to the plan. The great lords of war, Germain, Clinton, and Cornwallis, would bear the brunt of the recriminations for the failure of the southern strategy. No one thought of accusing the plan's architect, Thomas Brown. Yet, in the irony of history, Thomas Brown had the most difficult task of any of the principals. He had to explain to the Indians why they were being abandoned by their Father across the waters.

Although Governor James Wright professed to be distressed at the order to evacuate Savannah, he should not have been surprised. One of Guy Carleton's first decisions as commander in chief was to evacuate Savannah immediately and Charlestown as soon as possible. On May 23, 1782, Carleton wrote to the governors of East Florida and Georgia announcing his appointment. On the same day he notified General Leslie that a fleet of transports was on the way to evacuate Loyalists from Savannah and St. Augustine. On June 16 the Royal Georgia Assembly addressed a petition to General Leslie protesting against the abandonment of Georgia and East Florida and suggesting that the garrison of East Florida be sent to Savannah. Sir James Wright, John Graham, and Samuel Farley signed the petition. As if they knew that the request would be denied, they sent a second petition the same day, saying that if Georgia had to be evacuated, at least Florida should be retained as a haven for southern refugees. Georgians disliked the idea of migrating to cold Nova Scotia. Further, they had every intention of taking their slaves with them.[24]

Leslie had orders to send the troops to New York, but he decided that the King's Rangers were an exception. He would retain the Rangers in Charlestown in case Carleton decided to allow the refugees to go to Florida. In that event, he recommended that the Rangers go there.[25]

On July 1 a group of Savannah merchants came out to talk to Wayne under a flag of truce to learn what treatment they might expect when the British troops were gone. Wayne wisely consulted with Governor Martin, who was at Ebenezer for a special session of the Georgia Assembly. Prompted by Wayne, the Georgia Assembly resolved to grant Loyalists up to twelve months to terminate their business. Wayne promised that all who chose to stay would be protected. Under those conditions many Loyalists who had planned to leave changed their minds. Wayne advertised the opportunity to join the Georgia Continental Battalion as a means of regaining citizenship, and some took advantage of it. Major John Habersham was Wayne's liaison in formalizing the arrangements, and, as a member of the prewar establishment, he enjoyed a good relationship with the loyal Savannahians.[26]

The formal surrender of Savannah took place on July 11, 1782. Colonel James Jackson was given the honor of receiving General Alured Clarke's submission. The regular troops embarked for Charlestown and New York. The civilian refugees, estimated at about twenty-five hundred whites and four thousand blacks, waited for transportation at Tybee and Cockspur islands. The presence of Thomas Brown's Rangers nearby caused the victorious Georgians to feel less secure in their occupation of Savannah.[27]

General Greene was anxious for Wayne to join him outside Charlestown because of the augmentation of British troops there. Wayne shared some of the apprehension of Governor Martin and the assembly, which met in Savannah on July 13. He pointed out that Brown was only twelve miles away and could capture the entire Georgia government if Wayne left then. He correctly predicted that Brown's Rangers, together with the refugees and the Indians, were bound for St. Augustine and that they planned to settle permanently there.[28]

The minutes of the sitting Georgia Assembly betray a fear of Brown's corps: "Whereas the Situation of this barrier State absolutely requires a Military force for its defence, and whereas Lieut. Col. Brown with above 500 men composed of British, Refugees and Indians, etc. remains within a days March of the Town of Savannah," Wayne's troops must be allowed to remain in Georgia. The resolution depicted Brown as waiting for the removal of the American troops in order to "Plunder, burn and destroy." Major John Habersham added his plea that the Continentals be allowed to remain in Georgia.[29]

This chorus of concern about what Thomas Brown might do added to Nathanael Greene's problems. "I am at a loss to interpret Browne's intentions," he admitted to Habersham. "Whether he had orders to hover upon your coast to detain General Wayne there until General Leslie can give us a blow here, or whether for plundering—or mean revenge—I cannot tell." In any case, Greene needed the Continentals because if Greene were defeated in Carolina, the effect would be far greater than the depredations of Brown's corps in Georgia.[30]

The anxiety generated in the American camp by Thomas Brown was a better indication of his reputation than of his intentions. By July 20, his Indian allies had embarked for St. Augustine. By August 9, the evacuation was sufficiently far enough along that Wayne felt safe in leaving Savannah. A grateful assembly granted him an estate and gave another to General Greene.[31] The fortunes of war made both men Georgia planters while depriving Thomas Brown and his friends of that possibility.

Even in the final days of his troubled sojourn in Georgia, Brown resorted to his bankrupt strategy. He directed Colonel Thomas Waters, now his deputy in the Indian Department, to mount still another Indian offensive. In Waters's words, he was "to go up to the Cherokee and Creek Indians and attack the rebel settlements." Waters had a hard time persuading the Indians to fight at a time the British troops were giving up Georgia. He managed to collect enough Cherokees to make one sweep through the Ceded Lands. The raid had the intended effect of distracting the Georgians from the enemy on the coast. Even while the assembly asked for Continental troops to protect Savannah from Brown's Rangers on Tybee, that body could not afford to take Elijah Clarke's militia out of the backcountry. Symbolic of the reversal of roles wrought by the Revolution in the backcountry was the fact that Elijah Clarke now occupied Thomas Waters's plantation house. Unfortunately for the Cherokees, Waters's expedition brought another retaliation down upon that harassed nation. Andrew Pickens burned more Cherokee towns, and Elijah Clarke chased Waters down to Florida. He was accompanied by a thousand homeless Cherokees.[32]

Although the war was lost by the British in August 1782, the peace negotiations dragged on for another year. The southeastern Indians were immediately concerned about restoring their supply system. Wayne's and Martin's talks created division and confusion, especially among the Creeks. Alexander McGillivray, even though he was Brown's deputy, later stated that he had listened to the Americans' talks and ceased all hostilities in the summer of 1782. The evacuation of the British was a good reason for the Indians to defect. They did not abandon the British partly because of Brown's adroit management. While the transports were ferrying the refugees to Florida, Brown's messengers spread the word among the Creeks that St. Augustine was the new base of supplies. Daniel McMurphy, successor to George Galphin as Georgia's agent to the Creeks, reported that "all the traders and enemy Indians is either gone or will go to St. Augustine."[33]

Thomas Brown's first letter to the Earl of Shelburne was from Fort Picolata on the St. Johns River, dated September 25, 1782. By then he had removed his Rangers and his Indian friends to St. Augustine and marched to the St. Johns River. Brown's return to Florida must have resembled a homecoming. His patron, Governor Tonyn, was there to welcome him. When Brown offered to help the Georgia refugees settle along the St. Johns River, the governor gladly accepted. Thomas Brown knew the St. Johns frontier thoroughly; he had guarded it in 1777 and 1778. Before the arrival of the first refugees there were about a thousand white settlers and three thousand blacks in East Florida. The number of whites more than doubled. Governor Tonyn estimated that fifteen hundred white refugees and a thousand blacks came from Georgia. He was disappointed at the appearance and social standing of the Georgians. Although there were a few "respectable families," most of them were "intolerably indolent" country people. Evidently many of the "better sort" took advantage of the period of grace to settle their affairs in Georgia.[34]

Brown informed Lord Shelburne that he had followed General Leslie's orders to cancel all Indian offensive actions. He explained to Emistisiguo's Upper Creeks who had come to Florida with him that the king had decided to remove his troops to Florida so as to carry on the war more effectively. He gave them presents and sent them home satisfied. Lieutenant Governor Graham dismissed his contingent of Choctaws. Graham probably did not deserve to be Indian superintendent because he lacked experience, and immediately after making the trip to Florida he returned to Charlestown and requested and received a leave of absence. He had served king and country well in many political duties, however, and he had advanced his own money to pay for transportation of the refugees to Florida. He left an able man to carry on the affairs of the western district in Lieutenant Colonel John Douglass, the former Ranger and close friend of Thomas Brown.[35]

Brown's report on his Rangers for October 1782 reveals that some of them were still waiting for embarkation on St. Johns Island outside Charlestown. Captains William Wylly and Donald Cameron and Lieutenants Daniel Ellis, James Smith, John Anderson, and Daniel Egan were there. Major James Wright, Jr., and Captains Samuel Roworth, James Smith, John Marshall, and John Bond Randall were in Florida with Brown as were Lieutenants James Brown, William Jones, Archibald Cameron, and Jacob Obman.[36]

The first transport of Carolinians reached St. Augustine in October. Lieutenant Colonel Archibald McArthur came with them. The same ships took off Lieutenant Colonel Beamsley Glazier's Royal Americans. Brown lost a friend with Glazier's departure (Glazier must have told him how he had threatened to hang six prisoners if Brown were harmed after the surrender of Augusta), but Brown gained a new friend in McArthur, who was soon promoted to the rank of brigadier general.

The transports had difficulty in crossing the shallow sandbars at the entrance of St. Augustine harbor, "this horrid bar," McArthur called it, and most of the provisions were unloaded at the St. Johns. McArthur had to allocate the provisions equitably among the Georgia and Carolina refugees. He named Josiah Tattnall and John Douglass to administer to the Georgians and Colonels Elias Ball and James Cassells for the Carolinians. McArthur was pleased that Thomas Brown was willing to settle the Carolina refugees as he had those from Georgia.[37] Like most newcomers to Florida, McArthur liked the climate. He thought it was a great place "for a company or two of old fogies, they might smoke their pipes and tell their lies in great tranquility without fear of flux or ague." There was always the problem of rank when military men gathered together, and McArthur asked for help in determining seniority between Thomas Brown and Lieutenant Colonel John Hamilton of the North Carolina provincial regiment. Hamilton agreed to defer to Brown until official word was received. Governor Tonyn, who always coveted military authority, vainly offered to act as the general as well as the governor. Tonyn was as pleased with the character of the Carolinians as he had been disappointed with the Georgians. He provided accommodations for the merchants in town and for the planters in the country. Their coming was the dawn of "a happy era to this province." The ill winds of war had blown some good to Florida.[38]

When the second transport of Carolinians arrived in December it was almost too much of a good thing. McArthur's best estimate of the total number of refugees in Florida was 2,428 whites and 3,609 blacks. McArthur worried that there would not be enough provisions to go around. If additional supplies did not arrive in a timely fashion, a famine would ensue.[39]

If the refugees were the only dependents upon the British stores, the crisis would not have reached the proportions it did. The influx of Indian visitors, however, surpassed the number of whites. They came in answer to Thomas Brown's invitation. Brown estimated that three thousand Creeks visited Florida to pay their respects and sample Brown's wares between September and the end of the year. In December delegations from the northern tribes descended on St. Augustine. It was fortunate that Governor Tonyn was an old hand at the business of hosting Indians or he would not have been able to cope with the situation. As it was, he could scarcely enumerate, much less entertain, the tribes represented; in addition to Creeks, Cherokees, and Choctaws, there were "Mohawks, Senecas, Delawares, Shawnees, Manjoes, Tuscaroras, Yatanous," and other tribes from Fort Detroit.[40]

Thomas Brown, Tonyn, and McArthur received their visitors with the customary ritual. The chiefs expressed concern that the Great King might abandon them. Thomas Brown replied that Savannah and Charlestown had been evacuated so the war could be carried on elsewhere. The Indians should desist from fighting and go hunting but always be prepared to guard their lands against the rebels. Brown urged the tribes to form a confederacy. His listeners were well disposed toward the idea. If they had carried out the plan, the St. Augustine congress of 1782 would have merited a page in history instead of a footnote. Thomas Brown promised that traders would resume their business with St. Augustine as a base. He advised the Cherokees to move from their North Carolina villages to the Coosa, Chattahoochee, and Tennessee rivers, where they would be closer to the Upper Creeks. In the old days the Cherokees and Creeks would have maintained their distance from each other, but their common enemy united them. McArthur performed his part in the entertainment of the visitors. He reported that he had "paid them all military honors, shewed them the fort magazines and some explosions with shott and shells, with which they seemed highly pleased."[41]

Governor Tonyn's satisfaction was tempered with anxiety. "We feel severely the weight of their provisions," he reported, "should they in such trains repeat their visits, we shall be altogether without the means of supplying them." As the year ended, he wondered whether Florida could afford the unprecedented popularity it was experiencing.[42]

CHAPTER NINE

FLORIDA INTERLUDE,

1783–1785

 The year 1783 opened with promise of a bright future for East Florida, if not for the rest of British America. St. Augustine was beginning to look like a provincial capital with its three hundred houses huddled inside its old walls and its polyglot population. The town boasted a resident minister in the person of the exiled James Seymour. Seymour was invited to return to Augusta, where his loyalty to the king would be forgiven, but he declined in favor of the St. Augustine ministry. Georgian David Zubly set up a press in his house and in 1783 published John Tobler's *Almanack*, the first book produced in Florida. John Wells, Jr., of Charlestown gave the town a newspaper, the *East Florida Gazette*, from February 1783 to March 1784. The little settlements on the St. Marys and St. Johns rivers were frontier boom towns.[1]

Thomas Brown and his friends could look forward to a comfortable postwar future as Florida planters and gentlemen. Brown, aided by his £500 annual salary as superintendent, was especially resilient and enterprising. He leased a large, balconied residence on Charlotte Street appropriate to his position as a member of the Governor's Council. His patron, the governor, was generous in rewarding Brown. Many years later, Brown described ten tracts of land on the east side of the St. Johns River totaling one hundred thousand acres given to him "by that brave old warrior" Patrick Tonyn.[2]

Brown established the validity of his rank by reciting his military service to Sir Guy Carleton. He reminded Carleton that his commission dated from June 1, 1776. Since then he had raised twelve hundred men and estimated that nearly five hundred had been killed in service. The numbers, like most of those quoted by Brown, were generalizations meant to make a point. He asked that the commissions originally granted by Governor Tonyn to him and his men be confirmed by Carleton.[3]

Because the Indians had not made their peace with the Americans, Thomas Brown was still involved in their struggle. In February Brown wrote to Secretary of State Thomas Townshend that the Georgians demanded a cession of land between the Ogeechee and Oconee. They threatened to take it by force if necessary. The attitude of the Georgians was understandable. The same tract was sought by backcountrymen in 1773 when Governor Wright negotiated for the Ceded Lands. The backcountry faction was disappointed by the governor's failure to demand the territory as the price of peace in 1774. Since then the settlers had fought for the land and now they demanded it as the spoils of victory. Brown fully intended to frustrate the intentions of the Georgians. He asked for instructions as to how to act if the Creeks requested aid in repulsing the aggressors. Brown was still anxious to take the initiative against Pensacola. He estimated that six frigates could block the harbor and three hundred men could take the post. New Orleans was also ready for the taking.[4] Something might yet be accomplished.

The new governor of Georgia, Lyman Hall, had the same problem George Galphin had faced in his efforts to reach agreements with the Indians. Too many of his countrymen would rather fight than talk with them. When some of the Galphin faction among the Tallasees and Cussitas decided to test the sincerity of the talks of General Wayne and Governor Martin, they went to visit Augusta. They were disappointed at the poverty of the Georgians, they received only a few shirts and some rum as presents, and to make matters worse, their horses were stolen. Some who tried to protect their horses were beaten. No wonder that the Creeks decided to clasp the hand of Thomas Brown more firmly than ever.[5]

Brown's deputy, William McIntosh, wrote to say that a general meeting of the tribe had been held in Tuckabatchee town. The Creeks promised never to bury the hatchet or make peace with the rebels, French or Spaniards. They were determined to reject the Georgians' demand for the Oconee lands. They asked Brown for ammunition to prevent the whites from settling on those lands. Twenty horseloads for the Lower Creeks and thirty for the Upper Creeks would satisfy.[6]

Governor Hall's Georgia government proceeded with plans for an

Indian conference in Augusta. Hall invited General Greene to attend the important event, to be held within two or three miles of Augusta "at a place called the Spring," probably Indian Springs on the hill above Augusta. Greene named Anthony Wayne as his representative. The nearly bankrupt administration, faced with the problem of supplying presents to the Indians, decided to sell rice to the British in East Florida. The house and lot belonging to James Ingram were also sold to raise funds. In addition, all confiscated horses and slaves in Richmond County were sold to buy provisions for the expected visitors.[7]

Although preparations for the conference were begun in March, it was not until May 31 that talks in Augusta began. The mood of the Georgians was jubilant because the news of the preliminary peace agreement had reached them the week before. Augustans celebrated with a ball, illuminations, bonfires, rockets, "and every other demonstration of joy suitable to the occasion."[8]

A galaxy of war heroes represented the state as the talks began. Governor Hall, John Twiggs, Elijah Clarke, William Few, Edward Telfair, and Samuel Elbert met with eighteen Cherokee chiefs and a few Lower Creeks. The Indians were told that the Oconee would be the new boundary. The land in question was generally regarded as Creek land, so the Cherokees readily signed the treaty. The Creeks refused. Again they suffered the indignity of having their horses stolen. In spite of the repeated insults, fourteen Creeks were coaxed back to Augusta in November, and they agreed to the cession in a separate treaty. Tallasse King and the Fat King were the only leaders of standing to sign.[9] The state of Georgia needed the land to pay its war debts, and consistently during the next seven years Georgians maintained that the November 1, 1783, treaty was legal. During those years the Creek Nation, under the leadership of Alexander McGillivray, denied them the prize. In doing so, McGillivray sought protection from the hitherto despised Spanish. The man more than any other whom the Georgians blamed for the Creek-Spanish alliance was Thomas Brown. A revolutionary turn of events caused Thomas Brown, who as late as February 1783 was urging an attack on Pensacola, to advise the Creeks to make an alliance with Spain. The revolution was a diplomatic one. On January 20, 1783, Lord Shelburne's government signed the preliminary peace agreement with representatives of France and Spain. By the terms of the fifth article, East Florida was ceded to Spain. British citizens were allowed eighteen months to remove themselves, bag and baggage, from the province.[10]

This bad news shocked the Loyalists in Florida when they read Governor Tonyn's proclamation on April 21, 1783. It cast a pall over a brilliant military exploit carried out under the leadership of Colonel Andrew Deveaux, formerly of Beaufort, South Carolina. Deveaux determined to regain the Bahama Islands, which Spain had taken the year before. He recruited 220 Loyalists, white and black, and, with the approval of General McArthur, set out from St. Augustine. Before dawn he landed his small force on the eastern end of the island of New Providence. He fooled the Spanish garrison at Fort Montagu by making repeated trips back and forth to his vessels. His men would lie low on the way back to the transports, then pop up for the landing. Some of his volunteers were dressed like Indians, and they let out a few war whoops. The baffled Spaniards abandoned Fort Montagu. The governor, Don Antonio Caraco, sent out a flag from Nassau saying that peace between their countries had been concluded. Deveaux thought it was a trick and demanded and received the Spaniard's surrender.[11]

Thomas Brown played a part in this last military adventure of the war. One of Deveaux's two transports, the *Whitby Warrior*, was partly owned by Brown. Presumably, Brown was responsible for the name, and perhaps it betrayed a touch of nostalgia for the little seaport town he had left nearly a decade before. As it turned out, Don Antonio was right. The peace agreement had been signed and the Bahamas had been restored to England. The result was that the heroes of the belated conquest were not compensated for the cost of the expedition. The British residents of Nassau regarded Deveaux as their deliverer, however, and signed a petition to the king expressing the hope that he would be generously rewarded, even if he was a few weeks late.[12]

The incident was important in another respect. It reminded the Florida Loyalists that there was an alternative to migrating to Nova Scotia or Jamaica. First, they had to determine whether the Bahamas were suited to a plantation economy.

The news of the cession of Florida to Spain meant more to Thomas Brown than the need for him to find a new home. Brown was instructed to recall all of his deputies and commissioners from the Indian country. His Majesty's government was concerned that the Indians would turn on the British when they learned that they were going to be abandoned. To say that the instructions placed Brown in an awkward position is to understate the case. Three months before, Brown had sent traders among the Indians with the pledge that the British would never leave and that St. Augustine would be their base of supplies.[13] Furthermore, Brown's deputies had counseled war against the Spaniards for years. Now they were supposed to explain how it was that their enemies would be given St. Augustine.

The Florida Loyalists shared the opinion of the ministry in London. They, too, worried that the Indians would be angry, and a certain edge was added to their concern because they were convenient objects of the wrath of their former allies. The Commons House of Assembly addressed a formal request to Thomas Brown to exert his influence to keep the Indians friendly and the Floridians safe.[14]

Thomas Brown was still the good soldier. He did not delay in sending orders to white men to come at once to St. Augustine. But he gave vent to his frustration in a letter to Carleton: "The situation of our poor unfortunate allies most terribly affects me, they were ever faithful to me. . . . Your Excellency I hope will pardon this liberty of saying I now feel for my own honor."[15] Brown's sentiments, however sincerely felt, did not interfere with his grasp of reality. He invited the head men of the Creeks to Florida in the knowledge that the Indians would not harm white people in the interior while their chiefs were talking to Brown.

Just before the Creeks arrived and on the eve of Brown's most difficult talk, Sir Guy Carleton undermined Brown's authority by sending a directive that the local military commander, McArthur, should dispense all presents to the Indians. Brown wrote to Carleton that he had always distributed presents to the satisfaction of all the generals he had served under. The new method would "degrade him to the character of a storekeeper." The local general, McArthur, decided to disobey his superior officer in the matter of Indian diplomacy. "I must venture to deviate a little from the mode of delivering presents to the Indians," he wrote, "particularly at this critical juncture when the utmost attention is necessary in our conduct towards them." McArthur was not concerned that Brown would misuse the funds; his "character for integrity is so well established there is not the least danger of misapplication."[16] Carleton was surprised that there was a problem. He assured Brown that the orders were based on the king's instructions with regard to the Indians in Canada and were not meant to impute blame to Brown.[17]

Because the inhabitants of St. Augustine were nervous about hosting large numbers of Indians, Brown entertained them at Fort Picolata on the St. Johns. Far from displaying hostility, the Creeks asked to accompany their friends the English when they left Florida. General McArthur could scarcely believe this turn of events; he tried to explain it to Carleton: "However chimerical it may appear to us, they have very seriously proposed to abandon their country and accompany us."[18] Carleton received this startling information with equanimity. If the Indians insisted on going to the Bahamas, he said, transportation would be provided, but he could not imagine that they would be happy in that strange habitat, and every possible argument should be used to dissuade them.[19]

Thomas Brown's other concern during that summer of 1783 was the future of his own men, the deputies and commissioners recalled from the Indian country and the officers and men of his Rangers. The North and South Carolina regiments were on the verge of mutiny in May when they heard that they were to be shipped off to parts unknown without their consent. General McArthur made an example of the ringleaders, and that quieted the troops for a while. McArthur informed Carleton that the men were "extremely anxious" to know more about their destinies. Thomas Brown sent his own representative in the person of Captain William Wylly to London to make sure the Rangers were not forgotten.[20]

Brown recommended that the officers of the Indian Department be granted the same opportunities as the other military men. They had sacrificed property and distinguished themselves in the service. Because they had been involved in Indian warfare, they could expect no pardon or restitution from the Americans. Specifically mentioned by Brown were Captain Thomas Waters (who was also a colonel of militia), Commissary and Captain Alexander McGillivray, Commissary and Lieutenant John McDonald, and Commissary and Lieutenant Walter Scott.[21]

During July and August the Loyalists waited anxiously for the return of a party sent out by McArthur to inspect the Bahamas. General Carleton admitted that he did not know much about the Bahamas, so he put McArthur in charge of the islands. He recommended to the ministry that Loyalists who lost their property in America be granted compensatory estates in the Bahamas.[22]

Carleton agreed to treat Brown's officers of the Indian Department the same as military officers. As a special consideration, their salaries would be paid up to December 24, 1783, but they should leave when the troops were withdrawn in October 1783. Like other officers they were entitled to land in Nova Scotia or any other part of His Majesty's dominions. Carleton suggested that after the Rangers left Brown should remain behind to deal with the Indians.[23]

Carleton told McArthur to pay the troops through October 24. Any who preferred to be discharged at St. Augustine might stay there. Some Loyalists from New York had recently sailed for Abaco and Cat islands in the Bahamas; perhaps the Florida troops would want to go there. Others receiving the special consideration of pay through December 24 were former Ranger Samuel Roworth, now major of brigade, Colonel Andrew Deveaux, the hero of the mistimed conquest, and McArthur himself. Richard Pearis was granted a subsidy of a hundred pounds because of his services and because he was in great distress.[24]

As the deadline for their departure neared, the Florida Loyalists grew anxious. The word from the gentlemen who went to inspect the Bahamas was not good. Lieutenant John Wilson confirmed that gloomy report. The soil was too rocky and there were no tracts large enough to be cultivated as plantations. The islands would not support the plantation economy of Carolina or Georgia. Some men of the North Carolina regiment deserted rather than go to cold Nova Scotia or the rocky Bahamas. They were caught, and their ringleader was shot. Half of the North Carolina regiment decided to go to Nova Scotia, about forty wanted transportation to England, and only a few would go to the Bahamas. Two-thirds of the South Carolinians wanted to remain in Florida and presumably take their chances on being allowed to return to their state; the rest would go to Nova Scotia or the Bahamas. Most of the King's Rangers decided to go together to Abaco in the Bahamas.[25]

The civilians who watched the troops prepare to leave were increasingly uneasy. Governor Tonyn forwarded a memorial to Carleton signed by "the principal inhabitants" protesting the removal of troops before the civilians were provided for. One good reason for their anxiety was that large numbers of Creek Indians were expected to come visiting after they finished celebrating their annual green corn dance or "busk." The lieutenant governor, the council, and the Commons House of Assembly asked that some of the troops remain to prevent "murder and rapine" and that ships and supplies be provided to take them somewhere other than Nova Scotia or the Bahamas, neither of which was suited to Negro slavery. Among the council signers were Thomas Brown and Dr. Lewis Johnston.[26]

Thomas Brown informed Frederick Lord North, Thomas Townshend's successor as secretary of state, about the transition of Florida to Spain. Brown could not resist a personal note in his first letter: "I had the honor to be considered a son of your lordship and an emissary of administration sent to poison the minds of the virtuous citizens of America." He went on to say that "this honorable though to me unfortunate distinction" caused him to be "burnt, stabbed, scalped and otherwise wounded in ten different places." Brown sent his lordship a superb map of southeastern North America drawn for him by Joseph Purcell. The map, three years in the making, was, he said, "the only accurate one extant."[27]

On October 24, 1783, Brown sent Lord North a letter from Alexander McGillivray, recently chosen "King and Head Warrior." McGillivray warned that he could not "keep his people in the dark much longer." They had fought for nine years only to find their country betrayed to their enemies. Now the rebels were demanding land all the way to the Flint River. In his reply to McGillivray Thomas Brown gave directions that were historic in their implications. "I advised him," Brown wrote to North, "to enter into a negotiation with the Spanish Governor of Pensacola . . . for obtaining a supply of such arms and ammunition as would enable them to defend their territories." This important message was carried to McGillivray by one of Brown's most faithful friends, Martin Weatherford.[28] The turn of events that led to the revolutionary advice was simply that the British forces were about to deliver Florida to their former enemies. Thomas Brown and Alexander McGillivray were realists. The greatest threat to the Creek lands was the ever aggressive Georgians. The only available ally was Spain.

The Creek and Cherokee chiefs were reluctant to believe that their allies were actually abandoning them. They came to hear the bad word from their father, Thomas Brown. There was reproach as well as pathos in the talk delivered by the Raven on behalf of the Cherokees: "We never turned our backs on the Enemy but remembered your talks. We subsisted our Women and Children on acorns . . . and were determined to hold the English fast by the arm and like Men stand or fall with our friends . . . we have heard from the Virginians that the English have given up our lands and yours to be divided amongst their Enemies. The Peacemakers and our Enemies have talked away our land at a Rum drinking."[29]

The Upper Creeks delivered their message on December 30, 1783. In Brown's words, they were "disturbed beyond description" at the idea of being abandoned by the English. "I must confess, My Lord," he wrote to North, "I feel most sincerely for our poor, brave, faithful allies."[30] Brown attempted to placate them with presents. Six hundred Indians were given cloth, shirts, knives, saddles, and ammunition. He dissuaded them from their intention of going to the Bahamas. According to one of the Creeks, Brown told them that the great king of Spain was already in possession of this land and the English were leaving. Brown advised them to take the Spaniards by the hand, that they would be brothers and friends even as the English were.[31] Many years later Tallasse King, who had signed the November 1 Treaty of Augusta, recalled that he had been at the Florida meeting with Thomas Brown. Brown promised that the Americans would never get possession of the homeland of the Creeks.[32]

Only after the departure of the Indians did Brown's Rangers and the officers of the Indian Department take their leave for Abaco. On February 7, 1784, Governor Tonyn published a proclamation assuring the civilian population that shipping would be provided for them, that the Bahamas were open to occupation, and that evacuation had to be completed by March 19, 1785.[33]

Although it did not make much sense to withdraw one set of troops and send down another, that is what happened in Florida. Three companies of the Thirty-seventh Regiment arrived in St. Augustine from New York in November 1783. They and the detachment of royal artillery would stay until the arrival of the Spanish governor. Brown made a friend in Major George Beckwith of the Thirty-seventh. Because roving "banditti" were increasingly troublesome, Governor Tonyn raised two troops of provincial horse, much as he had done at the beginning of the war. These rangers rode under the command of Captain William Young.[34]

On May 6, 1784, Tonyn ordered the people to apply to Lieutenant Colonel William Brown at St. Augustine or Lieutenant Robert Leaver at St. Marys for directions regarding embarkation. Tonyn estimated that four thousand Loyalists had returned to the United States to take their chances there. About ten thousand claimed transportation to British ports. Many had departed by June 27, when the new Spanish governor arrived, but many still remained. Governor Vizente Manuel de Zespedes was welcomed by Patrick Tonyn and the four highest-ranking officials in Florida, Chief Justice John Hume, Brigadier General Archibald McArthur, Superintendent Thomas Brown, and Lieutenant Governor John Moultrie.

From the beginning there was a tension between the English and Spanish governors caused by the uncertainty about who was in charge. Zespedes was willing to concede that he had not formally arrived until all his baggage was on shore and the British stores were removed from the ancient Castillo de San Marcos. On July 12 the formal ceremony of transfer of authority took place. On July 14 Zespedes issued a proclamation reminding those who intended to depart that the treaty accorded them eighteen months, or until March 19, 1785, to put their affairs in order. Families should register with the governor's secretary, Carlos Howard; disputes would be settled by arbitration and enforced by the Spanish government. By a second proclamation, slaves had to be registered; unattached blacks would register themselves. Failure to do so would result in the individual becoming property of the government. These apparently straightforward announcements generated friction between Tonyn and Zespedes and were not enforced. The roving gangs of banditti, notably Daniel McGirth's band, took advantage of the confusion of authority to pillage the borderlands.[35]

The departing British officials honored the new administration with a banquet on July 14, 1784. Whatever personal problems there may have been between Tonyn and Zespedes, Thomas Brown and the new governor got along famously. Zespedes would later write in effusive Spanish that when he first met Brown, "I looked upon you with a liking which has gone on increasing with friendly intercourse, until it has grown into a high and lasting esteem."[36]

Another Spanish official who became a friend of Brown was Father Michael O'Reilly, who arrived in Florida with Zespedes's party. One of Brown's Indian friends became an accepted member of their social circle. Charles Fox Taylor was the son of a Captain Taylor, the natural son of Lord Holland, and the head queen of the Cherokees. The mixed-blood Taylor gave up his claim to a chiefdom in the Cherokee Nation to accompany Thomas Brown into exile.[37]

It is impossible to determine whether any other Indians migrated with Brown to the Bahamas. Charles Weatherford, the half-breed son of Martin Weatherford, later stated that the daughter of Creek Chief Perryman was Brown's concubine both in Florida and in the Bahamas. Perryman himself was the son of an Augusta trader, Theodore Perryman, and a Creek wife. Brown may have lived with an Indian woman, but Charles Weatherford was not a reliable witness—Benjamin Hawkins called him a "very bad man"—and moreover was hostile to Brown and Alexander McGillivray.[38]

Thomas Brown's most important service to Governor Zespedes was to induce a delegation of visiting Creeks to take Zespedes by the hand. Brown later told William Pitt that he "established a friendly intercourse between the Indians and Spaniards to prevent our unfortunate red allies being totally dependent on their implacable enemies the Americans." As a result, Zespedes made Alexander McGillivray, Brown's deputy, a colonel in the Spanish service. Brown was also instrumental in establishing the Creek trade with the firm of William Panton and John Leslie. Brown's friend and countryman Isaac Herbert had followed him to Florida and secured the position of storekeeper for Panton and Leslie. Herbert enjoyed the profitable business of supplying the Creeks and Cherokees during their Florida sojourn. Governor Zespedes agreed to continue the Panton-Leslie monopoly. The Georgia merchants, frustrated in their hopes of recovering the trade of the Indians as well as their land, had one more grievance against Thomas Brown.[39]

Governor Tonyn had fixed February 20, 1785, as the day for the evacuation of the transports. When it became evident that the deadline would not be met, nor would the treaty-imposed date of March 19, an extension was granted with July 19, 1785, as the final date. That day came and went, and the refugee colony on the St. Marys still remained.

The slow-departing British were offended at the overly hospitable reception accorded to Major General Nathanael Greene in April 1785, especially since Zespedes had not seen fit to banquet the British officials. Because Greene was principally responsible for expelling the Loyalists from Georgia and Carolina, he was not well received by those he passed along the way. A few remained at the St. Johns, where Greene and Benjamin Hawkins left their boat. The appearance of the refugees was wretched, and "under this veil of misery there is all the bitterness of party and malevolence of disappointment," Greene wrote his wife, the vivacious Caty.[40]

The journey from the St. Johns to St. Augustine was disagreeable, the landscape a range of pine barrens, the road only a footpath. Though Greene had attempted to keep the visit a secret, Governor Zespedes was expecting the Americans. He sent a guard to escort the visitors and met them himself with his wife and daughters beside him. "Compliments flew from side to side like a shuttle cock in the hands of good players," wrote Greene. His store of small talk was soon exhausted, but what he lacked in conversation he made up in bowing. The governor's wife, Maria Conception, was about fifty-five years of age but "as cheerful as a Girl of sixteen." The daughters were not beautiful, but with their "sweet, languishing eyes" they looked as though they "could love with great violence." As they sang and played the harpsichord, Hawkins admitted that he was "smitten." Greene was asked if he was married; he replied that he was. The admission "limited my gallantry." The dinner was amazing. Greene counted more than 150 different dishes served in seven courses over a five-hour period. It left him feeling like a "stuffed pig." The rest of the evening was spent companionably at cards.[41]

During his four-day stay Greene explored the town. He remarked that the houses were built of "a kind of conextion of shells." He had not seen tabby before. The houses were crowded together, but the orange trees interspersed among them relieved their appearance. There were enough newly arrived Spanish ladies to cause Greene to comment on their free behavior. "Our stay was too short to try experiments," he teased his wife. A military escort accompanied Greene's party to the Georgia border. At the St. Marys River the commodore of the Spanish fleet fired a salute to the departing guests. This attention was particularly galling to the refugees being boarded on their transports. Greene counted twenty sail in St. Marys harbor.[42]

Greene's visit was not altogether an innocent sightseeing expedition. When he returned to Georgia he reported to Governor Samuel Elbert and his council that he had learned on the highest authority that Thomas Brown had alienated the Indians from the American interest and joined them to the Spanish. A general Indian war threatened the Georgia frontier. Greene believed that "it would be the height of bad policy and folly in the extreme to solicit or urge a cession of land" while Brown was at St. Augustine. Greene's opinions were buttressed by depositions gathered from Indian traders and read to the council. Governor Elbert had entered the trading business and was angered by the inability of his agents to win over the Creeks. Except for Brown's animosity, Elbert might have expected that Alexander McGillivray would have turned to the Americans. McGillivray had once worked in Elbert's accounting house. Elbert's partner was Brown's nemesis Elijah Clarke. Clarke had been active in collecting statements from Indians who were opposed to the cession of the Oconee territory. He, too, blamed Brown. Georgia merchants used Brown's interference to explain their lack of profits and their inability to pay their debts to British merchants. The state of Georgia prepared a charge against Thomas Brown which was to be forwarded to the British government by Congress. If ever a person was anathema in Georgia it was Thomas Brown.[43]

Whether or not Governor Zespedes knew that he caused trouble in Georgia for his friend Thomas Brown, the information he gave Greene ended any chance of reconciliation for Brown. Brown tested the climate in a letter to James Habersham. Habersham's wife, Hester Wylly, was sister to Brown's two Ranger captains, and Brown maintained cordial relations with the eldest of the three Habersham brothers. Habersham acknowledged Brown's letter and said that his wife and he would like to see Brown before he left the continent, but he warned Brown not to come to Savannah, "as my Dear Sir there would be no salvation for you here, I must look for this happiness at some more favorable period." Habersham said that Brown was accused of being motivated by vengeance and hatred in turning the Indians against the Georgians. Habersham added a piece of intelligence. The Georgians intended to claim the free navigation of the Mississippi by negotiation with Spain if possible, by force if necessary: "The emigrations from the southern states to the waters of the Mississippi are incredible." It was the policy of Congress to foster this movement and to encourage hostilities, but Congress would disavow any "violent measures" to "mask our intentions." Habersham, whose brother Joseph was a member of Congress, concluded, "The Spanish and Indian commerce of the Eastern and Western branches of the river will amply repay for the loss of blood or toil in the conquest."[44]

The letter is an interesting early example of "manifest destiny" that would operate later in West Florida, Texas, and California. Zespedes considered it significant enough to send copies to the Spanish minister Don Diego de Gardoqui in New York, to Bernardo de Galvez in Mexico City, and to José de Galvez, the minister of the Indies, in Madrid. Thomas Brown informed Zespedes that he could obtain more information concerning the "notorious Intentions" of the Americans if the Spanish government wanted it, but the identity of "J.H." must be closely guarded. Zespedes guessed the surname of Brown's informant but was not sure which of the brothers it was. He suggested that if Brown had anything further to relate, it could be safely conveyed through Panton, Leslie and Company. Brown confided that the proper name of his correspondent was "James." James Habersham sent one other item of information. His brother Joseph, who was on the Ways and Means Committee in Congress, believed that the country was on the verge of bankruptcy; the government lacked energy and power. Georgians were escaping taxes by migrating "in shoals" to the Ohio and Mississippi rivers, "the land of promise." Habersham repeated his prediction that those hardy pioneers would constitute a ready army if the United States was obliged to use force to achieve its purposes.[45]

Thomas Brown was a member of Governor Tonyn's party, which left St. Augustine and reached St. Marys in early July. They had hoped to depart by the July 19 deadline. Brown wrote to Zespedes that little progress had been made in the embarkation of the Loyalists and he expected at least a three-week delay. His letter was unusually sentimental, apologizing for not saying good-bye. He said he could endure the ordinary vicissitudes of life as well as any man, "but on these occasions I know my own weakness. I must confess, I am less than woman." Brown was lavish in his expressions of gratitude for the various favors he had received from Zespedes and his lady. Zespedes would not be outdone in emotional expression: "I regret exceedingly therefore the departure, perhaps forever, of a friend in whose happiness I am greatly interested." Despite his affection for Brown, he hoped that the Loyalists would be gone in three weeks; if not, he would notify his government of the extraordinary delay.[46]

While Brown was waiting at St. Marys he was surprised by a visit from Zespedes's young son Antonio. The boy had taken passage from St. Augustine without his parents' permission. Brown wrote to the governor to ask him to pardon Antonio, for "his agreable society has greatly contributed to make our heavy hours pass more lightly." The repentant Antonio wrote to ask forgiveness, saying it was "a boyish prank which I never in my life expected to perform." He explained that the "principal end and object" was "to give an embrace to Colonel Brown." He also wanted to see the St. Marys River. In a separate letter, Antonio asked his mother to intercede for him. The incident reveals that Thomas Brown had outdone Nathanael Greene in winning a place in the bosom of the Zespedes family. The correspondence displays an aspect of Brown's character which he had no opportunity to express in his official dispatches. Georgians who depicted him as a bitter man consumed by hatred would have been surprised at his softness of heart. The governor admitted that his son's "recklessness" grieved him, but Brown's recommendation of which his son "knew how to take advantage" protected Antonio. He thanked Brown for the hospitality afforded "the thoughtless fugitive."[47]

Brown's last days in America were spoiled by a violent pain in his stomach, which prevented him from sitting at the table "without the most exquisite torment." Finally, on August 29, Governor Tonyn, who was bound for England, reported that the last transports of evacuees had departed. All the ships, Tonyn's included, had put to sea by September 11, but a change of wind delayed their passage. The *Cyrus*, Governor Tonyn's ship, sat down on its own anchor and had to undergo extensive repairs. Tonyn was forced to wait for the transports to return from Nassau before he could leave. Tonyn's last letter from St. Marys was dated November 10, 1785. He arrived in Portsmouth, England, after a passage of fifty-three days.[48]

The Florida interlude was a comparatively quiet one for Thomas Brown. He swam no rivers, rode on no campaigns, fired no shots at an enemy, and suffered no bodily injury. But Thomas Brown made perhaps his most significant contribution to history during those first years of peace. By attaching the Creek Indians to their former adversaries, the Spanish, he helped frustrate the westward movement of his former countrymen. Because Georgia was unable to achieve its long-sought objective, the possession of the Oconee territory, the state entered more readily into the federal alliance. It is interesting to speculate whether Brown's legendary reputation for villainy might have had more to do with his postwar Spanish connection than with his wartime activities.

CHAPTER TEN

A GENTLEMAN

PLANTER

 After eleven tumultuous years in America, Thomas Brown looked forward to an untroubled life in the balmy Bahamas. He thought of himself as a southerner and shunned the prospect of settling in the colder climate of Nova Scotia. Specifically, he was a southern planter. He had come to Georgia at the age of twenty-four with 150 white indentured servants to become a planter. In November 1785 he was thirty-five years old and his ambition was the same. Instead of indentured servants he claimed 170 slaves.

There were an estimated five thousand slaves in East Florida in 1785. British officials had attempted to prevent any slaves who were not the property of Loyalists from leaving Georgia or South Carolina. Slaves who had served with the British army in any capacity were promised their freedom. Georgians complained that slaves had been stolen from their masters and taken off to Florida as plundered property. On his accession to office, Governor Zespedes attempted to bring order into the confusion by requiring slaveowners to show proof of ownership. British officials objected that British law did not require owners to have written documentation. In the interest of harmony, Zespedes failed to enforce his decree. The situation was ripe for enterprising individuals to claim slaves as compensation for losses sustained in the war. Thomas Brown was not only enterprising, he was well placed with both the outgoing and incoming governors.[1] Brown was initially awarded two hundred acres on Abaco in the Bahamas, not enough to occupy 170 slaves and not nearly enough to satisfy his ambition. He would do better than that.[2]

Before his Rangers left Florida, some of them had decided to live as Brown's neighbors on Abaco. Abaco is a narrow, irregular, crescent-shaped island at the northern end of the Bahamas with a cluster of small islands inside the crescent and long sandbars outside. The island was virtually uninhabited before the arrival of the Loyalists. A colony of New York refugees settled at a place they named Carleton, in the northern sector of the island. The Rangers claimed land on the lower third of the island. Captain Joseph Smith, who had carried the crucial message from Brown to Cruger during the first Battle of Augusta, claimed land at a place called Spencer's Bight and expressed the hope that the soil would "yield equal to the Expectations." Near him were Captain Alexander C. Wylly, author of "The Sketch of the Siege of Savannah," Captain Donald Cameron, Richard Pearis and his son Ensign Richard Pearis, Jr., Conrad Pennybaker, drummer, and John Cornish, quartermaster. Brown's contingent of slaves was at work there in 1784. Brown's friend the Indian Charles Fox Taylor may have been in charge of them because he was listed as a settler in 1784 by Lieutenant John Wilson in an inspection tour of the island.[3]

Before Brown's arrival, Governor James Edward Powell announced grants of forty acres to every head of family and twenty acres for each member of the family. The Rangers waited until their colonel arrived to lodge a formal protest. Then they expressed their "great mortification" that the generous grants allowed to the officers who went to Nova Scotia would not be available to them.[4] Brown was bothered by the uneven distribution of compensations. For example, Lieutenant Governor John Graham, who was superintendent for a short time at the end of the war and who allowed his deputy John Douglass to do most of the work, was compensated for the loss of his superintendency by appointment to the position of comptroller of customs at Kingston, Jamaica. Brown would later complain to William Pitt, "At the close of the war had I been disposed to have joined the clamorous herd of petitioners for public favor, I possibly might have been as fortunate as many who never saw the face of an enemy but having at that time, neither health, talents or inclination for such a business, I presume I was overlooked or forgotten."[5]

Of course, Brown did not allow himself to be overlooked entirely. On December 16, 1783, Thomas Forbes presented a memorial on Brown's behalf requesting compensation for losses. Forbes left London before he accomplished anything and joined Brown in the Bahamas, where he became a partner of William Panton and John Leslie in the Indian trading business. Brown then relied on his brother Jonas to protect his interests. For Jonas it was a matter of safeguarding

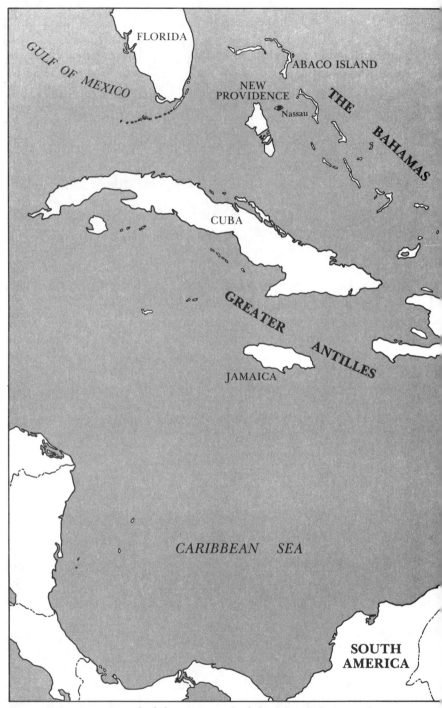

Brown's interests stretched from one end of the island chain to the
other. He owned plantations on Abaco, Grand Caicos, and St. Vincent.

THE WEST INDIES, CA. 1785

ATLANTIC

OCEAN

N

0   100   200 Miles
0   100   200   300 Kilometers

GRAND CAICOS
ISLAND

Santo Domingo   PUERTO RICO

HISPANIOLA

GREATER   ANTILLES

LESSER

ANTILLES

CARIBBEAN   SEA

ST. VINCENT
BARBADOS

SOUTH AMFRICA

his own interests after extending credit to help Thomas become established.[6]

The Abaco lands proved to be a disappointment. Lieutenant Wilson had been correct in describing Abaco as "nothing more than vegetable bodies rotted on the surface of the rocks." Jonas Brown had to advance more credit to permit experimental cotton cultivation. Jonas experienced an attack of anxiety when he happened to read a notice on July 21, 1787, that the deadline for filing claims was six months away. He sent a dispatch to his brother, but adverse winds delayed the vessel. On December 31, 1787, Jonas filed for Thomas, listing the expenses of settling Brownsborough and claiming compensation. He apologized to the commissioners on behalf of Thomas, explaining that ill health prevented the latter from coming to England in person. Jonas pleaded his brother's case again on January 19, 1788, in vain. Thomas Brown was not on the list of persons compensated. Frantic now, Jonas applied once more on November 17, 1788.[7]

Thomas Brown's deposition, taken by Lord Dunmore on November 27, 1787, arrived in time to bolster his case. In it he recited his personal history in America and added details about his current situation. Finding the soil on Abaco unsuitable, he had begun to transfer his slaves to Grand Caicos. On the way to that place, he was shipwrecked and spent four days with few provisions and no water before his party was rescued. As a result, he had contracted a violent fever which prevented him from going to England.[8]

The Bahama grants to Brown and others were delayed by confusion in land titles. The government had to buy the land from the heirs of John Colleton. That business was finished in 1787. John Murray, fourth Earl of Dunmore, arrived in October 1787 and prepared to begin the distribution of compensatory grants. The Loyalists greeted his arrival with eager anticipation. They had every reason to expect sympathetic treatment from Lord Dunmore. He was a fellow refugee, having served as governor of New York and then Virginia, where he led colonials against Indians in Lord Dunmore's War. Some might have wondered why so prominent a person would accept a minor post like the Bahamas. A clue was that a fellow passenger with the governor was John Miller, former trader to the Creek Indians in Pensacola. Miller intended to reestablish commerce with the western Indians with the governor as his silent partner. The obstacle that stood in their way was the monopoly the Spanish government had given to William Panton, John Leslie, and Thomas Forbes.[9]

Dunmore began issuing grants in 1788. Thomas Brown received more than anyone else. In 1788 he was given seven separate allotments of 100 acres each, in addition to one of 150 and one of 180, all on Abaco, which by that time he had abandoned. In March 1789 he received six grants on Grand Caicos, totaling 2,530 acres. In December of that year, he was awarded 2,180 additional acres on Grand Caicos. There were more grants on Abaco also. The grand total came to a staggering 6,290 acres, more than the 5,355 acres awarded to the governor and far more than the 1,773 acres Dunmore allotted to his son, Alexander Murray.[10]

To judge from his own testimony and that of Jonas, Thomas Brown's health was unusually poor during the first years in the Bahamas. He mentioned his bout of fever after being wrecked on the voyage to Grand Caicos. He had suffered from a stomach ailment during his last days in Florida. He also endured intermittent headaches as the result of the blows administered by the Liberty Boys in 1775. In an effort to gain relief from the terrible migraine attacks he submitted to the ancient operation called "trepanning," the removal from the skull of bits of bone, supposedly to relieve the pressure causing the headache. The surgery did not help. Whatever the health reasons that held him in the Bahamas, they did not prevent him from engaging in local politics, in international intrigue, and in romance, all at the time he was fulfilling his dream of becoming a colonial lord of the manor.

With the arrival of the first Florida refugees in 1783, a political schism developed between the old settlers and the newcomers. The refugees criticized Governor John Maxwell for his failure to grant representation in the assembly to the residents of the outer islands. The newcomers, calling themselves "American Loyalists," printed a notice in the *Bahamas Gazette* stating that they were not represented in the assembly and therefore did not consider themselves bound by any laws it passed. The principle was a familiar one to those who remembered the great debates in America a decade before. The Loyalists asked for a dissolution of the sitting assembly. They hoped for better things when Maxwell was replaced by Lieutenant Governor James Edward Powell, a former Georgian, but Powell disappointed them. After celebrating the king's birthday on June 4, 1785, they met again on June 8 and denounced Powell's conciliatory address to the assembly, claiming that he had broken his promise to dissolve that body.[11]

Powell died on February 6, 1786, and an interregnum ensued with John Brown, president of the council, acting as governor. It was during this year that Thomas Brown joined his fellow officers in protesting the unfair distribution of land. In September the *Gazette* carried an announcement by Brown, Josiah Tattnall, Thomas Stephens, Thomas Forbes, and Edmund R. Wegg warning trespassers to keep off their property on Little Abaco. The same issue noted that David Ramsay of Charleston (the new spelling was adopted when the town was incorporated after the war) had published a history of the late Revolution. This advertisement must have caught Brown's eye. He read Ramsay's history and then wrote Ramsay to defend his conduct and to set the record straight. Later in the year Loyalist Joseph Eve's newly invented cotton gin was displayed at Nassau. Brown would later publicly testify as to the utility of Eve's gin, which could clean a hundred pounds of cotton a day.[12] Unfortunately for his place in history, Eve did not receive the recognition of his invention which was accorded to Eli Whitney's version developed at Catherine Greene's plantation outside Savannah in 1793.

Brown could hardly avoid politics. His friend and former Georgian Josiah Tattnall was appointed judge of Court of Vice-Admiralty. William Wylly, the Ranger captain, became attorney general and took the lead in agitating for the rights of Loyalists. Brown and his friends hoped for better things when Lord Dunmore arrived to assume the governor's chair. Dunmore forwarded Brown's November 27, 1787, deposition to the commissioners on claims, but after that relations between the governor and Thomas Brown deteriorated rapidly.

Dunmore's assumption of office coincided with an uprising of blacks on the island of Abaco. Armed bands of "outlayers" roamed the island, robbing and plundering. A posse of whites caught up with the outlaws and hanged three of them. General Archibald McArthur was supposed to return to England with the men of the Thirty-seventh Regiment, but Dunmore persuaded him to stay because of the violence. Dunmore's enemies would soon claim that it was not the blacks he feared but an uprising of the American Loyalists. Dunmore issued a proclamation on November 7, 1787, offering a general pardon to fugitive blacks who would give themselves up to the authorities. He promised to investigate their claims to freedom. The American Loyalists complained that Dunmore subsequently took slaves from them and gave them to his friends.[13]

Dunmore further alienated the Loyalists by refusing to listen to their charge of fraud in the electoral process. Six Loyalists were denied seats even though they had a greater number of votes than their opponents. The provost marshal refused to recount the votes and declared the candidates representing the old inhabitants elected. Thereafter, other duly elected Loyalists boycotted the assembly in protest. The Loyalists hoped that Dunmore would call for new elections. Instead, he simply prorogued the session from November 1 to December 4, 1787.

The recently elected member from Abaco was Thomas Brown. He cast his lot with his fellow Loyalists by refusing to take his seat. The rump assembly called upon Attorney General William Wylly to go to Abaco and explain to Brown the error of his ways. Wylly was not about to lecture his colonel and told the governor as much. He said, "If the governor wished him to get a broken head, he could not have fallen upon a better expedient." Dr. Robert Scott, former surgeon to the Royal Artillery in St. Augustine, was another elected member who boycotted the assembly. The inhabitants of the island of Exuma elected Thomas Brown and Thomas Forbes to represent them on February 5. Both refused to take their places in the assembly. The Abaco Loyalists signed a memorial to the effect that they were unrepresented in the legislature and therefore subject to laws they had no share in making. They asked for a dissolution of the assembly, which had now been sitting for three years. Thomas Brown loaned his name to the protest. Lord Dunmore forwarded the memorial to Lord Sydney in London but added that he believed the reason the Loyalists wanted control of the assembly was to enact legislation enabling them to keep the slaves they had stolen in Florida. Furthermore, Dunmore had discovered a treasonous intent on the part of the Loyalists to separate the Bahamas from allegiance to Britain. In case of a war with America, he believed that the Loyalists would join the Americans against England.[14]

Dunmore stirred up more trouble in May 1788 when he sent a posse to Abaco to search for smuggled corn and to free slaves who had been abducted from Florida. The governor's man, Samuel Mackay, decided to make an example of the veteran Loyalist Richard Pearis, whose house guests at the time included Thomas Forbes and

Ranger Captain Joseph Smith. Even though he had no search warrant, Mackay broke open Pearis's storehouses and confiscated 401 bushels of corn. With Mackay's encouragement, some of the slaves went aboard the government boat, expecting to be set free. Other blacks ran away into the woods. Dunmore himself then made a special trip to Abaco. He interviewed thirty slaves but could determine that only one of them was "rebel property" wrongly taken from Florida. Planters on Abaco blamed him for causing confusion in the minds of the blacks on the island.[15]

Pearis, who was living on a government pension, informed the governor of another memorial being circulated which was critical of Dunmore. The memorial in question was addressed to William Pitt. It complained of the false seizure of slaves, argued that six of the fifteen members of the assembly had been fraudulently elected, and alleged that the public treasury had been plundered. Dunmore defended himself by forwarding evidence of the secret plans of the Loyalists. He cited testimony by a Loyalist named William Augustus Bowles that "there has been and is now a design to wrest this colony from the Dominion of Great Britain."[16] Dunmore would make good use of Bowles before the year 1788 was over. Then occurred a trivial incident that caused Dunmore to close the courts and declare that the colony was in a state of rebellion. In another context it would have passed unnoticed.

Former Ranger William Wylly had accepted the nonpaying position of attorney general when he came to Nassau in 1787. When he was told that he would have to take sides against the Loyalists, he resigned. On April 9, 1788, Wylly was in the company of Thomas Forbes when they met Chief Justice John Matson on the street. Wylly asked Matson to corroborate his assertion that he had told Wylly to "join a party." Matson said that he could not remember having said so. Wylly said, "Sir, you are a damned liar." The governor and council ordered Wylly arrested for treason. Wylly was tried but discharged when Matson refused to testify. Thereupon, Wylly sued for false arrest. It was then that Dunmore closed the courts and sent Matson off to England to explain the insurrectionary nature of conditions in the colony. The Loyalists named William Wylly their agent and dispatched him to London to counteract Matson's influence.[17]

It was in this anxious time of inflamed emotions that the Loyalists of Nassau put up Thomas Brown for election to the assembly. The governor's faction supported Alexander Murray, Dunmore's son.

The *Bahamas Gazette,* which was printed by John Wells, former publisher of the short-lived *East Florida Gazette,* carried an endorsement of Brown which reads like a modern campaign promotion: "He possesses a strength of understanding and an extent of information rarely equalled." The *Gazette* praised his "manly spirit" and noted that his "independent fortune" made him secure from corruption.[18] An unnamed but authoritative-sounding correspondent pledged his support for "General Brown," citing his "loyalty, ability, integrity, attachment to the Rights of the People, public spirit and property" as reasons to vote for him. Another testimonial called attention to the concern Brown displayed toward the suffering Loyalists and reminded readers that Brown had on a previous occasion defended the liberties of his countrymen with "courage and intrepidity."[19] One wonders if Brown was tempted to send these tributes to David Ramsay.

On February 5, 1789, Thomas Brown won the election by a vote of fifty-four to forty-one for Murray. Wells printed the names of the voters in the *Gazette,* possibly to forestall a recount such as had previously elected six of the governor's men. Brown sent a victory message to the *Gazette* thanking the "free, independent electors" of Nassau for the honor conferred upon him. He promised that he would serve and use his influence "to promote the general interests of the colony and to defend your Rights, Liberties and Privileges from encroachment or violation."[20] The statement was like a gauntlet flung before Dunmore.

Although the Loyalists won an important victory with Brown's election, they were not so fortunate in the outlying islands. Thomas Forbes was not allowed to take his seat for Abaco because of alleged irregularities in voting. This and other disputed returns caused the Grand Jury to protest the "clandestine manner" in which voting was conducted. The foreman of the jury was former Deputy Indian Superintendent John Douglass. Members included Thomas Forbes and John Mullryne Tattnall, staunch friends of Brown. The jury also protested that the governor had permitted "a considerable armed force" to depart for suspicious business in Florida.[21] Behind that presentment lay a tangled web of intrigue involving the mysterious William Augustus Bowles.

Thomas Brown knew a great deal about Bowles, enough to alarm him. In 1779, Bowles was an ensign in a regiment of Maryland Loyalists assigned to Major General John Campbell's army in West Florida. Military routine and discipline did not suit Bowles, and he deserted to join a party of Creeks who had come to see John Stuart, then in the last phase of his mortal illness. Bowles was befriended by Perryman, the chief who caused so much controversy the year before when he came at Governor Tonyn's call and accused Stuart's deputies of sending the other Creeks to Pensacola instead of East Florida. Bowles took a Cherokee girl as his wife and had one or more children by her. Then he added a daughter of Perryman as his second wife, and the pair produced a son, "Little Billy."[22] Interesting coincidences abound in the history of this period, and it might be recalled that Brown was said to be living with the daughter of Perryman in 1785. It would be too much to expect that the same daughter was involved. In any case, Brown did not need such an intimate feminine relationship to have learned about Bowles. He had known Perryman since 1776 and had fought beside him on the Florida frontier in 1777. He must have been aware that Bowles was later a member of Perryman's household.

When Brown's deputies Alexander McGillivray and William McIntosh summoned the Creeks to the defense of Pensacola, Bowles went along. Instead of being shot as a deserter, he was reinstated as an ensign. When Pensacola surrendered in May 1780, Bowles was paroled to New York with the rest of his regiment. After the war, he decided to go to the Bahamas rather than Nova Scotia. Like other provincial officers, he was entitled to half-pay and was granted five hundred acres on Eleuthera Island. The life of a planter appealed to him no more than that of the military. So in 1785 he returned to Perryman's village and Perryman's daughter and became a chief. He affected a cloth turban with an ostrich feather and carried a silver pipe tomahawk. Bowles shared the general distrust of the aggressive Georgians and on one occasion, according to his own testimony, went to Augusta to spy on the legislature there.[23]

In 1786 Alexander McGillivray sent the Creeks on the offensive to drive Georgia trespassers off the Oconee lands. Creek war parties roamed the frontier during 1787 causing Georgia to join the other states in a stronger union and also to increase the stridency of protests to Governor Zespedes in East Florida and Governor Arturo O'Neill in West Florida. O'Neill especially was alarmed at the success of the Creeks. He had never trusted McGillivray and worried that the Creeks would turn on Spain. Early in 1788 McGillivray learned that Spanish support was to be diminished.[24] Therefore, when

William Bowles walked into Coweta town with a promise to supply goods independently of Spain, he was welcomed. McGillivray himself went down to meet Bowles. Bowles distributed samples of goods from the Nassau firm of Miller, Bonamy and Company and promised to supply more. Despite his silent partnership in Panton, Leslie and Company, McGillivray gave Bowles reason to believe that a rival company would be well received.

Bowles returned to Nassau and conferred with Dunmore and Miller. As a result, two vessels were outfitted with arms, ammunition, and provisions. It was alleged that the military stores came out of the royal arsenal. The exact purpose of the expedition was not clear. Dunmore and Miller were anxious to strike a blow at William Panton and his associate Thomas Forbes by seizing Panton's stores in Florida. Bowles told his recruits that the objective of the mission was to attack Georgia. Because he had trouble enlisting enough men, Dunmore opened the prison to fill the quota of fifty.[25] Bowles drilled his little army on one of the outlying islands and then set sail for Florida.

Thomas Brown was so suspicious of Bowles's intentions that he refused to receive the Indians who accompanied Bowles to Nassau. Brown wrote to his friend Zespedes to warn him that Bowles "was the foolish instrument of veritable scoundrels." Brown expressed greater contempt for Dunmore than for Bowles. The governor was "as poor in money as in brains" and hoped to steal from Panton, Leslie warehouses; "no gentleman can deal with him without staining his reputation," said Brown.[26]

Zespedes appreciated Brown's warning. He sent a dispatch to McGillivray on October 8, 1788, informing him that "that constant friend of the Indians, Colonel Brown" said that Bowles could not be trusted and that his purpose was to ruin the firm of Panton, Leslie and to turn the Creeks against Spain. Zespedes asked McGillivray to capture Bowles and bring him in to St. Augustine or Pensacola. McGillivray expressed thanks for the timely information. It was true that Bowles had promised "great hopes of Succour and aid, beside many other fine things." When McGillivray had questioned him about his backers, Bowles denied that Dunmore was involved. If McGillivray saw him again, he would expose him as a "Needy Vagrant." Having had some acquaintance with Bowles in the defense of Pensacola, he would not treat him as a felon but "give him wholsome advice and dismiss him."[27]

As it turned out, Bowles's expedition failed without intervention by the Spanish or the Creeks. Bowles could not make up his mind whether to attack the Panton store at the St. Johns River or the one at St. Marks. His men grew tired of marching about, and most of them deserted and were arrested by the Spanish authorities. Bowles returned to Nassau and talked Dunmore and Miller into financing another nonmilitary expedition.

Bowles returned to the Creek country in 1789, claiming to represent the great King George III. A general council of Lower Creeks and Seminoles commissioned Bowles and several chiefs to go see the English king and ask him to restore his protection. Bowles and eight chiefs stopped at Nassau to confer with Lord Dunmore. William Panton described Bowles's companions as "two [or] three half Breeds of the Cherokees and a couple of Young fellows from the Creeks" and said that Bowles was put in jail for debt upon his arrival but released through Dunmore's influence. The presence of Bowles's party was grist for the Loyalists' anti-Dunmore campaign. Dunmore, who was already under heavy criticism by William Wylly in London, was not sure what reception Bowles might receive at the Court of St. James and detained the Indian delegation in Nassau. Bowles was considered an enemy of Spain, and William Pitt's policy was to maintain friendly relations with that country. But events played to Bowles's advantage in 1789. Spanish warships seized several British merchant vessels at Nootka Sound, Vancouver Island. The act was seen as a challenge for control of the Pacific coast of North America. William Pitt's attitude toward Spain changed correspondingly. Thus it was that Bowles's party was welcomed when, finally, after several misadventures, they reached England by way of Canada. Bowles entertained his listeners with stories of easy conquests of Spanish Florida, Louisiana, and even Mexico. The crisis ended when Spain gave up her pretentions to the region and signed the Convention of 1790 with England. Subsequently, it was reported in Nassau that the savages were now out of fashion and Bowles was snubbed by Pitt.[28]

The year of the Nootka crisis, 1790, was also the year of Alexander McGillivray's rapprochement with the new federal government of the United States. William Panton made a journey to the Creek country to warn McGillivray not to fall into an American trap, but McGillivray and twenty-six Creek chiefs and warriors had already left on their long journey to New York. The anxious Spanish authorities sent Carlos Howard to listen in on the negotiations. An equally concerned British government was represented by George

Beckwith, a friend of Thomas Brown's and later governor of St. Vincent Island. The Treaty of New York was signed on August 7, 1790. McGillivray gave up the long-disputed strip between the Ogeechee and Ocmulgee rivers in Georgia but refused to desert Panton and open trade with the Americans unless a war with England occurred. The United States promised not to take any Creek land without the consent of the Creek Nation. McGillivray was given a commission as brigadier general with an annual salary of $1,200 a year. McGillivray was satisfied with the treaty, and so was Panton, Leslie and Company. The Georgians were furious. They had already claimed the Oconee and wanted the Flint or at least the Ocmulgee as their new boundary.[29] It would take a personal visit from George Washington himself in 1791 to stop their grumbling.

It was against this background of Nootka and New York that the Spanish government made Thomas Brown an astonishing offer. Father Michael O'Reilly wrote to Brown on behalf of Zespedes's successor, Don Juan de Quesada, on August 15, 1790, to tell him that the king had approved the appointment of Brown as commandant of Spanish troops in Florida and superintendent of Indian affairs with a salary of $10,000 per year. Brown would be compensated for any costs incurred in removing from Grand Caicos to Florida. There would be no question raised about religion, and Brown would have liberty to retire whenever he chose. Father O'Reilly added his urgent request for Brown to come back: "Think only of the honors and advantages which await you." O'Reilly remembered Charles Fox Taylor and hoped that he, too, would return with Brown to Florida.[30]

Brown replied that he would consult with the British authorities because he could never enter the service of a foreign power without the permission of the king. He then wrote to William Pitt to request approval. His letter was a perceptive analysis of Spanish-Indian relations in America. Brown had played a part in securing for Alexander McGillivray an appointment as colonel in the service of Spain. McGillivray trusted Governor Zespedes and remained a steadfast ally while Zespedes was governor. When Zespedes notified the Creeks that another governor had been appointed to succeed him, however, they became less attached to the Spanish interests. At this juncture McGillivray concluded a treaty with the Americans. McGillivray had too many financial commitments to Panton, Leslie and Company ever to go over to the American side, but the Spanish government did not know that and was afraid of losing the allegiance of the Creeks. The extraordinary offer was extended because of Brown's influence with the Indians. Brown suggested that Pitt might confirm his credentials with Major General Alured Clarke, Lieutenant Governor John Moultrie, or Major James Wright, Jr., now Sir James after the death of his father, the governor.[31]

The Spanish proposition was tempting. Brown would have been assured of honors and wealth. He could have claimed the thousands of acres Governor Tonyn had given him in Florida and perhaps the tens of thousands the Indians had promised. Brown's expectations must have been high; he must have looked forward to a reply from London with keen anticipation. In his own words, "I received a letter from Mr. King, Undersecretary of State, to inform me that His Majesty was fully sensible of my fidelity, services, zeal, etc., etc. but I received no answer to my request."[32] J. Leitch Wright has suggested that Dunmore and Bowles had caused the British ministry to believe that Brown, as well as Panton, Leslie and Company were too friendly to the Spanish interest. In any case, in the anti-Spanish aftermath of the Nootka controversy, England was not in the mood to do any favors for Spain. Brown's faint praise was his answer. George Beckwith, who represented England as a witness to the Treaty of New York in 1790, was glad that Brown was not given permission to accept the Spanish proposition: "You might have been a greater or a richer man, but not half so happy."[33] Even though the opportunity passed, Brown felt honored by the offer.

The decade of the 1790s was a comparatively happy one for Thomas Brown. On Grand Caicos, at the eastern extremity of the Bahamas, Brown realized his dream of becoming a gentleman planter. His estate grew to eight thousand acres, and his work force numbered over six hundred slaves. Brown prided himself on being a considerate master. He would never set his people to work at a burdensome task like turning the heavy wheels of his grist and sugar mills. He allowed each person to cultivate a garden plot. If any wanted to marry a slave on another plantation, he would acquire that person and keep the family together.[34] His policy was never to sell his own people.

Whether Brown lived with an Indian princess after his removal to the Bahamas is uncertain. There is better evidence that he formed a close personal attachment to one of his servants. "Black Nancy" would later accompany the Brown family to England and return with them to St. Vincent. Brown remembered her in his will, giving her a house of her own to live in. It is likely that Brown was the father of her mulatto son, George, who accompanied her to England. Interracial liaisons were not unusual. James Gordon, Brown's partner from the Orkneys, was devoted to one of his slaves, who became his common-law wife and the mother of his son, John Rutherford Gordon. The couple settled on Crooked Island in the Bahamas in 1787 after sojourns in the Virgin Islands and Nova Scotia. Gordon was desolate when his wife died. He could not bring himself to bury her; instead, he dressed her body in velvet, adorned her with jewels, and placed her in a protective cage. This bizarre mausoleum became a Bahamian curiosity. Whether Thomas Brown had much social contact with Gordon is not known. Very likely there was a coolness between them. When Gordon had claimed reimbursement for expenses in transporting 149 settlers to Georgia, Jonas Brown, Jr., testified that Gordon had not put up his promised share of the costs and was not entitled to compensation. Instead of the £1,629 he asked for, Gordon was awarded £117.[35]

In 1789 Thomas Brown took a major step toward domesticity. The *Gazette* of October 3, 1789, announced the marriage of the colonel and Esther Farr of Nassau. Esther, or Hetty, was the sixteen-year-old daughter of Captain William Farr and his wife, Sarah. The Farrs were old inhabitants of Nassau, but Farr cast his vote in 1789 with the new settlers for his future son-in-law. Thomas Brown, aged thirty-nine, thus followed his father's example in taking a younger wife. Jonas, Sr., was fifty-six when he married twenty-one-year-old Sarah. In both cases, the marriages were happy, and in both the older partners outlived the younger.

In 1791 Hetty gave birth to their first child, Mary Frances. A year later a son was born and encumbered with the name Thomas Alexander Murray Brown. Why Brown should have named his first son after his political rival, Dunmore's son, is a mystery. The second son was given an even more unusual name, Charles Susan Baring Brown. The Barings were friends of the Browns, but young Charles must have regretted this particular method of honoring Mrs. Baring. A second girl was born to the Browns and she, too, was named Susan. As the younger girl, Susan Harriett was her father's favorite. Brown's household grew still larger when William Farr died and his widow, Sarah, and her sister Margaret moved in. Charles Fox Taylor, the Indian chief, was there, too.

Fortunately, Brown could support a retinue. He planted three thousand acres in cotton and a thousand in grapes, most of the latter pasturage for cattle. Seven hundred acres was set aside for corn to feed the hands. Brown allotted an entire acre to each slave for private gardening. On the rest of his land he planted trees to provide fencing and to act as a barrier against the constant winds. Brown may have been boasting when he claimed that his estate produced £20,000 annually; his property was valued at £108,000.[36]

Thomas Brown remembered his family in Whitby during these years. The patriarch, Jonas, outlived his young wife, Sarah, by almost two decades. She died in 1781, leaving him to care for their surviving children, Ann, Sarah, and George, at Newton House on the edge of the moors. Thomas Brown had never seen this new generation of his siblings. An unexpected honor befell Jonas in 1793 when he was in his seventy-sixth year. The eighth Viscount Montague drowned while on a hunting expedition in Shaffhausen, Germany. He had no heirs and so the title originally granted by King Henry VIII to Anthony Browne devolved upon Jonas, the ninth viscount. It was the second title for the family because in 1787 Jonas, Jr., had been honored by the king with knighthood. At the time brother Jonas was living in Kingston on the Hull with his bride of one year, Elizabeth Preston. Thomas remembered his father, brother, and sisters by sending them collections of shells from his island or pearls from Cuba and looked forward to the day he would see them again.[37]

Though the Caicos years were idyllic, it was Thomas Brown's destiny that quiet times did not last. When the British and French resumed their intermittent warfare in 1793, Caicos was dangerously exposed. The enemy was only 150 miles due south on the rebellion-torn island of Santo Domingo. William Pitt's government was so concerned about the security of the British West Indies that half the army was sent to the islands. The British people had to shoulder the burden of heavy taxation, a discouraging war on the Continent, and unrest in Ireland.

In America, old animosities subsided with new wars to worry about. Citizen Edmond Genet created a stir by enlisting Georgia veterans in a French scheme to invade Florida.[38] Genet was inhibited in his plans by Washington's Proclamation of Neutrality and forestalled by his recall to France. With Washington's permission, he chose to remain in America. One of Genet's recruits was Thomas Brown's old adversary, Elijah Clarke. Clarke had warmed to the idea of yet another descent into Florida. Frustrated by Genet's recall, he gathered his faithful veterans and invaded Creek territory instead of Florida, establishing the short-lived Trans-Oconee Republic. The Georgia militia had to be dispatched to fetch him back. Clarke's friends were of the opinion that the old hero was denied the recognition his exploits in the Revolution warranted. When Clarke died in 1799, the Augusta newspaper noted that David Ramsay's history ignored Clarke. The writer, General James Jackson, was certain that the British Colonels Cruger and Brown, both "gallant officers," would not forget Clarke and that Brown would "remember the White House, now Harrisburgh, as long as he exists."[39]

Many of Brown's fellow Loyalists returned to Georgia. Dr. Thomas Taylor was pardoned by the legislature, as were Colonel Thomas Waters and James Ingram. Ranger Captain Alexander C. Wylly took his wife and three children to St. Simons Island and lived out the rest of his life among the plantation gentry of the low country.[40] Isaac Herbert, who had embarked for Georgia from Whitby in 1775 and had served as Brown's storekeeper in Augusta and in Florida, lived quietly as a Wilkes County planter until 1795, when he moved to Augusta and opened a dry goods store on Broad Street. His business prospered so well that he was able to build a summer house on the hill near George Walton's College Hill residence.[41]

Brown's fellow colonizer of the Georgia backcountry, William Manson, returned home to the Orkneys after his adventures. His second marriage was to Elizabeth, daughter of the distinguished William Balfour of Trenabie. In 1789 William bought a handsome house in Kirkwall's principal street for his bride. Undoubtedly his good connections helped him obtain the position of comptroller of customs. In 1806 William Manson's daughter Mary married William Balfour of Elwick, forging another link between the two families.[42]

Unlike Dr. Taylor and Isaac Herbert, Thomas Brown could not return to America. He would not, he said, even if his "principles" would allow him to do so. Nor was he prepared to go home again, as Manson did. Staying where he was on Caicos, however, became increasingly less of an option. The renewal of the French war found him in a dangerously exposed situation. Brown was a fighter and prepared to defend his island and his people. He armed and drilled his black labor force. He constructed two forts for the defense of St. George's Harbor and bought fourteen cannon and installed them in the forts. He thus had a stronger fortification in Caicos than he had in the old days to defend Georgia. Although these defenses were not tested, French warships intercepted supply vessels bound for the Bahamas. The *Bahamas Gazette* of August 21, 1798, reported one such incident. A ship bound for Grand Caicos was wrecked on nearby West Caicos. Brown and other planters sent their boats to retrieve goods belonging to them. As the supplies were being transferred into the small boats, a French privateer came up under full sail. Four vessels made a run for it, but Brown's men decided to fight for possession of the wrecked ship. The all-black crew was armed only with a two-pounder cannon and muskets, but they drove off the Frenchmen repeatedly. The heavier armed privateer stayed out of range of Brown's defenders and used its cannon to sink Brown's boat. The valiant crew swam to shore. Brown told his father about the battle and said that he was so proud of his men that he did not mind the loss of his goods.[43]

The war came no closer, but Brown worried that it might. He was too near to rebellion-ravaged Santo Domingo. Then, too, the thin soil of Caicos would not continue to support cotton, despite his best efforts at planting trees and conservation. The death of Jonas Brown on March 28, 1799, caused Brown to decide to return to Whitby as soon as he could risk a sea passage. It had been a long time since he had seen his family and friends.

CHAPTER ELEVEN

WHITBY AND

ST. VINCENT

 Jonas Brown was eighty-two when he died at Newton House. He had prepared a will six years earlier, giving his plantation to the surviving children of his second marriage, Ann, Sarah, and George. The big house on Grape Lane went to his eldest son, Jonas; the rest of the property was to be evenly divided among the older offspring, Mary Cayley, Margaret Brown, and Thomas. Jane had died, and her share was assigned to her husband, Jonathan Lacy. Jonas left instructions that he wanted his funeral to be private and that there should be a minimum of trouble and expense. He charged the older sons and daughters with taking care of the younger ones. Jonas was buried with the dignity befitting a leading citizen of Whitby, in old St. Mary's Churchyard on the east cliff in the shadows of the ancient abbey.[1]

The Treaty of Amiens in 1801 brought a temporary peace to the high seas and allowed Thomas Brown to return with his family to England. He wrote to his brother on March 21, 1802, that a bout of fever had prevented his leaving earlier but that he would sail for Liverpool in June. He warned Jonas that he had put on weight but hoped "to present only a tolerable show of embonpoint." His nephew Edward Cayley had visited him at Caicos, and Brown liked him at once.[2]

Brown sounded like a doting father as he discussed proper schools for his four children. He worried whether the girls would like England. Mary, especially, was shy. "I am afraid she would suffer in health from leaving me," he said. Mary was already eleven and tall for her age. Tom was ten, Charles and Susan younger. Hetty Brown's mother, Sarah Farr, would go with them, as would some of their

193

favorite servants, including Black Nancy, the housekeeper. Her mulatto son, George, now a teenager, would make the trip. George was apprenticed to a Whitby sea captain, just as if he had been born and bred to the North Sea life, and eventually acquired a ship of his own. The arrival of the colonel's entourage in Whitby must have created a stir. Whitby was accustomed to heroes of the sea, but no native son had lived among Indians and fought against George Washington's troops and come home to tell about it. Brown purchased Newton House from the other family members and erected a monument on the grounds in honor of his father. He took his family to the church on the cliff in a fine coach. He rented a pew box in the prestigious upper gallery on the south side of the church.[3]

There were tender moments of family reunion. Faithful brother Jonas (Sir Jonas now) sat as magistrate for Sculcoats, near Hull. Young sister Sarah had married a wealthy London merchant named George Wilkinson on January 21, 1801. Thomas admired Sarah and was a frequent visitor at the Wilkinsons' house in fashionable Fitzroy Square in London. His half-sister Ann was also well married to a wealthy Yorkshire landowner named Peirson. Sisters Mary Cayley and Peggy Brown were still in Whitby. George Clubb, who had supervised the construction of Newton House, was on hand to greet the new master. He remained on the estate as a general factotum until his death in 1812.[4]

It was reported that the colonel tried to walk on the waters of Newton pond. Brown, always inventive, was fascinated by the buoyant qualities of cork. He attached a large piece of cork to each foot and stepped out of a boat, immediately turning upside down. The idea was good even if the part of the anatomy was badly chosen. Brown would later equip his workers in the West Indies with lifesaving cork belts and would recommend the device to the British navy.[5]

Thomas Brown would have noticed changes in Whitby over the past quarter-century. There was a new Tollbooth, as the town hall was called. A hundred houses and the Wesleyan Chapel on Henrietta Street had been buried when part of the east cliff collapsed in a landslide in 1787. The street had been cleared, and John Wesley himself had come to dedicate the new chapel. At the end of Henrietta Street a battery of cannon overlooked the North Sea. They were put there to ward off the famous American privateer John Paul Jones. They remained there in case one of Napoleon's warships ventured too close. The whaling industry had brought prosperity to Whitby. New banking houses had sprung up, three on Grape Lane, the street where Brown grew up. Jonas Brown's handsome, four-story house with its striking bottle-shaped staircase window, now the property of Sir Jonas Brown of Hull, was occupied by a firm of solicitors.[6]

Whaling had produced a new hero for Whitby. William Scoresby rivaled even the great Captain Cook in the estimation of the seafaring folk. In 1798 Scoresby had brought back oil from thirty-six whales, taken in a single voyage. The average for a voyage was five or six. In 1801 Scoresby built a larger and stouter ship in the Whitby yards and, in honor of Cook, named it the *Resolution*. Construction and outfitting cost Scoresby and his backers £8,000. The *Resolution* was launched in 1803, and Scoresby astounded the world by taking 194 whales in the next six years, showing an annual profit of more than twice the original investment. Scoresby equaled Cook as a navigator. He ventured through ice-choked waters no one else dared try. In 1806, Scoresby sailed to within 510 miles of the North Pole when the sea began to freeze around his ship and he reluctantly turned back. He had reached 81°30′ north latitude, higher than any sailing vessel had gone before. He had to break out of the ice by running his crew from one side of the ship to the other, rocking it loose. He invented the crow's nest in 1807—a leather box at the head of the topgallant mast for the lookout to spy for bowhead whales and shout "Thar she blows" and to sight channels through Arctic ice.[7]

Scoresby was a hero, but the Whitby men turned to Thomas Brown in 1803 when the Napoleonic wars were renewed. The Independent Volunteers of Whitby offered command of their corps to Lieutenant Colonel Thomas Brown. Seventy had already enrolled and more were expected.[8] It was a nice compliment, but a colonelcy in the home guards was too tame for a man who had swum rivers with Indians in warpaint at his side. Brown, however, might not have refused a better offer. He paid a courtesy call on his old patron, Governor Patrick Tonyn, at his residence on Park Street, near Grosvenor Square, in London. Tonyn still hoped to lead an army into battle. Brown mentioned Tonyn's aspiration in a letter to a comrade in arms from the Florida interlude, George Beckwith of the Thirty-seventh Regiment. Brown had done young Major Beckwith a favor, lending him money to return to England. Since then Beckwith had gone from one honor to another. He was England's unofficial representative in New York in 1790, observing the treaty negotiations with the Creek Indians. He was promoted to colonel in 1795, named governor of Bermuda in 1797, and raised to the rank of major general in 1798. Beckwith seemed genuinely glad to renew his acquaintance with Brown. In response to Brown's reference to Tonyn's eagerness for active service, Beckwith replied that he would prefer to serve under Brown's command than Tonyn's. Beckwith thought that Brown's services would be needed in the war with Napoleon. Brown must not let his martial ardor cool; "we must put our shoulders to the wheel." Meanwhile, Beckwith hoped that Brown might be able to enjoy a little time of quiet, the society of friends, and the comforts of his native country, "which after all is the best country in the world, and Yorkshire the best part of that."[9] Neither Brown nor Beckwith could have known when they corresponded in 1803 that within a year Tonyn would be dead, Beckwith would be named governor of St. Vincent, or Brown would receive a princely grant of land on St. Vincent in 1805.

The birth of their fifth child, George Newton Brown, was a happy event for the colonel and his lady. The middle name might have commemorated Newton House, or it might have been chosen to honor the memory of Adeline Newton Huntrodes of Bagdale Hall, Brown's maternal grandmother.

During this sojourn in England, Brown comported himself like the wealthy West Indian planter he was. His war record and his evident fortune opened society's doors to him. He was known to William Pitt, who was recalled to head the government in 1804 after a two-year hiatus. Brown lost no time in pressing his request for land on St. Vincent in exchange for his Caicos estate. Brown corresponded with Pitt's friend William Wilberforce about the management of slaves. Wilberforce, the great antislavery advocate, apparently approved of Brown's efforts to keep slave families together. Lord Francis Rawdon, once Brown's superior officer in Carolina, was now the Earl of Moira and mentioned as a possible successor to Pitt as prime minister. Brown cultivated a friendship with him and his sister Lady Charlotte Rawdon and Rawdon's kinsman Lord Kingston. On one occasion Kingston invited Brown to go on a vacation to Scotland. Kingston promised a diet of "fish and grouse and grouse and fish with a second course of mutton chops . . . with a pipe and a glass of punch brandy and rum . . . to finish the evening with."[10] It was a pleasant prospect.

Brown's oldest son, Tom, became well acquainted with the Beckfords. William Beckford, son of the lord mayor of London of the same name, gained fame in literary circles by writing an Oriental novel entitled *Vathek*. Beckford's "volatile imagination" has been compared to William Blake's and "the exotic character" of his work with that of the poet Keats.[11] Beckford squandered a fortune building a gothic mansion as exotic as his novel. The structure collapsed a few years after Beckford sold it to pay his debts. It was said of Beckford, "It never seemed to occur to him that his magnificent possessions in the West Indies entailed upon him the least responsibility."[12] The same could not be said of Thomas Brown. He had lived too long among his people on Caicos; his destiny was linked with theirs.

The year of Pitt's return to power, 1804, was crucial in Brown's career. King George III, "the good old King" in Brown's words, granted Brown's request for six thousand acres of land on St. Vincent. W. Hayes Bourne notified Brown of his good fortune on November 10, 1804. One month earlier, the king had appointed George Beckwith governor of St. Vincent.[13]

The lands in question were, until 1804, reserved for the so-called "black Caribs" of St. Vincent. These fiercely independent people were descendants of shipwrecked and escaped slaves who knew the meaning of freedom and were prepared to fight for it. The Caribs were inspired by the example of the rebellious blacks on Santo Domingo to resist British rule in 1795. The garrison of Royal Americans on the island was reinforced by the Forty-Sixth Regiment. The Caribs proved a match for the British in courage and even in tactics. Eventually, three thousand regulars, more than Archibald Campbell had in Georgia, were sent to the tiny island. General George Prevost, son of Augustine, gained the tainted distinction of eventually putting down the rebellion. It was only in 1804 that the government decided that the lands were forfeit and thenceforth the Caribs must be content with a reservation of 230 acres in the interior.[14] The Carib lands amounted to nearly one-quarter of the island. It was this princely tract of 6,000 acres that was awarded to Thomas Brown by a grant of June 8, 1805, signed by the colonial secretary, Lord Camden.

Thomas Brown must have been as eager to plant his colony on the forfeited Carib lands of St. Vincent as he had been thirty years earlier to claim his grants on the Indian Ceded Lands in Georgia. His experience in Georgia should have taught him that it was one thing to obtain a grant and quite another to occupy it. Squatters had already settled on the Carib land granted to Brown. The rather weak and vacillating Governor William Bentinck admitted that he lacked

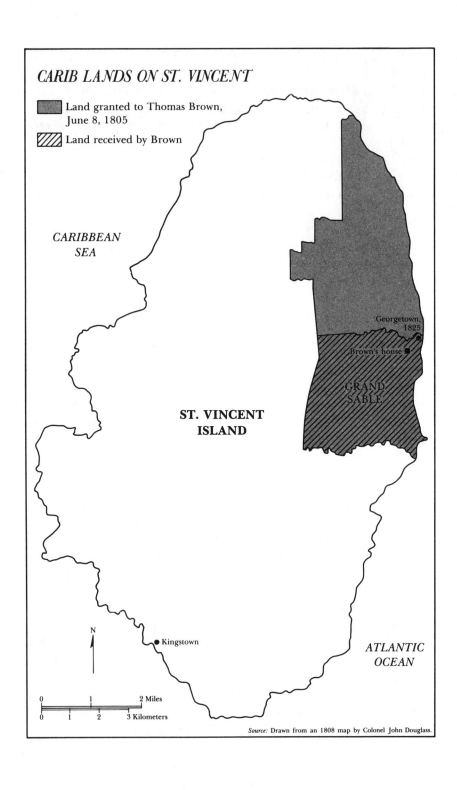

CARIB LANDS ON ST. VINCENT

■ Land granted to Thomas Brown,
June 8, 1805

▨ Land received by Brown

CARIBBEAN
SEA

Georgetown,
1825

Brown's house ■

GRAND
SABLE

ST. VINCENT
ISLAND

N

● Kingstown

ATLANTIC
OCEAN

0   1   2 Miles
0   1   2   3 Kilometers

Source: Drawn from an 1808 map by Colonel John Douglass.

authority to grant land, but he gave temporary permits to certain influential planters to occupy the Carib lands. These gentlemen immediately began sugar cultivation, which Bentinck complained was against the spirit of the arrangement but which he allowed to continue.[15]

Bentinck was reprimanded by Lord Camden for permitting settlement without authorization. Camden transmitted instructions to Beckwith, the new governor, on June 8, 1805, that six thousand acres from the Byera River to Morne Garon Mountains had been granted by His Majesty to Thomas Brown as of that date. Beckwith posted a notice that the grant had been awarded and then went on an extended visit to Barbados, supposing that Council President Drewry Ottley would clear off the squatters. Ottley took no action at first because the planters in question were friends of his and, finally, because he died. His successor, Robert Paul, decided to wait for Beckwith to do the unpleasant business. One of the planters, Alexander Cruickshank, was Speaker of the House; another, Andrew Ross, was a member of the Council. All were justices of the peace and officers in the militia. In their opinion, they had helped win the war against the Caribs and they deserved the forfeited territory more than did Brown, whatever his services in America. They addressed a petition to Brown asking him to sell them the land they were cultivating. He declined, explaining that he had a large contingent of blacks and needed the entire tract. The determined planters engaged a lobbyist, Dr. P. Colquhoun, to present their case in London. Brown was advised that it might take two years to remove the occupants by means of a lawsuit. He could not afford to wait.[16]

When Beckwith returned to St. Vincent in April 1806, he was dismayed to find the situation unchanged. He summoned up all the authority at his command to clear Brown's grant. He published the opinion of His Majesty's solicitor general that Governor Bentinck had no right to grant lands and issued a warrant on May 26, 1806, declaring that persons who continued to occupy the territory would be held in contempt.[17]

At the same time, Beckwith warned the ministry that he expected "very intemperate and improper proceedings" on the part of the planters. He was right; the land question became an obsession, influencing every measure introduced into the assembly by the government. Beckwith took stern measures. First, he removed the offending planters from office and then he dissolved the assembly on September 9,

1806, and called for new elections. Beckwith's faction won control of the House and squatter Cruickshank was defeated by a large majority in his bid for reelection.[18] Even that did no good.

Beckwith's flurry of activity was prompted by the arrival on the island of his old comrade in arms, Thomas Brown. Brown had written to Acting Governor Ottley on November 16, 1805, from Newton House expressing his anxiety that all should be in readiness for his arrival. He served notice that he was about to order his agents at Caicos to embark his people. He engaged a ship of four hundred tons to convey them and estimated that it would take three or four trips from Caicos to St. Vincent to transport them all. He intended to bring over 643 Negroes and fifteen white overseers. It would cost him £25,000 to make the crossing.[19] Hetty would make the long voyage with him to their new home. Mary, now a young lady of sixteen, would accompany them, but the younger children would finish their education in Whitby under the supervision of Mrs. Farr before they joined their parents. Edward and Tom Cayley, Brown's nephews, were members of the party. Edward would act as Brown's attorney and Tom as manager of the estate.

On May 2 Brown made an urgent personal appeal to the St. Vincent Council stating that he needed to occupy the grant immediately. There followed Beckwith's increasingly frantic series of proclamations, climaxed on October 22, 1806, by the notice that Brown's servants had arrived on the island and Brown had legal rights to occupancy.[20]

Even under the most extreme pressure, the planters refused to budge. Only one, John Gerald Morgan, agreed to yield seventeen hundred acres to Brown after the Caicos contingent had actually landed on St. Vincent and had no place else to go. Morgan had made little or no improvements on the property but hoped to be compensated by Brown or the government. Three witnesses testified that there were no buildings on the property and that cattle had been turned loose to keep down the vegetation. Nevertheless, Morgan demanded payment of £5,000 from Brown. It was a preposterous claim, but after a while it was taken seriously by the government. Morgan's estate was called Grand Sable. Alexander Cruickshank's Mount Bentinck adjoined Grand Sable; other estates were called Langley Park, Rabacca, Lot #14, Waterloo, Orange Hall, and Tourama.[21] The eight plantations that occupied the six thousand acres of the former Carib territory were separated from the lower half of the island by a rocky ridge that jutted into the sea. The rising ground behind this peninsula was called Mount Young, and twenty acres was designated there as a military reserve. A strip of land three chains wide along the coast was also retained by the crown.

The Brown party disembarked at Kingstown and made their way along the narrow coastal road on the eastern side of the island. When he climbed the last barrier, the Point Young ridge, Thomas Brown might have gazed down at his new possessions with mixed feelings. It was a splendid sight; the Carib plantations stretched for six miles along the gentle curve of the coast. Two miles inland the land rose sharply and formed the inaccessible wilderness of the Morne Garon Mountains. The highest peak was the brooding volcanic mountain 4,048 feet high called Soufriere. The mountains and the surf formed beautiful scenery, yet they could be dangerous. A hot fury rumbled in Soufriere's depths, and the prevailing easterly winds made the seacoast unsafe for sailing ships.[22]

Brown's elation at first sight of his new home must have been tempered by frustration. Despite his friend Beckwith's best efforts, little more than one-fourth of his promised grant was available to him. His support in high places had been firm enough while he was in London to represent his own interests. In his absence his agent, John Turnbull, had less political clout. William Pitt's death in January 1806 was a blow to Brown's cause. The first indication that Brown was losing influence was contained in a dispatch from Downing Street to Beckwith dated October 3, 1806. The Lords Commissioners of the Treasury were beginning to have doubts about the wisdom of the six-thousand-acre grant to Brown. If Brown had actually taken possession of the Carib tract he could keep it. If he had not, then Beckwith should not deliver it until the Lords Commissioners made up their minds.[23] Beckwith and Brown must have uttered imprecations regarding the Lords Commissioners, the obdurate squatters, and fate in general.

At Brown's suggestion, Beckwith sent for Colonel John Douglass, the engineer of Fort Cornwallis and former deputy superintendent of Indian affairs, to survey Brown's grant. Douglass's commission was dated October 8, 1807. Douglass worked rapidly and completed his map by February 1808. The back line was especially difficult because it ran along mountains and across steep ravines. Douglass's map revealed the actual situation of the squatters on Brown's grant. Brown occupied the southernmost tract. He had already erected sugar works and planted cane. His house, as well as "Negro houses," were shown, and there were structures, probably warehouses, on the ocean or "shipping bay." The colonel's neighbor was Robert Brown. "Mr. Cruickshanks Sugar Works" were next, then Dr. John Smith's house, Robert Sutherland's house and sugar works, and the house of recently deceased Andrew Ross. The planters scored points with the Lords Commissioners by defending widow Ross's right to remain on her husband's plantation. All the plantations cultivated sugarcane. The area must have looked then much as it does today, an extensive plain between the mountains and the sea, with continuous fields of cane. Only on Brown's Grand Sable plantation was there evidence of coffee cultivation. Patches of woodland interrupted the cane fields.[24]

Even as he labored at establishing his army of workers on the fraction of his grant, Brown suffered an emotional blow. Hetty, his child bride and wife of eighteen years, died on April 9, 1807. The best evidence of his devotion to her was his decision not to bury her body in that uncertain land with his title still in question. He had her body prepared for transport to England. Mary remained on St. Vincent, perhaps because she had taken a fancy to Thomas Weatherall, one of Brown's overseers. The colonel accompanied his wife's remains to Whitby in June 1808. She was buried as befitted the mistress of Newton House. After resting in state in the old parish church for two days, her body was interred near Jonas in the churchyard near the ancient abbey ruins.[25]

After a family reunion at Newton House with Mrs. Farr, Tom, Charles, Susan, and George, the colonel went down to London to attend to business. He took lodgings in the fashionable Holylands Hotel on the Strand near Somerset House. Jonas, Jr., had stayed there when he was attending to family matters in London. The Holylands Coffee House was one of the first coffee houses in Europe. A travelers' guide in London, written in 1793, had high praise for Holylands: "In this House every convenience is consistent with appearance and if the charges be now and then a little above par, the advance should be excused by the style in which everything is performed."[26] Brown was clearly living above his means; his finances were in a critical condition. He owed a fortune for transporting his people and setting up his plantation. He and his family had always dealt with John Moss, the Liverpool banker, and Brown turned to Moss again to borrow £20,000. He had to pledge to Moss his lifetime half-pay as lieutenant colonel. Two years later, Brown's indebtedness to Moss had increased to £35,000.[27]

A major setback to Brown's chances of winning possession of his grant was the naming of his friend and advocate George Beckwith as governor of Barbados on October 8, 1808. That was the beginning of Beckwith's glory years. He was responsible for the conquest of the island of Martinique in 1809, received the thanks of the House of Lords on April 14, 1809, and was knighted on May 1. In 1810 he won new honors for the conquest of Guadeloupe.[28] As his fortunes waxed, Brown's waned.

The new governor of St. Vincent, Sir Charles Brisbane, arrived on the island in January 1809. He too was a hero, having commanded the expedition that captured the Dutch island of Curaçao. He was met with a chorus of pleas by the planters on Brown's grant to intercede on their behalf. He agreed with their contention that they had as much right to the land as Brown did. Brown's services in America were unknown and unimportant to them; their services in the recent Carib war were well remembered on the island. Brisbane was persuaded that the dispossessed planter James Gerald Morgan was entitled to £5,000 for yielding the Grand Sable plantation to Brown and that Brown should pay. Brown's managers challenged that sum as exorbitant. Morgan had erected no structures and had merely kept cattle on the property. Brisbane was sympathetic to the plight of the widow, Ann Ross, and gave her money to send her son to England for his education. Finally, Brisbane did not trust the Douglass map and had the tract surveyed a second time. The two men who did the work complained that they ran the back line at the risk of their lives only to find that the new survey corresponded with that done by Douglass.[29]

Meanwhile, the Lords Commissioners of the Treasury had finally made their decision. On June 13, 1809, their secretary, George Harrison, informed Brisbane that it was the intention of their Lordships that Brown be granted 2,330 acres of cultivable land in the Carib country, including the roughly 1,700 acres he already had. The planters occupying the grant could keep 3,670 acres. One-half of the appraised value would be paid to Brown as compensation for the loss of the land, and the other half would be retained by the government.[30] The judgment seemed eminently fair to Charles Shephard, who wrote a history of St. Vincent in 1831: "Colonel Browne received a part of this money, amounting to about £25,000, the remainder was at the disposal of the Government; by this judicious arrangement the land was divided into eight large estates, the different claimants were apparently satisfied, and a great and permanent increase of the revenue had been secured."[31]

Unfortunately for Thomas Brown, Governor Brisbane made no effort to increase Brown's holdings from the 1,700 actually in his possession to the 2,330 he was supposed to receive. Even worse, Brisbane reserved 172 acres for a new town on Brown's property. Only 20 acres and a narrow strip along the seacoast had been so designated in Lord Camden's original grant. Nor was the anticipated £25,000 forthcoming. Brisbane appointed a committee to decide the amount of the award to Morgan, the original occupant. The committee decided that £5,000 was due Morgan out of Brown's account. Brown's attorneys on St. Vincent, Edward Cayley and Johnson Littledale, objected that the committee consisted of interested parties and stated that the value of the property when Brown received it was more nearly £500. The government proceeded to withhold £5,450 from Brown's award but assigned only £1,000 to Morgan and kept the rest.[32]

Attorney Colquhoun, who represented the Carib planters in London, was also Brisbane's confidant. It was a shock to them both when Brisbane received new orders from Downing Street dated February 2, 1810. On the face of it, the letter was innocuous enough, but the first few words were enough to alarm Brisbane: "Upon the application of Col. Browne," the instructions were sent out. The implication was that Brown (he added the final "e" at this time) had gained the ear of Lord Liverpool, secretary of state. The letter referred to the Douglass survey and directed the governor to deduct the lands granted to the different occupants and then grant the residue of 6,000 acres of cultivable land to Brown in a manner agreeable to Brown. The letter was signed by Cecil Jenkinson, Liverpool's secretary. Accompanying the letter was a schedule of the amount of land assigned to each planter. Brown's share was 4,287 acres. This statement bore the signature of George Harrison, secretary of the Lords Commissioners of the Treasury, and was dated February 2, 1810. The Jenkinson letter was little more than a reiteration of the previous year's instructions, except that it referred to Douglass's plat rather than Brisbane's survey and it stipulated that the lands assigned to Brown should be agreeable to him. The accompanying schedule considerably enlarged the acreage due Brown from 2,330 to 4,287. The arithmetic of the two dispatches was not consistent; the second assumed a larger total acreage than 6,000.[33]

Brisbane suspected foul play immediately and confided to Colquhoun, "There appears something so completely outre in this decision that I am at a loss to account for it, particularly so when you mention nothing of such an order. Probably Brown is playing crooked tricks and has smuggled these orders thro the obedience of some of the clerks by bribery and has had address enough to escape your vigilance." Colquhoun was equally distressed: "This is precisely what your exertions were trying to obviate, because the above distribution will take up all the eligible Land in the Charaib Country." It would later become evident that Brisbane wanted some of the "eligible land" for himself. On July 10, 1810, Colquhoun informed George Harrison that Brisbane believed that the February 2 dispatches were fabrications.[34]

In London, Brown did not comport himself any differently than before. He wrote to his son Tom on March 16, 1810, that he was pushing an appeal through the House of Lords. Presumably the appeal would have forced Brisbane to follow directions in a way that would be to Brown's advantage. When the appeal procedure was finished, he intended to return to St. Vincent. He had heard from Tom Cayley that there were good prospects for the sugar crop. He could not resist dropping the names of those with whom he was dining: Lady Charlotte Rawdon, Lord and Lady Mount, and his old friends Lord and Lady Kingston. There was other happy news from St. Vincent that year. Mary had lost her shyness sufficiently to accept a proposal of marriage from Tom Weatherall.[35]

On December 6, 1810, Brown interceded with Lord Liverpool on behalf of some of his old friends in the Bahamas. They felt neglected by the government because of a long delay in appointing a governor. They informed Brown that they intended to petition the king if they did not hear from Lord Liverpool soon. Brown was ready to discuss the matter at Liverpool's convenience. Whether as a result of Brown's influence or not, Charles Cameron was named governor.[36]

During that same December 1810 Brown began to write a book entitled "Stratagems of War." Between December 28 and March 26, 1811, Brown delivered 177 sheets of manuscript to the shop of Thomas Steele, scrivener, in Chancery Lane. The colonel became a familiar figure to Steele and his assistants. That fact was of crucial importance in Brown's impending litigation.[37]

By March 1811, Brisbane was in London insisting on a criminal prosecution of Brown. Brown attempted to call on Brisbane at the Clarendon Hotel, where the governor was staying, but was told that Brisbane was out. Brown had learned from George Harrison the object of Brisbane's mission. On March 7, 1811, Brown made a sworn deposition before a magistrate "that of the contents of two letters said to be written, the one by George Harrison, Esq., Secretary to the Treasury and the other by Lord Liverpool to the Governor of Saint Vincent he is totally ignorant."[38]

In due time, Harrison forwarded the statement to Vicary Gibbs, the attorney general, who gathered depositions from Brisbane, George Harrison, Cecil Jenkinson, and the clerks in Thomas Steele's establishment. It was Brown's misfortune that Gibbs was his prosecutor. Gibbs had a reputation for harshness and severity. His biographer noted that "his manner was so caustic and bitter and sometimes so rude and uncivil" that his reputation was deserved.[39]

Brown was evidently shocked and embarrassed to receive a summons to appear for trial at Westminister Hall in February 1812. Brown admitted that he and other St. Vincent residents had employed Steele's clerks to draw up documents but denied that the two papers in question were done at his direction. Brown submitted his honorable record to prove that he was incapable of such an act. He expressed "great abhorrence and detestation" at the idea of forgery even if the kingdom of Great Britain could be so obtained. Brown suggested that Steele's books be checked.[40]

It was too late for that. Gibbs had obtained a deposition from Steele to the effect that Brown had indeed brought the two documents to be copied. Steele named the two clerks who actually did the work. Steele's books contained the damning notation that on February 2, 1810, a "Fair Copy Statement of Crown Grant" was charged to Brown's account.[41]

The trial on February 22 was sensational but short. Brown was defended by James Alan Park, who was noted not for his eloquence but for his piety and sincerity. His defect, according to his biographer "was a certain irritability about trifles, which too frequently excited the jocularity of the bar." Brown stoutly maintained his innocence and stated that he had received the documents in good faith. He knew the identity of the high official who gave him the papers but had been advised by thirteen out of fifteen of friends whom he had consulted not to reveal the name. Brown's attorney adopted the strategy of simply bringing in prominent character witnesses to testify to Brown's integrity. Thus Lord Moira, Sir Alured Clarke, Deputy Indian Superintendent Charles Shaw, and others praised Brown as a man of honor.

To his surprise, Brown was not called upon to speak in his own behalf. One possible reason is that the stress had begun to show. Among the documents relating to the trial is a scribbled note stating that Lord Moira believed that Brown was "a little deranged" during the trial. In his correspondence with his family Brown referred to the excruciating headaches that plagued him from time to time and were caused by the blows he received in 1775. He took laudanum to relieve the pain. Whether pain, drug, or stress was the cause of Brown's derangement, he was not put on the stand.[42]

Gibbs, the prosecutor, charged that Brown "unlawfully, knowingly and fraudulently did falsely make, forge and counterfeit and cause and procure to be falsely made, forged and counterfeit" the two documents in question, namely the Cecil Jenkinson letter of February 2, 1810, and George Harrison's schedule of land allotment of the same date. The prosecutor took some liberty with the facts, stating that the government gave Brown £30,000 and assigned him nearly three thousand acres, that he was at first satisfied with this arrangement, but that he "very soon resolved, by the present fraud to get the money and also the additional number of acres." Brisbane was presented as one who was completely taken in by Brown's scheme and was in the process of carrying out the fraudulent orders when he became involved in a dispute with Brown's agents on the island which led him to seek the advice of the home government. Thus, quite by accident, he discovered the fraud.[43]

If Brown had been allowed to testify, he would have pointed out that he was awarded £20,000 rather than £30,000, and 2,330 acres rather than 3,000. Even then he had not been allowed (and would not be allowed) to occupy more than 1,700 acres. Brisbane suspected "crooked tricks" from the first and took the initiative in uncovering the wrongdoing. These facts were not germane to the trial, except that the jury received the impression that Brown was unreasonable not to have been satisfied with such a generous arrangement. The prosecutor called Harrison and Jenkinson to testify that they had not signed the documents, Brisbane to state that he had received them, and Steele and his clerks to affirm that Brown had copies of the documents made.

Lord Ellenborough, the presiding judge, instructed the jury that the testimony to Brown's good character could not outweigh the evidence. The jury had to decide whether a forgery had been perpetrated and whether Brown "superintended" the fraud. Thus instructed, the jury spent only a few minutes in deliberation before returning a verdict of guilty.[44]

The transcript of the trial concludes with the terrible sentence, "The said Thomas Browne for his Offences aforesaid whereof he is Impeached and Convicted as aforesaid be Imprisoned in his Majesty's Gaol of Newgate for the Term of two years now, next ensuing and he the said Thomas Browne is Now Committed to the Custody of the Keeper of the said Gaol of Newgate to be by him kept in safe Custody in Execution of this Judgment."[45]

Thomas Brown, lieutenant colonel of the King's Rangers and superintendent of Indians, was thus disgraced in the eyes of the world. London newspapers broadcast the story of the trial. The *Augusta* (Georgia) *Chronicle* reprinted the report from the *London Star* with the note that many Augustans would doubtless remember Thomas Brown,[46] but there was no editorial gloating.

After his conviction, Brown wrote an interesting letter to one Litchfield in the Treasury Office. He admitted to being "a total stranger to the forms and practice of a court of judicature" and wondered if he should have revealed the name of the person responsible. In any case, that person had promised to write a letter that would clear Brown of blame. Brown's letter was forwarded to Gibbs, the crusty prosecutor, who thought that "the whole story has so much of improbability in it and carries as much the air of fiction as any that can be imagined." Still, he thought it worthwhile to check out Brown's story. Accordingly, one of his assistants called on Brown in the King's Bench and asked for the name of the guilty person. Brown replied that he would have to consult the friends who had previously advised him not to divulge the name. If he decided to reveal the name, he would first insist that the person leave England. The man from the attorney general's office doubted that the public interest would be served by that solution.[47]

Whether Brown's friends advised him against it, or whether the story was a work of fiction as the attorney general thought, there is no evidence that anyone else was later implicated in the affair. What conclusions can be drawn from this bizarre episode in Brown's career?

There appears to be no doubt that Brown brought the false documents to Steele's shop for copying. When he denied doing that, he was lying or his memory failed him. Brown's defense was that someone in a government office was responsible. If Brown knew that the letters were forged, regardless of who arranged it, he would still have been culpable in the eyes of the court. There is the possibility that Brown was telling the truth, that someone gave the documents to him and he did not know they were forged. This would have explained Brown's complete lack of furtiveness in his dealings with Steele and his staff. They remembered him smoking comfortably while he waited for his papers. He continued to use the same stationers after the forged documents were copied and, in fact, invited the authorities to check Steele's books. These do not seem to be the actions of a man with something to hide.

There is also the puzzling fact that the forged documents would not have helped Brown appreciably. He would have had no more money from the government, and the additional acreage would not have been cultivable. Why he would have risked his reputation to gain a dubious advantage is the puzzle.

Finally, there is the testimony of Brown's entire career. Anyone familiar with his life would not have believed him capable of a crooked trick, as Brisbane (who did not know Brown) called it. In fact, Brown's first defense was to send his accusers the résumé of his exploits during the Revolution and his subsequent career, including the testimonials he had received from time to time. How could such a person be capable of so devious an act? Only Brown knew the truth. His friends had to decide whether there was a flaw in his character or whether he was the victim of a bureaucratic nightmare. Before the world, he stood convicted. Charles Shephard, historian of St. Vincent and a contemporary of Brown's, phrased his opinion as circumspectly as possible: "During a long and protracted discussion of claims and counter claims, which lasted until the year 1809, an unfortunate act of misconduct on the part of the Colonel occurred, which alienated the liberal views of His Majesty's Government from him."[48]

Although sentenced to Newgate, Brown was incarcerated in the King's Bench Prison, which primarily housed debtors. Brown was in debt to the amount of £35,000, and this may have been the reason he was assigned to the King's Bench. Conditions in the English jails had not improved measurably since James Edward Oglethorpe exposed their evils a century earlier. The King's Bench Prison contained about two hundred rooms, which were rented to the inmates. Eight of the rooms were state rooms and brought a higher fee. Upon arrival the prisoner was expected to pay a commitment fee. Although it was illegal to refuse to admit a prisoner who could not pay this fee, the marshal of the King's Bench was known to have done so.

In 1813, when a parliamentary committee inspected the prison, about eighty rooms were occupied singly. There were six to eight persons in the other rooms because the prisoners could sell shares in rooms they rented. The practice was so profitable that former prisoners continued to rent and to let out their rooms after they left jail. Nonprisoners, including turnkeys and other staff members, rented out rooms. Women and children were not allowed in the prison, and yet the committee discovered 180 women and children living there. The marshal, of course, received his share of the fees. The committee was of the opinion that the £2,600 per year which the marshal collected was "surely too much to be drawn from the pockets of debtors." Although the law forbade prison keepers to act as publicans, the marshal made £872 a year on the gin, wine, and ale sold in prison. Except to collect his fees, the marshal rarely set foot in the prison.

According to an ancient but curious tradition, those who could pay for the privilege could live outside the prison, provided that they remained within two and a half miles. Others might purchase the privilege of absenting themselves from nine in the morning until nine at night. No effort was made to clean the prison. There were no allowances for fuel, bedding, or blankets. There was no infirmary, no medicine for the sick. The committee discovered a man dying of jaundice in a room that housed five men, two women, and two children. In short, the King's Bench Prison was a grim and terrible place for those who could not bribe privileges for themselves.[49]

Thomas Brown served out the two-year sentence in the King's Bench. Extant letters dated April 7, 1812, and December 28, 1814, were both from the King's Bench. How he fared is not recorded. Apparently, there were some dangerous moments. Brown later recalled that while in prison his life was threatened on two occasions. A man named Matthew Daly saved him "from the poinard [sic] of a crew of desperate assassins." Daly, whose uncle possessed a considerable estate in Ireland, also helped Brown with a timely loan; otherwise, as Brown put it, "I should certainly have been starved for want of money."[50]

During the first year of Brown's imprisonment, fate dealt another cruel turn. His daughter Mary, the shy girl who hated to be away from her father, died at St. Vincent, probably giving birth to her first child, Anne Hetty. Her husband, Brown's overseer Tom Weatherall, brought Mary's body to Whitby for burial, even as Thomas had transported Hetty. Space was at a premium in the crowded churchyard on the cliff, and Mary was buried in the same grave as her mother. Many years later one of the residents of Whitby remembered that Tom Weatherall was so overcome with grief that he left the burial site quickly, putting spurs to his horse.[51]

Thomas Brown's bad luck in 1812 extended even farther. On April 30, 1812, the long-dormant Mount Soufriere suddenly erupted, spewing volcanic ash over the entire northern end of the island. The weight of the falling debris crushed an overseer's house on the Grand Sable plantation, killing a man named Phillips. The Speaker of the St. Vincent Assembly transmitted a list of estimated losses sustained by the Carib land planters. The damage to Brown's property was put at £7,392. Brown received £1,580 compensation from the government. He might have complained that he was awarded a lower percentage than the other planters and would have been justified in suspecting Governor Brisbane of discrimination.[52]

When Charles Brisbane returned to St. Vincent on August 7, 1812, he immediately turned unwelcome attention upon Brown's Grand Sable estate. Brisbane's conduct from the beginning demonstrated a hostile attitude toward Brown. After the forgery trial Brisbane was actively opposed to Brown. He wrote to the secretary of state, Lord Bathurst, on November 6, 1812, that he had decided to lay out a town and build a church on the Grand Sable estate and had reserved 132 acres out of the 1,700 acres for that purpose. Brown's nephew Tom Cayley and son-in-law Tom Weatherall forcibly prevented a survey being made. Cayley declared his firm determination to die on the spot rather than yield the best part of Brown's property. There were more than six hundred blacks working at Grand Sable, and the managers could not afford to give up any more land. Brisbane announced his determination to send troops to take over Grand Sable.[53]

Cayley and Weatherall immediately appealed to Bathurst, explaining that Brown had received the tract of 1,700 acres as part of a grant of 6,000 acres. Confident of receiving the entire 6,000 acres, Brown had moved his servants from Caicos to St. Vincent at enormous expense. The original grant contained no reservation except 20 acres for a military post on Mount Young. Nevertheless, Brisbane had arbitrarily decided to take the most highly cultivated portion of Grand Sable for a town.[54]

Bathurst sharply reprimanded Brisbane for acting without authorization. Brisbane excused himself and proceeded to give a curiously inexact version of the history of Brown's property. The grant of 1,700 acres, he declared, was obtained by forged dispatches and on that grant land was reserved for a church, fort, barracks, and shipping place. The statement is remarkable. Brisbane claimed authorization for his town on the basis of a document for which he had prosecuted Brown. He chose to ignore the valid instructions he had received in 1809 from George Harrison on behalf of the Lords Commissioners of the Treasury that Brown was entitled to 2,330 acres of cultivable land.[55]

Brisbane was persistent and had his way. The town carved out of Brown's estate was called Georgetown. The principal street was named Regent Street in honor of the prince regent. Incredibly, Brisbane tried to acquire a 700-acre portion of Brown's tract for himself. He was prevented from seizing it when Brown's managers again protested to the government. Brisbane continued his efforts to detach a third part of Brown's estate until Brown's death.Then Brown's heirs took up the struggle.[56]

It was an arbitrary justice that demanded that Thomas Brown serve two years in prison for attempting to enlarge his property but failed to protect his rights to maintain what was legally his. Brisbane refused to permit Brown to claim the 2,330 acres due him and succeeded in reducing the amount in Brown's possession. The princely estate on Caicos was a matter of the past, although Brown maintained a cattle farm there. Brown's great expectations were gradually diminishing.

As his sentence in the King's Bench neared an end, Brown's thoughts turned to the future. He was sixty-four in 1814, but his health was good, except for the painful headaches that were souvenirs of the cruel ministrations of the Liberty Boys. He followed the progress of the war in America as well as he could in the newspapers. On December 29, 1814, he wrote to the prime minister, Lord Liverpool, offering his services. He was confused about the identity of the General Jackson who commanded the American forces on the southern frontier. He explained that Jackson "is a man whom I obliged when in Georgia to scamper off for safety from the field of battle."

Actually James Jackson, Brown's adversary, had died in 1806. This was a different Jackson, and the British would learn more about him on January 8, 1815, on the bloody plain outside New Orleans.

In his letter Brown assumed that the Americans would reject the Treaty of Ghent and that the war would continue. He recited his war record without the restraints of modesty. He said of the Indians, "I commanded them as Superintendent and led their kings and warriors to battle in twenty five different actions with invariable success." He took credit for attaching them to the Spanish interests after the war. He was convinced that he could once again rally the southern Indians against the Americans: "There is no person in Great Britain who possesses interest and influence to detach these Indians from the Americans except myself." He required only the assistance of a regiment of light troops with two howitzers and suitable supplies for the Indians such as they were accustomed to receiving during the last war. Brown suggested that Sir Alured Clarke was prepared to give references. Apparently Sir Alured had not lost faith in Brown as a result of the forgery trial. The letter was postmarked "the King's Bench," however, and that must have been a consideration in Liverpool's decision not to take Brown up on his offer.[57]

Apparently Liverpool had the courtesy to respond to Brown about another matter, as did his Royal Highness, the Duke of York. Both officials expressed interest in Brown's lifesaving cork belts, which he had devised for the use of his workers in St. Vincent. Loading casks of sugar on vessels was a tricky business along the windward shore. Brown's life belts had saved several men who were unable to swim. When three hundred Englishmen were lost in the sinking of a transport vessel near Falmouth, Brown argued that cork belts would have saved many. Brown suggested that the belts might also be used by a small war party in crossing a river to surprise an enemy. A cork could be inserted into the muzzle of the rifle and a feather into the flintlock. That was what his Rangers had done, he explained, but, of course, his Rangers were excellent swimmers and did not need lifesaving devices.[58]

During the year 1814, Brown penned a letter to his daughter Susan, which provides a glimpse at a different facet of his character. He was a loving father and not ashamed to express his feelings. The salutation speaks volumes. He addressed Susan as "My dearest Puss." She was not too old for a pet name that must have been bestowed in childhood. Brown would send a cask of sugar to Newton House so that Mrs. Farr could preserve fruit. He suggested a recipe for apple dumplings, American style. There was a message for eldest son, Tom, who, at age twenty-two, was still at Newton House but was about to begin his career in the ministry. Susan's aunt Sarah Wilkinson was well and in Brown's opinion "an uncommon clever woman." She was uncommonly hospitable, also, as events would prove. Brown wished that he could assist her financially, "but at present I am incapable." As soon as he had the funds, he would ask Mrs. Farr to let Susan come to London with Tom. They could stay with Uncle Jonas and Aunt Elizabeth in Hull, with Brown's half-sister Ann in Lincoln, and with the Wilkinsons in Fitzroy Square. Brown would take delight in showing her the sights of London. Lord and Lady Kingston were still loyal to Brown, and Susan would stay with them at Norfolk on the way home. She should keep a journal of everything worthy of observation. The letter ended as sensitively as it began: "Give your Grandmama a kiss for me and believe me my darling your ever most affectionate father."[59]

When his two-year sentence was over, Brown had almost insuperable financial obstacles to overcome. He owned £31,943 to John Moss, the Liverpool banker. If it was not reduced to £15,000 by June 30, 1817, he would lose his property in St. Vincent to Moss.[60] In this exigency he thought of his Indian lands in Florida. They would bring him wealth beyond reckoning, if only he could capitalize on his claim. He wrote to an old acquaintance in Spanish Florida that he intended to return there and begin to cultivate the extensive territory his red children had given him. He proposed to sell naval stores to the government of the United States as well as to Spain. He could dispose of large tracts and plant sea island cotton on the rest. He hoped to greet his friend in person, "provided you think I can do it with safety." Whether he was worried about lingering animosities or the unsettled conditions in Florida in that year is not clear. In any case, he did not return to Florida, but he never gave up hope of claiming his wilderness empire.[61] A less chimerical asset was Newton House, and the decision to sell it must have been painful. He had to give up Whitby or St. Vincent, and the latter's potential sugar production outweighed the sentimental value of the former. Brown's family bid their sad farewells to their friends in Whitby and accepted the hospitality of the Wilkinsons in Fitzroy Square while they waited to return to St. Vincent. Tom would not accompany them. He had wooed and won a minister's daughter, Anne McElreath. They were married in 1817, and Tom began his ministry, assisting his father-in-law in the village of Ellerburn in Yorkshire. A year later their first child was born. The Reverend Thomas then acquired a church of his own in Thornton, near Ellerburn and not far from Whitby.[62]

Thus John Moss of Liverpool became master of Newton House. He had long since earned Brown's animosity; "that scoundrel Moss," Brown called him, and he wanted no more dealings with Moss. He found another banking house in the firm of Nathaniel Chauncey, Robert Lang, and Phillip Lucas, which agreed to assume Brown's remaining mortgage of £19,365 with the St. Vincent property as collateral.[63] The new loan rescued Brown from embarrassment as well as harassment. It was said that Brown had to hide from his creditors in the Mint or some such place of refuge. Brown's grandson wrote that Brown had to leave England to avoid his creditors and therefore returned to St. Vincent. Apparently, Brown appealed to the House of Lords for the remainder of the money due him from the government but never received the entire amount. Exactly how much he was owed is a matter of dispute. When his agent, Matthew Daly, wrote him that the Treasury was supposed to pay £5,000, Brown quickly corrected him: "The sum their Lordship are indebted to me is Forty Thousand pounds for the lands of mine sold by their lordships."[64] As with his lands in Florida, Brown's claims upon the government remained an unrealized asset.

Thomas Brown left England for the last time in 1817, never to return. His mother-in-law, Sarah Farr, his sons Charles and George, his daughter Susan, and Nancy, his black housekeeper went with him. Tom Cayley had done all that Brown could have wished as the manager of Grand Sable. A tunnel had been cut through the hard rock of the Mount Young peninsula, permitting the coastal road to reach Brisbane's new town on the Grand Sable estate. The tunnel gave Brown's workers access to the sheltered bay south of the promontory where ship loading was easier.[65]

Brown built a proper mansion for himself and his family and named it Montague House in honor of his ancestor Sir Anthony Browne, Viscount Montague, master of horse for King Henry VIII. The house overlooked the broad plain of sugarcane. From his veranda, Brown could see the rolling surf, and along the shore ran the windward highway. The little village of Georgetown was struggling into existence out beyond Brown's sugar mills. Governor Brisbane obtained money for a new church, and the Carib lands were duly christened Charlotte Parish.[66]

Ironically, the church, completed in 1820 and dedicated to the Trinity, was Brisbane's one benefaction to the Brown family. After the colonel's death, the Reverend Thomas Alexander Murray Browne would become the rector of the parish. The church and its cemetery were clearly visible from Brown's house. The house sat on an elevation, and behind it the slopes of Morne Garon Mountains rose sharply. Brown must have reflected about his career and his search for a permanent home, from Whitby to Brownsborough to St. Augustine, Abaco, and Grand Caicos. Grand Sable was the most beautiful location of all. A visitor in 1846 would write, "St. Vincent is full of lovely little valleys and the isolated knolls offering the most exquisite sites for houses and presenting the most delightful panoramic views."[67] Brown confided to his brother Jonas that his estate produced more than five hundred heavy hogsheads of sugar each year, valued at twelve to fifteen thousand pounds sterling. His sugar, he boasted, always found ready buyers. It was usually the first sugar to be sold on the English market, and it was bought before it was unloaded. His statement is borne out by the record. In 1828 Grand Sable shipped out 650,717 pounds of sugar, 11,297 gallons of rum, and 14,595 gallons of molasses. During that year there were 661 blacks working on the plantation.[68]

Brown displayed an affection for his black workers reminiscent of his relationship with his "red children." He gave certificates of freedom to those who, as he put it, "had during the whole of their lives given the most unequivocal proofs of their regard and affection" for him. He set aside an annuity for his oldest and most faithful servant, Nancy, and gave her a house on the plantation. Many of his servants had adopted the name Browne; in his will, he remembered Charlotte Browne, Mary, her daughter, Sally, the widow of the late Simon Browne and nurse to Brown's son, Tom. Two of his legatees were still managing his cattle farm on Caicos, Maurice Moore Browne and Cyree Browne. If the Brownes are well represented on St. Vincent today, it is because they had a good start.[69]

By 1821 Brown was able to tell his brother that one more good crop would clear him of debt, except for £2,500 he owed to one Robinson and about £2,000 to various individuals in London who had come to his aid when he was in need. Among the happy experiences of these autumn years was the marriage of his daughter Susan to Allan MacDowall in the year 1818. MacDowall was one of a proud clan of Highlanders from western Scotland, which, according to one of his descendants, "by marriages retrieved the effects of the persecutions of Robert the Bruce, their cruel enemy." MacDowall owned a 350-acre estate called Park Hill on which he cultivated arrowroot.[70]

The last years of Brown's life were marred by a bitter quarrel with his mother-in-law. Brown told Jonas that she had deserted him at a time he was so ill he nearly died. She took the two boys to London with her. Brown forgave George, who in the meantime had written "a very penitential letter"; Charles, on the other hand, was old enough to know better. In vain had Brown written to Charles to quit his life of idleness in London and return to his duty in St. Vincent. Brown was convinced that Mrs. Farr hoped to get the generous allowance Brown had always given the two boys. Therefore, he sent George's allowance to Tom, his oldest son, and cut off Charles completely.

Sarah Farr made a clean sweep of things when she left. She took all the household articles from the mansion and persuaded two house servants to accompany her. Brown told his brother, "She has not left me a knife, fork, spoon or either table or bed linen which I had sufficient for six families." He intended to have his agent, Matthew Daly, prosecute Mrs. Farr for theft. He had recovered from his severe illness, but he still suffered from headaches. "The only relief I ever experienced," he told Jonas, whose wife, Elizabeth, suffered from migraines, "was from a person's emptying a pail of cold water upon my head. . . . It revives a person most wonderfully and the shock has a most powerful effect." He recommended the treatment to Mrs. Brown.[71]

Brown was in the same angry mood when he wrote to his son Tom. "Is it not a severe reflection of my family for two of my sons to permit themselves to be enveigled away by an unprincipled woman . . . from the duty they owed their parent confined to his bed by sickness?" He asked Tom to take care of George's needs, but Charles would not receive a shilling until "that ungrateful, unnatural vagabond" returned to his duty. As for Mrs. Farr, he never wanted her name mentioned again.[72]

In his letters to his brother Jonas and son Tom, Brown rejected the notion that his agent, Matthew Daly, might be cheating him. But he finally concluded that the man he had esteemed as his most loyal friend had indeed been guilty of robbing him and of forging his name. He resolved to have no more agents; he would henceforth entrust his affairs to Jonas and Tom.[73]

During the twilight of his life Thomas Brown must have enjoyed the company of Anne Hetty Weatherall, his granddaughter, and of Susan's two sons, his grandsons. He had close friends on the island, particularly John Mowbray, who provided companionship during the final years. And, of course, there were Susan and her husband, Allan, to fill his family circle. He had sent for his books and papers, and he may have busied himself with writing. If so, his manuscripts have not survived.

By a happy coincidence, William Wylly, captain in the King's Rangers and attorney general of the Bahamas, was appointed chief justice of St. Vincent in 1822. The two old soldiers had much to talk about: their last campaign in Georgia, the Florida transition, the political battle against Dunmore in the Bahamas. Brown could acquaint Wylly with his own problems with the current government of St. Vincent, and Wylly might have told Brown about the antislavery campaign in the Bahamas he waged. The colonel must have been flattered that Wylly had done him the honor of naming his first son Thomas Brown Wylly.[74]

Thomas Brown died on August 3, 1825, at the age of seventy-five. His passing was reported in the London *Gentleman's Magazine*. It is not known how many of his old friends paid their respects at his funeral. The colonel was buried in the family plot near Trinity Church. Susan could see the grave from the window of her house.[75]

CHAPTER TWELVE

THE LEGEND AND

THE MAN

 The black legend associated with Thomas Brown began to form before his death. The story told by David Ramsay in 1786 that he hanged thirteen prisoners while gloating over their suffering and then handed the other prisoners over to the Indians for torture, which he specifically denied, became more terrible with each telling. Georgia's first historian, Hugh M'Call, began the embellishment: "Feelings had long been banished from his remorseless bosom, and their place inhabited by a fiend of darkness."[1] The Reverend William Bacon Stevens added a note which others copied when he wrote that Brown was "smarting in body and mind, under painful wounds and remembered indignities and true to a nature which gloated in revenge, immediately spread around Augusta detachments of troops and Indians."[2] M'Call suggested, and Stevens stated explicitly, that Brown's infamous behavior was directly attributable to his mistreatment at the hands of the Liberty Boys. The facts make the theory plausible. But the early Georgia historians did not have access to Thomas Brown's papers, in which he continually denied having been guilty of atrocities and maintained that he was not motivated by petty vengeance. He usually added the thought that the severity of his treatment in 1775 would have justified retribution, if he had been so inclined.

The metamorphosis into legend was complete with William Gilmore Simms's "Joscelyn: A Tale of the Revolution," published in 1867. Simms used Brown as the protagonist of his novel. He was portrayed as a monomaniac even before the episode of August 2, 1775; indeed, he brought the attack on himself by the obnoxious speeches which Simms put in his mouth. After the tarring and feath-

219

ering, Brown evolved into a crazed fanatic, as in the passage, "The madman had become endowed with a speech of fire, which sped like a lightning shaft through the assemblage." Simms pictured Brown, in his famous confrontation with Drayton, as deliberately wearing vestiges of tar and feathers to stir up sympathy. The novel concluded with a hand-to-hand combat between Brown, the villain, and Stephen Joscelyn, the hero.[3] The historian Charles Colcock Jones, Jr., achieved the ultimate blend of romance and history in *The History of Georgia* published in 1883. Brown had become thoroughly evil. "Of all the inhuman characters developed during this abnormal period so replete with murder, arson, theft, brutality and crimes too foul for utterance," wrote Jones, "none can be named more notorious than Thomas Brown, Loyalist and colonel in his majesty's service." Jones elaborated on the theme established by his predecessors: "Revenge was the passion sweeter than all others. To his ears the dying groans of the republican were more enjoyable than strains of purest melody."[4]

Jones's version of the black legend became official history. It was bolstered by the evolution of another legend. For a century the Ezechiel Harris House on upper Broad Street in Augusta had been identified as nothing more or less than what it was, the house of Harris, a tobacco merchant, built around 1797. By 1938, however, the house had become the old "White House of the Revolution, or the Mackay House, built in 1750." A guidebook to Augusta printed in that year referred to the circular stairway in the central hall, leading to the attic: "From an immense iron hook in this attic the aforementioned patriots were dropped down the well of the staircase to their deaths. It is said that if one stands on the stairway and counts 13, he will hear a groan." Thus the groans were introduced into history as ghostly incriminations against Thomas Brown.[5]

In 1946 the Richmond County Historical Society was organized to preserve the house. The society turned the building over to the state, which sponsored an extensive restoration. Historical architects, who did not challenge the prerevolutionary dating of the structure, decided that the circular staircase was a later addition and placed the stairway on the back porch. They also revealed that the original color was blue, not white. These revelations were reconciled with the legend. The ghosts of the patriots obligingly groaned on the back stairs. It was explained that the term "white house" was used in slavery days to refer to the big house where the white folk lived and that was why this blue house was the "White House."

Hundreds of tourists visited the house, advertised as "the Mackay House, the shrine of the American Revolution." They heard how the terrible Thomas Brown hanged thirteen prisoners, one for each of the thirteen colonies, and delivered the other prisoners to the Indians for torture. They listened for the groans on the stairs and peered tentatively into the attic, as if they might be intruding on the spirits of the dead heroes. Among others, I never thought to question the identity of the house. In 1975, however, a historian employed by the State Office of Historic Preservation discovered that the house was not the Mackay House after all, but the Ezechiel Harris House. Governor George Busbee denounced the house as a hoax and gave it to a local committee, which turned it over to the city of Augusta. After recovering from their initial anger and embarrassment, Augustans decided that the house was not at fault and that an eighteenth-century structure should be treasured. It became the headquarters of Historic Augusta, Inc., a preservation organization, and more than ever it is a source of pride to the Harrisburg neighborhood.[6]

Although banished from the house, Thomas Brown and the ghosts are not forgotten. The Mackay House was, after all, on the same tract of land as the Harris House. The old stories persist. In 1984 the *Atlanta Constitution* featured an article entitled "Tory's Revenge" in the "Georgia History" column. The account repeated the familiar story of revenge. Thirteen were hanged, "one victim for each of the colonies." The rest were tortured by Indians. The article concluded, "Browne's fate? It is not known, but few colonists wished him well."[7]

Historians eventually began to distinguish between fact and legend. E. Merton Coulter continued to portray Brown as a monster: "Now he took vengeance, tardy though terrible. He scourged and murdered the patriots . . . and he harried and devastated all the surrounding country." Coulter's history was written in 1933, and he saw no reason to revise his opinion in the editions of 1947 and 1960.[8]

The first to question the accuracy of the traditional account was Kenneth Coleman, Coulter's successor as the dean of Georgia historians. Writing in 1958, Coleman distinguished between Tory and Whig versions of the Mackay House hangings.[9]

Gary Olson's treatment of Brown was scholarly and dispassionate. Focusing on the early phases of the war, Olson credited Brown with

222 : The King's Ranger

formulating the plan that became the southern strategy. He concluded that it might have worked if it had been supported properly in 1776.[10]

The most objective and thorough treatment of Brown was a master's thesis written by Martha Condray Searcy in 1972. She had access to the Browne family papers and portrayed her subject in human dimensions. She deferred to tradition by admitting that Brown might have hanged his prisoners for "sheer pleasure" but adds that he might have been carrying out the standing order requiring hanging for those who had broken their paroles. Searcy revealed Brown as an effective military leader, skillful in Indian diplomacy and highly regarded by his superiors. She recognized his role in the establishment of the Panton, Leslie Company in the Florida Indian trade as a contribution of historic importance.[11]

In a later, carefully documented study of the Georgia-Florida border warfare, Searcy compared Brown's Rangers with the Georgia Regiment of Horse and found the former superior in *esprit de corps*, discipline, and skill in guerrilla tactics and credited the leadership qualities of Thomas Brown.[12]

Bernard Bailyn devoted a chapter to Thomas Brown and William Manson in his Pulitzer-prize-winning *Voyagers to the West*. Although Bailyn was primarily interested in Brown's colonization efforts, he also described the wartime activities of "Bloody Colonel Brown." He unaccountably put the number of those alleged to have been hanged by Brown at nineteen and concluded that the truth of the hanging and torturing "cannot be definitely established." But he correctly observed that it was generally believed to be true by Georgia Whigs.[13]

Brown and hundreds of other Loyalists populate the pages of Robert S. Lambert's monumental *South Carolina Loyalists in the American Revolution* (1987). Lambert was primarily interested in numbers and motivation. He concluded that about one-fifth of South Carolina's free population became Loyalists during the Revolution. He admits that they "left little literary evidence that would inform us of their reasons for supporting the British effort to suppress the rebellion." Although Brown is peripheral to his study, Lambert assumes that Brown "yearned for revenge against those who had treated him so brutally in Augusta." He acknowledges that Brown's plan, abetted by Kirkland and promoted by the southern governors, provided the basis for the planning that led to the temporary recovery of Georgia and South Carolina for the crown.[14]

What, then, is Thomas Brown's place in history? There were many places and many moments. On these occasions, he was an active participant, at times influencing the course of history by his leadership and personality.

The opening of Georgia's Ceded Lands in 1773 was an important episode in the colonial history of the province. There were hundreds of prospective settlers, but Thomas Brown's colonizing effort was the most ambitious. Frustrated by the Creek uprising from locating on the Ceded Lands, he established Brownsborough, a settlement that rivaled Augusta for a decade. Perhaps because Brown was a magistrate, court was held in Brownsborough; elections and court sessions alternated between the two towns.

In 1775, when Georgians were taking sides and most of the Loyalists were inclined to maintain a prudent silence, Thomas Brown plunged boldly into the fray. By actively campaigning for a loyal association, he became a marked man. It was no accident that he was singled out for special attention by the Liberty Boys on August 2, 1775. The incident marked the effective beginning of the Revolution in the Georgia backcountry. The way Brown faced his adversaries was a study in courage. The brutal treatment he received compelled the sympathy even of his enemies and cast a stigma on the liberty faction.

After his escape from Georgia, Brown entered South Carolina's history. Whig spokesmen William Henry Drayton and William Tennent recognized Brown as their most implacable and dangerous opponent. By his oratory and example, he assumed a position of leadership which Lord William Campbell acknowledged. Whether or not Brown originated the plan to rescue the backcountry Loyalists by bringing Indians into the war in cooperation with the king's troops, he was certainly one of the first proponents of the strategy. He convinced both Lord William Campbell and Governor Patrick Tonyn of the plausibility of the plan. Although the likelihood of success diminished with the passage of time, the plan evolved into the southern strategy adopted by Lord George Germain and Sir Henry Clinton.

Brown's prolonged sojourn among the Creeks in 1776 demonstrated his adaptability and laid the foundation for a new career. He treated the Indians with respect and affection and was accepted by them as a brother and, later, as their "father." Brown emerged from the forests to take command of his Rangers and to lead them in a new kind of military campaign, a combination of foraging and fighting. Brown kept sight of his objective, the redemption of the interior. He sent his Rangers on distant raids and maintained communication with Loyalists in the Carolina up-country.

Brown's foraging expeditions provoked the state of Georgia into three successive invasions of Florida. In each of these campaigns Brown's Rangers bore the brunt of the fighting. At Fort McIntosh, Thomas Creek, and Alligator Creek the Rangers distinguished themselves. The invading Georgians, for whom the sun and swamps were as dangerous as the enemy, must have wondered how "Burntfoot Brown" had become so well accustomed to the miserable climate and terrain. Brown's versatility was demonstrated by the record of his first four years in America. He was his father's assistant in Whitby in 1774, a Georgia planter in 1775, a resident among the Creeks in 1776, and a swamp fighter in 1777.

Desertion and low morale were not as evident among the Rangers as among the Continental light horse. A negative factor was that the Rangers could not return to their homes, but Brown's leadership must have been positive. The Rangers maintained an *esprit de corps* that survived defeat and exile.

The exodus of the Carolina Loyalists to Florida in 1778 was a major event of that year. Georgians were baffled by the apparently inexplicable folk march. They could not have known that Thomas Brown claimed responsibility for initiating the migration. At Governor Tonyn's request, he sent his Rangers to summon key leaders with whom he had maintained contact. The influx of Loyalists provided Florida with another regiment of rangers but decimated the strength of the Loyalists in the Carolina up-country.

Thomas Brown and his Rangers were not the principal actors in the British reconquest of Georgia under Lieutenant Colonel Archibald Campbell, but the invasion itself was the fruition of Brown's plan, formulated in 1775. The Indian offensive was poorly coordinated, and too few Loyalists rallied to the king's standard. Even as a lesser actor in the drama he helped write, Brown influenced events by his attack on the Whig militia at the Burke County jail. After participating in the Battle of Briar Creek, the invasion of South Carolina, and the siege of Savannah, in none of which actions he played a pivotal role, he was promoted to the ranks of the movers and shakers. John Stuart was a giant in American colonial history. Thomas Brown was asked by the king's minister to succeed where Stuart had failed. Stuart was blamed for being too sedentary; Thomas Brown was ordered to lead the Indians.

Nothing in this war went exactly as planned. The six-month delay in the official notification of Brown's appointment resulted in confusion in the Indian Department at the time of Clinton's invasion of the South. Brown enjoyed Clinton's confidence, thanks partly to Governor Tonyn's glowing reports, and Brown would have had a wider scope for the play of his fertile imagination if Clinton had remained in the southern theater. The idea of using Indians in warfare was abhorrent to many professional soldiers. General Augustine Prevost was never comfortable with the strategy. Charles Lord Cornwallis was a complete stranger to the peculiar brand of guerrilla warfare that had become typical of the southern frontier. He made a firm decision not to call upon Indians, thus excluding Brown from the privileged position he enjoyed under Clinton. Brown's authority was further threatened by Cornwallis's equally firm decision to remove him from command of the Rangers. In reprimanding Brown and James Wright, Jr., for recruiting former Whigs, Cornwallis was not only fussy but unrealistic. He had much to learn about the southern style of warfare; switching sides was commonplace. In fact, Cornwallis soon issued an order that paroled rebels must take up arms in the king's service, thus causing many Whigs who would have remained quiet to resume the rebellion.

Elijah Clarke's raid on Augusta in September 1780 had the effect of restoring Brown to the center of action. Kings Mountain was the direct result of the attack on Augusta. That battle forced Cornwallis to change his mind about the employment of Indians. The Cherokee offensive in the winter of 1780–81 was evidence of Brown's influence in that nation, which had suffered so much earlier in the war and yet was willing to suffer again.

On the other side of the southern frontier and in answer to Brown's instructions, the Creeks were mobilized in defense of Pensacola. In addition, Brown's Indian allies ranged the frontier from the Gulf to the Great Lakes, interdicting American travelers on the Ohio and Mississippi. Joseph Purcell's magnificent map of the southeastern region was a memorial to the extensive empire that was the jurisdiction of Thomas Brown in the beginning of the year 1781. It is interesting to speculate what the subsequent history of the American

Southeast might have been if the war had ended on the basis of *uti possidetis* in the early weeks of 1781.

Augusta was the key to British control of the frontier, as Governor Sir James Wright repeated endlessly to his superiors. Nevertheless, Brown was left to defend the town as well as he could without reinforcement because John Harris Cruger did not receive the orders to abandon Ninety-Six and join Brown. The Cherokees were beaten too badly to be of help; the Creeks were too late. After Brown's defeat the reestablishment of a Whig government in Augusta strengthened Georgia's claim to independence in the subsequent peace negotiations.

Thomas Brown's role during the final months of the war in Georgia was much like his earlier career in Florida. His Rangers rode as foragers and raiders, sometimes with the assistance of Indians, sometimes not. After the British surrender of Savannah and until the final evacuation at Tybee, Brown was regarded as the chief menace by the Georgia legislature.

In Florida, Thomas Brown enjoyed the prestige of a returning hero and member of the royal council. He was active in settling the newcomers along the St. Johns River. He received huge grants of land from Governor Tonyn and somehow acquired 170 slaves. If the peace negotiators had left Florida in English hands, Brown's comfortable future would have been assured. The decision to surrender Florida to Spain forced Brown into one of the most difficult of all his roles. He had to explain to England's Indian allies that the king still loved them but that they were being abandoned to their enemies. Brown succeeded in reconciling thousands of visiting Indians to their fate. Skills in diplomacy have seldom been put to sterner tests.

Brown enjoyed a close personal relationship with the Spanish Governor Zespedes and his family. Brown was Zespedes's mentor in Indian affairs. He used his enormous influence with the Creeks to attach the Creek interest to Spain. He was instrumental in establishing the firm of Panton, Leslie and Company as suppliers of Creek goods. Georgia Indian merchants such as Samuel Elbert and Elijah Clarke blamed Brown for alienating the Creeks, though the Georgians' anti-Indian war record might have had something to do with the Creeks' postwar attitude.

Thomas Brown was a study in resilience; he started anew in the Bahamas. After a short stay on Abaco he established a prosperous plantation on Grand Caicos. He was affiliated with the Loyalist faction in its political struggle with Lord Dunmore, and he defeated Dunmore's son in a test of strength for a seat in the assembly. He alerted his friends Florida Governor Zespedes and Creek Chieftain Alexander McGillivray to the machinations of Dunmore and William Bowles.

During the war with France, Brown turned Caicos into a fortress. Undisturbed by enemies, he raised a family and managed his plantation. He took pride in keeping his colony of slaves as a large family, none to be sold elsewhere. He was determined to keep them together in St. Vincent, even though that decision cost him a fortune, years of litigation, grief, and public disgrace.

As Colonel Brown, hero of the American war and prosperous West Indian planter, Thomas Brown returned to the town he had left a quarter-century before. He never intended to remain in Whitby permanently. His primary concern was new land for his plantation workers. By extraordinary coincidences the Carib territory on St. Vincent was declared forfeit and a personal friend was made governor of the island. In what seemed the climax of a career of oversized land grants, Thomas received a bona fide award of six thousand acres of prime land.

A combination of bureaucratic bungling, ill-will, and bad luck denied Brown his prize. His attempt to use the bureaucracy to protect his interests failed. Although the extent of his complicity in the matter of the fraudulent document is impossible to determine, it seems that Brown prevailed upon allies in the government to produce the document that would force a reluctant Governor Charles Brisbane to do his duty and convey to Brown the land that was legally his. The ploy had the opposite effect. Brown never received the property to which he was entitled, and he suffered the humiliation of a trial, a guilty verdict, and a term in the King's Bench Prison.

Thomas Brown survived even these setbacks. He paid off a staggering debt, partly by selling his father's estate, and on St. Vincent Island at last lived the life he had long sought, that of a gentleman planter. If for no other reason, the controversy over the Carib lands ensured him a place in the history of St. Vincent.

Because he figured in so many pivotal events in the southern theater of the American Revolution, Thomas Brown deserves to be ranked among the major characters of the war in that sector. He is entitled to a complete portrait rather than the crude caricature tradition has shaped. As a member of a distinguished family, he accepted leadership roles as a natural responsibility. As an officer, he was respected by his men and praised by his superiors; as a Ranger, he was daring, courageous, and resourceful; as Indian superintendent, he was diplomatic and sensitive to the interests of his charges. His friendships were lasting; he was a faithful husband and loving father. These would be some of the features of a proper sketch.

Americans tend to relegate the losers of the Revolution, the Loyalists, to oblivion. Thomas Brown's career demonstrates that the Revolution was but one episode, however traumatic, in the lives of those who were exiled. Brown, the loser, fared as well as or better than many of the winners. Brown, the villain, was a hero in the Bahamas and in England.

Finally, his life reminds us of the power and persuasiveness of those myths that substitute for history. The atrocity stories attributed to Thomas Brown served at least two purposes. They justified, after the fact, the injuries inflicted upon Brown, and Thomas Brown, as monster, symbolized the cruelty of the British government and vindicated the rebellion.

Americans no longer need that particular psychological crutch. It is time for Thomas Brown to emerge from the exaggerations of myth and into the light of history.

EPILOGUE

 The Reverend Thomas Alexander Murray Browne inherited his father's estate in St. Vincent as well as the claims to the extensive but nebulous tracts in Florida. Brown's will directed Thomas to give an annuity of £500 to Jonas Brown because "hitherto it had never been in his power to manifest the sincere regard which he had borne to his dearest brother." Brown remembered "his dearest sister Margaret Browne" and his half-brother George Brown with smaller annuities.[1]

Since his marriage in 1817, Thomas and Anne had lived in Ellerburn, Thornton, and Nunnington, villages close together in Yorkshire's North Riding. They had five children: Thomas Alexander, George McIntosh, Charles William, Margaret Elizabeth, and Anne Henrietta. Thomas's wife, Anne, died in 1824 giving birth to their fifth child. She was forty-one; he was thirty-two. He had a memorial to her placed on the wall of her father's church in Middleton, twelve miles from Nunnington, where it may be seen today.[2]

Thomas married again before he moved with his family to St. Vincent. He sent Thomas Alexander to Codrington College in Barbados to be prepared for the ministry. Thomas managed to purchase from the government most of the land reserved by Governor Brisbane after the latter's death in 1829. A terrible hurricane devastated the island in 1831. Although Grand Sable survived, Thomas accumulated debts that were passed on to his son, the Reverend Thomas Alexander Browne, when Thomas died in 1839. A memorial was installed in his church in Georgetown with the inscription "Sacred to the memory of The Rev. Thomas Alexander Browne: Rector of this Parish, whose humble, charitable spirit borne on the wings of Christian faith and hope took heavenly flight April 24th, 1839, aged 47. Also to the memory of his father Lieut. Colonel Thomas Browne who died August 3rd, 1825."[3] Thomas Alexander Browne was forced to sell most of Grand Sable in 1846 to pay debts on the estate. He then returned to England and to the practice of the ministry in his father's old parish at Ellerburn. A publication of his survives, *Skeleton Lectures on the Catechism with Analysis of the Confirmation Service*, printed in London in 1855. He died in Ellerburn on March 29, 1864. His headstone was taken from the Newton House quarry.[4]

The colonel's second son, George Newton Brown, was a writer as well as an amateur painter. He received some recognition for a poem he wrote in the Yorkshire dialect in 1833. At the time, he lived near Nunnington, where his brother Thomas had served as curate. By profession he was a lawyer and later was employed in the management of the Midland Railway Company. On one occasion he went to St. Vincent to help his brother with his financial problems and to visit his sister Susan.

A writer named Charles Day traveled through St. Vincent in 1846 and recorded that there was "a Yorkshireman named Brown, a superannuated cooper, who had a grant of land from an estate, which he has faithfully served, and has married a Carib woman, by whom he had three children, is the owner of a good thatched house in the settlement (Sandy Bay) and is virtually domiciled amongst the Caribs." He saw a volume of *Chamber's Edinburgh Journal* in Brown's hut.[5]

The identity of this particular Brown is a mystery. The most likely candidate is the colonel's half-brother George. He was the only member of the family who could be described as "superannuated" in 1846. It is significant that he continued to spell his name without the final "e." He might well have come to St. Vincent to claim the annuity provided in the colonel's will.

The question of the validity of the ancestral title has haunted the family. According to a genealogical chart in the Thomas Alexander Browne Collection, Jonas, Jr., inherited his father's title as ninth Viscount Montague. Because Jonas had no children the title passed to the Reverend Thomas A. M. Browne. In turn, his son, the Reverend Thomas A. Browne, became the eleventh viscount. Upon his death at Ellerburn in 1864 the title passed to the second son of the Reverend Thomas A. M. Browne, George McIntosh Browne. George married Jean McLeod in Trinity Church, Georgetown, St. Vincent, when he was twenty-seven and she was twenty. They lived for a while in Kentishtown, the artists' section of London, then returned to St. Vincent, where they owned sixty acres of the once extensive Grand Sable tract. Their children were given family names: George Alexander, Susan McDowall, Montague, Anne, Thomas Newton, McKereth, McLeod.

George McIntosh Browne was the last to claim the title. According to the standard guide to the English peerage, the title became extinct after the drowning death in 1793 of George Samuel Brown, the eighth viscount. A genealogical chart of the family in the Waddington Papers, Whitby Musuem, indicates that Jonas Brown's great-grandfather was disinherited during the reign of Queen Mary for becoming a Protestant and, therefore, the title could not have passed to Jonas. Family members in the twentieth century have not given up hope that the title may yet be validated.[6]

BIOGRAPHICAL
SKETCHES OF
SOME LEADING
FIGURES

Balfour, Nisbet. Born Dunbog, Scotland, 1743; died Dunbog, 1823. His father was John, third Lord Balfour of Burleigh. He entered the army as an ensign in 1761 and was promoted to lieutenant in 1765 and captain in 1770. He was wounded at Bunker Hill. He distinguished himself in the New York campaign and was promoted to major by brevet. He fought at Elizabethtown, Brandywine, and Germantown. With the rank of lieutenant colonel, he went south with Clinton. After the fall of Charlestown, he was assigned the post at Ninety-Six. Many thought him haughty and arrogant; he would never have consorted with Indians in the way Thomas Brown did. He enjoyed the complete confidence of Cornwallis. When Cornwallis moved into the up-country, Balfour was assigned the Charlestown command. He incurred the wrath of the Americans by hanging Isaac Hayne. After the war he was promoted to the rank of colonel and aide-de-camp to the king. He served on the commission that heard the Loyalists' claims for compensation. When the war with France broke out in 1793, he was made major general and fought in France under his old comrade Lord Rawdon. He was made lieutenant general in 1798 and general in 1803. He retired to his family seat at Dunbog, where he died.

Beckwith, George. Born 1753; died London, 1823. The son of Major General John Beckwith, George was appointed ensign in the Thirty-seventh Regiment, which embarked for America in 1771. He was promoted to lieutenant in 1775 and major in 1781. From 1787 to 1791 he was unofficial British minister in the United States. During that time he was an interested observer of the negotiations leading to the Treaty of New York. He was made lieutenant colonel in 1790, colonel in 1795, major general in 1798. He held the latter rank when renewing acquaintance with Thomas Brown. In October 1804 he was made governor of St. Vincent and, in 1808, governor of Barbados. He won recognition by commanding the expedition that captured Martinique in 1809 and was rewarded by being made a Knight of Bath. In 1810 he captured Guadeloupe. He gave up his post at Barbados in 1814 and was appointed to command the forces in Ireland from 1816 until 1820 with the rank of full general.

Bowles, William Augustus. Born Frederick, Maryland, 1763; died Havana, Cuba, 1805. At the outbreak of the Revolution Bowles was commissioned ensign in the Maryland Loyalist Regiment, which was ordered to Pensacola in 1778, where he became acquainted with the Creek Indians. After the war he became involved in the plot to wrest control of the Creek trade from Panton, Leslie and Company. Failing in this effort, Bowles was arrested by Spanish officials and held in Spain. He was sent to the Philippines in 1795 but quarreled with the governor there, who returned him to Spain. On the way, he managed to escape and made his way to London and then back to the Indian country. He raised an army of Creeks and Seminoles and captured the Spanish fort at St. Marks. After peace was temporarily restored in Europe in 1802, Bowles no longer enjoyed the encouragement of the British. He was seen as a threat by the American agent, Benjamin Hawkins, who used his influence among the Creeks to cause Bowles to be handed over to his enemies, the Spanish authorities. Bowles died in Havana's Morro prison.

Brisbane, Charles. Born 1769(?); died St. Vincent, 1829. Brisbane went to sea in a ship commanded by his father in 1779 at the age of ten if we are to believe the tentative birth date in the *Dictionary of National Biography*. He saw action in several battles and was badly wounded in 1782. He was promoted to the rank of lieutenant in 1790 and later served under Nelson in the Mediterranean and, like Nelson, lost an eye. He got his own ship in 1794 and, while escorting troopships, sighted a Dutch squadron. He left the transports and was responsible for the capture of enemy ships. Instead of being court-martialed he was promoted and received the thanks of the admiralty. After a short period of peace, he again saw action in the West Indies. He was wounded in the siege and capture of Curaçao in 1807. For this service, Brisbane was knighted and given the governorship of St. Vincent, a post he held until his death in 1829. Brisbane's arrival in St. Vincent was welcomed by the planters occupying the Carib lands, but it was a sad day for Thomas Brown.

Cameron, Alexander. Born Scotland (date unknown); died Savannah, Georgia, 1781. Cameron's real name, according to John Richard Alden, was MacLeod. He was related to John Stuart by marriage. He emigrated with other Highlanders to Darien, Georgia, and was a resident there in 1737. He served as an ensign in the Cherokee War and was stationed at Fort Prince George. After the war he was employed by John Stuart as an agent to the Cherokees. In 1768 he was made deputy superintendent. He was known among the Cherokees as "Scotchie" and enjoyed great influence over them. He fathered at least three children of mixed blood. His disappointment at receiving the western part of the southern Indian Department, especially when Thomas Brown, a raw novice in Indian affairs, was assigned the eastern, is perfectly understandable. Cameron's wartime career has been traced in this volume.

Campbell, Archibald. Born Inveraray, Scotland, 1739; died London, 1791. Campbell was the son of James Campbell of Inveraray, Argyllshire, commissioner of the Western Isles of Scotland. He was appointed ensign in the Corps of Engineers in 1758, lieutenant in 1759, and captain-lieutenant in 1763 while serving in the West Indies. He was chief engineer in Bengal, India, from 1768 to 1772 and was promoted to lieutenant colonel in 1772. He returned to Inverneill, Scotland, and was elected to Parliament from 1774 until 1780. Meanwhile, he helped organize the second battalion of the Seventy-first Regiment as lieutenant colonel. He was captured when his ship blundered into Boston Harbor after the British had left in June 1776 and experienced harsh treatment during his two years as a prisoner. He was exchanged for Ethan Allen on May 6, 1778, just in time to be given command of the important Georgia expedition. After his adventures in Georgia, he was promoted (belatedly in his opinion) to the rank of brigadier general. He was made lieutenant governor of Jamaica in 1781 and governor in 1782. He provided Admiral Rodney his best troops as marines and so shared in the glory of the victory over DeGrasse in the Battle of the Saintes in 1782. In 1785 he was made Knight of Bath and in 1786 sent to India as governor of Madras. He resigned that post in 1789 and returned home. He died in 1791 and was buried with honors in Westminister Abbey.

Campbell, Lord William. (Birth date unknown); died Southampton, England, 1778. Fourth son of the fourth Duke of Argyll, William entered the navy and rose to the rank of captain in 1762. In the following year he married Sarah Izard, daughter of the wealthy merchant planter Ralph Izard. In 1766 he was named governor of Nova Scotia and in 1773 governor of South Carolina. He arrived in Carolina on June 17, 1775, after the revolutionary movement had begun. He took refuge on a British warship on September 15. He and his wife withdrew to Jamaica. He joined Sir Henry Clinton's attack on Charlestown in June 1776. After the failure of that effort, he returned to Southampton, England, where he died.

Carleton, Guy. Born 1724; died, 1808. Carleton served under Jeffrey Amherst in the capture of Louisburg in 1758 and in that year was promoted to colonel and joined James Wolfe's staff. He was wounded in the Battle of Quebec. In 1766 he was appointed lieutenant governor of Quebec and became governor in the following year. In 1770 he returned to England and was promoted to major general in 1772. He is said to have drafted the Quebec Act of 1774, which made him popular when he returned to Canada as governor in 1775. He is credited with retaining the loyalty of the French Canadians when the Revolution began. Carleton was successful in expelling the Montgomery-Arnold expedition from Canada but failed to penetrate New York and therefore was shunted aside in favor of John Burgoyne. He was knighted, promoted to major general, and allowed to return to Ireland in 1777. When the Rockingham ministry came to power, he was given military command in America. He reached New York on May 5, 1782, and prepared to end hostilities. On November 25, 1783, he evacuated New York for England. He was again named governor of Quebec in 1786. In that year, he had been made Lord Dorchester and antagonized Americans by his encouragement of Indian resistance to western expansion. He lived in retirement in England from 1796 until his death.

Clarke, Alured. Born 1745(?); died Llangollen, England, 1832. The son of Charles Clarke, baron of the exchequer and nephew of Alured Clarke, dean of Exeter, he obtained an ensign's commission in the Fiftieth Foot in 1759. After serving in Germany, he was promoted to lieutenant. In 1767 he was named captain in the Fifth Foot in Ireland. In 1775 he was made lieutenant colonel of the Fifty-fourth Regiment and sent to New York with General Howe. In 1777 he commanded the Seventh Fusiliers, then was made muster master of the Hessian troops, succeeding the defeated Burgoyne. He was ordered south to take command in Savannah in 1782 and served as Thomas Brown's superior. From there he went to Jamaica as lieutenant governor and served until 1790, acting as governor in the last year. Promoted to major general, he was assigned to Quebec from 1791 to 1793. In 1795 he cooperated in the capture of the Dutch colony in South Africa. He continued on to India, where he served as commander in chief from 1798 until 1801, when he returned to England. He renewed his association with Thomas Brown and testified to Brown's good character during the forgery trial. In 1830 he was one of the two oldest generals in the British army and was honored with the rank of field marshal.

Clarke, Elijah. Born North Carolina (date unknown); died Richmond County, Georgia, 1799. Elijah Clarke moved to Georgia's Ceded Lands in 1773 and was a signer of the loyal petition in 1774. When the Revolution began, Clarke was a captain in the militia. He was wounded in an Indian skirmish in 1776 and again at the encounter with Brown at Alligator Bridge in 1778. Promoted to the rank of lieutenant colonel, Clarke helped defeat Boyd's Loyalists at Kettle Creek in 1779. In 1780 he attacked Thomas Brown in Augusta and retreated in the face of British reinforcements. His friends from the North Carolina mountains caught Ferguson's Loyalists at Kings Mountain. Clarke commanded the Georgia militia during the Battle of Fort Cornwallis. He was made colonel of militia in 1781 and spent the last year of the war chasing after Indians. He claimed Thomas Waters's property by right of conquest. In 1786 he was promoted to brigadier general of militia and called upon to defend the frontier against McGillivray's Creeks. In 1792 Clarke was raised to the rank of major general. "Citizen" Edmond Genet recruited Clarke as part of a scheme to invade Spanish Florida on behalf of revolutionary France. Genet's recall and bungled negotiations doomed that project. Undaunted, Clarke took his followers into Creek territory and set up the Trans-Oconee Republic. Georgia Governor George Mathews sent the militia to fetch Clarke back. Clarke continued to plan other adventures until stopped by death.

Clinton, Henry. Born Newfoundland, 1738(?); died Gibraltar, 1795. He was the only son of Admiral George Clinton, governor of Newfoundland and later of New York, where Henry grew up. He saw action on the continent in the Seven Years' War. In 1766 he became colonel of the Twelfth Regiment and was promoted to major general in 1772 through the influence of his cousin the Duke of Newcastle. He was part of the British force that reached Boston as reinforcements for Gage in 1775. He won praise for his gallantry in leading a column up Bunker Hill. As lieutenant general he became second in command to General William Howe. After the failure of the Charlestown expedition in 1779, Clinton returned to New York and helped plan the strategy for the Battle of Long Island. Later he captured Newport, Rhode Island, in a well-executed operation. After that he returned to England to be knighted but also to be disappointed that Burgoyne was picked instead of him to command the Canada expedition. In March 1778 Clinton was named Howe's successor and ordered to begin the southern campaign. Clinton's Charlestown expedition has been called the one solid British triumph of the war. Clinton returned to the North leaving Cornwallis in command in the South. The two quarreled bitterly over strategy. Whereas Cornwallis received a sympathetic reception in England, Clinton bore the brunt of criticism for losing the war. He tried to get a parliamentary inquiry but was refused. In 1793 he was promoted to full general and made governor of Gibraltar. It is almost certain that Thomas Brown would have had greater freedom of action under Clinton than he was allowed under Cornwallis.

Cornwallis, Charles. Born 1738; died India, 1805. Strangely, Cornwallis was not blamed by the government or the British people for the disastrous Virginia campaign that led to Yorktown. In May 1782 he was exchanged for Henry Laurens. In 1786 he accepted the governor generalship of India as Warren Hastings's successor. He won a reputation as a brilliant general and civil administrator. He was made first Marquess Cornwallis in 1793, and in 1797 he was sworn in as governor general and commander in chief of Ireland. In 1805 he returned to India but died soon after arrival.

Cruger, John Harris. Born New York, 1738; died London, 1807. John Harris Cruger succeeded his father as a member of the New York City Council and was mayor of New York in 1764. A son-in-law of Oliver DeLancey, he raised a Loyalist battalion and went south under Lieutenant Colonel Archibald Campbell. He was stationed at Sunbury until called by General Prevost to help defend Savannah against the Franco-American siege in 1779. In August he succeeded Nisbet Balfour at Ninety-Six and in September marched to Thomas Brown's relief in the first siege of Augusta. He gallantly defended Ninety-Six against Nathanael Greene's forces until rescued by Rawdon. He again distinguished himself at Eutaw Springs. After the war, Cruger lived in London. It is likely that he renewed acquaintances there with Thomas Brown.

Cunningham, Robert. Born Pennsylvania (date unknown); died New Providence, 1813. Robert Cunningham was a recognized leader soon after he settled on the Saluda River in the late 1760s. He was captain of militia, deputy surveyor, and justice of the peace. Like Moses Kirkland, he joined the regulator movement. Andrew Pickens believed that Cunningham should have been given a commission by the South Carolina Provincial Congress. He was a leader with Brown and Robinson of the loyal movement in 1775. He was arrested for that activity by the Council of Safety. After his release, he maintained contact with Thomas Brown and helped send Loyalists to Florida in 1778, though he did not go himself. Instead, he was elected to the South Carolina Senate by the voters of the Saluda District. He did not take his seat. Cunningham proved of great help to Nisbet Balfour in recruiting men in the Ninety-Six District for a loyal regiment. Balfour recommended him to Cornwallis as a man of great influence. Cornwallis appointed him brigadier general and put him in command of the militia of the Ninety-Six District in November 1780, much to the chagrin of Moses Kirkland. After the evacuation of Charlestown he went to Nova Scotia, then to East Florida, and from there to London to present his claims for compensation. He was awarded £1,080 and half-pay as a brigadier general. He settled on the island of New Providence in the Bahamas.

Dunmore, John Murray, fourth Earl of. Born Scotland, 1732; died Ramsgate, England, 1809. Dunmore was one of sixteen Scottish peers elected to sit in Parliament in 1761. In 1770 the Earl of Hillsborough appointed him governor of New York. After only eleven months there he was named governor of Virginia. His first clash with the Whig faction occurred when he dissolved the House of Burgesses in 1773 for proposing a Committee of Correspondence. In 1774, as his problems mounted, he issued a call to the militia to go on an expedition against the Indians. He personally led a contingent that reached the Shawnee country after that tribe had been defeated by Colonel Andrew Lewis. In the face of increasing hostility, Dunmore withdrew to a warship on June 1, 1775. In November he proclaimed freedom for all slaves who would join him. On January 1, 1776, he bombarded Norfolk. He was finally defeated at Gwynn's Island in the Chesapeake and returned to England to take a seat in the House of Lords. His controversial career as governor of the Bahamas from 1787 to 1796 has been treated in this volume.

Elbert, Samuel. Born Savannah, Georgia, or Prince William Parish, South Carolina, 1740; died Savannah, 1788. By 1769, when he married Elizabeth Rae, daughter of the prosperous trader John Rae, Elbert was a leading Savannah merchant. In 1774 he served as captain of the Georgia Grenadiers. In 1775 he was elected to the revolutionary Council of Safety and in the following year commissioned lieutenant colonel, then colonel in Georgia's Continental battalion. He took part in the abortive invasions of Florida and assumed command of the Continentals in 1778, when General Lachlan McIntosh was transferred to the northward. Elbert served under General Robert Howe when Savannah fell to Archibald Campbell and fought bravely at Briar Creek. Elbert was a prisoner of war from March 1779 until June 1781. He was then promoted to brigadier general and served under Washington at Yorktown. After the war, he attempted to rebuild his mercantile business in Savannah. In 1785 he was elected governor of Georgia; one of his concerns was the intermittent Creek Indian war. Elbert died at Rae's Hall, his home north of Savannah.

Galphin, George. Born County Armagh, Ireland, ca. 1709; died Silver Bluff, South Carolina, 1780. Galphin emigrated to South Carolina in 1737, and his career spanned Augusta's colonial history. He immediately entered the Georgia Indian trade and, despite his previous marriage to Catherine Sanderson, he lived with Metawney, a woman of high standing among the Creek Indians. She was only one of several who bore him children. Galphin became a partner in the firm of Brown, Rae and Company, which dominated the Augusta trade. Galphin was one of those credited with maintaining peaceful relations with the Creeks during the Great War for Empire and with prevailing upon them to come in to Augusta in 1763 to sign a treaty. In 1765 Galphin and John Rae were responsible for recruiting settlers in Ireland for the township of Queensborough on the Ogeechee. Galphin was supposed to be reimbursed from the sale of the Ceded Lands in 1773, but because he joined the Revolution, his claim was rejected by England and finally paid by the United States government in 1850. In addition to his Indian wives, Galphin had children by two of his black slaves. He provided for all of his offspring in his will. He died at his home in Silver Bluff on the Savannah River.

Germain, George Sackville. Born 1716; died 1785. He was known as Lord George Sackville from 1720 until 1777 and as Lord Germain from then until he became Viscount Sackville in 1782. He became secretary of state for the American colonies in 1775 and remained in that position during Lord North's administration.

Habersham, James, Jr. Born Savannah, 1745; died Savannah, 1799. The son of James Habersham of Yorkshire and Savannah, young James entered business as junior partner of his cousin Joseph Clay. Later he formed a partnership with his brother-in-law Richard Wylly. James was more moderate in his zeal for the new order than his brothers. When Savannah fell in 1778, he took his family to Virginia. After the war he returned to Savannah, where he served as Speaker of the first General Assembly. James was unsuccessful in his efforts to restore his father's plantation at Silk Hope to prosperity. He risked his reputation by corresponding secretly with Thomas Brown in 1785.

Habersham, John. Born Savannah, 1754; died Savannah, 1799. John, the youngest of the three sons of James Habersham, Sr., was twenty-one when his father's death allowed him to embrace the revolutionary movement openly. He joined the Georgia Continental battalion as lieutenant, then major. He was taken prisoner when Savannah fell in 1778 and exchanged in 1779, only to be captured again in 1780, when Charlestown surrendered. He rejoined his unit in 1781 and served under Anthony Wayne in the liberation of Savannah in 1782. On one occasion he duped a party of Loyalists and Indians by pretending to be Thomas Brown. After the war he served in the Continental Congress. He spent the last ten years of his life as a planter and collector of the port of Savannah.

Habersham, Joseph. Born Savannah, 1751; died Savannah, 1815. The second of the three Habersham brothers followed his father and older brother James into the mercantile trade. He was one of the protestors at Tondee's Tavern in 1774. He was a leading member of the conservative wing among the Georgia Whigs. In the heat of political debate, he ran his sword through one of the radical members of the assembly, a deed for which he was tried and acquitted. He served as General Lachlan McIntosh's second in the famous duel with Button Gwinnett. When Savannah was overrun by the British, he became a refugee until the end of the war. He was elected to the state assembly and served as a delegate to the Georgia convention that ratified the United States Constitution in 1788. In 1795 President Washington appointed him postmaster general of the United States, and he held the position until 1801. In 1802 he became the first president of the Savannah branch of the national bank.

Jackson, James. Born Devonshire, England, 1757; died Washington, D.C., 1806. A protégé of John Wereat, James Jackson joined the Revolution early and rose to the rank of lieutenant colonel. In 1780 he fought a duel with acting Governor George Wells in which Wells was killed. Jackson took part in the siege of Fort Cornwallis and was rewarded with command of his "legion" of troopers. He fought Brown in the Ogeechee swamps outside Savannah; both sides claimed victory. Jackson led the victorious Whigs into Savannah after the surrender of that town. Jackson served in the state legislature during the 1780s; he was elected to the first session of the United States Congress as a member of the House and served in the Senate from 1793 to 1795 and again from 1801 to 1806. He resigned in 1795 to return to Georgia to oppose the Yazoo land sales. He organized Georgia's first real political party and was elected governor in 1798.

Kirkland, Moses. (Birth date unknown); died at sea, 1787. Kirkland was one of the early settlers of the Ninety-Six District. By selling rum to Indians, dealing in fraudulent land grants, and operating a sawmill and a ferry on the Saluda, he amassed a small fortune and settled down to a planter's life on Stevens Creek, a tributary of the Savannah River. He was one of the regulators in 1768 who organized to maintain order in the up-country. He received a commission from the South Carolina Provincial Congress in 1775 but changed sides when the Council of Safety named James Mayson to command the militia in his district. This book has traced Kirkland's association with Brown in formulating the plan which he attempted to convey to General Thomas Gage in 1775 and succeeded in putting before General Henry Clinton in 1778. Kirkland achieved his wish when he was given command of a militia regiment in 1780 with the rank of lieutenant colonel. He commanded Ninety-Six while Lieutenant Colonel John Harris Cruger marched to Brown's relief in September of that year. When he heard that Robert Cunningham had been promoted over him to the rank of brigadier general, however, he resigned his commission. When Savannah was evacuated, he took his family to Jamaica. He was lost at sea while on a voyage to England to press his claim for compensation. Kirkland undoubtedly had some leadership qualities, but he suffered from the accurate perception that he was regarded as not quite a gentleman.

Lee, Henry "Light Horse Harry." Born Virginia, 1756; died Cumberland Island, Georgia, 1818. Lee graduated from Princeton at the age of seventeen. In 1776 he was commissioned a captain in the Virginia cavalry. His unit joined George Washington's army outside Philadelphia in 1777. Washington admired Lee's soldierly qualities, and the two formed a lasting friendship. He was cited by Congress for gallantry and authorized to enlist two troops of horse to serve as Lee's Legion. Congress voted him a medal after the Paulus Hook engagement and promoted him to lieutenant colonel. Lee's Legion was sent south to join Nathanael Greene's army in January 1781. Greene detached Lee to join Francis Marion in an attack on Georgetown, South Carolina, in January. Lee rejoined Greene and covered the retreat into North Carolina, skirmishing with Tarleton's cavalry. After the pitched battle at Guilford, Lee was again detached to operate against the outposts, Fort Walton (April 15–23), Fort Motte (May 12), Fort Granby (May 15), and Augusta. His role in the Battle of Fort

Cornwallis has been described earlier. Lee admired Brown as a worthy foe; without Lee's precautions Brown would certainly have met Grierson's fate. Lee saw action at Ninety-Six and Eutaw Springs. He left his troops for a short while to carry dispatches to Washington at Yorktown and then returned to join his command outside Charlestown. Lee left the army in February 1782 suffering from fatigue. He married his cousin Matilda Lee and served in Congress from 1785 to 1788. From 1792 to 1795 he was governor of Virginia. He commanded the forces sent by Washington to quell the Whiskey Rebellion in Pennsylvania in 1795. In 1799 he again served in Congress. He delivered the famous eulogy for Washington, "first in war, first in peace, first in the hearts of his countrymen." Like so many, Lee was a land speculator and a chronic debtor. He was imprisoned for debt in 1808–9 and used the time to write the classic account of his campaigns. In 1812 he was injured by a mob in Baltimore when trying to defend a friend. He went to the West Indies for his health but grew worse. On his return, he stopped at Dungeness on Cumberland Island, the home of the widow of Nathanael Greene. He died and was buried there. His remains were transferred in 1913 to Washington and Lee University. After his first wife died in 1790 he married Anne Hill Carter. Their son, born in 1807, was Robert E. Lee.

McGillivray, Alexander. Born 1750, in Little Tallasee; died Pensacola, 1793. His mother was Sehoy Marchand, said to be the daughter of a French officer and a Creek mother; his father was the prominent Augusta trader Lachlan McGillivray. At the age of fourteen he went to Charlestown for his education. Later, he worked in Samuel Elbert's office in Savannah. This book has noted McGillivray's rise to prominence as John Stuart's deputy and then as Thomas Brown's. In June 1784 McGillivray entered into an agreement with the Spanish government giving Spain control of the Creek trade. The British firm of Panton, Leslie and Company acted as Spain's exclusive agent. Thomas Brown used his influence to make these arrangements. With Spanish aid, McGillivray launched a war on the Georgia frontier in 1786 in an effort to drive the settlers across the Ogeechee River. McGillivray and the Georgians, for different reasons, welcomed the inauguration of George Washington as the head of a stronger government. McGillivray was persuaded to go to New York to sign a treaty ceding the strip between the Ogeechee and Oconee. McGillivray lived the life of a gentleman planter. He owned three plantations, had sixty slaves, two wives, and two children. He died of "gout in the stomach" and pneumonia and was buried with Masonic honors in the garden of William Panton.

McIntosh, Lachlan. Born Invernesshire, Scotland, 1727; died Savannah, 1806. Young McIntosh accompanied his father to Georgia in 1736 as one of the original settlers of Darien. In 1748 he went to Charlestown and was be-

friended by Henry Laurens. He returned to Georgia to tend to his successful rice plantations. McIntosh was a Whig who disliked the radical
features of the revolutionary constitution and government. He was given
command of the Georgia Continental Battalion in 1776 and engaged in
the abortive invasions of Florida in 1776 and 1777. The failure of the
latter expedition led to his famous duel with Button Gwinnett. When
Gwinnett was killed, the radical faction raised such a hue and cry that
McIntosh was transferred northward. General Washington sent him back
in 1779 to protect the new Whig government in Augusta, and again McIntosh was caught up in factional politics and again removed from command in Georgia. He served under General Benjamin Lincoln in the siege
of Charlestown and was captured when that city fell. After his exchange
in 1781, he conducted a vigorous campaign to clear his name against the
allegations that led to his second transfer and was cleared of all charges
by the Georgia Assembly and by Congress. He was mollified by appointment to the rank of major general. His financial losses during the war
were considerable, and like many other winners of the war, he could
never recover from a crushing burden of debt.

Pickens, Andrew. Born Paxtang, Pennsylvania, 1739; died Pendleton District, South Carolina, 1817. Pickens moved south with his parents and
settled on Waxhaw Creek. In 1761 he served under James Grant's expedition against the Cherokees. After peace was restored, he moved to Long
Cane Creek in the Ninety-Six District. He was a captain in the Whig
militia in 1775. He was promoted to colonel and, with Elijah Clarke and
John Dooly, defeated Boyd's Loyalists at Kettle Creek in 1779. After
Charlestown surrendered, Pickens and his men took the parole. When his
plantation was plundered, he took up arms again and fought at Cowpens
under Daniel Morgan. We have seen the part he played in the capture of
Fort Cornwallis in 1781. Immediately after Brown's surrender, Pickens
marched to assist Greene at Ninety-Six and, with Greene, was forced to
withdraw at Rawdon's approach. He was wounded at Eutaw Springs but
recovered in time to engage in punitive raids against the Cherokees in
1782. After the war, he served in the state legislature and in the United
States Congress. He was regularly called upon to negotiate with the Indians. After living for a number of years at his plantation on the Oconee
River in Georgia, he returned to the Pendleton District of South
Carolina. It is said that Pickens seldom smiled and never laughed.

Prevost, Augustine. Born Geneva, 1723; died England, 1786. Prevost joined
the Sixtieth Foot as a major in 1756 and was dangerously wounded at
Quebec in 1759. In 1761 he was advanced to the rank of lieutenant colonel and in 1775 to full colonel. Commanding the British forces in East
Florida, he participated in the invasion of Georgia and took overall command of that province in 1779 as major general. His younger brother

Lieutenant Colonel James Mark Prevost distinguished himself at Briar Creek in that year, and Augustine's moment of triumph was the defense of Savannah in October 1779. He returned to England, where he died. His son George also served in the Sixtieth Foot and took part in the subjugation of the black Caribs on St. Vincent. In 1811 he was promoted to the rank of lieutenant general and made governor general of Canada. He commanded the British forces in the invasion of New York and was checked at Plattsburg in 1814.

Rawdon, Lord Francis. Born Ireland, 1754; died Malta, 1826. Rawdon fought at Bunker Hill, taking command of a company when his captain was hit. He served as aide to Sir Henry Clinton and took part in the battles of Long Island, White Plains, and Fort Washington. In 1778 he was promoted to lieutenant colonel and authorized to raise a provincial regiment called the Volunteers of Ireland. He joined Clinton in South Carolina in 1780 and remained there under Cornwallis. He distinguished himself in the Battle of Camden. When Cornwallis moved into Virginia, Rawdon was left behind to cooperate with Lieutenant Colonel Nisbet Balfour in maintaining control of South Carolina and Georgia. Rawdon attacked the Americans under Greene at Hobkirk's Hill in April 1781. John Harris Cruger did not receive Rawdon's orders to evacuate Ninety-Six and join Brown in Augusta. Rawdon had to march his men through a killing heat to rescue Cruger from Greene's siege. Failing health forced him to sail for England in July 1781. He must have become acquainted with Thomas Brown, who was on parole in Charlestown at that time. Rawdon was only twenty-seven when he left Carolina. He was elevated to the peerage as Baron Rawdon in 1783. In 1789 his mother succeeded to the barony of Hastings, and Rawdon added the surname Hastings to his own. In 1793 he succeeded his father as Earl of Moira and in that year served as major general in the war against Napoleon. He was promoted to lieutenant general in 1798 and full general in 1803. Rawdon was on friendly terms with the Prince of Wales, who drained him of money. Whether Thomas Brown joined this circle on occasion is not known, but he was at least on its fringes. He counted Rawdon as a friend and corresponded with the Prince of Wales. In 1813 Rawdon, now known as the Earl of Moira, was made governor general of India and served with distinction there until 1824. For the last two years of his life he was governor of Malta.

Robinson, Joseph. Born Virginia (date unknown); died Prince Edward Island (date unknown). Robinson was a cut above many of his neighbors in education. When he moved into the Carolina up-country from Virginia, he brought his personal library with him. He was made deputy surveyor, justice of the peace, and mayor of militia in the "New Acquisition" above Ninety-Six. As such, his social position was comparable to Thomas

Brown's. Robinson was the reputed author of the loyal counterassociation oath which Brown energetically promoted. Robinson was one of the trio, with Brown and Robert Cunningham, who defied Drayton and Tennent in 1775. After the collapse of the loyal movement of 1775, Robinson remained at large. He worked his way through the Cherokee country to West Florida and then to St. Augustine. He helped organize his fellow refugees as the South Carolina Royalists and served as their commander with the rank of lieutenant colonel. The commanding officer, Colonel Alexander Innes, served as aide to General Clinton until 1780, when he took active charge of the corps. Robinson was permitted to retire from service in 1781 on half-pay. After the war, Robinson went to Jamaica but stayed only one year before going to the province of New Brunswick. In 1785 he established a successful farm on the Kennebecasis River northeast of Saint John. He became lieutenant governor of Prince Edward Island and moved to Charlottetown.

Tonyn, Patrick. Born 1725; died London, 1804. Tonyn joined his father's regiment, the Sixth (Inneskilling) Dragoons, in 1744 and became a captain in 1751. He fought in Germany during the Seven Years' War and in 1761 was made lieutenant colonel of the 104th Foot, a unit that was disbanded after the war. In 1774 he succeeded John Moultrie as governor of East Florida and maintained that post until England ceded Florida to Spain. He was twice promoted during the war, to the rank of colonel in 1777 and to major general in 1781. He never ceased hoping for military glory, but it eluded him. He was promoted to full general in 1798, when he was seventy-three and too old for active service. He was one of Thomas Brown's staunchest supporters.

Walton, George. Born Goochland or Cumberland County, Virginia, 1749 or 1750; died Augusta, 1804. Walton was reared by an uncle after his father died. In 1769 he struck out on his own, moving to Savannah to learn law. In 1772 he began a successful practice. Walton was an early leader of the revolutionary movement and served as president of the Council of Safety. He was elected to Congress in 1776 and, with Button Gwinnett and Lyman Hall, signed the Declaration of Independence. When the British forced Congress to leave Philadelphia, Walton was honored by election to the three-man Executive Committee, which did the business of Congress in 1776 and 1777. Walton returned to Georgia and as colonel in the militia took part in the 1778 invasion of Florida. He was severely wounded in the Battle of Savannah on December 28 and recuperated as a prisoner in Sunbury until 1779. Walton was asked by General Benjamin Lincoln to go to Augusta to establish a constitutional government. Walton was elected governor for the brief session at the end of 1779, best known for its request to remove General Lachlan McIntosh from the state. Despite criticisms stemming from this incident, Walton was elected to the office of chief justice in 1783. He moved to Augusta and was active in building up that town. In 1789 he was elected governor. He was the foremost among the town's delegates to welcome President George Washington to Augusta in 1791. In 1795 he was appointed to complete the unexpired U.S. Senate term of James Jackson. Walton disagreed with Jackson regarding the Yazoo Act, perhaps because many of his friends and relatives were involved in the scheme. Walton was another of those land-poor heroes of the war who could not overcome chronic indebtedness. When he died he was honored and mourned by his fellow citizens, but the sheriff sold his property to clear the debts.

Wayne, Anthony. Born Chester County, Pennsylvania, 1745; died Erie, Pennsylvania, 1796. Wayne was a tanner before the Revolution. As colonel of a Pennsylvania battalion, he saw action on the Canadian frontier and in 1776 commanded Fort Ticonderoga. In 1777 he was promoted to brigadier general and joined Washington's army at Morristown. He commanded the Pennsylvania Line at Brandywine, Paoli, Germantown, and Monmouth. He won lasting fame for his daring capture of the post at Stony Point in 1779 and during the following year conducted raids along the lower Hudson. In 1781 Wayne marched south to take part in the Yorktown campaign after which he joined Greene on January 4, 1782. Greene immediately sent him to Georgia, where he began the final siege of Savannah, a campaign that earned him promotion to major general. He was given a plantation by a grateful Georgia but failed as a rice planter. He was elected to the first Congress in 1791, but his seat was declared vacant because of election irregularities. In 1794 he led the expedition that defeated the Ohio Indians at Fallen Timbers and forced them to sign the Treaty of Greenville. He died at Erie on his return from Detroit.

Wells, George. Born Philadelphia (date unknown); died Augusta, 1780. Wells, a "practitioner of phisick," arrived in the Georgia backcountry in 1771. When Savannah merchants protested British policy in 1774, Wells's name headed the list of subscribers in St. George Parish maintaining their loyalty to the king. Wells and his friends were disappointed by Governor James Wright's decision not to ask for the Oconee strip as a condition of peace in 1774. George Galphin accused Wells of plotting to kill the Indians who came in to sign the treaty in order to start an Indian war. In 1776 Wells was a colonel of militia and a political ally of Button Gwinnett. Wells helped draw up the radical constitution of 1777 and stood as Gwinnett's second in the fatal duel with Lachlan McIntosh. Wells organized petitions demanding McIntosh's transfer out of Georgia. Wells was taken prisoner when Savannah fell but was exchanged early in 1779. Back in Augusta Wells vigorously opposed the ad hoc government headed by John Wereat. He was joined by George Walton in October 1779. They were successful in establishing a rival government and in ousting General Lachlan McIntosh. Wells was elected to the assembly in 1780 and honored by election to the presidency of the council. In February the assembly voted to send Governor Richard Howley to Congress and designated Wells to act as governor in his absence. Wells was killed in a duel with Major James Jackson. Wells was a turbulent and controversial character, but he helped set Georgia's democratic course for at least a decade.

Wright, James. Born London, 1716; died London, 1785. Wright came with his father to Charlestown around 1730. By 1740 he was a practicing attorney and served for a time as attorney general. In 1757 he was sent to London to act as agent for Carolina. There he was appointed lieutenant governor of Georgia in 1760 and governor in 1761. Wright was the host to three other colonial governors and hundreds of Indians in 1763 in the signing of the Treaty of Augusta, which opened the backcountry to settlement. He was an enthusiastic promoter of expansion and went personally to London to arrange a second major land cession in 1773. This was the treaty that so directly influenced Thomas Brown's life and the future of Georgia. Wright was created a baronet in 1772 while in England. Without the support of troops, Wright's authority broke down, and he was placed under house arrest by the Whigs in 1776. He made his escape on a British war vessel in February. Wright was a leading agitator for the reconquest of Georgia and returned in July 1779 after at least part of the state had been restored. After a brief illusion of victory in 1780, the royal cause collapsed again in spite of Wright's best efforts to attract help from the generals. After the war Wright was made head of a board of American Loyalists seeking compensation for their losses. His own losses were huge, £33,000 plus his salary as governor. He was given an annual pension of £500 in compensation but did not live to enjoy it. He was buried in the north cloister of Westminster Abbey.

APPENDIX

MUSTER ROLLS,

KING'S RANGERS

The following rolls were compiled by Murtie June Clark from records in the Carleton Papers (PRO 30/55), the Ward Chipman Papers in the Public Archives of Ontario, Ottawa (PAC MG 23, D1), and the British Military Records also in the Public Archives of Ontario (PAC RG81, "C" Series):*

Muster, Lieutenant Colonel Thomas Brown's Company, King's Rangers, June 24, 1779

Nr	Rank	Name/Remarks
1	Lieut Colonel	Brown, Thomas
1	Capt-Lieut	Barclay, John
1	Lieutenant	Brown, James
1	Ensign	Prevost, G. M.
1	Chaplain	Stewart, James
1	Adjutant	Browne, James C.
1	Qtr-Mstr	Cameron, Donald
1	Surgeon	Clark, John
1	Sergeant	Adamms, Aach, died Oct. 27
2	Sergeant	Brooks, Thomas, enlisted Aug. 3
3	Sergeant	Wilson, David, enlisted Aug. 3
1	Corporal	Advison, Phillip
2	Corporal	Bryson, Hawkins
3	Corporal	McKnight, Moses
1	Private	Middlebrook, James
2	Private	George, Henry, died Sept. 19, 1779
3	Private	Ward, Banjamin
4	Private	Bush, John
5	Private	Barker, Moses

*Murtie June Clark, *Loyalists in the Southern Campaign of the Revolutionary War*, 2 vols. (Baltimore: Genealogical Publishing Co., 1981), 1:49–85. Reprinted with permission of the Genealogical Publishing Co.

6	Private	King, Wallis
7	Private	McBride, Edward
8	Private	Deems, Aba
9	Private	Stone, Elias
10	Private	Hutchison, Joseph
11	Private	Hodge, Benjamin
12	Private	Wallis, Joseph
13	Private	Dugelere, John
14	Private	Rickman, John
15	Private	McGovern, Thomas
16	Private	Johnston, Edward
17	Private	Holt, Reuben
18	Private	Cooke, David
19	Private	Parke, Andrew
20	Private	Allgood, William, deserted Sept. 23
21	Private	Mills, Henry, deserted Sept. 23
22	Private	Burch, John
23	Private	Barry, Thomas
24	Private	Longford, Moses
25	Private	Hog, James
26	Private	Curler, John, deserted Sept. 25
27	Private	McIntire, John
28	Private	Pedlar, John
29	Private	Handcocke, John
30	Private	Hunter, William
31	Private	Vincent, John
32	Private	Winfield, Curtis
33	Private	Prichard, John, enlisted July 3
34	Private	Finley, Jonathan
35	Private	Holt, Barry
36	Private	Carrol, John
37	Private	Hooper, William

Additional Listing:

1	Drummer	Burgess, Benjamin, enlisted Aug. 24
1	Volunteer	Cornish, John, enlisted Aug. 24
4	Sergeant	Norrington, Nathaniel, enlisted July 3, deserted Aug. 24
4	Corporal	Howell, Pat, enlisted July 3
38	Private	McBride, James, enlisted July 3, deserted Aug. 24
39	Private	Mullon, Henry, enlisted July 3, deserted Aug. 24
40	Private	Lynch, James, enlisted July 3, deserted July 28
41	Private	Nappleer, John
42	Private	Smith, John
43	Private	Mills, Jeremiah, deserted Sept. 14
44	Private	Symonds, Moses
45	Private	Lyman, John

46	Private	Sutherland, Gibson, dead July 15
47	Private	Huston, Jacob, dead July 17
48	Private	Prue, Edward, dead Aug. 18

Plus 3 contingent men

Note: Privates 1–32 enlisted June 25, 1779.

Attest: Thomas Brown, Lieutenant Colonel, King's Rangers
Rigdon Brice, Deputy Muster Master, Provincial Forces

Source: Carleton Papers, #10243.

Muster, Lieutenant Colonel Thomas Brown's Company,
King's Rangers, Savannah, Nov. 29, 1779

Nr	Rank	Name/Remarks
1	Lieut Colonel	Brown, Thomas, commissioned June 1, 1776
1	Lieutenant	Brown, James C.
1	Ensign	Prevost, George A., absent with leave
1	Chaplain	Stewart, James, commissioned June 24, 1779
1	Adjutant	Brown, James, commissioned June 1, 1779
1	Qtr-Mstr	Cornish, John, commissioned Nov. 17, 1779
1	Surgeon	Allen, John
1	Sergeant	Adams, Archibald, died Oct. 27, 1779
2	Sergeant	Brooks, James
3	Sergeant	Wilson, David
1	Corporal	Davidson, Philip
2	Corporal	Hawkins, Bryan
3	Corporal	Hodges, Benjamin
1	Drummer	Harrison, John
1	Private	Carroll, John
2	Private	King, Willis
3	Private	Barker, Moses
4	Private	Pigg, Henry
5	Private	Vincent, John
6	Private	Burt, John
7	Private	Stone, Elias
8	Private	Ward, Benjamin
9	Private	Winfield, Curtis
10	Private	Hugbe, John
11	Private	Roper, Will
12	Private	Deane, Absalom
13	Private	McCowan, Thomas
14	Private	Finlay, John
15	Private	McIntyre, John
16	Private	McBride, Edward
17	Private	Fidler, John
18	Private	Burgess, Benjamin

19	Private	Prichard, John
20	Private	Willis, Joseph
21	Private	Langford, Moses
22	Private	Berry, Thomas
23	Private	Koll, Beverly
24	Private	Handcock, John
25	Private	Hunter, William
26	Private	Swords, John
27	Private	Burch, John, sick, Regimental hospital
28	Private	Cook, David, sick, Regimental hospital
29	Private	Rickman, John, in General hospital
30	Private	McKnight, Moses, died Oct. 10, 1779
31	Private	George, Henry, died Sept. 19, 1779
32	Private	Holt, Reubin, died Nov. 10, 1779
33	Private	Lynch, James, died July 29, 1779
34	Private	Sutherland, Gibson, died July 15, 1779
35	Private	Huten, Jacob, died July 17, 1779
36	Private	Price, Edward, died Aug. 17, 1779
37	Private	Middlebrook, Edward, deserted
38	Private	Napier, John, deserted July 20, 1779
39	Private	Hogg, James, deserted Sept. 21, 1779
40	Private	Allgood, Will, deserted Sept. 23, 1779
41	Private	Curtis, John, deserted Nov. 13, 1779
42	Private	Mills, Henry, deserted Sept. 14, 1779
43	Private	Norrington, Nathan, deserted Aug. 24, 1779
44	Private	Howell, Patrick, deserted Aug. 24, 1779
45	Private	McBride, James, deserted Aug. 24, 1779
46	Private	Mullen, Henry, deserted Aug. 24, 1779
47	Private	Smith, John, deserted July 24, 1779
48	Private	Miles, Jeremiah, deserted July 24, 1779
49	Private	Symonds, Moses, deserted Sept. 14, 1779
50	Private	Lynn, John, deserted Sept. 14, 1779

Attest: Rigdon Brice, Deputy Muster Master, Provincial Forces
James Caldwell Brown, Lieutenant, King's Rangers

Source: PAC, RG8I "C" Series, Vol 1898.

Muster, Lieutenant Colonel Thomas Brown's Company, King's Rangers,
Augusta, Apr. 24, 1781, 61 days, Apr. 25–June 24, 1781

Nr	Rank	Name/Remarks
1	Lieut. Colonel	Brown, Thomas
1	Lieutenant	Ellis, Daniel
1	Ensign	Douglass, Benjamin, promoted Feb. 23, 1781
1	Adjutant	Brown, James Calder
1	Chaplain	Stewart, James

1	Surgeon	Allen, John
1	Qtr-Mstr	Cornish, John
1	Sergeant	Mitchell, Thomas
2	Sergeant	Fields, Charles
3	Sergeant	Hawkins, Bryan
1	Corporal	Rickman, John
2	Corporal	Barker, Moses
3	Corporal	Longford, Moses
1	Drummer	Mortimore, John
1	Private	Martindale, John
2	Private	Davids, James
3	Private	McBride, Edward
4	Private	Holt, Beverly
5	Private	Winfield, Curtis
6	Private	Cooke, David
7	Private	Pigg, Henry
8	Private	Finley, John
9	Private	Vincent, John
10	Private	Swords, John
11	Private	Hancock, John
12	Private	Pritchet, John
13	Private	Ward, Benjamin
14	Private	Pearce, Parker
15	Private	Thompson, Jonathan
16	Private	Campbell, Gilbert
17	Private	Smyth, Thomas
18	Private	Adams, William
19	Private	Adams, Jacob
20	Private	Battoe, Peter
21	Private	Shirley, James
22	Private	Matthews, Reuben
23	Private	Cochran, Robert
24	Private	Heaton, William
25	Private	Stone, Charles
26	Private	Langham, James
27	Private	Taylor, Richard
28	Private	Parker, John
29	Private	Shirley, Martin
30	Private	Bernard, Thomas
31	Private	Ferguson, John
32	Private	Bryant, William
33	Private	Johnston, William
34	Private	Perry, Richard
35	Private	Rapids, William
36	Private	Dean, Absalom, died Apr. 14, 1781
37	Private	Burch, John, died Apr. 18, 1781
38	Private	Davis, John, deserted Apr. 14, 1781

39	Private	Doudy, Richard
40	Private	Konig, Willis, killed Apr. 20, 1781
41	Private	Dowland, John, enlisted Jan. 28, 1781
42	Private	McCann, Patrick
43	Private	Davidson, John, enlisted Mar. 24, 1781
44	Private	West, Gabriel, enlisted Mar. 30, 1781
45	Private	King, John, enlisted Apr. 19, 1781
46	Private	Allgood, William, prisoner with rebels
47	Private	Harness, William, prisoner with rebels
48	Private	Villett, Giles, died Dec. 18, 1780
49	Private	Frail, John, died Dec. 21, 1780
50	Private	Slacks, Patrick, died Dec. 28, 1780

Mustered: 1 Lieut Colonel, 1 lieutenant, 1 ensign, 3 sergeants, 3 corporals, 1 drummer, and 40 effective private men.

Attest: John Jenkins, Deputy Muster Master
Daniel Ellis, Lieutenant King's Rangers

Source: PAC, RG8I "C" Series, Vol 1898

Muster, Lieutenant Colonel Thomas Brown's Company, King's Rangers, Savannah, Oct. 24, 1781, 61 days, Oct. 25–Dec. 24, 1781

Nr	Rank	Name/Remarks
1	Lieut. Colonel	Brown, Thomas
1	Lieutenant	Ellis, Daniel
1	Ensign	Douglas, Benjamin
1	Chaplain	Stewart, James, Charlestown
1	Adjutant	Ellis, Daniel
1	Qtr-Mstr	Cornish, John, Charlestown
1	Surgeon	Allen, John
1	Mate	Booth, Thomas
1	Sergeant	Mitchell, Thomas
2	Sergeant	Fields, Charles
3	Sergeant	Ball, William
1	Corporal	Cook, David
2	Corporal	Hogain, James
3	Corporal	Clibborn, Ephraim
1	Drummer	Brooks, James
1	Private	Banard, Thomas
2	Private	Swords, John
3	Private	Pritchet, John
4	Private	Stone, Charles
5	Private	Dowland, John
6	Private	King, John
7	Private	Smyth, Thomas
8	Private	Shirley, James

9	Private	Berry, Thomas
10	Private	Gibson, John
11	Private	Gunns, Andrew
12	Private	Roberts, Hat
13	Private	Holton, Richard
14	Private	Carroll, John
15	Private	Bruce, Simeon
16	Private	Dwyer, Jacob
17	Private	Ferligue, Peter
18	Private	Smith, John
19	Private	Pritchet, Edward
20	Private	Throughgood, John
21	Private	Carr, William
22	Private	Spindler, Boston
23	Private	Reynor, William
24	Private	Wall, Drury
25	Private	Blaylocke, John
26	Private	Smyth, William
27	Private	Bates, Thomas
28	Private	Belin, Nicholas
29	Private	Franks, Joseph
30	Private	Flanagan, John
31	Private	Riggings, Buchhannon
32	Private	Rickman, John*
33	Private	Langford, Moses*
34	Private	Mortimore, John*
35	Private	Martindale, John*
36	Private	Winfield, Curtis*
37	Private	Finley, Jonathan*
38	Private	Vincent, John*
39	Private	Hancock, John*
40	Private	Ward, Benjamin*
41	Private	Thompson, Jonathan*
42	Private	Campbell, Gilbert*
43	Private	Adams, William*
44	Private	Adams, Jacob*
45	Private	Batton, Peter*
46	Private	Longhorn, James*
47	Private	Taylor, Richard*
48	Private	Shirley, Martin*
49	Private	Ferguson, John*
50	Private	Repito, William*
51	Private	Allgood, William*
52	Private	Harness, William*
53	Private	Dayley, George
54	Private	Saxton, Matthew
55	Private	Small, Thomas

56	Private	Tomlin, Thomas, enlisted Sept. 3, 1781
57	Private	Long, William, enlisted Sept. 3, 1781
58	Private	Baker, William, enlisted Sept. 14, 1781
59	Private	Dougherty, John, enlisted Sept. 16, 1781 with the British Legion
60	Private	Owens, Terry, enlisted Sept. 18, 1781, with the British Legion
61	Private	Jones, William, died Oct. 19, 1781
62	Private	Latimer, George, died Oct. 12, 1781
63	Private	Henderson, Richard, died Oct. 23, 1781
64	Private	Brewer, William, died Oct. 22, 1781
65	Private	Bryant, William, transferred to Captain Wyley's Company Oct. 25, 1781
66	Private	Billings, John, died Sept. 10, 1781
67	Private	O'Niel, John, deserted Oct. 8, 1781
68	Private	Fuz, William, died Sept. 28, 1781
69	Private	Wyberm, John, died Oct. 8, 1781
70	Private	Dicks, Hendrick, died Sept. 14, 1781
71	Private	Moon, William, transferred to Capt. Marshall's Company Oct. 25, 1781
72	Private	Murdocks, William (same as Moon)
73	Private	North, Thomas, recruiting
74	Private	Starnes, John, enlisted Sept. 13, 1781

*Prisoners with rebels.

Mustered: 1 lieut colonel, 1 lieut, 1 ensign, 1 adjutant, 1 surgeon, 1 mate, 3 sergeants, 3 corporals, 1 drummer, 39 effective private men.

Attest: John Jenkins, Deputy Muster Master, Provincial Forces
Daniel Ellis, Lieutenant

Source: PAC, RG8I "C" Series, Vol 1898.

Muster, Lieutenant Colonel Thomas Brown's Company, King's Rangers, Savannah, Apr. 24, 1782, 61 days, Apr. 25–June 24, 1782

Nr	Rank	Name/Remarks
1	Lieut. Colonel	Brown, Thomas
1	Lieutenant	Ellis, Daniel
1	Ensign	Douglas, Benjamin
1	Chaplain	Stewart, James
1	Adjutant	Brown, James C.
1	Qtr-Mstr	Waldron, Gifford
1	Surgeon	Allen, John
1	Mate	Booth, Thomas
1	Sergeant	Mitchell, Thomas
2	Sergeant	Bruce, Simeon
3	Sergeant	Bryant, William

1	Corporal	Cook, David
2	Corporal	Hagan, James
3	Corporal	Clibborn, Ephraim
1	Drummer	Brooks, James
1	Private	Owens, Terry
2	Private	Bunard, Thomas
3	Private	Pritchet, John
4	Private	Stone, Charles
5	Private	King, John
6	Private	Smyth, Thomas
7	Private	Shirley, James
8	Private	Berry, Thomas
9	Private	Gums, Andrew
10	Private	Robert, Het
11	Private	Holton, Richard
12	Private	Carroll, John
13	Private	Duyre, Jacob
14	Private	Smyth, John
15	Private	Pritchett, Edward
16	Private	Thoroughgood, John
17	Private	Carr, William
18	Private	Zeyner, William
19	Private	Wall, Henry
20	Private	Smyth, William
21	Private	Bates, Thomas
22	Private	Franks, Joseph
23	Private	Flannagan, John
24	Private	Sexton, Matthew
25	Private	Small, Thomas
26	Private	Long, Thomas
27	Private	Baker, William
28	Private	Daugherty, John
29	Private	Dixon, William
30	Private	Evans, William
31	Private	Elmore, James
32	Private	Haines, John
33	Private	Haines, James
34	Private	Leach, James
35	Private	Hudson, Richard
36	Private	Jackson, Thomas
37	Private	Francis, John
38	Private	King, Robert
39	Private	Jones, John
40	Private	Browne, George
41	Private	North, Thomas

Mustered at Savannah, Apr. 24, 1782.

Mustered: 1 lieut colonel, 1 lieut, 1 ensign, 1 chaplain, 1 adjutant, 1 quarter master, 1 surgeon, 1 mate, 3 sergeants, 3 corporals, 1 drummer, 40 effective private men.

Attest: John Jenkins, Deputy Muster Master, Provincial Forces
Daniel Ellis, Lieutenant King's Rangers

Source: PAC, RG8I "C" Series, Vol 1898.
Note: The Georgia Loyalists merged with the King's Rangers in 1782.

Muster, Major James Wright's Company, King's Rangers, Savannah, Apr. 24, 1782, 61 days, Apr. 25–June 24, 1782

Nr	Rank	Name/Remarks
1	Major	Wright, James
1	Lieutenant	Peterson, William
1	Ensign	Johnston, William
1	Sergeant	Eggleton, Thomas, on command
2	Sergeant	Marshall, John
3	Sergeant	Jones, William
1	Corporal	Boyle, Roger
2	Corporal	Hughes, Joseph
3	Corporal	Hunt, Jonathan
1	Drummer	Pennybaker, Conrad
1	Private	Lawrence, John
2	Private	Lavine, Simon
3	Private	Damarine, George
4	Private	Scanline, Patrick
5	Private	Devent, Bernard
6	Private	Moore, Hugh
7	Private	Rudd, William
8	Private	Thomas, Evan
9	Private	Robinson, Robert
10	Private	Robinson, Henry
11	Private	Strahan, William
12	Private	Ponse, Joseph
13	Private	Henderson, Peter
14	Private	Donnavan, John
15	Private	Falconberg, Frederick
16	Private	Barclay, Jacob
17	Private	Mathiney, James
18	Private	Scott, John, on command
19	Private	Busby, Simeon
20	Private	Miniham, Charles
21	Private	Moore, James
22	Private	Billings, John
23	Private	Wealt, John
24	Private	MacCay, William
25	Private	Hayes, Gamiel

26	Private	Gunter, William
27	Private	Jones, Thomas
28	Private	Grizzle, John
29	Private	DeCrouse, Peter
30	Private	Hughes, Joseph
31	Private	Cadet, John

Mustered at Savannah, Apr. 24, 1782.

Mustered: 1 major, 1 lieutenant, 1 ensign, 2 sergeants, 3 corporals, 1 drummer, 30 effective private men.

Attest: John Jenkins, Deputy Muster Master, Provincial Forces
James Wright, Major
William Peterson, Lieutenant King's Rangers

Source: PAC, RG8I "C" Series, Vol 1898.

Muster, Captain Donald Cameron's Company, King's Rangers, Augusta, Apr. 24, 1781, 61 days, Apr. 25–June 24, 1781

Nr	Rank	Name/Remarks
1	Captain	Cameron, Donald
1	Lieutenant	Cameron, Archibald, commissioned Feb. 23, 1781
1	Sergeant	Fitten, Thomas
2	Sergeant	Fenton, Jacob
3	Sergeant	Litby, John
1	Corporal	McDonough, Philip
2	Corporal	Stewart, William
3	Corporal	Reed, Jones
1	Drummer	Love, William
1	Private	Smyth, George
2	Private	Barfield, Daniel
3	Private	Ryan, Anthony
4	Private	Berry, Thomas
5	Private	Nichols, Thomas
6	Private	Gormon, James
7	Private	Sharp, John
8	Private	Miller, Richard
9	Private	Lindsay, Benjamin
10	Private	Hall, John
11	Private	Edmonds, Thomas
12	Private	Hilezendigen, Christian
13	Private	Pronectus, Henry
14	Private	Mendoselly, Benjamin
15	Private	Boise, Christian
16	Private	Gervais, John
17	Private	Fugate, Josiah
18	Private	Battaline, Joseph

19	Private	Sarlotte, Francis
20	Private	Condolly, Francis
21	Private	Consales, John
22	Private	Ferra, John
23	Private	Fatis, Peter
24	Private	Trualle, Christopher, on command
25	Private	Consales, Simeon
26	Private	Nusaw, Raphel, on command
27	Private	Allen, William
28	Private	LeRoy, Philip
29	Private	McCosta, James
30	Private	Petter, Manuel
31	Private	Furnwel, Richard
32	Private	Calvina, Francis
33	Private	Coleman, Daniel
34	Private	Coarson, David
35	Private	Hupham, Abraham
36	Private	Augus, Josento
37	Private	Clyne, Peter
38	Private	Coarson, Samuel, enlisted Mar. 10, 1781
39	Private	Buchannon, John, enlisted Mar. 3, 1781
40	Private	Temple, Thomas, enlisted Mar. 5, 1781
41	Private	Saxton, Philip, killed Sept. 15, 1780
42	Private	Roza, Angilo, killed Jan. 15, 1781
43	Private	Franks, Jacob, killed Sept. 15, 1780
44	Private	Drummond, William, killed Sept. 25, 1780
45	Private	Tiddy, John, killed Jan. 1, 1781
46	Private	Bond, Nicholas, died Dec. 10, 1780
47	Private	McDonald, Donald, died Oct. 20, 1780
48	Private	Page, James, killed Sept. 15, 1780
49	Private	Rockery, Richard, killed Sept. 15, 1780
50	Private	Smith, Martial, killed Sept. 14, 1780

Mustered at Augusta, Apr. 24, 1781, 1 captain, 1 lieutenant, 3 sergeants, 3 corporals, 1 drummer, 38 effective private men.

Attest: John Jenkins, Deputy Muster Master, Provincial Forces
Donald Cameron, Captain, King's Rangers

Source: PAC, RG8I "C" Series, Vol 1898.

Muster, Captain Donald Cameron's Company, King's Rangers, Savannah, Oct. 24, 1781, 61 days, Oct. 25–Dec. 24, 1781

Nr	Rank	Name/Remarks
1	Captain	Cameron, Donald
1	Lieutenant	Cameron, Archibald

1	Sergeant	Feele, Thomas
2	Sergeant	Fenton, Jacob
3	Sergeant	Stewart, William
1	Corporal	Reed, Jonas
2	Corporal	Barfield, Daniel
3	Corporal	Baese, Christian
1	Drummer	Galleher, Charles
1	Private	Cansaller, Simon
2	Private	Smith, George
3	Private	Nicholas, Thomas
4	Private	Gormon, James
5	Private	Sharp, John
6	Private	Miller, Richard
7	Private	Hall, John
8	Private	Edwards, Thomas
9	Private	Nebzendagen, Christian
10	Private	Primertus, Henry
11	Private	Mindouly, Benjamin
12	Private	Jarvis, John
13	Private	Fugah, Josiah
14	Private	Battinie, Joseph
15	Private	Lindsay, Benjamin
16	Private	Canealiaus, John
17	Private	Ferraw, John
18	Private	Fatis, Peter
19	Private	Troall, Christopher
20	Private	Allan, William
21	Private	Peter, Manuel
22	Private	Cavenaugh, Francis
23	Private	Huppan, Abraham
24	Private	Birmingham, John
25	Private	Dayton, John, enlisted Sept. 9, 1781
26	Private	Ryan, Anthony, dead, Aug. 24, 1781
27	Private	Berry, John
28	Private	David, James
29	Private	Holloway, Joseph, enlisted Sept. 22, 1781
30	Private	Coarsen, David, prisoner with rebels
31	Private	Coarsen, Samuel, prisoner with rebels
32	Private	Coleman, Daniel, prisoner with rebels
33	Private	Buchhannon, John, prisoner with rebels
34	Private	Condially, Francis, prisoner with rebels
35	Private	Franks, Anthony, enlisted Sept. 18, 1781
36	Private	Black, Joseph, enlisted Sept. 18, 1781
37	Private	McCosta, James, enlisted Sept. 18, 1781
38	Private	McDonaugh, Philip, prisoner with rebels
39	Private	Sarlotte, Francis, on command

Mustered at Savannah, Oct. 24, 1781: 1 captain, 1 lieutenant, 3 sergeants, 3 corporals, 1 drummer, 31 effective private men.

Attest: John Jenkins, Deputy Muster Master, Provincial Forces
Archibald Cameron, Lieutenant, King's Rangers

Source: PAC, RG8I "C" Series, Vol 1898.

Muster, Vacant Company, King's Rangers, Savannah, Apr. 24, 1782, 61 days, Apr. 25–June 24, 1782

Nr	Rank	Name/Remarks
1	Lieutenant	Cameron, Donald
1	Ensign	Cameron, Archibald
1	Sergeant	Frilee, Thomas
2	Sergeant	Fenton, Jacob
3	Sergeant	Stewart, William
1	Corporal	Boise, Christian
2	Corporal	Nichols, Thomas
3	Corporal	Berry, John
1	Drummer	Galekow, Charles
1	Private	Consales, Simeon
2	Private	Smyth, George
3	Private	Gorman, James
4	Private	Sharp, John
5	Private	Edwards, Thomas
6	Private	Hylsendagon, Christian
7	Private	Prinectus, Henry
8	Private	Gervas, John
9	Private	Battadine, Joseph
10	Private	Lindsay, Benjamin
11	Private	Candiolly, Francis
12	Private	Consallus, John
13	Private	Ferray, John
14	Private	Fatis, Peter
15	Private	Allen, William
16	Private	Petter, Manuel
17	Private	Calvina, Francis
18	Private	Burningham, John
19	Private	Deyton, William
20	Private	Upham, Abraham
21	Private	Franks, Anthony
22	Private	Black, Joseph
23	Private	Charlotte, Francis
24	Private	Davidoe, James

25	Private	Mundowley, Benjamin, absent with leave in Charlestown
26	Private	Frowal, Christopher, on command

Mustered at Savannah, Apr. 24, 1782: 1 lieutenant, 1 ensign, 3 sergeants, 3 corporals, 1 drummer, 24 effective private men.

Attest: John Jenkins, Deputy Muster Master, Provincial Forces

Source: PAC, RG81 "C" Series, Vol 1898.

Muster, Captain Andrew Hewat's [sic] Company, King's Rangers, Savannah, Apr. 24, 1782, 61 days, Apr. 25–June 24, 1782

Nr	Rank	Name/Remarks
1	Captain	Hewat [sic], Andrew
1	Lieutenant	Eagan, Daniel
1	Ensign	Waldron, Lefferd
1	Sergeant	Wyatt, John
2	Sergeant	Dobbins, James
3	Sergeant	Hopkins, William
1	Corporal	Finney, John
2	Corporal	Thomas, William
3	Corporal	Whitehouse, Joseph
1	Drummer	Hansler, David
1	Private	Neuel, Samuel
2	Private	Doral, Thomas
3	Private	Delk, David
4	Private	Ladson, John
5	Private	Kennedy, James
6	Private	Dumay, Stephen
7	Private	Bowen, Thomas
8	Private	Bates, Ezekiel
9	Private	Kelly, James
10	Private	Triplet, John
11	Private	Simmory, William
12	Private	Stine, Bartholomew
13	Private	Teakin, John
14	Private	Horry, John
15	Private	Hamilton, John
16	Private	Williams, John
17	Private	Stevenson, John
18	Private	McGraw, John
19	Private	Taylor, George
20	Private	Jones, Jonathan
21	Private	Rogers, Baxton
22	Private	Proby, John

23	Private	Hughes, George
24	Private	Mallett, John
25	Private	Gesup, Thomas
26	Private	Gordon, Robert
27	Private	Hopkinson, James
28	Private	Wallace, William
29	Private	Moor, John
30	Private	Graham, William
31	Private	Aikin, David
32	Private	Ballintine, James
33	Private	McDonald, Alexander

Mustered at Savannah, Apr. 24, 1782: 1 captain, 1 lieutenant, 1 ensign, 3 sergeants, 3 corporals, 1 drummer, 33 effective private men.

Attest: John Jenkins, Deputy Muster Master, Provincial Forces
Andrew Hewat(sic), Captain
Daniel Eagan, Lieutenant
Lefferd Waldron, Ensign

Source: PAC, RG8I "C" Series, Vol 1898.

Muster, Captain Andrew Johnston's Company, King's Rangers, Savannah, Nov. 29, 1779

Nr	Rank	Name/Remarks
1	Captain	Johnston, Andrew
1	Lieutenant	Ellis, Daniel
1	Ensign	Andersen, John
1	Sergeant	Hayes, James
2	Sergeant	Files, Thomas
3	Sergeant	Fenten, Jacob
1	Corporal	McDonnagh, Philip
2	Corporal	Sexten, Philip
3	Corporal	Davids, James
1	Drummer	Gallihue, Charles
1	Private	Fitner, Abram
2	Private	Mindowly, Benjamin
3	Private	Malonly, Michael
4	Private	Bond, Nicholas
5	Private	Baker, William
6	Private	Smith, George
7	Private	Banfield, Daniel
8	Private	Ryan, Anthony
9	Private	Franks, Joseph
10	Private	Franks, Jacob
11	Private	Drummond, William

12	Private	Hobson, Thomas
13	Private	Reed, Jones
14	Private	Nott, Robert
15	Private	Nichols, Thomas
16	Private	German, James
17	Private	McDonald, Donald
18	Private	Miller, Richard
19	Private	Stewart, William
20	Private	Smith, Marshel
21	Private	Page, James
22	Private	Lindsay, Benjamin
23	Private	Edwards, Thomas
24	Private	Ludlike, John
25	Private	Mitzendigen, Christopher
26	Private	Pronishes, Henry
27	Private	Rocherie, John
28	Private	Calem, Thomas
29	Private	Cloyne, Peter
30	Private	Boyce, Christopher
31	Private	Duban, William
32	Private	Neugent, Michael
33	Private	Sharp, John, in confinement
34	Private	Smith, Thomas, in confinement
35	Private	Hupham, Abraham, sick in Regimental hospital
36	Private	Hall, John, sick in Regimental hospital
37	Private	Loyal, Richard, sick in Regimental hospital
38	Private	Miller, Henry, sick in Regimental hospital
39	Private	Calibie, Robert, sick in Regimental hospital
40	Private	Roberts, William, died Nov. 6, 1779
41	Private	Snodgrass, Benjamin, died Nov. 6, 1779
42	Private	Gross, ———, died Oct. 17, 1779
43	Private	Thomas, John, died, Aug. 20, 1779
44	Private	McMillen, George, died Aug. 25, 1779
45	Private	Prevale, James, prisoner with rebels
46	Private	Coins, Thomas, prisoner with rebels
47	Private	Henning, William, prisoner with rebels
48	Private	Burch, John, deserted Sept. 12, 1779
49	Private	Davis, George, deserted Sept. 12, 1779
50	Private	Webb, Alexander, deserted Nov. 21, 1779
51	Private	Robinson, John, deserted Nov. 21, 1779
52	Private	Bullen, Gasper, deserted Nov. 21, 1779

Note: Privates 1–42 paid to Oct. 24, 1779.

Attest: Rigdon Brice, Deputy Muster Master, Provincial Forces
Andrew Johnston, Captain, King's Rangers

Source: PAC, RG8I "C" Series, Vol 1898.

Muster, Captain Robert Law's Company, King's Rangers, Augusta, Apr. 24, 1781, 61 days, Apr. 25–June 24, 1781

Nr	Rank	Name/Remarks
1	Captain	Law, Robert
1	Lieutenant	Anderson, John
1	Sergeant	Perkins, John
2	Sergeant	Hayes, James
1	Corporal	Brown, Joseph
1	Private	Gregory, James
2	Private	Blaney, Matthew
3	Private	Bugg, John
4	Private	Swords, William
5	Private	Farrier, James
6	Private	LeBreton, Peter
7	Private	Oreugus, Enus
8	Private	McKenly, Jeremiah
9	Private	Matthews, John
10	Private	Dees, Claudius
11	Private	Bellington, Anthony
12	Private	Pendigrass, Patrick
13	Private	Proudlove, William
14	Private	Roundtree, Alexander
15	Private	Johnston, Clark
16	Private	Johnston, John
17	Private	Johnston, Benjamin
18	Private	Walmar, Henry, deserted Oct. 1, 1781
19	Private	Jones, William, died Feb. 7, 1781
20	Private	Henning, William, with the rebels
21	Private	Private, John, with the rebels
22	Private	Ryan, James, died Jan. 1, 1781
23	Private	Cooney, Jacob, died Sept. 18, 1780
24	Private	Crider, Christian, killed Sept. 14, 1780
25	Private	Cabstead, Jacob, died Sept. 15, 1780
26	Private	Starky, William, died Sept. 20, 1780
27	Private	Bartonfield, Christopher, killed Sept. 16, 1780
28	Private	Cooke, Archibald, killed Sept. 16, 1780
29	Private	Gardner, John, died Oct. 21, 1780
30	Private	Ryan, William, deserted Oct. 6, 1780

Mustered at Augusta, Apr. 24, 1781: 1 captain, 1 lieutenant, 2 sergeants, 1 corporal, 17 effective private men.
Attest: John Jenkins, Deputy Muster Master, Provincial Forces
John Anderson, Lieutenant, King's Rangers
Source: PAC, RG8I "C" Series, Vol 1898.

Muster, Captain Robert Law's Company, King's Rangers, Savannah, Oct. 24, 1781, 61 days, Oct. 25–Dec. 24, 1781

Nr	Rank	Name/Remarks
1	Captain	Law, Robert
1	Ensign	O'Halloran, John
1	Sergeant	Hayes, James
2	Sergeant	Perkins, John
3	Sergeant	Flemming, John
1	Corporal	Blaney, Matthew
2	Corporal	Matthews, John
3	Corporal	Burbitt, Peter
1	Drummer	Canning, James
1	Private	Billington, Anthony
2	Private	Dees, Claudius
3	Private	Artogus, Enos
4	Private	Farrow, James
5	Private	Brown, Allen
6	Private	McKinley, Jeremiah
7	Private	Syar, Joseph
8	Private	Corney, Cornelius
9	Private	Tonnackan, James
10	Private	Elder, John
11	Private	Lundie, John
12	Private	Lundie, Zachariah
13	Private	Meanars, Nathan, enlisted Sept. 1, 1781
14	Private	Harris, William, enlisted Sept. 1, 1781
15	Private	Brown, John, enlisted Sept. 8, 1781
16	Private	Good, Lewis, enlisted Sept. 5, 1781
17	Private	Herman, John, enlisted Aug. 27, 1781
18	Private	Marshall, Joseph, enlisted Aug. 28, 1781
19	Private	Gathen, Reuben, enlisted Aug. 27, 1781
20	Private	Lillycroft, James, enlisted Sept. 3, 1781
21	Private	McConkoy, Patrick, enlisted Sept. 3, 1781
22	Private	Arent, Richard, enlisted Sept. 8, 1781
23	Private	Arent, John, enlisted Sept. 8, 1781
24	Private	Quinlan, Patrick, enlisted Sept. 22, 1781
25	Private	Cells, William, enlisted Sept. 3, 1781
26	Private	Leach, John, enlisted Oct. 20, 1781
27	Private	Brooks, James, enlisted Oct. 3, 1781
28	Private	Elidge, John, enlisted Oct. 4, 1781
29	Private	Gregory, James, died Oct. 1, 1781
30	Private	Swords, William, deserted June 3, 1781
31	Private	LeBreton, Peter, prisoner with rebels
32	Private	Pendergrass, Patrick, prisoner with rebels

33	Private	Proudlove, William, prisoner with rebels
34	Private	Kenning, John, prisoner with rebels
35	Private	Privatt, John, prisoner with rebels
36	Private	Crater, Christian, died Sept. 14, 1780
37	Private	Cubstead, Jacob, died Sept. 15, 1780
38	Private	Bartonfield, Christian, died Sept. 16, 1780
39	Private	Johnston, John, killed May 3, 1781
40	Private	Roundtree, Alexander, deserted May 30, 1781
41	Private	Cook, Archibald, killed Sept. 14, 1780
42	Private	Gardner, John, killed Oct. 21, 1780
43	Private	Bryan, William, deserted Oct. 1, 1780
44	Private	Johnston, Clark, deserted May 6, 1781
45	Private	Johnston, Benjamin, deserted May 6, 1781
46	Private	Holman, Henry, deserted Oct. 1, 1780
47	Private	Jones, William, died Feb. 9, 1781
48	Private	Ryan, James, died Jan. 1, 1781
49	Private	Cooney, Jacob, died Sept. 18, 1780
50	Private	Starkey, William, died Dec. 20, 1780
51	Private	Brown, Joseph, deserted May 30, 1781
52	Private	Bugge, John, prisoner with rebels

Mustered at Savannah, Oct. 24, 1781: 1 captain, 1 ensign, 3 sergeants, 3 corporals, 1 drummer, 28 effective private men.

Attest: John Jenkins, Deputy Muster Master, Provincial Forces
Robert Laws, Captain, King's Rangers

Source: PAC, RG8I "C" Series, Vol 1898.

Muster, Captain Robert Law's Company, King's Rangers, Savannah, Apr. 24, 1782, 61 days, Apr. 25–June 24, 1782

Nr	Rank	Name/Remarks
1	Captain	Law, Robert
1	Lieutenant	Brown, James
1	Sergeant	Dowland, John
2	Sergeant	Hayes, James
3	Sergeant	Gass, John
1	Corporal	Flemming, John
2	Corporal	Oram, Henry
3	Corporal	Matthews, John
1	Drummer	Canning, John
1	Private	Billington, Anthony
2	Private	Cooney, Cornelius
3	Private	Lundie, Zachariah
4	Private	Manners, Nathan
5	Private	Harris, William
6	Private	Jonathan, Thomas

7	Private	Harmon, John
8	Private	Lillycraft, John
9	Private	Quinland, John
10	Private	Leaver, Jacob
11	Private	Grant, Solomon
12	Private	Ward, William
13	Private	Fanning, Patrick
14	Private	Aaron, Moses
15	Private	Syar, William
16	Private	Burdett, Patrick
17	Private	Ball, William
18	Private	Vaughn, John

Mustered at Savannah, Apr. 24, 1782: 1 captain, 1 lieutenant, 3 sergeants, 3 corporals, 1 drummer, 18 effective private men.
Attest: John Jenkins, Deputy Muster Master, Provincial Forces
Robert Law, Captain
John Brown, Lieutenant, King's Rangers

Source: PAC, RG8I "C" Series, Vol 1898.

Muster, Captain Joseph Marshall's Company, King's Rangers, Augusta, Apr. 24, 1781, 61 days, Apr. 25–June 24, 1781

Nr	Rank	Name/Remarks
1	Captain	Marshall, Joseph
1	Lieutenant	Brown, James Calder
1	Sergeant	Underwood, Augustus
2	Sergeant	Caughlin, James
1	Corporal	Thomas, Isaac, promoted Apr. 25, 1781
2	Corporal	Oglesby, William
3	Corporal	Sanford, John
1	Drummer	Harrison, John
1	Private	Johnston, Caleb
2	Private	Boyd, Henry
3	Private	Freeman, John
4	Private	Williams, Evan
5	Private	Allen, James
6	Private	Hammett, John
7	Private	Gunn, Jesse
8	Private	Hulveston, Godfrey
9	Private	Bennett, James
10	Private	McClain, John
11	Private	Carter, Vincent
12	Private	Campbell, Abram
13	Private	Baldwin, David, deserted Mar. 30, 1781
14	Private	Cumming, John

15	Private	Forth, Henry
16	Private	Clay, Nathan
17	Private	Brady, William
18	Private	Adams, Robert
19	Private	Stallions, Zekiel
20	Private	Smyth, James
21	Private	Barrow, Reuben
22	Private	Davis, Jesse, confined for desertion
23	Private	Floyd, Paramin, killed Sept. 14, 1780
24	Private	Stevans, Benjamin, killed Sept. 14, 1780
25	Private	Vines, Jacob, killed Sept. 14, 1780
26	Private	Bonnell, John, killed Sept. 14, 1780
27	Private	Lawdon, William, killed Sept. 14, 1780
28	Private	Moore, Alexander, killed Sept. 14, 1780
29	Private	Asbridge, James, killed Sept. 14, 1780
30	Private	Davis, Hezekiah, killed Dec. 20, 1780
31	Private	Adams, Solomon, killed Oct. 5, 1780
32	Private	Mangum, Samuel, killed Nov. 12, 1780
33	Private	Floyd, Thomas, with the rebels
34	Private	Hodge, John, deserted Nov. 3, 1780
35	Private	Hodge, Willoughby, deserted Nov. 3, 1780
36	Private	King, Joel, deserted Jan. 27, 1781
37	Private	Trapp, Moses, deserted Jan. 24, 1781
38	Private	Robertson, Thomas, deserted Jan. 24, 1781
39	Private	Leggett, John, deserted Jan. 24, 1781
40	Private	Sibley, John, deserted Mar. 2, 1781

Mustered at Augusta, Apr. 24, 1781: 1 captain, 1 lieutenant, 2 sergeants, 3 corporals, 1 drummer, 21 effective private men.

Attest: Joseph Marshall, Captain, King's Rangers
James Brown, Lieutenant, King's Rangers
Source: PAC RG8I "C" Series, Vol 1898.

Muster, Captain Joseph Marshall's Company, King's Rangers, Savannah, Oct. 24, 1781, 61 days, Oct. 25–Dec. 24, 1781

Nr	Rank	Name/Remarks
1	Captain	Marshall, Joseph
1	Lieutenant	Smyth, James, on command
1	Sergeant	Underwood, Augustus
2	Sergeant	Coughlin, James
3	Sergeant	Clements, James
1	Corporal	Boyd, Henry
2	Corporal	Williams, Evan
1	Drummer	Harrison, John

1	Private	McClain, John
2	Private	Helvston, Godfrey
3	Private	Floyd, Peter
4	Private	Barbar, Abram
5	Private	McElvy, Andrew F.
6	Private	Moore, Burgess
7	Private	West, Gabriel
8	Private	Delemar, Patrick
9	Private	Murdocks, Anthony*
10	Private	Moran, William*
11	Private	Boovey, William, enlisted Sept. 6, 1781
12	Private	Slocum, John, enlisted Sept. 14, 1781
13	Private	Fitzgerald, Michael, enlisted Aug. 29, 1781
14	Private	Crosby, Germain, enlisted Sept. 25, 1781
15	Private	Boyd, Robert, enlisted Mar. 26, 1781 taken prisoner in May 1780, now returned from the rebels

Prisoners with rebels:

16	Private	Thomas, Isaac
17	Private	Oglesby, William
18	Private	Stanford, John
19	Private	Jackson, Joseph
20	Private	Hazelwood, James
21	Private	Hogg, John
22	Private	Saunders, George
23	Private	Thompson, John
24	Private	Mosely, Robert
25	Private	Webster, Benjamin
26	Private	Travis, William
27	Private	Walker, William
28	Private	Seber, Joseph
29	Private	Davis, Chesly
30	Private	Waggstaff, William
31	Private	Meadows, John
32	Private	Ellis, James
33	Private	Forth, Henry
34	Private	Adams, Robert
35	Private	Smith, James
36	Private	Barrow, Reuben
37	Private	Floyd, Thomas
38	Private	Roeberry, John

Mustered at Savannah, Oct. 24, 1781: 1 captain, 3 sergeants, 2 corporals, 1 drummer, 15 effective private men.

*Transferred to the Colonel's Company, Oct. 25, 1781.

Attest: John Jenkins, Deputy Muster Master, Provincial Forces
Joseph Marshall, Captain, King's Rangers
Source: PAC RG8I "C" Series, Vol 1898.

Muster, Captain Joseph Marshall's Company, King's Rangers, Savannah, Apr. 24, 1782, 61 days, Apr. 25–June 24, 1782

Nr	Rank	Name/Remarks
1	Captain	Marshall, Joseph
1	Lieutenant	Smith, James
1	Sergeant	Underwood, Augustus
2	Sergeant	Fitzgerald, Michael
3	Sergeant	Harkness, George
1	Corporal	Boyd, Henry
2	Corporal	Williams, Evan
3	Corporal	Moore, Burgess
1	Drummer	Jeffries, Young
1	Private	Harkness, John
2	Private	McClain, John
3	Private	Floyd, Peter
4	Private	Leba, Andrew Francis
5	Private	Spindler, Boston
6	Private	Delamore, Patrick
7	Private	West, Gabriel
8	Private	Murdock, Antone
9	Private	Moran, William
10	Private	Boovey, William
11	Private	Slocum, John
12	Private	Boyd, Robert
13	Private	Sparks, James
14	Private	Spratt, James
15	Private	Stowell, Miller
16	Private	Williams, John
17	Private	Hover, Godlep
18	Private	Smyth, John
19	Private	Neill, James
20	Private	Smyth, George
21	Private	Harris, Joseph
22	Private	Whitlock, (illegible)

Mustered at Savannah, Apr. 24, 1782: 1 captain, 1 lieutenant, 3 sergeants, 3 corporals, 1 drummer, 22 effective private men.
Attest: John Jenkins, Deputy Muster Master, Provincial Forces
Joseph Marshall, Captain, King's Rangers
Source: PAC RG8I "C" Series, Vol 1898.

Muster of the Officers, Privates, Women, Children, and Servants of the late King's Carolina Rangers, settled at Country Harbour, Nova Scotia, June 12, 1784

Nr	Rank	Name/Remarks
1	Captain	Marshall, Joseph
2	Lieutenant	Ellis, Daniel
3	Lieutenant	Cameron, Archibald
4	Ensign	Douglas, Benjamin
5	Ensign	Waldron, Liffert
6	Private	Campbell, John
7	Private	Hopkins, William
8	Private	Dobbins, James
9	Private	Fenton, Jacob
10	Private	Files, Thomas
11	Private	Miles, Armstead
12	Private	Cook, David
13	Private	Clyburn, Ephraim
14	Private	Crozier, Mar.
15	Private	Slime, Barth
16	Private	Nowland, John
17	Private	Brooks, James
18	Private	Berry, Thomas
19	Private	Bates, Thomas
20	Private	Hayes, Gamaliel
21	Private	Boyle, Roger
22	Private	Balantine, James
23	Private	Finney, John
24	Private	Hamilton, John
25	Private	Oven, John
26	Private	Stevenson, John
27	Private	Jessop, Thomas
28	Private	Saunders, George
29	Private	Reyonoure, William
30	Private	Furney, John
31	Private	Smith, George
32	Private	Jarvis, John
33	Private	Stewart, William
34	Private	Lindsay, Benjamin
35	Private	Gallihow,
36	Private	Hytzendeger, Chris
37	Private	Upham, Abraham
38	Private	Young, Thomas
39	Private	Birmingham, John
40	Private	Thorogood, Lovet

41	Private	Williams, John
42	Private	Lawrence, John
43	Private	Holly, John
44	Private	Boyd, Henry
45	Private	Redmond, William
46	Private	Yellow, Gilbert
47	Private	Black, Peter
48	Private	Morris, William
49	Private	Swiney, Roger, gone to Halifax since last muster
50	Private	Connor, Peter
51	Private	McIntyre, Charles
52	Private	Gordon, Robert, died since last muster

Women

1	Marshall, Mrs.
2	Grant, Margaret
3	Smith, Mrs.
4	Upham, Mrs.
5	Filue, Mrs.
6	Campbell, Mrs.
7	Clyburn, Mrs.
8	Cook, Mrs.
9	Nowland, Mrs.
10	Brooks, Mrs.
11	Norris, Mrs.

Children above 10:

1	Norris, John
2	Nowland, John
3	Nowland, Sarah

Children under 10:

1	Marshall, Joseph
2	Clybourn, John
3	Cook, David
4	Brooks, Margaret
5	Brooks, Nelly
6	Campbell, Mary

Servants:

1	Dick	Captain Marshall
2	Sue	Captain Marshall

3	Charlotte	Captain Marshall
4	Mobly	Lieut Cameron
5	Prince	Ensign Douglass
6	Nero	Ensign Douglass
7	Patty	Ensign Waldron

Attest: Joseph Marshall, Captain, late King's Carolina Rangers
Archibald Cameron, Lieutenant
William Shaw, Muster Master, Provincial Forces

Source: PAC, MG23, D1, Vol 24.

Muster, Captain John Bond Randall's Company, King's Rangers, Savannah, Apr. 24, 1782, 61 days, Apr. 25–June 24, 1782

Nr	Rank	Name/Remarks
1	Captain	Randall, John Bond
1	Lieutenant	O'Banan, Jacob Daniel
1	Ensign	Robertson, William
1	Sergeant	Bocher, Jonathan
2	Sergeant	Strange, David
3	Sergeant	Hardin, John
1	Corporal	Lee, Ambrose
2	Corporal	Acord, Lewis
3	Corporal	Cope, Thebert
1	Drummer	Ferry, Philip
1	Private	Doran, Groves
2	Private	Stayley, Timothy
3	Private	Busby, Miles
4	Private	Beartrap, Miles
5	Private	Roxberry, Edward
6	Private	Johnston, Thomas
7	Private	Smyth, Charles
8	Private	Evans, David
9	Private	Arnold, Thomas
10	Private	Shuption, Christian
11	Private	Zippero, Samuel
12	Private	Cloner, Benjamin
13	Private	Lackner, Frederick
14	Private	Ott, Gotlis
15	Private	Gittins, Richard
16	Private	Bryan, William
17	Private	Williams, Benjamin
18	Private	Dupree, Peter
19	Private	Stewart, James
20	Private	Miller, John
21	Private	Giger, Jacob
22	Private	Hall, Jesse

23	Private	Hill, John
24	Private	Rickey, Benjamin
25	Private	Redman, William
26	Private	Williams, Nathan
27	Private	McGuire, James
28	Private	Bailey, Christopher
29	Private	Throughgood, Lovet
30	Private	Murphey, John
31	Private	Cannon, Philip
32	Private	Williams, John
33	Private	Bolten, William
34	Private	Carr, Francis
35	Private	Smyth, Joseph
36	Private	Allen, John
37	Private	Baker, Benjamin

Mustered at Savannah, Apr. 24, 1782: 1 captain, 1 lieutenant, 1 ensign, 3 sergeants, 3 corporals, 1 drummer, 37 effective private men.

Attest: John Jenkins, Deputy Muster Master, Provincial Forces
John Bond Randall, Captain
Jacob Daniel O'Banan, Lieutenant
William Robertson, Ensign, King's Rangers

Source: PAC, RG8I "C" Series, Vol 1898.

Muster, Captain Samuel Rowarth's Company, King's Rangers, Savannah, Nov. 29, 1779

Nr	Rank	Name/Remarks
1	Captain	Rowarth, Samuel
1	Lieutenant	Cameron, Donald, sick in quarters
1	Sergeant	Armistead, Joseph
2	Sergeant	Smith, Samuel
3	Sergeant	Poille, Henry
1	Corporal	Deal, Jacob
1	Drummer	Duley, Lawrence
2	Drummer	Fields, William
1	Private	Baner, John
2	Private	Turney, John
3	Private	Chandler, John
4	Private	Spangs, George
5	Private	Ryneck, Andrew
6	Private	Smith, Jonathan
7	Private	Savage, Henry
8	Private	Minear, Robert
9	Private	Gareau, Anthony

10	Private	Turner, George
11	Private	Myling, William
12	Private	Gresius, Michael
13	Private	George, Francis
14	Private	Ward, Henry
15	Private	Sheareau, John
16	Private	Morrey, William
17	Private	Cameron, James, sick
18	Private	Green, John, sick in Regimental hospital
19	Private	Lee, Edward, sick in General hospital
20	Private	Busby, Ben, sick in General hospital
21	Private	Tibee, Enoch, sick in General hospital
22	Private	Green, Joshua, died Oct. 19, 1779
23	Private	Price, Benjamin, died Sept. 21, 1779
24	Private	Miller, Joseph, died Aug. 19, 1779
25	Private	Bulgen, Joseph, died July 30, 1779
26	Private	Pugh, Lewis, prisoner with rebels
27	Private	McGee, Thomas, deserted Sept. 1, 1779
28	Private	Mitchell, James, deserted Aug. 22, 1779
29	Private	Simmons, Moses, deserted Aug. 22, 1779
30	Private	McGee, Thomas, deserted Aug. 7, 1779
31	Private	Stackey, Thomas, deserted July 4, 1779
32	Private	Malay, William, deserted July 2, 1779
33	Drummer	Downey, John, died Oct. 7, 1779

Attest: Rigdon Brice, Deputy Muster Master, Provincial Forces
Samuel Rowarth, Captain King's Rangers

Source: PAC RG8I "C" Series, Vol 1898.

Muster, Captain Samuel Rowarth's Company, King's Rangers, Augusta, Apr. 24, 1781, 61 days, Apr. 25–June 24, 1781

Nr	Rank	Name/Remarks
1	Captain	Rowarth, Samuel
1	Lieutenant	Jones, William
1	Sergeant	Armistead, Joseph
2	Sergeant	Tweedle, John
1	Corporal	Calverass, George
2	Corporal	Turner, George
3	Corporal	Minear, John
1	Drummer	Watters, John
1	Private	Potter, Thomas
2	Private	Webster, John
3	Private	Fields, William
4	Private	Sherrow, John

5	Private	Ryneck, Andrew
6	Private	Stewart, William, on command
7	Private	Ferney, John
8	Private	Dusteberry, Henry
9	Private	Rockett, John
10	Private	Canty, Michael
11	Private	Scott, William, on command
12	Private	McGau, Owen
13	Private	Dooley, Lawrence
14	Private	Gough, Henry
15	Private	Maling, William
16	Private	Manuel, John
17	Private	Garrow, Anthony
18	Private	Spangs, George
19	Private	Boydd, John
20	Private	Bryant, Robert
21	Private	Gough, Nathaniel
22	Private	Sharpton, Joseph
23	Private	Combs, Stephen
24	Private	Smith, Jonathan
25	Private	Pugh, Lewis
26	Private	Gibson, William
27	Private	Bell, William
28	Private	Cameron, James
29	Private	Chandler, John
30	Private	Mattocks, Mordecai
31	Private	George, Frank
32	Private	Gracias, Michael
33	Private	Smyth, Frank, deserted Mar. 15, 1781
34	Private	Hadcocks, Thomas
35	Private	Morris, William
36	Private	Brazeel, William
37	Private	Morris, William, Jun.
38	Private	Marshall, Isaac, enlisted Feb. 6, 1781
39	Private	Curtis, James, enlisted Feb. 6, 1781
40	Private	Peterson, William, enlisted Feb. 6, 1781
41	Private	Peterson, Thomas, enlisted Feb. 6, 1781
42	Private	Wiltshire, Benjamin, returned from desertion, Apr. 24, 1781

Mustered at Augusta, Apr. 24, 1781: 1 captain, 1 lieutenant, 2 sergeants, 3 corporals, 1 drummer, 39 effective private men.

Attest: John Jenkins, Deputy Muster Master, Provincial Forces
Samuel Rowarth, Captain
William Jones, Lieutenant King's Rangers

Source: PAC, RG8I "C" Series, Vol 1898.

*Muster, Captain Samuel Rowarth's Company, King's Rangers, Savannah,
Oct. 24, 1781, 61 days, Oct. 25–Dec. 24, 1781*

Nr	Rank	Name/Remarks
1	Captain	Rowarth, Samuel
1	Lieutenant	Jones, William
1	Sergeant	Armistead, Joseph
2	Sergeant	Calverass, George
3	Sergeant	Smith, Jonathan
1	Corporal	Turner, George
2	Corporal	Morriss, William
3	Corporal	Menere, John
1	Drummer	Waters, John
1	Private	Fields, William
2	Private	Sherrow, John
3	Private	Stewart, William, recruiting in Charlestown
4	Private	Ferney, John
5	Private	Dusteberry, Henry
6	Private	Dooly, Lawrence
7	Private	Maling, William
8	Private	Spangs, George
9	Private	Pew, Lewis
10	Private	Gibson, William
11	Private	Cameron, James
12	Private	George, Frank
13	Private	Greaves, Michael
14	Private	Brazil, William
15	Private	Garraw, Antoyne
16	Private	Webster, Thomas*
17	Private	McCarty, Michael*
18	Private	Chandler, John, prisoner with rebels
19	Private	Rocket, John, prisoner with rebels
20	Private	McGan, Owen
21	Private	Bell, William
22	Private	Potter, Thomas
23	Private	Boyd, John
24	Private	Boyd, Robert
25	Private	Pitcinton, William
26	Private	Marshall, Isaac
27	Private	Curtis, James
28	Private	Gough, Henry
29	Private	Gough, Nathaniel
30	Private	Manuel, John
31	Private	Combs, Stephen
32	Private	Wiltshire, Benjamin
33	Private	Sharpton, Joseph

34	Private	Mattocks, Mordaica
35	Private	Haddrik, Thomas

Mustered at Savannah, Oct. 24, 1781: 1 captain, 1 lieutenant, 3 sergeants, 2 corporals, 1 drummer, 11 effective private men.

*Returned from being prisoner with rebels, back pay 122 days from June 25–Oct. 24, 1781.

Attest: John Jenkins, Deputy Muster Master, Provincial Forces
Samuel Rowarth, Captain
William Jones, Lieutenant King's Rangers

Source: PAC, RG8I "C" Series, Vol 1898.

Muster, Captain Samuel Rowarth's Company, King's Rangers, Savannah, Apr. 24, 1782, 61 days, Apr. 25–June 24, 1782

Nr	Rank	Name/Remarks
1	Captain	Rowarth, Samuel
1	Lieutenant	Anderson, John
1	Qtr-Mstr	Campbell, John
1	Sergeant	Grant, Gilbert
2	Sergeant	Smith, Michael
3	Sergeant	Bryan, Hawkins
1	Corporal	Huggins, David
2	Corporal	McBride, Edward
3	Corporal	Colter, Uriah
1	Trumpeter	Nole, Christian
1	Private	Outlaw, George
2	Private	Hall, Thomas
3	Private	Cumming, John
4	Private	Adair, Bernard
5	Private	Leroy, Philip
6	Private	Fannon, Joseph
7	Private	Hunter, John
8	Private	Wedgewood, John
9	Private	Thark, Robert
10	Private	Connor, Peter
11	Private	Harris, Benjamin
12	Private	Johnston, Caleb
13	Private	Pearce, Parker
14	Private	Cochran, John
15	Private	Pigg, Henry
16	Private	Tate, Jeremiah
17	Private	Tate, William
18	Private	Hammet, John
19	Private	Goff, John
20	Private	Clark, Thomas

21	Private	Gunn, Jesse
22	Private	Cheevers, Ezekiel
23	Private	Browning, John
24	Private	Current, William
25	Private	Berry, William
26	Private	Howell, Thomas
27	Private	Garroway, James
28	Private	Rowarth, Joseph
29	Private	Clarke, William
30	Private	Vines, Harbert
31	Private	Nusaw, Raphell
32	Private	Mullen, Robert
33	Private	Green, Richard
34	Private	Sherrow, John
35	Private	Barker, Moses
36	Private	Carey, Laughlin
37	Private	Scott, William

Mustered at Savannah, Apr. 24, 1782: 1 captain, 1 lieutenant, 1 quarter master, 3 sergeants, 3 corporals, 1 trumpeter, 37 effective private men.

Attest: John Jenkins, Deputy Muster Master, Provincial Forces

Source: PAC, RG8I "C" Series, Vol 1898.

Muster, Captain Joseph Smith's Company, King's Rangers, Savannah, Nov. 29, 1779

Nr	Rank	Name/Remarks
1	Captain	Smith, Joseph
1	Sergeant	Cornett, Joseph
2	Sergeant	Lloyd, William
3	Sergeant	Haytell, Henry
1	Corporal	Owens, John
2	Corporal	Martin, Archibald
1	Drummer	Black, Peter
1	Private	Whitman, Richard
2	Private	Tate, Jeremiah
3	Private	Mondale, James
4	Private	Ballroop, Augustine
5	Private	King, Herbert
6	Private	Gibbs, Stephen
7	Private	Smith, Benjamin
8	Private	Tate, William
9	Private	Stapleton, George
10	Private	Berry, William
11	Private	Wood, James
12	Private	Jones, William
13	Private	Higgenbottom, Lachlan

14	Private	McCarey, Lachlan
15	Private	Kelly, Thomas
16	Private	Duncan, James
17	Private	Lane, James, sick, Regimental hospital
18	Private	Garret, Matthew, sick, Regimental hospital
19	Private	Price, John, sick, Regimental hospital
20	Private	Harris, William, Regimental hospital
21	Private	Price, Elijah, sick, Regimental hospital
22	Private	Wood, James, sick, Regimental hospital
23	Private	Laster, William, died Oct. 25, 1779
24	Private	Hart, Edward, died Oct. 25, 1779
25	Private	Strothers, Keith, died Sept. 2, 1779
26	Private	Weakfield, Henry, died Sept. 4, 1779
27	Private	Bennett, William, died Sept. 9, 1779
28	Private	Edwards, John, died Sept. 15, 1779
29	Private	McLane, John, died Sept. 27, 1779
30	Private	Martin, William, died Sept. 2, 1779
31	Private	Benton, James, died Sept. 3, 1779
32	Private	Kirkendel, Simeon, died Sept. 5, 1779
33	Private	Blair, James, died Sept. 8, 1779
34	Private	Whitual, Simon, died Sept. 8, 1779
35	Private	Hynes, Richard, died Sept. 5, 1779
36	Private	Mitchell, John, died Sept. 5, 1779
37	Private	Hardis, Isaac, deserted Nov. 16, 1779
38	Private	Neale, Matthew, deserted Oct. 25, 1779
39	Private	Watson, Peter, deserted Oct. 25, 1779
40	Private	Windferd, Joseph, deserted Oct. 25, 1779
41	Private	Kennady, James, deserted Nov. 16, 1779
42	Private	Brown, George, deserted Nov. 14, 1779
43	Private	Thomas, John, deserted Nov. 14, 1779
44	Private	Perdew, William, deserted July 22, 1779
45	Private	Mealing, Josiah, deserted July 22, 1779
46	Private	Neal, Thomas, deserted July 22, 1779
47	Private	Tellison, Benjamin, deserted July 30, 1779
48	Private	Trent, William, deserted Aug. 7, 1779
49	Private	Townsend, Henry, deserted Aug. 7, 1779
50	Private	Trout, John, deserted Aug. 7, 1779
51	Private	McLane, Richard, deserted Aug. 15, 1779
52	Private	Collard, Thomas, deserted Aug. 20, 1779
53	Private	Childers, William, deserted Aug. 8, 1779
54	Private	Lynn, John, deserted Aug. 8, 1779

Mustered at Savannah, Nov. 29, 1779.

Note: Privates 1-43 received pay to Oct. 24, 1779.

Attest: Rigdon Brice, Deputy Muster Master, Provincial Service
Joseph Smith, Captain, King's Rangers

Source: PAC, RG8I "C" Series, Vol 1898.

Muster, Captain Joseph Smith's Company, King's Rangers, Augusta, Feb. 23, 1781, 60 days, Feb. 24–Apr. 24, 1781

Nr	Rank	Name/Remarks
1	Captain	Smith, Joseph
1	Ensign	Pearis, Richard, promoted Feb. 8, 1781
1	Sergeant	Cornet, Joseph
2	Sergeant	Baker, William
3	Sergeant	Paxton, William
1	Corporal	Gibs, Stephen
2	Corporal	Thornton, Joseph
3	Corporal	Whitmore, Richard
1	Drummer	Black, Peter
1	Private	Vines, Herbert
2	Private	Tate, William
3	Private	Tate, Jeremiah
4	Private	McCary, Lachlan
5	Private	Owings, John
6	Private	Wedgewood, John
7	Private	Whaley, Charles
8	Private	Stapleton, George
9	Private	Wright, Nathan
10	Private	Brooks, Robert
11	Private	Berry, William
12	Private	Kelly, Thomas
13	Private	France, Abram
14	Private	Jones, John
15	Private	Jones, Britain
16	Private	Hover, John
17	Private	Lane, James
18	Private	Ware, Thomas
19	Private	Cryder, Christain
20	Private	Greer, William
21	Private	Febigur, John
22	Private	Hutt, John
23	Private	Barrs, William
24	Private	Syfrett, Philip
25	Private	Price, John
26	Private	Yellow, Gilbert
27	Private	Knight, Jacob
28	Private	Fielder, Peter
29	Private	Wetsail, Martin
30	Private	Wilkens, William
31	Private	Marr, Martin
32	Private	Duncan, James
33	Private	Jones, William

34	Private	Barry, Richard
35	Private	Parker, John
36	Private	Turner, John, enlisted Feb. 20, 1781
37	Private	Morris, Patrick, enlisted Feb. 20, 1781
38	Private	Hillburn, John, enlisted Feb. 20, 1781
39	Private	Moore, Joseph, enlisted Feb. 20, 1781
40	Private	White, James, enlisted Feb. 23, 1781
41	Private	Davis, William, enlisted Feb. 23, 1781
42	Private	Ackley, John, enlisted Feb. 3, 1781
43	Private	Owenby, Arthur, enlisted Feb. 10, 1781
44	Private	Owenby, Thomas, enlisted Feb. 10, 1781
45	Private	Dampier, Daniel, enlisted Feb. 10, 1781
46	Private	Perkins, William, enlisted Feb. 18, 1781
47	Private	Thompson, William, prisoner with rebels
48	Private	Stroud, Julius, prisoner with rebels
49	Private	Linnen, William, prisoner with rebels
50	Private	Smith, Benjamin, prisoner with rebels
51	Private	Nigh, Wolf, prisoner with rebels
52	Private	Vessels, James, prisoner with rebels
53	Private	Collins, Peter, prisoner with rebels
54	Private	Rhodes, Christian, deserted Feb. 5, 1781
55	Private	Red, Jacob, deserted Feb. 5, 1781
56	Private	Carne, Adam, deserted Feb. 5, 1781
57	Private	Evenelle, John deserted Feb. 5, 1781
58	Private	Price, Elijah, died Dec. 20, 1780
59	Private	Martin, Archey, killed Dec. 20, 1780
60	Private	Jackson, Jordan, killed Dec. 20, 1780

Mustered at Augusta, Feb. 23, 1781: 1 captain, 1 ensign, 3 sergeants, 3 corporals, 1 drummer, 46 effective private men.

Attest: John Jenkins, Deputy Muster Master, Provincial Forces
Joseph Smith, Captain, King's Rangers

Source: PAC, RG8I "C" Series, Vol 1898.

Muster, Captain Joseph Smith's Company, King's Rangers, Augusta, Apr. 24, 1781, 61 days, Apr. 25–June 24, 1781

Nr	Rank	Name/Remarks
1	Captain	Smith, Joseph
1	Lieutenant	Hybert, John, recruiting in Charlestown
1	Ensign	Pearis, Richard
1	Sergeant	Connell, Joseph
2	Sergeant	Baker, William
3	Sergeant	Paxton, William
1	Corporal	Gibbs, Stephen
2	Corporal	Thornton, Joseph

3	Corporal	Whitman, Richard
1	Drummer	Black, Peter
1	Private	Vines, Harbert
2	Private	Tate, William
3	Private	Tate, Jeremiah
4	Private	McCary, Lachlin
5	Private	Owens, John
6	Private	Wedgewood, John
7	Private	Whaley, Charles
8	Private	Stapleton, George
9	Private	Wright, Nathan
10	Private	Brooks, Robert
11	Private	Berry, William
12	Private	Kelly, Thomas
13	Private	France, Abram
14	Private	Jones, John
15	Private	Jones, Brittain
16	Private	Hover, John
17	Private	Lane, James
18	Private	Ware, Thomas
19	Private	Cryder, Christian
20	Private	Greer, William
21	Private	Febiger, John
22	Private	Hull, John
23	Private	Barrs, William
24	Private	Syfrett, Philip
25	Private	Price, John
26	Private	Yellow, Gilbert, absent with leave
27	Private	Knight, Jacob
28	Private	Felder, Peter
29	Private	Wetsail, Martin
30	Private	Wilkins, William
31	Private	Marr, Martin
32	Private	Duncan, James
33	Private	Jones, William
34	Private	Thompson, William, prisoner with rebels
35	Private	Stroud, Julius, prisoner with rebels
36	Private	Linen, William, prisoner with rebels
37	Private	Smith, Benjamin, prisoner with rebels
38	Private	Nigh, Wolf, prisoner with rebels
39	Private	Vessels, James, prisoner with rebels
40	Private	Collins, Peter, prisoner with rebels
41	Private	Barry, Richard, recruiting
42	Private	Parker, John
43	Private	Turner, John
44	Private	Morris, Patrick
45	Private	Hillburn, John

46	Private	Moore, Joseph, on furlough
47	Private	White, James
48	Private	Davis, William
49	Private	Ashley, John
50	Private	Ownby, Arthur, on furlough
51	Private	Ownby, Thomas, on furlough
52	Private	Dampier, Daniel
53	Private	Perkins, William
54	Private	Price, Elijah, died Dec. 20, 1780
55	Private	Martin, Archy, killed Dec. 24, 1780
56	Private	Jackson, Jordan, killed Dec. 24, 1780

Mustered at Augusta, Apr. 24, 1781: 1 captain, 1 ensign, 3 sergeants, 3 corporals, 1 drummer, 40 effective private men.

Attest: John Jenkins, Deputy Muster Master, Provincial Forces
Joseph Smith, Captain, King's Rangers

Source: PAC, RG8I "C" Series, Vol 1898.

Muster, Captain Joseph Smith's Company, King's Rangers, Savannah, Oct. 24, 1781, 61 days, Oct. 25–Dec. 24, 1781

Nr	Rank	Name/Remarks
1	Captain	Smith, Joseph
1	Lieutenant	Hybert, John
1	Ensign	Pearis, Richard
1	Sergeant	Cornett, Joseph
2	Sergeant	Baker, William
3	Sergeant	Paxton, William, prisoner with rebels
1	Corporal	Whitmore, Richard
2	Corporal	Gibbs, Stephen, prisoner with rebels
3	Corporal	Thaxton, Joseph, prisoner with rebels
1	Drummer	Black, Peter
1	Private	Yellow, Gilbert
2	Private	Owins, John
3	Private	Stapleton, George
4	Private	Kelly, Thomas
5	Private	Lane, James
6	Private	Ware, Thomas
7	Private	Cryder, Christian
8	Private	Price, John
9	Private	Duncan, James
10	Private	Owenby, Arthur
11	Private	Owenby, Thomas
12	Private	Dampier, Daniel
13	Private	Barrs, William

14	Private	Brooks, Robert
15	Private	Thompson, William
16	Private	Holly, Jonathan
17	Private	Cotter, David
18	Private	Raiman, William
19	Private	Hawkins, Samuel
20	Private	Wallace, James
21	Private	McCalep, Robert, enlisted Sept. 4, 1781
22	Private	Cox, John, enlisted Sept. 7, 1781
23	Private	Cox, Joel, enlisted Sept. 7, 1781
24	Private	Jones, John, returned from being a prisoner with the rebels, Oct. 2, 1781, back pay from June 25–Oct. 24, 122 days
25	Private	Wright, Nathan*
26	Private	Jones, Brittain*
27	Private	Hovver, John*
28	Private	Greer, William*
29	Private	Hull, John*
30	Private	Knight, Jacob*
31	Private	Felder, Peter*
32	Private	Wetsel, Martin*
33	Private	Wilkins, William*
34	Private	Marr, Martin*
35	Private	Morris, Patrick*
36	Private	Barry, Richard*
37	Private	Parker, John*
38	Private	Turner, John*
39	Private	Hillburn, John*
40	Private	Moore, Joseph*
41	Private	White, James*
42	Private	Davis, William*
43	Private	Stroud, Julius*
44	Private	Linn, William*
45	Private	Smyth, Benjamin*
46	Private	Nigh, Wolf*
47	Private	Vessels, James*
48	Private	Collins, Peter*
49	Private	Febiger, John*

Mustered at Savannah, Oct. 24, 1781: 1 captain, 1 lieutenant, 1 ensign, 2 sergeants, 1 corporal, 1 drummer, 24 private men.

*Prisoner with rebels.

Attest: John Jenkins, Deputy Muster Master, Provincial Forces
Joseph Smith, Captain
John Hybart, Lieutenant King's Rangers
Source: PAC, RG8I "C" Series, Vol 1898.

Muster, Captain Joseph Smyth's [sic] Company, King's Rangers, Savannah, Apr. 24, 1782, 61 days, Apr. 25–June 24, 1782

Nr	Rank	Name/Remarks
1	Captain	Smyth, Joseph [sic]
1	Lieutenant	Hybert, John
1	Sergeant	Clements, James
2	Sergeant	Damphire, Daniel
1	Corporal	Whitmore, Richard
2	Corporal	Owens, John
3	Corporal	Kelly, Thomas
1	Drummer	Black, Peter
1	Private	Holley, Jonathan
2	Private	Yellow, Gilbert
3	Private	Stapleton, George
4	Private	Lane, James
5	Private	Cryder, Christian
6	Private	Price, John
7	Private	Duncan, James
8	Private	Owenby, Arthur
9	Private	Owenby, Thomas
10	Private	Thompson, William
11	Private	Reynolds, William
12	Private	Hawkins, Samuel
13	Private	Cox, John
14	Private	Barnes, William
15	Private	Cox, Joel
16	Private	Jones, John

Mustered at Savannah, Apr. 24, 1782: 1 captain, 1 lieutenant, 2 sergeants, 3 corporals, 1 drummer, 16 effective men.

Attest: John Jenkins, Deputy Muster Master, Provincial Forces

Source: PAC, RG8I "C" Series, Vol 1898.

Muster, Captain Alexander Campbell Wylly's Company, King's Rangers, Savannah, Nov. 29, 1779

Nr	Rank	Name/Remarks
1	Captain	Wylly, Alexander Campbell
1	Sergeant	Slade, Josiah
2	Sergeant	Rowell, David
1	Corporal	Clayburn, Ephraim
2	Corporal	Churchill, Charles
1	Drummer	Ball, William
1	Private	Hazelwood, Thomas

2	Private	Harris, Benjamin
3	Private	Daley, George
4	Private	Bullen, Young
5	Private	Cutlaw, George
6	Private	Huggans, David
7	Private	Hogg, John
8	Private	Buckly, George
9	Private	Connor, Peter
10	Private	Lewis, John
11	Private	Mills, James
12	Private	Moore, Burges
13	Private	Saxten, Matthew
14	Private	Bladen, William
15	Private	Ebey, Andrew F. L.
16	Private	Blalock, William
17	Private	Saunders, George
18	Private	Ball, William
19	Private	Jackson, Joseph
20	Private	Berry, John
21	Private	Haggan, James, sick in Regimental hospital
22	Private	Stupe, Abraham, sick in Regimental hospital
23	Private	Stokes, Bentley, sick in Regimental hospital
24	Private	Stewart, Bryan, sick in General hospital
25	Private	Johnston, Edward, sick in General hospital
26	Private	Brunsten, Alexander, in town
27	Private	Brunsten, William, in town
28	Private	Wall, Michael, prisoner with rebels, July 15
29	Private	Ellis, James, prisoner with rebels, July 15
30	Private	Browning, John, prisoner with rebels, July 15
31	Private	Wagstaff, William, prisoner with rebels, July 15
32	Private	Liber, Joseph, prisoner with rebels, July 15
33	Private	Connely, John, died Sept. 3, 1779
34	Private	Werridge, John, died Nov. 16, 1779
35	Private	Price, John, died Sept. 1, 1779
36	Private	Davies, Christy, deserted July 5, 1779

Attest: Rigdon Brice, Deputy Muster Master, Provincial Services
Alexander C. Wylly, Captain, King's Rangers

Source: PAC, RG8I "C" Series, Vol 1898.

Muster, Captain Alexander Campbell Wylly's Company, King's Rangers, Augusta, Apr. 24, 1781, 61 days, Apr. 25–June 24, 1781

Nr	Rank	Name/Remarks
1	Captain	Wylly, Alexander C., on command
1	Lieutenant	Smith, James
1	Ensign	O'Wateran, John, recruiting

1	Sergeant	Ball, William
2	Sergeant	Grant, Gilbert
3	Sergeant	Smith, Michael, on command
1	Corporal	Cleburn, Ephraim
2	Corporal	Low, William
3	Corporal	Bladen, William
1	Drummer	Galewho, Charles
1	Private	Conner, Peter
2	Private	Hazelwood, Thomas
3	Private	Harris, Benjamin, on command
4	Private	Huggins, David, on command
5	Private	Dailey, George
6	Private	Outlaw, George
7	Private	Hogg, John
8	Private	Buckley, George, on command
9	Private	Hagin, James
10	Private	Lewis, John
11	Private	Mills, James
12	Private	Moore, Burges
13	Private	Saxton, Matthew
14	Private	Saunders, George, on command
15	Private	Bailey, William
16	Private	Browning, John
17	Private	Libra, Andrew F.
18	Private	Johnston, Edward
19	Private	Thompson, John
20	Private	Harrington, John
21	Private	Berry, John
22	Private	Jackson, Joseph
23	Private	Tanner, Joseph
24	Private	Small, Thomas
25	Private	Ryggins, Buckingham
26	Private	Mosely, Robert
27	Private	Flanegan, John
28	Private	Mullen, William
29	Private	Travis, William
30	Private	Roeberry, John
31	Private	Fitner, Everheart
32	Private	Webster, Benjamin
33	Private	Caturn, John
34	Private	Browne, Thomas
35	Private	Franks, Joseph
36	Private	Walker, William

Prisoners with rebels:

37	Private	Lebar, Joseph
38	Private	Davis, Chesley

39   Private   Wagstaff, William
40   Private   Meadows, John
41   Private   Ellis, James

Mustered at Augusta, Apr. 24, 1781: 1 lieutenant, 2 sergeants, 3 corporals, 1 drummer, 32 effective private men.

Source: PAC, RG8I "C" Series, Vol 1898.

Muster, Captain Alexander C. Wylly's Company, King's Rangers, Savannah, Oct. 24, 1781, 61 days, Oct. 25–Dec. 24, 1781

Nr	Rank	Name/Remarks
1	Captain	Wylly, Alexander C.
1	Lieutenant	Brown, James C.
1	Cornet	Anderson, John
1	Sergeant	Grant, Gilbert
2	Sergeant	Smyth, Michael
3	Sergeant	Bryant, Hawkins
1	Corporal	Lowe, William
2	Corporal	Huggins, David
3	Corporal	McBride, Edward
1	Trumpeter	Red, Christian
1	Private	Conner, Peter
2	Private	Harris, Benjamin
3	Private	Outlaw, George
4	Private	Buckley, George
5	Private	Mills, James
6	Private	Bailey, William
7	Private	Browning, John
8	Private	Muller, William
9	Private	Bladen, William
10	Private	Tanner, Joseph
11	Private	Smyth, George
12	Private	Jones, William
13	Private	Curren, William
14	Private	Fielding, Thomas
15	Private	Gibson, Gideon
16	Private	Childs, James
17	Private	Colter, William
18	Private	Rainy, Michael
19	Private	Hall, John
20	Private	McPherson, Alexander
21	Private	Clark, John
22	Private	Clark, Thomas
23	Private	Clark, William
24	Private	Barrier, John

25	Private	Hunter, John
26	Private	Roche, William, died Oct. 20, 1781
27	Private	Adier, Barnard
28	Private	Christian, Peter
29	Private	Pearce, Parker
30	Private	Barker, Miles
31	Private	Pigg, Henry
32	Private	Cochran, John
33	Private	Scott, William
34	Private	Vines, Herbert
35	Private	Berry, William
36	Private	Wedgewood, John
37	Private	McCarey, Laughlin
38	Private	Tate, Jeremiah
39	Private	Tate, William
40	Private	Gunn, Jesse
41	Private	Johnston, Caleb
42	Private	Cumming, John
43	Private	Hammet, Jacob
44	Private	Lowry, Philip
45	Private	Nuesa, Raphail
46	Private	Harvel, Thomas, enlisted Sept. 1, 1781
47	Private	Sealey, Gideon, enlisted Sept. 5, 1781
48	Private	Green, Richard, enlisted Sept. 10, 1781
49	Private	Andrews, John, enlisted Sept. 10, 1781
50	Private	Francisco, John, enlisted Sept. 10, 1781
51	Private	Whaley, Charles, deserted Oct. 1, 1780

Mustered at Savannah, Oct. 24, 1781: 1 captain, 1 lieutenant, 1 cornet, 3 sergeants, 3 corporals, 1 trumpeter, 50 effective private men.

Attest: John Jenkins, Deputy Muster Master
Alexander C. Wylly, Captain King's Rangers

Source: PAC, RG8I "C" Series, Vol 1898.

Muster, Captain Alexander C. Wylly's Company, King's Rangers, Savannah, Apr. 24, 1782, 61 days, Apr. 25–June 24, 1782

Nr	Rank	Name/Remarks
1	Captain	Wylly, Alexander C.
1	Ensign	Jones, William
1	Sergeant	Armistead, Joseph
2	Sergeant	Calveras, George
3	Sergeant	Turner, George
1	Corporal	Morris, William
2	Corporal	Garrow, Anthony
3	Corporal	Mailing, William

1	Drummer	Waters, John
1	Private	Fields, William
2	Private	Webster, Thomas
3	Private	Ferney, John
4	Private	Disterbury, Henry
5	Private	Duley, Lawrence
6	Private	McCarty, Michael
7	Private	Spangs, George
8	Private	Pew, Lewis
9	Private	Cameron, James
10	Private	Frank, George
11	Private	Gresiers, Michael
12	Private	Brazill, William
13	Private	Smyth, Jonathan
14	Private	Horn, John
15	Private	Howell, Robert
16	Private	O'Bryan, John
17	Private	Bailey, William
18	Private	Gibson, Gideon
19	Private	Mills, James
20	Private	McPherson, James
21	Private	Stanton, William
22	Private	Tilley, Josiah
23	Private	Irwin, William
24	Private	Walker, William
25	Private	Traverse, Aaron

Mustered at Savannah, Apr. 24, 1782: 1 captain, 1 ensign, 3 sergeants, 3 corporals, 1 drummer, 25 efffective private men.

Attest: John Jenkins, Deputy Muster Master, Provincial Forces
Alexander C. Wylly, Captain
William Jones, Ensign King's Rangers

Source: PAC, RG8I "C" Series, Vol 1898.

NOTES

1. From Yorkshire to Georgia

1. The genealogical chart of the Brown family is in TAB. Another version is in the Waddington Papers, 8:220–21, Whitby Museum.

2. William Jayns Weston, *The North Riding of Yorkshire* (Cambridge, Eng.: University Press, 1919), 48, 61–62.

3. Information on Bagdale Hall, Adeline Huntrodes, her daughter Margaret, and Margaret's two marriages was provided by A. A. Berends, keeper, Whitby Museum, from an examination of Percy Burnett Papers, Whitby Museum.

4. Information on Thomas Brown's birth and baptismal dates was provided by A. A. Berends, who searched parish records. Berends suggested that the Browns might have gone through a Quaker phase; see Waddington Papers, 8:380.

5. A. A. Berends searched the muster rolls of Whitby registered ships to ascertain the names of Jonas Brown's ships. For Manson's voyage in the *Flora*, see A. A. Berends, "The Stone Horse Had Like to Been Down," *Whitby Literary and Philosophical Society Annual Report, 1982*, 16–19. Jonas and Thomas Brown of Whitby are listed as owners of the *Prince Frederick*, a ship of 140 tons, John Fletcher, master, which embarked from Savannah with a cargo of rice, pitch, "lignum vitae," and mahogany on May 7, 1766 ("A list of Ships and Vessels Entered Inwards at the Port of Savannah in Georgia between the 5th day of April 1766 and the 5th day of July following," *GHS Collections*, 8:Appendix).

6. It is recorded of Jonas Brown's pumping system that "it perhaps could not be in the power of man to devise any thing more easy, artful, and ingenious" (Lionel Charlton, *History of Whitby* [York: A. Ward, 1779], 357–58).

7. Hugh P. Kendall, *The Streets of Whitby and Their Associations* (Whitby: Whitby Literary and Philosophical Society, 1976), 19–20; William Page, ed., *The Victoria History of the County of York North Riding*, 2 vols. (London: Constable, 1914, 1923), 2:507–12.

8. J. Geoffrey Graham, *Captain James Cook, "Servant and Friend" of Captain John Walker* (Whitby: Abbey Press, 1986), 3–8. Walker's House in Grape Lane is now a museum honoring Cook. The location of Jonas

Brown's house was ascertained by A. A. Berends from local tax records. On July 23, 1986, Berends conducted me to the handsome house built by Jonas Brown in Grape Lane.

9. Information obtained from a tape-recorded history of St. Mary's Church available to visitors, July 23, 1986, Whitby, England.

10. Graham, *Captain James Cook*.

11. Jonas Brown to Nathaniel Cholmley, April 23, 1773, Dartmouth Papers, Staffordshire Record Office, Stafford, England.

12. Thomas Brown to Nathaniel Cholmley, April 23, 1773, ibid.

13. Kendall, *Streets of Whitby*, 13–14; Waddington Papers, 8:376–77, 382–83.

14. Information about Newton House was obtained on a visit to the house in June 1983. Andrew Summerbell conducted me on a tour of the house and grounds. The mansion is used for school groups as a base for exploring the moors. For Jonas's marriage date, see Waddington Papers, 9:221.

15. A copy of Wright's proclamation was filed with Thomas Brown's postwar claims for compensation, PRO, AO 13/34. The notice of the *Marlborough*'s sailing was first published in *Etherington's York Chronicle* on May 6, 1774.

16. The passenger list is in PRO, T 47/10; a slightly different list was filed with Brown's claim, PRO, AO 13/34.

17. *Etherington's York Chronicle*, July 28, 1775.

18. Jonas Brown, Jr.'s, knighthood was reported in the *Yorkshire Journal*, May 11, 1787, Waddington Papers, 61:54; the cost of establishing Brown's colony was reported in Brown's claim, PRO, AO 13/34.

19. George Barry, *History of the Orkney Islands* (London: Printed for Longman, Hurst, Rees and Orme, 1808), 335, 345. Orcadians were also described as healthy and hardy and capable of abstemious and laborious life; they practiced the Presbyterian religion "without bigotry, enthusiasm or zeal" (J. Storer Clouston, *A History of Orkney* [Kirkwall: W. R. Mackintosh, 1932], 361–63). Clouston describes the Orcadians' outmoded farming methods. See also Alexander Fenton, *The Northern Isles, Orkney and Shetland* (Edinburgh: Donald, 1978), 49–51.

20. Lydia Austin Parrish, "Records of some Southern Loyalists, being a collection of manuscripts about some 80 families, most of whom immigrated to the Bahamas during and after the American Revolution," typescript in Widener Library, Harvard University, microfilm in P. I. Yonge Library, University of Florida, Gainesville, pp. 343–45. See also The Case of James Gordon, in United Empire Loyalists: Enquiry into the losses and services in consequence of their loyalty: Evidence in the Canadian Claims, Archives of Ontario (microfiche, 1984), 792–97. Gordon stated that he went to America in 1772 in consequence of a proclamation from Sir James Wright. Wright's

proclamation was not issued until June 11, 1773, and time elapsed before Gordon could make arrangements with the Browns and take voyage to America. On November 16, 1773, James Gordon reserved three tracts on the Ceded Lands totaling five thousand acres (Robert S. Davis, Jr., ed., *The Wilkes County Papers, 1773–1833* [Easley, S.C.: Southern Historical Press, 1979], 12).

21. Edward J. Cashin, "Sowing the Wind: Governor Wright and the Georgia Backcountry on the Eve of the Revolution," in Harvey H. Jackson and Phinizy Spalding, eds., *Forty Years of Diversity: Essays on Colonial Georgia* (Athens: University of Georgia Press, 1984), 233–50.

22. "List of Papers Relative to My Memorial about Indian Affairs and with Some Notes and Remarks Thereon," in Wright to Hillsborough, received December 12, 1771, Ms. CRG, 28, pt. 2B:669–73; also in *CRG*, 28, pt. 2:358–60.

23. Kenneth Coleman, *Colonial Georgia: A History* (New York: Charles Scribner's Sons, 1976), 226–27.

24. Philip Yonge, "A Map of the Lands Ceded to His Majesty by the Creek and Cherokee Indians at a Congress Held in Augusta the 1st June 1773," in Edward J. Cashin, ed., *Colonial Augusta: "Key of the Indian Countrey"* (Macon, Ga.: Mercer University Press, 1986), 22. Wright put the total acreage of the Ceded Lands above the Little River at 1,616,298 (Wright to Dartmouth, August 10, 1773, Ms. CRG, 38, pt. lA:80; William Bartram, *Travels of William Bartram*, ed. Mark Van Doren (New York: Dover, 1928), 53–54.

25. Wright to Edward Barnard, n.d., "Instructions to Edw'd Barnard, Esquire, Captain of the Troop of Rangers to be raised to keep good order amongst and for the protection of the Inhabitants in the new Ceded Lands above Little River," in claim of Thomas Waters, PRO, AO 13/37.

26. *Georgia Gazette*, February 2, 1774.

27. Ibid.; see also Wright to Dartmouth, January 31, 1774, Ms. CRG, 38, pt. 1:163–71.

28. *Georgia Gazette*, March 30, April 13, 1774.

29. *CRG*, 12:406–10; John Richard Alden, *John Stuart and the Southern Colonial Frontier: A Study of Indian Relations, War, Trade, and Land Problems in the Southern Wilderness, 1754–1775* (1944; rpt. New York: Gordian Press, 1966), 309–10.

30. Resolutions of St. Paul Parish, *Georgia Gazette*, October 12, 1774; other resolutions in *Georgia Gazette*, September 28, 1774.

31. For a sketch of Hammerer's career see "Appendix C: British Missionaries," in Alden, *John Stuart*, 353–55.

32. *Georgia Gazette*, October 26, 1774.

33. Extract of a letter from Charlestown, November 11, 1774, letter from

Charlestown, June 27, 1774, in Peter Force, ed., *American Archives*, 4th ser., 6 vols. (Washington, D.C.: U. St. Clair and Peter Force, 1837–46), 1:974, 451.

34. Council Minutes, August 30, 1774, *CRG*, 12:406–7.

35. *Georgia Gazette*, October 19, 1774; Force, ed., *American Archives*, 4th ser., 1:1137; Alden, *John Stuart*, 311; Wright and Stuart to Dartmouth, October 21, 1774, Ms. CRG, 38, pt. 1B:335.

36. Petition of the Inhabitants of St. George and St. Paul, including the ceded lands in the Province of Georgia—July 31, in *NYHS Collections*, 5:181; Edward J. Cashin, "'The Famous Colonel Wells': Factionalism in Revolutionary Georgia," *GHQ* 58, Suppl. (1974):137–56.

37. Extract of a letter from Savannah to a gentleman in Philadelphia, December 9, 1774, in Force, ed., *American Archives*, 4th ser., 1:1033–34.

2. Shaping a Southern Strategy, 1775

1. Beckwith to Hope, September 24, 1803, TAB.

2. W. Calvin Smith, "Georgia Gentlemen: The Habershams of Eighteenth-Century Savannah" (Ph.D. dissertation, University of North Carolina, 1971), 2–4; *GHS Collections*, 8:7; Joseph Clay advertised that the *Marlborough* was loading rice for London and "the Markets" *(Georgia Gazette*, November 23, 1774); Susannah Wylly Memorial, August 11, 1784, in Hugh Edward Egerton, *The Royal Commission on the Losses and Services of American Loyalists, 1783–1785* (1915; rpt. New York: Arno Press and the New York Times, 1969), 171–72.

3. State of the Claim of Jonas Brown of Whitby, Col. Thomas Brown and James Gordon . . . , American Loyalists, Audit Office Transcripts, vol. 28, Transcribed for the New York Public Library, 1900; Wright to Dartmouth, August 17, 1775, Ms. CRG, 38, 1B:564; Supplemental Memorial of Lieutenant Colonel Thomas Brown, PRO, AO 13/34; Thomas Brown to Jonas Brown, Sr., November 10, 1775, Browne Family Papers in possession of Joan Leggett of Oxford, England, a descendant of Brown.

4. Narrative of William Manson, n.d., D 2/9/10 Balfour Papers, Kirkwall Public Library, Kirkwall, Scotland. I am indebted to Robert S. Davis, Jr., for a copy of Manson's narrative and to Heard Robertson of Augusta, who also had copies of the material pertinent to Georgia; for Manson's career in Georgia see Robert S. Davis, Jr., "The Last Colonial Enthusiast: Captain William Manson in Revolutionary Georgia," *Atlanta Historical Journal* 28 (Spring 1984): 23–38.

5. Manson's vessel, the *Arundel*, "entered outward" on December 12, 1774, but Manson was not aboard. He signed a deed for two hundred acres

of land in Wrightsborough on January 23, 1775. Witnesses were George Walton and William Belcher (Georgia Colonial Conveyance Book CC-1, 419–20, Colonial Records of Georgia, 1750–1802, Georgia Department of Archives and History, Atlanta. Manson returned to England on the *Georgia Packet*.

6. Waldo P. Harris III, "Locations Associated with Daniel Marshall and the Kiokee Church," *Viewpoints, Georgia Baptist History* 6 (1978): 25–44; grantees to land on the Kiokee may be found in Marion R. Hemperley, *English Crown Grants in St. Paul Parish in Georgia, 1755–1775* (Atlanta: State Printing Office, 1974).

7. Supplemental Memorial of Thomas Brown, PRO, AO 13/34.

8. Parrish, "Records of some Southern Loyalists," 343–45.

9. Weston, *North Riding*, 58–60.

10. Harry J. Carman, ed., *American Husbandry* (New York: Columbia University Press, 1939), 339.

11. Ibid., 340–52.

12. A description of Augusta in 1779 is in Colin Campbell, ed., *Journal of an Expedition against the Rebels of Georgia in North America under the Orders of Archibald Campbell Esquire Lieut. Colol. of His Majesty's 71st Regimt. 1778* (Darien, Ga.: Ashantilly Press, 1981), 54–55; Campbell's map showing the town of Augusta is in *GHS Collections* 8:following p. 32.

13. John A. Chapman, *History of Edgefield County from the Earliest Settlements to 1897* (1897; rpt. Spartanburg, S.C.: Reprint Company, 1980), 140.

14. "Unfinished Memories of Robert Mackay," in Mackay-Stiles Papers, vol. 42, Southern Historical Collection, University of North Carolina, Chapel Hill.

15. Robert Mackay to Mary Mackay, January 8, 10, 1775, Mary Mackay to Robert Mackay, January 19, 1775, ibid.

16. Hammond to John Lewis Gervais, June 22, 1777, in Mamie Norris Tillman and Hortense Woodson, eds., *The Hammond Family of Edgefield District* (Edgefield, S.C.: Advertiser Press, 1954), 4.

17. Mary Mackay to Robert Mackay, March 22, 1775, Mackay-Stiles Papers.

18. Robert Mackay to Mary Mackay, January 24, 1775, ibid.; *Georgia Gazette*, January 11, 1775.

19. Kenneth Coleman, *The American Revolution in Georgia, 1763–1789* (Athens: University of Georgia Press, 1958), 46–49.

20. Carman, ed., *American Husbandry*, 339.

21. Bartram, *Travels*, 54, 259, 264–67; Robert S. Davis, Jr., "Captain Edward Barnard and the Ceded Lands Rangers," *Georgia Pioneers Genealogical Magazine* 15 (February 1978): 20–22; Pay Bill of His Majesty's troop of Rangers Commanded by Captain Edward Barnard, March 13, 1775, in Loyalist Claim of Thomas Waters, PRO, AO 13/36-A.

22. Stuart to Gage, January 18, March 27, 1775, General Thomas Gage Papers, WLCL.

23. Wright to Gage, June 7, 27, 1775 (forged), ibid.; Robert W. Gibbes, *Documentary History of the American Revolution* (1853; rpt. 3 vols in 1. New York: New York Times and Arno Press, 1971), 1:100; John Drayton, *Memoirs of the American Revolution*, 2 vols. (1821; rpt. New York: New York Times and Arno Press, 1969), 1:346–50, 357.

24. *Georgia Gazette*, May 17, June 7, 21, July 12, 1775.

25. Wright to Dartmouth, July 29, 1775, *GHS Collections*, 3:200–201; Ms. CRG, 38, 1B:536–38.

26. Wright to Dartmouth, June 20, 1775, Ms. CRG, 38, 1B:475.

27. Drayton, *Memoirs*, 1:292–98.

28. Stuart to Gage, July 9, 1775, Gage Papers; Gage to Stuart, September 12, 1775, in Tonyn to Clinton, June 10, 1776, Sir Henry Clinton Papers, WLCL.

29. Drayton, *Memoirs*, 1:308–9.

30. Ibid., 312.

31. Campbell to Gage, July 1, 1775, Gage Papers; Campbell to Dartmouth, July 19, 1775, Clinton Papers.

32. Grierson to Wright, *CRG*, 12:434–37. William Thomson went to Georgia in 1775 to claim land left him by his father. According to his claim, he rode with Lieutenant Colonel Brown and the Indians; he was captured but escaped. He returned to England until the British reoccupied Georgia in 1779 (PRO, AO 13/37/352–74).

33. Grierson to Wright, *CRG*, 12:434–37; Hugh M'Call, *The History of Georgia, Containing Brief Sketches of the Most Remarkable Events Up to the Present Day (1784)*, 2 vols. (1811, 1816; rpt. 2 vols. in 1, Atlanta: A. B. Caldwell, 1909), 288–89; Brown to Cornwallis, July 16, 1780, PRO, AC 30/11/2.

34. Drayton, *Memoirs*, 1:322–23.

35. Ibid., 324.

36. Thomas Brown to Jonas Brown, November 10, 1775, letter in possession of Joan Leggett of Oxford, England; Gibbes, *Documentary History*, 1:143–44.

37. Thomas Brown to Jonas Brown, November 10, 1775, in possession of Joan Leggett.

38. Ibid.; Brown to Cornwallis, July 16, 1780, Cornwallis Papers, PRO, CO 30/11/2.

39. Pension claims of James Hall and Caleb Johnson, Revolutionary War Pension Claims, Record Group 15, National Archives; *Georgia Gazette*, August 30, 1775.

40. David Fanning, "Col. David Fanning's Narrative of His Exploits and Adventures as a Loyalist of North Carolina in the American Revolution

. . . ," in Walter Clark and Stephen B. Weeks, eds., *The State Records of North Carolina*, 22 (Goldsboro, N.C.: Nash Brothers, 1907), 182.

41. Wilson to Grierson, August 6, 1775, Grierson to Wright, August 6, 1775, Ms. CRG, 38, 1B:584–86; Wright to Dartmouth, August 17, 1775, *GHS Collections*, 3:18.

42. Thomas Brown to Jonas Brown, November 10, 1775, in possession of Joan Leggett; Andrew Pickens narrative, August 28, 1811, Sumter Papers, vol. 1, vv, Draper Collection, Wisconsin Historical Society, Madison.

43. Drayton to Council of Safety, August 16, 1775, in Gibbes, *Documentary History*, 1:140–43; Robert Stansbury Lambert, *South Carolina Loyalists in the American Revolution* (Columbia: University of South Carolina Press, 1987), 38.

44. Tennent to Henry Laurens, August 21, 1775, Drayton and Tennent to Council of Safety, August 24, 1775, in Gibbes, *Documentary History*, 1:145–46, 149–54, 156–57.

45. Tennent to Laurens, August 20, 1775, to Council of Safety, September 1, 1775, to Council of Safety in Savannah, September 10, 1775, Drayton to Council of Safety, August 21, 1775, in ibid., 145–46, 149–54, 164–66, 168–69.

46. Tennent to Council of Safety, September 1, 1775, Drayton to Council of Safety, August 30, September 11, 1775, Proclamation dated August 30, 1775, in ibid., 162–63, 163–64, 164–66, 171–75.

47. Drayton to Council of Safety, September 11, 1775, in ibid., 171–75.

48. Brown to Lord William Campbell, October 18, 1775, Clinton Papers; Charles Drayton to William Henry Drayton, September 16, 1775, Extract from an intercepted letter of Frederick George Mulcaster to Governor Grant, September 29, 1775, in Gibbes, *Documentary History* 1:183–84, 196–98.

49. Washington to Major General Philip Schuyler, December 24, 1775, in John C. Fitzpatrick, ed., *The Writings of George Washington from the Original Manuscript Sources, 1745–1799*, 39 vols. (Washington, D.C.: U.S. Government Printing Office, 1931–44), 4:178–80; Stuart to Gage, October 3, 1775, in Drayton, *Memoirs*, 1:296–98.

50. Treaty of Ninety-Six, September 16, 1775, signed by William Henry Drayton, Thomas Fletchall, John Ford, Thomas Greer, Evan McLaurin, Benjamin Wofford; Drayton to Council of Safety, September 17, 1775, in Gibbes, *Documentary History*, 1:184–91.

51. Brown to Campbell, October 18, 1775, Clinton Papers.

52. Ibid.

53. Lord William Campbell to Brown, November 3, 1775, TAB.

54. Drayton to Council of Safety, September 17, 1775, to Cunningham, September 21, 1775, to Cameron, September 26, 1775, in Gibbes, *Documentary History*, 1:187–91, 191–92, 194–95.

55. Cunningham to Drayton, October 5, 1775, in ibid., 200.

56. A Fragment of a Journal Kept by Rev. William Tennent . . . , August 2, 1775, to September 15, 1775, in ibid., 225–39.

57. Thomas Brown to Jonas Brown, November 10, 1775, in possession of Joan Leggett.

58. Martha Condray Searcy, "Thomas Browne: Loyalist" (M.A. thesis, Louisiana State University, 1972), 31–32.

59. Declaration by the Authority of Congress, November 19, 1775, in Gibbes, *Documentary History*, 1:210–14; *Georgia Gazette*, November 29, 1775.

60. Agreement for a Cessation of Arms . . . , November 22, 1775, James Mayson to William Thomson, November 24, 1775, Williamson to Drayton, November 25, 1775, Richard Richardson to Henry Laurens, December 12, 1775, in Gibbes, *Documentary History*, 1:214–19, 239–41; *Georgia Gazette*, December 6, 20, 1775.

61. Campbell to Dartmouth, January 1, 1775, Brown to Tonyn, May 8, 1776, Clinton Papers.

62. Baikia Harvey to Thomas Baikia, December 30, 1775, Balfour Papers.

63. Bernard Bailyn, *Voyagers to the West* (New York: Knopf, 1986), 553–54; *Etherington's York Chronicle*, July 28, 1775.

64. Viola Root Cameron, *Emigrants from Scotland to America, 1774–1775* (Baltimore: Genealogical Publishing Co., 1965), 93–95.

65. *Georgia Gazette*, December 20, 1775.

66. Taylor to Mr. Morrison, December 26, 1775, in Margaret Wheeler Willard, ed., *Letters on the American Revolution, 1774–1776* (Boston: Houghton Mifflin, 1925), 245–46; Taylor to Rev. Dr. Percy, January 13, 1776, Miscellaneous Papers, WLCL.

67. William Manson to his mother, April 8, 1776, Balfour Papers; Minutes of Council of Safety, January 2, 1776, *GHS Collections*, 5:25, 67.

68. Dr. Thomas Taylor to Rev. Dr. Percy, January 13, 1776, Miscellaneous Papers, WLCL.

69. Minutes of Council of Safety, July 25, 1776, *GHS Collections*, 5:82.

3. Testing the Plan, 1776

1. Wright to Clinton, February 21, 1776, Clinton Papers; Wright to Royal Council of Georgia, n.d., *RRG*, 1:269–72.

2. Coleman, *American Revolution in Georgia*, 69–70.

3. *RRG*, 1:274–77; George White, *Historical Collections of Georgia: Containing the Most Interesting Facts, Traditions, Biographical Sketches, Anecdotes,*

Etc., Relating to Its History and Antiquities, from Its First Settlement to the Present Time (New York: Pudney and Russell, 1855), 96–98.
4. *Georgia Gazette,* February 7, 1776.
5. Tonyn to Clinton, May 21, 1776, Clinton Papers.
6. Gage to Stuart, September 12, 1775, in Tonyn to Clinton, June 10, 1776, Clinton Papers. General Sir William Howe sent a sloop to convey Stuart to Cape Fear (Tonyn to Clinton, February 15, 1776, ibid.).
7. Brown to Tonyn, February 24, 1776, ibid.
8. Tonyn to Clinton, February 15, 1776, Clinton to Tonyn, March 20, 1776, in Clinton Letterbook, January 11, 1776, to December 29, 1776, ibid.
9. Tonyn to Clinton, April 15, 1776, ibid.
10. Stuart to Clinton, May 9, 1776, PRO, CO 5/77; Stuart to Germain, March 5, 1778, PRO, CO 5/79.
11. Stuart to Clinton, May 9, March 15, 1776, in K. G. Davies, ed., *Documents of the American Revolution, 1770–1783: Colonial Office Series,* 21 vols. (Shannon: Irish University Press, 1972–81), 12:135–37, 76–79; Tonyn to Clinton, June 8, 1776, East Florida Papers, typescripts of documents in PRO, CO, 5/556–57, Library of Congress.
12. Brown to Tonyn, May 2, 1776, Clinton Papers.
13. Brown to Tonyn, November 8, 1776, East Florida Papers. For a study of Galphin's career, see John McKay Sheftall, "George Galphin and Indian-White Relations in the Georgia Backcountry during the American Revolution" (M.A. thesis, University of Virginia, 1983).
14. George Galphin to Willie Jones, October 26, 1776, in Force, ed., *American Archives,* 5th ser., 3:648–50. The culprit's name is given as Thomas Few in the Journal of the Council of Safety, May 14–16, 1776, *RRG,* 1:122–23, 125, 128; it is Thomas Fee in David H. Corkran, *The Creek Frontier, 1540–1783* (Norman: University of Oklahoma Press, 1967), 297.
15. Records of Talks between Commissioners of the Continental Congress and the Southern Indians, Secretary of State, Continental Congress, 1774–79, Department of Cultural Resources, Division of Archives and History, Raleigh, N.C.
16. To His Excellency General Lee, Commander in Chief, etc.: The Petition of the Inhabitants of the Parish of St. George, and St. Paul, including the Ceded Lands in the Province of Georgia, July 31, 1776, *NYHS Collections,* 2:181–82.
17. Taitt to Tonyn, May 3, 1776, Brown to Tonyn, May 8, 1776, Clinton Papers.
18. Brown to Tonyn, May 8, 1776, ibid.; Tonyn to Howe, February 24, 1778, HMC, 1:197–99. For the date of Brown's commission, see Brown to Carleton, January 11, 1783, ibid., 3:322–23.
19. Brown to Cornwallis, July 16, 1780, Clinton Papers.

20. In 1771 Emistisiguo complained to John Stuart that Adam Tapley was one of those trading illegally in the woods. See Proceedings of Congress with Upper Creeks, 29 October–2 November, in Stuart to Hillsborough, December 29, 1771, Davies, ed., *Documents*, 3:212–28; Testimony of Joseph Ironmonger, October 31, 1776, in Force, ed., *American Archives*, 5th ser., 3:651; Galphin to Jones, October 26, 1776, ibid., 648–50; Williamson to Drayton, June 27, 1776, in Gibbes, *Documentary History*, 2:22–23.

21. Taitt to Stuart, July 7–10, 1776, in Davies, ed., *Documents*, 12:156–62.

22. Tonyn to Germain, October 30, 1776, East Florida Papers.

23. Tonyn to Germain, July 19, 1776, ibid.; Extract of a letter from Savannah, July 11, 1776, in Force, ed., *American Archives*, 5th ser., 1:181.

24. Minutes of Council of Safety, May 14, 1776, *RRG*, 1:122; Henry Stuart to John Stuart, May 7, August 25, 1776, in Davies, ed., *Documents*, 12:191, 208.

25. James H. O'Donnell III, *Southern Indians in the American Revolution* (Knoxville: University of Tennessee Press, 1973), 38; Henry Stuart to John Stuart, August 25, 1776, in Davies, ed., *Documents*, 12:191–208.

26. Francis Salvador to Drayton, July 18–19, 1776, in Gibbes, *Documentary History*, 2:24–26.

27. Henry Laurens to John Laurens, August 14, 1776, in *NYHS Collections*, 2:216–29; John Rutledge to Constitutional Assembly, September 19, 1776, in Force, ed., *American Archives*, 5th ser., 2:19.

28. Campbell to Germain, July 8, 1776, in Davies, ed., *Documents*, 12:165–66.

29. Drayton to Salvador, July 24, 1776, Williamson to Drayton, August 22, 1776, in Gibbes, *Documentary History*, 2:28–30, 32; Galphin to Jones, October 26, 1776, in Force, ed., *American Archives*, 5th ser., 3:648–50; Charles Lee to Edmund Pendleton, July 7, 1776, in ibid., 1:95.

30. Testimony of Joseph Ironmonger, October 31, 1776, in Force, ed., *American Archives*, 5th ser., 3:651.

31. Stuart to Dartmouth, January 19, 1776, PRO, CO 5/77; Council Minutes, July 25, 1776, *RRG*, 1:165; Brown to Tonyn, November 8, 1776, PRO, CO 5/557.

32. Lee to Rutledge, August 1, 1776, to Board of War and Ordinance, August 27, 1776, to Gen. John Armstrong, August 27, 1776, in *NYHS Collections*, 2:186–87, 241–47; Martha Condray Searcy, *The Georgia-Florida Contest in the American Revolution, 1776–1778* (University, Ala.: University of Alabama Press, 1985), 61–62.

33. Lachlan McIntosh to William McIntosh, October 22, 1776, *GHS Collections*, 12:15–16.

34. George Galphin to Willie Jones, October 26, 1776, with depositions of George Barnes, John Lambeth, and Joseph Ironmonger, October 21, 1776,

in Force, ed., *American Archives*, 5th ser., 3:648–51; Tonyn to Germain, October 30, 1776, PRO, CO 5:557.

35. Stuart to Germain, October 26, 1776, PRO, CO 5/78.
36. Ibid.
37. Stuart to Germain, November 24, 1776, PRO, CO 5/78.
38. Brown to Stuart, September 29, 1776, PRO, CO 5/78.
39. Testimony of George Barnes and John Lambeth, October 21, 1776, in Force, ed., *American Archives*, 5th ser., 3:650–51; McIntosh to Howe, October 22, 1776, *GHS Collections*, 12:14–15.
40. McIntosh to Howe, November 19, 1776, to Marbury, November 25, 1776, to Lt. Col. Habersham, November 27, 1776, to Henry Laurens, November 8, 1776, to Lt. Wilson, December 13, 1776, *GHS Collections*, 12:18–22.
41. McIntosh to Howe, December 13, 1776, January 7, 1777, to Captain Richard Winn, January 10, 1777, ibid., 12:31–32, 35–36; McIntosh's talk, December 23, 1776, PRO, CO 5/78, also in Antonio J. Waring Collection, Georgia Historical Society, Savannah.
42. Brown to Tonyn, November 8, 1776, PRO, CO 5/557.

4. Frontier War, 1777–1778

1. Tonyn to Perryman, January 12, 1777, PRO, CO 5/557. The best account of the confusing border warfare is Searcy, *Georgia-Florida Contest.*
2. Lewis Butler and Stewart Hare, *The Annals of the King's Royal Rifle Corps*, vol. 1: Butler, *The Royal Americans* (London: Smith, Elder and Co., 1913), Appendix II, "Memoir of Major Patrick Murray," 207.
3. Tonyn to Prevost, January 17, 1777, Prevost to Tonyn, January 11, 1777, Tonyn to Prevost, January 13, 1777, Prevost to Tonyn, January 16, 1777, Tonyn to Prevost, January 19, 1777, PRO, CO 5/557.
4. Tonyn to Chief Warriors of Creek Nation, February 8, 1777, to Brown, February 5, 1777, PRO, CO 5/557.
5. Winn to Col. Francis Harris, February 17, 1777, Bostick to McIntosh, February 18, 1777, Lachlan McIntosh Papers, New-York Historical Society.
6. McIntosh to Howe, February 19, 1777, to Screven, February 19, 1777, *GHS Collections*, 12:41.
7. Brown to Tonyn, February 20, 1777, List of the Garrison of Fort McIntosh on the St. Tilla [sic] River surrendered Prisoners of War this 18th February 1777 . . . , PRO, CO 5/557.
8. McIntosh to Bostick, February 20, 1777, *GHS Collections*, 12:42.
9. Brown to Tonyn, February 20, 1777, PRO, CO 5/557.

10. McIntosh to Washington, April 13, 1777, *GHS Collections*, 12:45–47.

11. Council Minutes, February 21, 1777, *RRG*, 1:224–25.

12. Papers respecting the Augustine Expedition in April 1777, *GHS Collections*, 12:61–63.

13. Ibid.

14. Lyman Hall to Roger Sherman, June 1, 1777, in Thomas Gamble, *Savannah Duels and Duellists, 1733–1877* (Savannah: Review Publishing Company, 1923), 15; Charles F. Jenkins, *Button Gwinnett, Signer of the Declaration of Independence* (New York: Doubleday, Page, 1926), 152–53; for the factional dispute see Hazard Pamphlets, Rare Book Room, Library of Congress.

15. For Elbert's correspondence during the expedition see *GHS Collections*, 5, pt. 2:19–35.

16. Brown to Tonyn, May 15, 1777, in Charles E. Bennett, *Southernmost Battlefields of the Revolution* (Bailey's Crossroads, Va.: Privately published, 1970), 7–9.

17. Brown to Tonyn, May 18, 1777, in ibid., 13–15.

18. Murray's memoirs cited in ibid., 15; Tonyn to Germain, June 18, 1777, in ibid., 16–17.

19. Elbert to McIntosh, May 25, 1777, *GHS Collections*, 12:64–66.

20. Tonyn to Germain, June 16, 1777, PRO, CO 5/557.

21. Howe to Prevost, April 1, 1777, to Tonyn, May 4, 1777, Prevost to Howe, June 14, 1777, HMC, 1:100, 107; Prevost to Tonyn, June 29, 1777, PRO, CO 5/557.

22. Prevost to Howe, June 14, November 1, 1777, HMC, 1:119–20, 147–48.

23. Howe to Stuart, January 13, 1777, in Davies, ed., *Documents*, 14:28–30.

24. Stuart to Germain, January 23, 1777, to Howe, April 13, 1777, Taitt to Stuart, May 23, 1777, to Brown, May 23, 1777, in ibid., 14:34–35, 68–69, 93–95, 95–66.

25. Tonyn to Germain, June 16, 1777, in ibid., 116–18; Germain to Tonyn, April 2, 1777, Howe to Tonyn, May 4, 1777, PRO, CO 5/557.

26. Prevost to Clinton, July 11, 1778, HMC, 1:271–72.

27. Stuart to Germain, October 6, 1777, in Davies, ed., *Documents*, 14:192–95.

28. Robert S. Davies, Jr., "George Galphin, and the Creek Congress of 1777," *Proceedings and Papers of the Georgia Association of Historians 1982* (Marietta, Ga.: Georgia Association of Historians, 1983), 13–29; Sheftall, "George Galphin," 33; McIntosh to Cameron, July 6, 1777, Waring Collection.

29. Taitt to Brown, May 23, 1777, in Davies, ed., *Documents*, 14:95–96;

Tonyn to Stuart, August 31, 1777, PRO, CO 5/557; Searcy, *Georgia-Florida Contest*, 113.

30. Sheftall, "George Galphin," 35.

31. Lila M. Hawes, ed., "Minutes of the Executive Council, May 7 through October 14, 1777," *GHQ* 34(1950):108–9.

32. Rutledge to Gentlemen, August 30, 1777, John Rutledge Papers, University of South Carolina, South Caroliniana Library, Columbia, S.C.; Tonyn to Stuart, August 31, 1777, PRO, CO 5/557. For the view that Stuart was plotting the assassination of Galphin see Davis, "Galphin and the Creek Congress," 13–29.

33. Elbert to Baker, August 16, 1777, to McIntosh, August 16, 1777, Thomas Addis Emmet Collection, New York Public Library.

34. Treutlen to Hancock, June 19, 1777, John Adam Treutlen Papers, Georgia Historical Society, Savannah; Wereat to Walton, August 30, 1777, *GHS Collections*, 12:66–72.

35. Rutledge to Gentlemen, August 30, 1777, Rutledge Papers; Stuart to Germain, October 6, 1777, in Davies, ed., *Documents*, 14:192–95.

36. Introduction, Davies, ed., *Documents*, 14:20–21.

37. Introduction, ibid., 15:13.

38. Stuart to Germain, January 23, 1778, in ibid., 15:32–34.

39. Howe to Sir, September 4, 1777, Papers of the Continental Congress, 1774–89, Georgia State Papers, 1777–88, Library of Congress; Washington to Howe, January 13, 1778, in Fitzpatrick, ed., *Writings of Washington*, 10:300–302.

40. Minutes of the Executive Council, July 14, 1777, *GHQ* 34 (March 1950): 27.

41. Memorial of Lord William Campbell and others to Lord George Germain, August 1777, in Davies, ed., *Documents*, 14:182–84. The "others" were Governor James Wright and Lieutenant Governors William Bull and John Graham.

42. Germain to Clinton, March 8, 1778, Headquarters Papers of the British Army in America, Colonial Williamsburg Foundation, Williamsburg, Va. (microfilm), 9:996.

43. Ibid.

44. Prevost to Howe, February 12, 1778, Brown to Tonyn, February 19, 1778, HMC, 1:193, 195.

45. Tonyn to Howe, February 24, 1778, ibid., 197–99.

46. Brown to Tonyn, March 13, 1778, Tonyn to Howe, March 31, 1778, Headquarters Papers, 9:1014, 1058.

47. Prevost to Howe, March 31, 1778, ibid., 1035; Tonyn to Howe, April 4, 1778, Prevost to Howe, April 5, 1778, ibid., 10:1068, 1069; William Moultrie, *Memoirs of the American Revolution. So Far as It Related to the States*

of North and South Carolina and Georgia. 2 vols. (1802; rpt. New York: Arno Press, 1968), 1:203–4.

48. Prevost to Howe, March 18, 1778, HMC, 1:211–12; Howe to Moultrie, April 7, 1778, in Moultrie, *Memoirs*, 1:203–4.

49. Brown to Prevost, April 10, 1778, HMC, 1:227, Headquarters Papers, 10:1081.

50. Brown to Germain, March 10, 1780, PRO, CO 5/81.

51. Brown to Tonyn, April 16, 1778, Headquarters Papers, 10:1100; Minutes of the Executive Council, April 13, 1778, *RRG*, 2:73; Houstoun to Sir, April 16, 1778, Papers of the Continental Congress, 1774–89, National Archives.

52. Fanning, "Narrative," 185.

53. Tonyn to Howe, April 29, 1778, Clinton to Prevost, June 3, 1778, Headquarters Papers, 10:1133, 1203.

54. Tonyn to Howe, May 1, 1778, to Brown, April 18, 1778, ibid., 1143, 1107.

55. Clinton to Tonyn, June 3, 1778, ibid., 1024.

56. John Fauchereau Grimké, "Journal of the Campaign to the Southward, May 9th to July 14th, 1778," *SCHGM* 12 (April, July, October 1911): 60–69, 118–34, 190–206.

57. Ibid., 132, 192.

58. Brown to Tonyn, June 30, 1778, Headquarters Papers, 10:1027; Prevost to Clinton, September 25, 1778, HMC, 1:302; Grimké, "Journal," 134.

59. Brown to Tonyn, June 30, 1778, Capt. Alex Shaw to Tonyn, July 1, 1778, Headquarters Papers, 11:1247, 1255; Butler, *Royal Americans*, 305; Grimké, "Journal," 192.

60. The Case of the Inhabitants of East Florida (St. Augustine, 1784), P. K. Yonge Library, University of Florida, Gainesville; Prevost to Clinton, July 11, 1778, HMC, 1:271–72; Tonyn to Stuart, July 3, 1778, quoted in Bennett, *Southernmost Battlefields*, 35–36; Charles Loch Mowat, *East Florida as a British Province, 1763–1784* (1943; rpt. Gainesville: University of Florida Press, 1964), 163.

61. Prevost to Clinton, September 25, 1778, Clinton to Prevost, May 2, 1779, HMC, 1:302, 427; Butler, *Royal Americans*, 326–27.

62. White, *Historical Collections of Georgia*, 615–16, 524–25.

63. M'Call, *History of Georgia*, 366–67. There is some confusion of facts in M'Call's account. For example, he wrote that Daniel McGirth led the Rangers at Midway.

64. Searcy, *Georgia-Florida Contest*, 163–64.

65. Tonyn to Stuart, September 8, 1778, PRO, CO 5/80.

66. Tonyn to Germain, April 29, 1778, in Davies, ed., *Documents*, 15:111–12; William McIntosh to Stuart, April 3, 1778, PRO, CO 5/79; Germain to Stuart, December 2, 1778, PRO, CO 5/80.

67. Stuart to Germain, December 4, 1778, PRO, CO 5/80.
68. Taitt to Germain, August 6, 1779, ibid.

5. *The Plan Unfolds, 1779*

1. Moses Kirkland to Clinton, October 13, 1778, in Randall M. Miller, ed., "A Backcountry Loyalist Plan to Retake Georgia and the Carolinas, 1778," *SCHM* 75 (1974): 207–14; Prevost to Howe, March 10, 1778, PRO, CO 55/9; Campbell, ed., *Journal*, xii, 82.

2. Campbell, *Journal*, xi; Carlisle, Clinton, and Eden to Campbell, November 3, 1778, marked "Most Secret," in ibid., 6. The Carlisle Peace Commission was set up by the British government on April 12, 1778, to negotiate a peaceful settlement of the American war. Original members of the commission were the Earl of Carlisle, William Eden, and Commodore George Johnstone. The latter was replaced by Sir Henry Clinton. The commission was authorized to establish civil governments on a temporary basis. Documents relating to the commission are in B. F. Stevens, ed., *Facsimiles of Manuscripts in European Archives Relating to America, 1773–1783, with Descriptions, Editorial Notes, Collations, References, and Translations*, 25 vols. (London: Malby and Sons, 1889–98).

3. Prevost to Germain, January 18, 1779, in Stevens, ed., *Facsimiles*, 12:1251; Clinton to Stuart, October 27, 1778, Headquarters Papers, 13:1492.

4. Campbell to the Earl of Carlisle, in Stevens, ed., *Facsimiles*, 1:113; Alexander A. Lawrence, "General Robert Howe and the British Capture of Savannah in 1778," *GHQ* 36 (December 1952):303–27. Campbell's proclamation is in Campbell, *Journal*, 35.

5. Campbell, *Journal*, 37.

6. Prevost to Germain, January 18, 1779, in Stevens, ed., *Facsimiles*, 12:1251.

7. Campbell to Eden, January 19, 1779, in ibid., 1252; "On Mr. Prevost's Conduct in Georgia, 1779," unsigned, Lord George Germain Papers, WLCL.

8. Campbell to Germain, January 19, 1779, in Campbell, *Journal*, 41–44. Campbell fancied the phrase about snatching a stripe and a star. He used it in a letter to Carlisle, January 19, 1779, in ibid., 1:113.

9. Campbell, *Journal*, 48; Prevost to Clinton, January 19, 1779, Headquarters Papers, 14:1691.

10. Campbell, *Journal*, 49; Paul Leicester Ford, ed., *Proceedings of a Council of War Held at Burke Jail, Georgia, January 14, 1779, with a Narrative of the Subsequent Proceedings and the Proclamation Issued by Lieut. Col. James Ingram* (Brooklyn: Historical Printing Club, 1890); M'Call, *History of Georgia*, 390–91.

11. Campbell, *Journal*, 52.
12. Sheftall, "George Galphin," 51.
13. Ibid., 49; Campbell, *Journal*, 56.
14. Davis, "Last Colonial Enthusiast," 28–31; Doyce B. Nunis, Jr., "Colonel Archibald Campbell's March from Savannah to Augusta, 1779," *GHQ* 45 (September 1961):275–87; Robert S. Davis identified the writer in the Nunis article as Lt. John Wilson; see Davis, *Encounters on a March through Georgia in 1779* (Sylvania, Ga.: Partridge Pond Press, 1986), 10–13.
15. James Seymour to the Rev. Mr. Morice, Secretary to the Society for the Propagation of the Gospel, April 26, 1781, British Empire Church Records, S.P.G. Sup., Letters and Papers, American Colonies II (1680–85), Georgia and Virginia), University of Texas Library, Austin; Thomas Taylor to Madam, November 9, 1779, Balfour Papers.
16. Campbell, *Journal*, 55–58; Sheftall, "George Galphin," 51.
17. Moses Wheatley (or Whitley) was Joseph Robinson's brother-in-law (Lambert, *South Carolina Loyalists*, 69). Wheatley was exchanged for a Captain Celeron on May 21, 1779 (William Moultrie to Gen. Prevost, May 21, 1779, in Moultrie, *Memoirs*, 1:457–58); Campbell, *Journal*, 58, 60; M'Call, *History of Georgia*, 400.
18. Campbell's message was conveyed by way of Prevost to Indians, March 13, 1779, PRO, CO 5/80.
19. Campbell to Clinton, March 4, 1779, Headquarters Papers, 15:1797.
20. Campbell, *Journal*, 63–64.
21. Seymour to Morice, April 26, 1781, British Empire Church Records.
22. Prevost to Clinton, March 1, 1779, Headquarters Papers, 15:1783.
23. Campbell, *Journal*, 68, 71; *Royal Georgia Gazette*, March 11, 1779; Otis Ashmore and C. H. Olmstead, "The Battles of Kettle Creek and Briar Creek," *GHQ* 10 (June 1926):125.
24. Campbell to Lt. Col. James Mark Prevost, March 4, 1779, in Campbell, *Journal*, 75–76; the MacAlister incident in ibid., 77. The American General Lincoln was disgusted at the butchery of MacAlister, writing, "My soul abhors such inhuman deeds," in a letter to Williamson, February 16, 1779, Benjamin Lincoln Papers, Massachusetts Historical Society, Boston.
25. Germain to Campbell, March 13, 1779, to Prevost, March 13, 1779, in Stevens, ed., *Facsimiles*, 12:1270, 1271.
26. Prevost to Indians, March 13, 1779, PRO, CO 5/80.
27. M'Call, *History of Georgia*, 409–10.
28. Jacob Moniac to Stuart, April 16, 1779, PRO, CO 5/80. It is interesting to speculate on the identity of the British colonel. Thomas Brown and Joseph Robinson are the most likely candidates (Taitt to Germain, August 6, 1779, PRO, CO 5/80). According to Jacob Moniac, McGillivray barely man-

aged to escape between two lines of fire (Moniac to Stuart, April 16, 1779, ibid.).

29. *Virginia Gazette*, May 1, 1779; C. F. W. Coker, ed., "Journal of John Graham, South Carolina Militia, 1779," *Military Collector and Historian* 19 (Summer 1967):41. According to Graham, Hammond had five hundred mounted men. A British source stated that Hammond had two hundred men against forty Indians and ten whites (Commissioners to Germain, May 10, 1779, PRO, CO 5/80). General Andrew Williamson, who was in a position to know, said that Hammond had three hundred men and Pickens two hundred (Williamson to Lincoln, March 26, 1779, Lincoln Papers).

30. *Virginia Gazette*, May 1, 1779. Majors Spurgeon and Sharpe of the Carolina Loyalists were killed.

31. Cameron to Germain, May 10, 1779, PRO, CO 5/80; Germain to Cameron, April 5, 1780, PRO, CO 5/81.

32. Germain to Stuart, June 2, 1779, Cameron to Germain, March 26, 1779, PRO, CO 5/80. Campbell saw at least one Indian chief while at Augusta, according to Lt. John Wilson (Davis, *Encounters on a March through Georgia*, 42).

33. *South Carolina and American General Gazette*, February 25, 1779.

34. Lincoln to Jay, February 27, 1779, Papers of the Continental Congress, 1774–89, National Archives Microfilm Publications, 247; Washington to Henry Laurens, March 20, 1779, in Fitzpatrick, ed., *Writings of Washington*, 14:266.

35. Prevost to Clinton, April 16, 1779, Tonyn to Clinton, May 1, 1779, Clinton to Cameron, April 29, 1779, Headquarters Papers, 16:1925, 1969, 1955; Clinton to Prevost, May 2, 1779, HMC, 1:427; Germain to Cameron, April 5, 1780, PRO, CO 5/81.

36. Tonyn to Clinton, May 29, 1779, to Prevost, May 29, 1779, Headquarters Papers, 16:2026–27; Prevost to Clinton, June 16, 1779, ibid., 17:2056.

37. Germain to Brown and Cameron, June 25, 1779, PRO, CO 5/242, also in Clinton Papers.

38. Cameron to Clinton, October 15, 1779, Headquarters Papers, 19:2372; Germain to Cameron, April 5, 1780, Brown to Germain, December 31, 1779, PRO, CO 5/81. As early as July 3, 1779, the *Virginia Gazette* carried the news that Brown had been named Stuart's successor.

39. Council at Black Swamp, April 19, 1779, in Moultrie, *Memoirs*, 1:374–75; *South Carolina and American General Gazette*, April 9, 1779; Lincoln to John Jay, June 4, 1779, Lincoln Papers; Rutledge to Williamson, April 11, 1779, in Moultrie, *Memoirs*, 1:372–73.

40. For an account of Lincoln's movements see his Warrant Book, Rare Book Room, New York Public Library, and John Fauchereau Grimké, "Or-

der Book of John Fauchereau Grimké," *SCHGM* 15 (April and July 1914): 82–90, 124–32; Lincoln to Moultrie, May 6, 1779, to Cols. Walton, Few, and Dooly, May 10, 1779, to Jay, June 4, 1779, Lincoln Papers; M'Call, *History of Georgia*, 420–22.

41. Butler, *Royal Americans*, 212–13; Extracts of letter from Captain Henry, May 23, 1779, PRO, CO 5/80.

42. Prevost to Clinton, June 11, July 14, 30, 1779, Headquarters Papers, 17:2046, 2119, 2151.

43. *Virginia Gazette*, August 14, 1779; *Royal Georgia Gazette*, August 19, 1779; Prevost to Clinton, July 30, 1779, Headquarters Papers, 17:2151; HMC, 1:483.

44. Charles M. Lefferts, *Uniforms of the American, British, French, and German Armies in the War of the American Revolution* (Old Greenwich, Conn.: We, Inc., 1971), 22; Prevost to Clinton, July 30, 1779, Headquarters Papers, 17:2151; Heard Robertson, "Notes on the Muster Rolls of Lieutenant Colonel Thomas Brown's Battalion of Loyalist Provincial Rangers, 1776–1782," *Richmond County History* 4 (1972):5–15.

45. Prevost to Clinton, July 30, 1779, Headquarters Papers, 17:2154; Brown to Cornwallis, July 16, 1780, Cornwallis Papers, PRO 30/11/2.

46. Clinton to Prevost, August 10, 1779, Headquarters Papers, 18:2183.

47. Lincoln to McIntosh, July 15, 1779, Lincoln Papers.

48. Cashin, "'The Famous Colonel Wells,'" 146–47.

49. Wright to Germain, November 5, 1779, Ms. CRG, 38, pt. 2:206–9; Prevost to Clinton, September 8, 1779, Headquarters Papers, 18:2262.

50. Washington to Conrad Alexandre Gerard, May 1, 1779, to Brig. Gen. Charles Scott, May 5, 1779, to the president of Congress, May 11, 1779, to Benjamin Lincoln, February 27, 1780, in Fitzpatrick, ed., *Writings of Washington*, 14:270, 498, 15:40, 18:55.

51. Journal of the Siege of Savannah in Prevost to Germain, November 1, 1779, in Stevens, ed., *Facsimiles*, 23:2020. For a general account of the siege, see Alexander A. Lawrence, *Storm over Savannah: The Story of Count D'Estaing and the Siege of the Town in 1779* (Athens: University of Georgia Press, 1951), and Journal of the Siege of Savannah by the French troops under Count D'Estaing from September to October 18, 1779, in Stevens, ed., *Facsimiles*, 23:2010. "A Sketch of the Blockade" is in ibid., 23:2015. Wylly's "Plan of Attack and the Fortification of Savannah" is in the DeRenne Collection, University of Georgia Libraries, Athens.

52. Butler, *Royal Americans*, 214–18; George Fenwick Jones, "A Note on the Victor at Springhill Redoubt," *GHQ* 64 (Fall 1979): 377–79.

53. Richard C. Cole, "The Siege of Savannah and the British Press, 1779–1780," *GHQ* 65 (Fall 1981): 189–202; Bobby Gilmer Moss, *Roster of South Carolina Patriots in the American Revolution* (Baltimore: Genealogical Publishing Co., 1983), 423.

54. Cameron to Clinton, December 18, 1779, Headquarters Papers, 20:2489; Prevost to Clinton, November 6, 7, 1779, HMC, 2:59. George Prevost later gained doubtful distinction by putting down the Carib revolt on St. Vincent and by his abortive invasion of New York during the War of 1812.
55. Brown to Germain, December 31, 1779, PRO, CO 5/81.

6. The Plan as the Southern Strategy, 1780

1. Brown to Germain, March 10, 1780, PRO, CO 5/81.
2. Wright to Germain, February 18, 1780, *GHS Collections*, 3:275–76; Banastre Tarleton, *A History of the Campaigns of 1780 and 1781 in the Southern Provinces of North America* (London: T. Cadell, 1787), 5–6.
3. Brown to Germain, March 19, 1780, PRO, CO 5/81.
4. Prevost to Germain, February 11, 13, 17, 1780, HMC, 2:88–89, 91. Prevost informed Germain of the death of the veteran Lieutenant Colonel Lewis V. Fuser in St. Augustine.
5. Wright to Paterson, February 14, 1780, Ms. *CRG* 38, pt. 2:77–81.
6. David Ramsay, *History of South Carolina from Its First Settlement in 1670 to the year 1808*, 2 vols. (1858; rpt. Spartanburg, S.C.: Reprint Co., 1968), 2:183–87; Clinton to Wright, February 19, 1780, HMC, 2:92; Clinton to Tonyn, February 19, 1780, Headquarters Papers, 21:2587.
7. Clinton to Innes, February 19, 1780, HMC, 2:92–93.
8. Brown to Germain, March 18, 1780, PRO, CO 5/81.
9. Wright to Clinton, June 2, 1780, HMC, 2:106, 134; Wright to Clinton, April 20, 1780, Headquarters Papers, 21:2693.
10. Brown to Clinton, April 24, 1780, Clinton Papers; William McIntosh to Brown, March 20, 1780, Waring Collection.
11. Major A. S. DePeyster to Brown, April 5, 1780, Headquarters Papers, 12:2672.
12. Clinton to Clarke, May 20, 1780, to Wright, May 20, 1780, Headquarters Papers, 23:2754, 2756.
13. Butler, *Royal Americans*, 327.
14. Ibid., 325.
15. Brown to Germain, May 25, 1780, Germain Papers; Sheftall, "George Galphin," 57.
16. Brown to Cornwallis, June 18, 1780, Cornwallis Papers, PRO 30/11/2.
17. An Act for the more speedy and effectually settling and strengthening this State, January 23, 1780, *CRG*, 19, pt. 2:130–40.
18. Wereat to McIntosh, January 19, 1780, Peter Force Papers, ser. 7E, 3, Library of Congress.

19. Council Minutes, February 5, 18, May 23, 1780, *RRG*, 2:213–14, 222–23, 247–48; Gamble, *Savannah Duels and Duellists*, 37–40.

20. For Williamson's career and reputation, see Edward J. Cashin, "The Trembling Land: Covert Activity in the Georgia Backcountry during the American Revolution," in *Proceedings and Papers of the Georgia Association of Historians 1982* (Marietta, Ga.: Georgia Association of Historians, 1983), 31–39.

21. Davis, "Last Colonial Enthusiast," 31; Wright to Balfour, August 19, 1780, Ms. CRG, 38, pt. 2:421.

22. Brown to Cornwallis, June 18, 1780, Cornwallis Papers, PRO 30/11/2.

23. Parrish, "Records of some Southern Loyalists," 346; Seymour to Morice, April 26, 1781, British Empire Church Records; *Georgia Gazette*, March 13, 1783.

24. Cornwallis to Clarke, July 2, 1780, to Balfour, July 3, 1780, Cornwallis Papers, PRO 30/11/78.

25. Brown to Cornwallis, June 18, 1780, ibid., PRO 30/11/2, 166–68.

26. Balfour to Cornwallis, June 24, 27, 1780, ibid., PRO 30/11/2, 200–203.

27. Balfour to Cornwallis, June 24, 1780, ibid., PRO, CO 30/11/2; list of military stores sent from Fort Seneca to Ninety-Six, August 1, 1780, ibid., PRO 30/11/103.

28. Wright, Jr., to Cornwallis, July 15, 1780, Wright to Cornwallis, July 9, 31, 1780, ibid., PRO 30/11/2, 256–57, 160–61.

29. Germain to Brown, June 5, 1780, ibid., PRO, CO 5/81; Brown to Cornwallis, July 16, 1780, ibid., PRO, CO 30/11/2.

30. Brown to Cornwallis, July 16, 1780, ibid., PRO 30/11/2.

31. Cornwallis to Brown, July 2, 1780, to Clarke, July 24, 1780, ibid., PRO 30/11/78.

32. Cornwallis to Cruger, August 5, 31, 1780, ibid., PRO 30/11/79, 12–13, 50–51.

33. Disqualifying Act of July 1, 1780, in *RRG*, 1:348–63; Wright to Germain, July 17, 1780, *GHS Collections*, 3:307–9.

34. Brown to Cruger, August 6, 1780, Cornwallis Papers, PRO 30/11/62, 6–7; M'Call, *History of Georgia*, 481; Moultrie, *Memoirs*, 240.

35. Cruger to Cornwallis, August 7, 1780, Cornwallis Papers, PRO 30/11/63, 22.

36. Gates to the president of Congress, October 16, 1780, Papers of the Continental Congress.

37. Pension claim of Joshua Burnett, Revolutionary War Pension Claims, Record Group 15, National Archives.

38. Thomas S. Woodward, *Woodward: Reminiscences of the Creek or Muscogee Indians, Contained in Letters to Friends in Georgia and Alabama* (1859;

rpt. Birmingham: Birmingham Book Exchange, 1939), 59. Although Woodward, an Alabama pioneer who knew Taitt's son Davy, refers to David Taitt as John Tate, there is no doubt that he is referring to Stuart's deputy.

39. Brown to Cruger, September 15, 1780, Cornwallis Papers, PRO 30/11/64.

40. Elizabeth Lichtenstein Johnston, *Recollections of a Georgia Loyalist* (1901; rpt., ed. Arthur Wentworth Eaton, Spartanburg, S.C.: Reprint Co., 1972), 68–69.

41. Robert Mackay, "Unfinished Memoirs of Robert Mackay," Mackay-Stiles Papers, vol. 42.

42. Brown to Clinton, December 17, 1780, Clinton Papers.

43. *Royal Gazette* (South Carolina), March 23–27, 1782; Brown to Cruger, September 15, 1780, Cornwallis Papers, PRO 30/11/64.

44. Printed account of the siege, September 23, 1780, enclosed in Charles Shaw to Germain, September 24, 1780, PRO, CO 5/82.

45. Cruger to Cornwallis, September 16, 1780, Cornwallis Papers, PRO 30/11/64.

46. M'Call, *History of Georgia*, 485.

47. Printed account, PRO, CO 5/82; Wright to Commons House of Assembly, September 27, 1780, *CRG*, 15:625–26; Cornwallis to Germain, September 21, 1780, PRO, CO 5/183; Cruger to Balfour, September 19, 1780, Cornwallis Papers, PRO 30/11/64; Lieutenant William Stevenson to Mrs. Susannah Kennedy, September 25, 1780, Draper Collection, 4 1780 vv; Cornwallis to Germain, September 23, 1780, PRO, CO 5/183.

48. Printed account of the siege, September 23, 1780, PRO, CO 5/82; Wright to Germain, October 17, 1780, *GHS Collections*, 3:321–22. The names of the victims were listed by M'Call: Henry Duke, John Burgamy, Scott Reeden, Jordan Ricketson, ——— Darling, and two brothers named Glass, *History of Georgia*, 486. According to R. B. Darling of Swainsboro, Georgia, the first name of Darling was Ephraim. Mr. Darling is a direct descendant of both Ephraim Darling and Chesley Bostick.

49. Clark to Thomas Sumter, October 29, 1780, Sumter Papers, Draper Collection, 7 vv 75; William Campbell to William Preston, December 12, 1780, "Preston Papers," *Virginia Magazine of History and Biography* 27 (July and October 1919):314–16; Cruger to Cornwallis, September 28, 1780, Cornwallis Papers, PRO 30/11/64.

50. Stephen Heard to Dear Sir, March 2, 1781, Revolutionary Papers, University of Georgia Libraries, Special Collections, Athens.

51. M'Call, *History of Georgia*, 488; Rutledge to Delegates of the State of South Carolina, November 20, 1780, Joseph Barnwell, ed., "Letters of John Rutledge," *SCHGM* 17 (October 1916): 142–45.

52. Brown to Ramsay, December 25, 1786, in White, *Historical Collections of Georgia*, 615; *Augusta Chronicle*, October 9, 1887.

53. Cornwallis to Clinton, December 3, 1780, Cornwallis Papers, PRO 30/11/72, 57–64; Tarleton, *History of the Campaigns,* 192.

54. From Camp near Gilbert Town to Gates, October 4, 1780, Gates to President of Congress, October 10, 1780, Gates Letterbook, 126, Horatio Gates Papers, New-York Historical Society.

55. Cornwallis to Clinton, December 3, 1780, PRO, CO 5/81.

56. Rawdon to Clinton, October 28, 1780, PRO, CO 5/183.

57. Cornwallis to Clinton, December 3, 1780, PRO, CO 5/182; Claim of Moses Kirkland, American Loyalists, Audit Office Transcripts, vol. 28, Transcribed for the New York Public Library, 1900.

58. Graham's report on the Ceded Lands, November 8, 1780, Cornwallis Papers, PRO 30/11/4.

59. Wright to Cornwallis, November 20, 1780, Cruger to Cornwallis, November 8, 1780, ibid.

60. Brown to Cornwallis, December 17, 1780, Clinton Papers; Cornwallis to Clinton, December 29, 1780, HMC, 2:225. According to a Virginia trader named William Springstone, the Raven received a war talk from Colonel Brown and agreed to go to war immediately "with the inhabitants of Virginia and Carolina settled on the Western Waters" (Deposition of William Springstone, in "Preston Papers," 313–14.

61. Brown to Cornwallis, December 17, 1780, Clinton Papers; Declaration of the Account of Lieutenant Colonel Thomas Brown as Superintendent of Indian Affairs in the Atlantic Department of the Southern District of North America from July 1, 1779, to December 31, 1784, July 9, 1791, PRO, AO 1 1531/9; see also PRO, T 1 601/298–306; A New Map of the Southern District of North America by Joseph Purcell (1781), PRO, CO 700/N. America 15.

7. The Plan Fails, 1781

1. Brown to Ramsay, December 25, 1786, in White, *Historical Collections of Georgia,* 2:617.

2. Clanosee and Ancoo (Cherokee messengers) to Col. Joseph Martin, April 28, 1781, Talk of the Tassel to Commissioners, July 26, 1781, Tennessee Papers, Draper Collection, ixx43; ixx47.

3. O'Donnell, *Southern Indians,* 114.

4. Greene to Benjamin Few, December 16, 1780, Nathanael Greene Papers, WLCL.

5. Morgan to William Davidson, January 26, 1781, Gates Papers.

6. Wright to Germain, January 26, 1781, *GHS Collections,* 3:332–33.

7. Seymour to Mr. Morice, April 26, 1781, British Empire Church Records; Claim of John Douglass, PRO, AO 13/34.

8. Brown to Balfour, January 23, 1781, Cornwallis Papers, PRO 30/11/62; Brown to Ramsay, December 25, 1786, in White, *Historical Collections of Georgia*, 2:616.

9. M'Call, *History of Georgia*, 512; Shaw to Germain, February 14, 1781, PRO, CO 5/81; Brown to Balfour, January 23, 1781, Cornwallis Papers, PRO 30/11/62.

10. Brown to Balfour, January 23, 1781, PRO 30/11/62.

11. M'Call, *History of Georgia*, 513.

12. Brown to Ramsay, December 25, 1786, in White, *Historical Collections of Georgia*, 2:617.

13. Shaw to Germain, February 14, 1781, PRO, CO 5/81; Brown to Balfour, January 23, 1781, Cornwallis Papers, PRO 30/11/62; Balfour to Brown, February 9, 1781, ibid., PRO 30/11/109.

14. Wright to Germain, March 6, 1781, Waters to Wright, February 20, 26, 1781, Brown to Wright, February 2, March 4, 1781, Ms. CRG, 38, pt. 2:469-79; Wright to Cornwallis, April 23, 1781, Cornwallis Papers, PRO 30/11/5.

15. Brown to Germain, August 9, 1781, PRO, CO 5/82.

16. Wright to Germain, April 24, 1781, *GHS Collections*, 3:346-47.

17. *Royal Georgia Gazette*, April 26, 1781.

18. Seymour to Mr. Morice, April 26, 1781, British Empire Church Records.

19. Pickens to Greene, February 19, 1781, Greene to Pickens, March 8, 1781, Greene Papers, WLCL.

20. Pickens to Greene, April 8, 1781, Greene to Pickens, April 15, 1781, to Sumter, March 30, 1781, ibid.

21. Greene to Lee, April 4, 1781, to Washington, May 14, 1781, ibid.

22. Brown to von Porbeck, May 1, 1781, quoted in Council Minutes, May 8, 1781, Ms. CRG, 38, pt. 2:524-25.

23. Claim of John Douglass, PRO, AO 13/34; *South Carolina Royal Gazette*, May 30, 1781.

24. Council Minutes, May 8, 1781; Wright to Germain, April 2, 1781, *CRG*, 12:499-503, 343-44.

25. M'Call, *History of Georgia*, 514-15; Thomas Taylor to John Wesley, February 28, 1782, Earl of Shelburne Papers, WLCL.

26. Pickens to Greene, May 1781, Lee to Green, May 22, 1781, original bound in William Johnson, *Sketches of the Life and Correspondence of Nathanael Greene* (Charleston: A. E. Miller, 1822).

27. Henry Lee, *Memoirs of the War in the Southern Department of the United States* (New York: University Publishing Company, 1869), 352-55.

28. Lee to Greene, May 22, 1781, Pickens to Greene, May 25, 1781, Greene Papers, Perkins Library, Duke University, Durham, N.C.; Lee, *Memoirs*, 356.

29. *South Carolina Royal Gazette,* May 26–30, 1781; Grierson to Brown, May 20, 1781, TAB. Brown kept Grierson's letter among his personal papers, but it is not known what happened to Grierson's valuable object.

30. The best account of the battle is in Lee, *Memoirs,* 356–70; see also Joseph Johnson, *Traditions and Reminiscences Chiefly of the American Revolution in the South* (Charleston: Walker and James, 1851), 354–61; M'Call, *History of Georgia,* 514–23; Claim of Samuel Williams in Second Report of the Bureau of Archives, United Empire Loyalists: Enquiry into the Losses and Services in Consequence of their Loyalty: Evidence in the Canadian Claims, Archives of Ontario (microfiche, 1984), 704; Claim of Richard Pearis, 190–93; Claim of Henry Williams, 695.

31. Lee, *Memoirs,* 360; Lee to Greene, June 4, 1781, Greene to Pickens, June 5, 1781, Greene Papers, Duke.

32. Pickens and Lee to Brown, May 31, 1781, Brown, to Pickens and Lee, n.d., in Lee, *Memoirs,* 367.

33. Tarleton Brown, *Memoirs* (Barnwell, S.C.: People Press, 1894), 25.

34. Pickens to Greene, June 2, 1781, Andrew Pickens Papers, South Caroliniana Library, University of South Carolina, Columbia; also in Greene Papers, Duke.

35. Pickens and Lee to Brown, June 3, 1781, Brown to Pickens and Lee, June 3, 1781, Pickens and Lee to Brown, June 4, 1781, in Lee, *Memoirs,* 367; Johnson, *Traditions,* 360.

36. Brown to Pickens and Lee, June 4, 1781, Pickens and Lee to Brown, June 5, 1781, Brown to Pickens and Lee, June 5, 1781, in Lee, *Memoirs,* 368; "Articles of Capitulation Proposed by Lieutenant Colonel Thomas Browne and Answered by General Pickens and Lieutenant Colonel Lee," in ibid., 368–69. Although specific numbers are hard to determine, one authority states that Brown commanded 330 Rangers and militia and 300 Indians. The same source puts rebel losses at about 40 and British at 52 killed and 334 captured (Mark Mayo Boatner III, *Encyclopedia of the American Revolution* [New York: David McKay, 1966], 50–51).

37. Lee, *Memoirs,* 370.

38. Ibid., Johnson, *Traditions,* 361; Brown, *Memoirs,* 25; White, *Historical Collections,* 611.

39. Lee to Brown, June 7, 1781, Miscellaneous Papers, WLCL.

40. Thomas Taylor to John Wesley, February 28, 1782, Shelburne Papers.

41. Pension Claim of Micajah Brooks, Revolutionary War Pension Claims, National Archives; Statement of Samuel Beckaem, Force Papers. A history of the Beckaem statement is in Robert S. Davis, Jr., *Georgia Citizens and Soldiers of the American Revolution* (Easley, S.C.: Southern Historical Press, 1979), 167.

42. Proclamation of June 9, 1781, Greene Papers, Duke.

43. Wright to Balfour, June 11, 1781, *GHS Collections,* 3:355–56; Ramsay, *History of South Carolina,* 1:213; Wright to Germain, June 12, 1780, Ms. CRG, 38, pt. 2:532; Rawdon to Cornwallis, Cornwallis Papers, PRO 30/11/6, 174–77.

44. Balfour to Greene, September 3, 1781, HMC, 2:327.

45. Fletchall, Robinson, and McLaurin to Germain, April 19, 1782, PRO, CO 5/82.

46. Greene to Clay, July 24, 1781, Greene Papers, WLCL; for a study of Greene's involvement in Georgia affairs see Edward J. Cashin, "Nathanael Greene's Campaign for Georgia in 1781," *GHQ* 61 (Spring 1977): 43–58.

47. Brownson to Greene, August 29, 1781, Greene Papers, Duke.

48. Wright to Balfour, July 27, 1781, Headquarters Papers, 29:3651.

49. Balfour to Wright, August 1, 1781, ibid., 3655.

50. Wright to Balfour, July 27, August 16, 1781, ibid., 3651, 32:3693.

51. Wright to Clinton, October 16, 1781, ibid., 33:3824; Wright to Germain, December 18, 1781, to Knox, February 12, 1782, *GHS Collections,* 3:360–61, 366–67.

52. Claim of William Goodgion, PRO, AO 13/35.

53. Governor Wright's expense account, March 27, 1782, Ms. CRG, 38, pt. 2:605–32. The list is barely legible. Robert S. Davis has remedied the problem by reprinting the account in *Georgia Citizens and Soldiers,* 179–94; *Royal Georgia Gazette,* December 20, 1781.

54. Brown to Germain, August 9, 1781, PRO, CO 5/81.

55. Nathan Brownson to Great Warriors and Beloved Men of the Creek Nation, n.d., in Mrs. J. E. Hays, ed., "Indian Treaties, Cessions of Land in Georgia, 1705–1837," 157, typescript in Georgia Department of Archives and History, Atlanta.

56. "Talk from the Cherokee Nation delivered by the Raven of Chotte [sic] at Savannah the 1st September, 1781," in Brown to Germain, April 6, 1782, PRO, CO 5/81.

57. Wright to Clarke, October 10, 1781, Brown to Clinton, October 28, 1781, PRO, CO 5/81.

58. Germain to Leslie, February 6, 1782, Headquarters Papers, 35:4120; Declaration of the Account of Lieutenant Colonel Thomas Brown as Superintendent of Indian Affairs in the Atlantic Department of the Southern District of North America from 1 July 1779 to 31 December 1784, PRO, AO 1/1531/9.

59. *Royal Georgia Gazette,* October 4, 1781.

60. Johnston, *Recollections,* 69–72.

61. Memorial of William Wylly, August 10, 1784, in Egerton, *Royal Commission on the Losses and Services of American Loyalists,* 170–71.

62. Johnston, *Recollections,* 69–72; M'Call, *History of Georgia,* 531–33; *Royal Georgia Gazette,* November 8, 1781.

63. Greene to Paston Gould, November 9, 1781, Greene Papers, WLCL.
64. M'Call, *History of Georgia;* 533.
65. Brownson to Greene, December 15, 1781, Greene Papers, Duke; Greene to Brownson, January 7, 1782, Greene Papers, WLCL.
66. Brown to [Alexander Leslie], December 5, 1781, Headquarters Papers, 33:3930, also in HMC, 2:359–60.
67. *Royal Georgia Gazette,* December 13, 1781; Thomas Taylor to John Wesley, February 23, 1782, Shelburne Papers, 66:665.

8. The Last Campaign, 1782

1. Wright to Clinton, January 2, 1782, Leslie to Clinton, February 1, 1782, Headquarters Papers, 35:4005, 4096.
2. Farquhar Bethune to Germain, January 28, 1782, Brown to Clinton, October 28, 1781, PRO, CO 5/81.
3. Greene to Martin, January 9, 1782, Greene Papers, WLCL; Council Minutes, January 5, February 5, 1782, *RRG*, 2:296–97, 316–17; Assembly Minutes, January 10, 1782, *RRG*, 3:64.
4. John Martin to Friends and Brothers, January 11, 1782, to Wayne, January 19, 1782, in "Official Letters of Governor John Martin, 1782–1783," *GHQ* 1 (December 1917):282–87.
5. Wayne to Greene, January 17, 1782, Greene Papers, WLCL.
6. Brown to George Yonge, n.d., PRO, CO 5/81.
7. Governor John Martin, Proclamation, February 20, 1782, HMC, 2:401. Specifically excepted from pardon were Samuel Douglass, Thomas Gibbons, David Zubly, John Glen, Lachlan McGillivray, John Fox, Jr., George Fox, Luke Mann, Levi Sheftal, Nathaniel Hall, Alexander Wright, Basil Cooper, John Smith, George Cuthbert, Francis Codington, David Delegal, Philip Delegal, Christopher Tribner, Jacob Buhler, James Pace, Philip Dill, Andrew McLean, John Douglass, James Seymour, and John Charles Lucina.
8. Wayne to Greene, February 22, 1782, Greene Papers, WLCL.
9. *Royal Georgia Gazette,* March 14, 1782.
10. Wayne to Greene, March 15, April 1, 1782, Greene Papers, WLCL.
11. Martin to Wayne, March 14, 1782, in "Official Letters of Governor John Martin," 295–96.
12. Martin to Greene, March 15, 1782, in ibid., 299–300.
13. Taylor to John Wesley, February 28, 1782, Shelburne Papers, 66:665; Brown to Germain, April 6, 1782, PRO, CO 5/81.
14. M'Call, *History of Georgia,* 535–37; Martin to Greene, February 9, 1782, Greene Papers, WLCL.
15. Wayne to Greene, April 1, 1782, Greene Papers, WLCL.

16. Wayne to Greene, April 18, 1782, ibid.; *Royal Georgia Gazette,* April 25, 1782.

17. Habersham to Wayne, February 8, 1782, Anthony Wayne Papers, Perkins Library, Duke University, Durham, N.C.; Wayne to Greene, May 18, 1782, Greene to Wayne, April 21, 1782, Greene Papers, WLCL.

18. Wayne to Greene, May 24, 1782, Greene to Wayne, May 28, 1782, Greene Papers, WLCL; *Royal Georgia Gazette,* May 23, 1782; M'Call, *History of Georgia,* 541–43.

19. *Gazette of the State of Georgia,* March 6, 1783.

20. Brown to Liverpool, December 29, 1814, Additional Manuscripts 38, 260, British Museum, London.

21. Wayne to Greene, May 27, 1783, Greene Papers, WLCL.

22. M'Call, *History of Georgia,* 543–45. According to Captain Patrick (Paddy) Carr, some of the Creeks returned to their upper towns and "went straight to Thomas Graham's house . . . and killed him. He was the most active man in tarring and feathering Brown" (Carr to Martin, August 22, 1782, in "Official Letters of Governor John Martin," 339).

23. Brown to Carleton, October 9, 1782, PRO, CO 30 55/51.

24. Carleton to Leslie, May 23, 1782, HMC, 2:494–95; Address of the Upper and Commons House of Assembly to Lieut. Gen. Alexander Leslie, June 16, 1782, ibid., 527.

25. Leslie to Carleton, July 18, 1782, Headquarters Papers, 35:5093.

26. Resolution, July 4, 1782, *RRG,* 3:121–22; Lee, *Memoirs,* 561–62; Orders, Headquarters, Savannah, July 11, 1782, Wayne Papers.

27. Wayne told Greene that six thousand souls, white and black, were camped at Tybee (Wayne to Greene, June 30, 1782, Greene Papers, WLCL); M'Call, *History of Georgia,* 551–52.

28. Wayne to Greene, July 17, 1782, Greene Papers, WLCL.

29. Resolution, July 31, 1782, *RRG,* 3:167.

30. Greene to Habersham, August 2, 1782, Greene Papers, WLCL.

31. Graham to Clinton, July 20, 1782, Headquarters Papers, 35:5108; Wayne to Greene, August 12, 1782, Clay to Greene, August 6, 1782, Greene Papers, WLCL.

32. Memorial of Thomas Waters, PRO, AO 13/38; Council Minutes, July 31, 1782, *RRG,* 3:166–71; Clark to Martin, May 29, 1782, Emmet Collection.

33. Randolph C. Downes, "Creek-American Relations 1782–1790," *GHQ* 21 (June 1937):142; McMurphy to Martin, September 22, 1782, in Hays, ed., "Creek Indian Letters." For Martin's talk to the Creeks, July 19, 1782, see "Official Letters of Governor John Martin," 313–15.

34. Brown to Shelburne, September 25, 1782, PRO, CO 5/82; Tonyn to Carleton, October 11, 1782, HMC, 3:163.

35. Brown to Shelburne, September 25, 1782, PRO, CO 5/82; Brown to

Leslie, September 30, 1782, Tonyn to Carleton, October 11, 1782, Graham to Carleton, December 2, 1782, George Rose to Carleton, March 13, 1783, HMC, 3:40, 163, 247, 398.

36. Wilbur Henry Siebert, *Loyalists in East Florida, 1774 to 1785: The Most Important Documents Pertaining Thereto, Edited with an Accompanying Narrative*, 2 vols. (Deland: Florida State Historical Society, 1929), 1:375.

37. McArthur to Leslie, October 30, 1782, HMC, 3:192–93.

38. Tonyn to Carleton, November 13, 1783, McArthur to Carleton, January 9, 1783, HMC, 3:220, 319–22.

39. McArthur to Carleton, January 9, 1783, HMC, 3:319–22, also in PRO, CO 30 55/60.

40. Tonyn to Carleton, December 23, 1782, HMC, 3:276–77.

41. Brown to Carleton, January 12, 1783, PRO, CO 30 55/60; Brown to Thomas Townshend, January 12, 1783, PRO, CO 5/82; McArthur to Carleton, January 9, 1783, HMC, 3:319–22.

42. Tonyn to Carleton, December 23, 1782, HMC, 3:276–77.

9. Florida Interlude, 1783–1785

1. Siebert, *Loyalists in East Florida*, 1:118; Mowat, *East Florida as a British Province*, 135–39; J. Leitch Wright, Jr., *British St. Augustine* (St. Augustine: Historic St. Augustine Preservation Board, 1975), 38–41; Daniel R. Schafer "'. . . not so gay a Town in America as this . . .' 1763–1784," in Jean Parker Waterbury, ed., *The Oldest City, St. Augustine: Saga of Survival* (St. Augustine: St. Augustine Historical Society, 1983), 119–23.

2. Last will and testament of Thomas Brown, March 8, 1821, in document entitled "In the West Indies Estates Court (St. Vincent), Filed 17th October 1872, Re Browne exparte Dobree, Supplemental, Abstract of the title of Thomas A. Browne and George McIntosh Browne to Grand Sable Estate in the Island of St. Vincent," Lester A. Browne Papers, Kingstown Courthouse, St. Vincent; for Brown's Charlotte Street residence, see Map of St. Augustine and description of houses by Mariano de la Rocque, 1788, St. Augustine Historical Society. The building which houses the St. Augustine Historical Society occupies the site of Brown's residence and is modeled after the de la Roque description.

3. HMC, 3:322–23.

4. Brown to Townshend, February 25, 1783, PRO, CO 5/82.

5. Council Minutes, *RRG*, 2:509–14.

6. William McIntosh to Brown, April 14, 1783, Waring Collection.

7. Hall to Greene, March 19, 1783, Greene Papers, Duke; *RRG*, 2:483, 490–92.

8. *Georgia Gazette,* May 29, 1783.
9. Hays, ed., "Indian Treaties," 129–31.
10. Mowat, *East Florida as a British Province,* 141.
11. Sandra Riley, *Homeward Bound: A History of the Bahama Islands to 1850 with a Definitive Study of Abaco in the American Loyalist Plantation Period* (Miami: Island Research, 1983), 132; *East Florida Gazette,* April 16–May 3, 1783.
12. Riley, *Homeward Bound,* 134. Brown and Thomas Forbes appointed Jonas Brown as their agent to claim compensation for losses sustained by the *Whitby Warrior* (Parrish, "Records of some Southern Loyalists," 188).
13. Brown to Carleton, April 28, 1783, PRO, CO 30 55/68.
14. East Florida Commons House of Assembly to Lt. Col. Thomas Brown, April 19, 1783, HMC, 4:40.
15. Brown to Carleton, April 28, 1783, ibid., 58–59.
16. McArthur to Carleton, May 19, 1783, ibid., 88–90.
17. Carleton to Brown, June 19, 1783, ibid., 164.
18. McArthur to Carleton, May 19, 1783, ibid., 88–90.
19. Carleton to McArthur, June 19, 1783, ibid., 164–66.
20. McArthur to Carleton, May 20, 1783, ibid., 934.
21. Brown to Carleton, July 20, 1783, PRO, CO 30 55/63.
22. Carleton to McArthur, July 29, 1783, HMC, 4:247–48.
23. Carleton to Brown, August 22, 1783, ibid., 291.
24. Carleton to McArthur, August 22, 1783, ibid., 292–94. By a fortuitous coincidence, Roworth and Deveaux were in-laws. The Ranger married Deveaux's sister.
25. McArthur to Carleton, September 7, 12, 1783, ibid., 340, 350–51.
26. McArthur to Carleton, September 12, 13, 1783, ibid., 350–51, 358; Resolution of Council, August 13, 1783, PRO, CO 5/82.
27. Brown to Lord North, June 4, 1783, PRO, CO 5/82; "A New Map of the Southern District of North America from surveys taken by the Compiler and others . . . For Lieut. Colonel Thomas Brown His Majesty's Superintendent of Indian Affairs by Joseph Purcell," PRO, CO 700/N. America 15.
28. Brown to North, October 24, 1783, PRO, CO 5/82; Receipt to Weatherford dated October 23, 1783, in Brown to Hon. Lords Commissioners of the Treasury, February 15, 1785, PRO, T 1/601/298–306.
29. Talks from Little Turkey and Headmen of Overhill Cherokees to Lt. Col. Thomas Brown, November 17, 1783, Brown to Hons. Lords Commissioners of the Treasury, February 15, 1785, PRO, T 1/601/298–306.
30. Brown to North, January 8, 1784, PRO, CO 5/82.
31. John W. Caughey, *McGillivray of the Creeks* (Norman: University of Oklahoma Press, 1959), 114.
32. William Vesey Munnings to Liverpool, December 12, 1811, PRO, CO 23/58/88.

33. Brown to North, February 15, 1784, PRO, CO 5/82; Riley, *Homeward Bound,* 15.
34. Mowat, *East Florida as a British Province,* 143.
35. Siebert, *Loyalists in East Florida,* 1:161–75; Helen Hornbeck Tanner, *Zespedes in East Florida, 1784–1790* (Coral Gables: University of Miami Press, 1963), 37–40.
36. Zespedes to Brown, July 18, 1785, in Joseph Byrne Lockey, *East Florida, 1783–1785,* ed. John Walton Caughey (Berkeley and Los Angeles: University of California Press, 1949), 569–70.
37. Brown to William Pitt, November 27, 1790, PRO, CO 23/30.
38. Caughey, *McGillivray of the Creeks,* 211.
39. Brown to Pitt, November 2, 1790, PRO, CO 23/30; Tanner, *Zespedes,* 35–36; for Herbert's role see PRO T 1/601/334. Herbert was called Brown's "amanuensis" in the Spanish census of 1784, St. Augustine Historical Society.
40. Greene to Catherine Littlefield Greene, April 14, 1785, Greene Papers, WLCL.
41. Ibid.
42. Ibid.
43. Thomas Brown to Zespedes, August 18, 1785, in Lockey, *East Florida,* 688–89.
44. Ibid.
45. Ibid., Zespedes to Brown, August 22, 1785, Brown to Zespedes, December 20, 1785, Joseph Byrne Lockey Collection, P. K. Yonge Library, University of Florida, Gainesville.
46. Brown to Zespedes, July 10, 1785, Zespedes to Brown, July 18, 1785, in Lockey, *East Florida,* 568–70.
47. Brown to Zespedes, August 15, 1785, in Lockey, *East Florida,* 679–80; Antonio de Zespedes to [Governor] Zespedes, July 31, 1785, Lockey Collection; Zespedes to Brown, August 19, 1785, in Lockey, *East Florida,* 680.
48. Brown to Zespedes, August 18, 1785, in Lockey, *East Florida,* 688; Brown to Zespedes, September 1, 1785, Lockey Collection; Tonyn to Sydney, August 29, 1785, PRO, CO 5/561; Mowat, *East Florida as a British Province,* 147.

10. A Gentleman Planter

1. Coleman, *American Revolution in Georgia,* 145–46; Patricia C. Griffin, "The Spanish Return: The People-Mix Period, 1784–1821," in Waterbury, ed., *Oldest City,* 185–86.

2. An account of the Cotton Plantations in the Bahamas Islands as they now stand on the 1st of November, 1785, PRO, CO 23/30/334.

3. Riley, *Homeward Bound*, 156–57.

4. Petition delivered to him that day signed by Lieutenant Colonel Thomas Brown and others in John Brown to Lord Sydney, March 18, 1786, PRO, CO 23/15.

5. Brown to William Pitt, November 2, 1790, PRO, CO 23/30.

6. Thomas Forbes was authorized to present a memorial on behalf of Brown, December 16, 1783, in Petition of Jonas Brown, PRO, AO 13/38; Riley, *Homeward Bound*, 156.

7. Petition of Jonas Brown, December 31, 1787, Jonas Brown to J. Forster, November 17, 1788, PRO, AO 13/38.

8. Thomas Brown's Deposition, November 27, 1787, PRO, AO 13/34.

9. J. Leitch Wright, Jr., *William Augustus Bowles, Director General of the Creek Nation* (Athens: University of Georgia Press, 1967), 28. The anticipation of some planters might have been tempered with concern over Dunmore's efforts to recruit slaves for his "Ethiopian Regiment" in Virginia; see Malcolm Bell, Jr., *Major Butler's Legacy: Five Generations of a Slaveholding Family* (Athens: University of Georgia Press, 1987), 32.

10. A list of tracts of land granted to the Inhabitants of the Bahama Islands from the 8 day of April 1788 to 31 day of December 1789, PRO, CO 23/30/216; copies of ten of Brown's grants were obtained from Bahamas Registry Office, Nassau, by Joan Leggett of Oxford, England, and made available to me October 29, 1986.

11. *Bahamas Gazette*, May 7–14, June 4–11, 1785.

12. Ibid., September 9–16, November 25–December 2, 1786, December 21–24, 1790, January 4–7, 1791. Brown to Ramsay, December 25, 1786, in White, *Historical Collections of Georgia*, 615.

13. Riley, *Homeward Bound*, 168–70.

14. Ibid., 171–72.

15. Ibid., 176.

16. Ibid., 175.

17. Ibid., 172–77.

18. Thelma Peterson Peters, "The American Loyalists and the Plantation Period in the Bahama Islands" (Ph.D. dissertation, University of Florida, 1960), 95–97.

19. Parrish, "Records of some Southern Loyalists."

20. *Bahamas Gazette*, February 7–14, 1789.

21. Ibid., February 21–28, 1789.

22. Wright, *Bowles*, 13.

23. Ibid., 24.

24. Caughey, *McGillivray*, 35.

25. Wright, *Bowles*, 31.

26. Caughey, *McGillivray*, 203; a Spanish translation of the letter is in the P. K. Yonge Library, University of Florida, Gainesville.

27. Caughey, *McGillivray*, 205, 207.

28. Ibid., 296; Wright, *Bowles*, 50.

29. Coleman, *American Revolution in Georgia*, 251–52.

30. Brown to Pitt, November 2, 1790, PRO, CO 23/30.

31. Ibid.

32. Brown to Liverpool, December 29, 1814, Additional Manuscripts, 38,260, British Museum.

33. J. Leitch Wright, Jr., *Britain and the American Frontier, 1783–1815* (Athens: University of Georgia Press, 1975), 63–65; Beckwith to Brown, May 8, 1803, TAB.

34. Substance of various documents delivered to Mr. Brown and Mr. Huskisson for Mr. Pitt's consideration by Col. Browne, 1805, PRO, CO 260/19.

35. Peters, "American Loyalists," 345; for reference to Black Nancy and her son George, see Waddington Papers, 8:381.

36. Petition of Lt. Col. Brown to Rt. Hon. Earl of Camden, n.d., PRO, CO 260/19; for family names and other information see *Bahamas Gazette*, October 3, 1789, Waddington Papers, 8:381, and Document entitled "In the West India Estates Court (St. Vincent), filed 17 October 1872, Re Browne Exparte Dobree, Supplemental, Abstract of the Title of Thomas A. Browne and George McIntosh Browne, to Grand Sable Estate in the Island of St. Vincent," Lester A. Browne Papers.

37. Brown to Jonas Brown, Sr., August 1, 1796, TAB. The succession of Jonas, Sr., to the title of Viscount Montague was reported in the *York Courant*, according to an entry in Waddington Papers, 9:385. Descendants of the family are skeptical that the title was valid.

38. Charles E. Bennett, *Florida's "French" Revolution, 1793–1795* (Gainesville: University Presses of Florida, 1981), 19–31.

39. *Augusta Chronicle*, December 28, 1799.

40. Edith Duncan Johnston, *The Houstouns of Georgia* (Athens: University of Georgia Press, 1950), 315–16.

41. *Augusta Chronicle*, October 31, 1795, January 23, 1796, December 23, 1797, April 17, 1802.

42. B. H. Hossak, *Kirkwall in the Orkneys* (Kirkwall: William Peace and Son, 1900), 198, 341. See also Balfour Papers. Manson's house was still standing at the time of my visit to Kirkwall, July 5, 1983. In excellent condition, it serves as the Customs House in Kirkwall.

43. *Bahamas Gazette*, August 21, 1798; Brown to Jonas Brown, Sr., August 8, 1798, to Earl of Camden, n.d., PRO, CO 260/19.

11. Whitby and St. Vincent

1. Transcript of will of Jonas Brown, May 30, 1793, Waddington Papers, 61:248.
2. Brown to Jonas Brown, Jr., March 21, 1802, TAB.
3. Waddington Papers, 8:381-83.
4. Ibid.; *Yorkshire Journal*, May 11, 1787.
5. Waddington Papers, 8:381–83; Brown's letter about the lifesaving devices was printed in the *London Morning Chronicle*, December 31, 1814.
6. Kendall, *Streets of Whitby*, 6–18. A. A. Berends has examined the title deeds and has determined that the house was Jonas Brown's property, inherited from an aunt, Jane Linskill, and passed on by him to his son Sir Jonas Brown of Hull.
7. Clarence Preston, *Captain William Scoresby, 1760–1829: Whitby's Most Successful Whaler* (1964; rpt. Whitby: Whitby Library and Philosophical Society, 1972), 15–18.
8. Mr. Richardson to Brown, August 18, 1803, TAB.
9. Beckwith to Brown, January 2, April 10, May 8, August 25, 1803, TAB.
10. Kingston to Brown, July 29, 1805, TAB. Moira is mentioned as possible prime minister in Philip Whitwell Wilson, *William Pitt the Younger* (Garden City, N.Y.: Doubleday, Doran, 1930), 321. Brown's connection with Wilberforce is cited in G. Ellis to Brown, October 14, 1804, TAB.
11. Robert J. Gemmett, *William Beckford* (Boston: Twayne, 1977), 83.
12. "William Beckford (1759–1844)," in *DNB*, 2:85.
13. Bourne stated that Pitt had consented to the grant and that it was not necessary to trouble Lord Moira on the subject (Bourne to Brown, November 10, 1804, TAB). Charles Shephard, *An Historical Account of the Island of St. Vincent* (1831; rpt. London: Frank Case, 1971), 179–80.
14. For a history of the Carib War, see Shephard, *Historical Account*, 36–176.
15. Proclamation of Governor H. W. Bentinck, June 27, 1805, in Beckwith to Rt. Hon. William Windham, May 20, 1806, PRO, CO 260/20.
16. Proclamations of Governor George Beckwith, May 3, 1805, May 2, 16, 1806, J. R. Dasent to Beckwith, April 23, 1806, printed opinion of His Majesty's Solicitor General A. Piggott that Bentinck had no authority to grant lands, citing letter of Camden to Beckwith, June 12, 1805, Brown to Beckwith, July 3, 1805, PRO, CO 260/20.
17. Printed warrant holding persons who occupy lands in contempt, May 26, 1806, PRO, CO 260/20.
18. Beckwith to Windham, July 21, 1806; Protest signed by Alexander Cruickshank, Andrew Ross, Sebastian French, Thomas Patterson, Robert Sutherland, and Alexander Cumming, July 9, 1806, Proclamation dissolv-

ing assembly, September 9, 1806, Beckwith to Windham, October 4, 1806, PRO, CO 260/20.

19. Brown to Edward Cooke, January 10, 1805, to President Drewry Ottley, November 16, 1805, PRO, CO 260/19.

20. Minutes of Proceedings of Privy Council, May 2, 1806, PRO, CO 260/21; Beckwith's Proclamation giving Brown occupancy, October 22, 1806, PRO, CO 260/22.

21. John Carmichael et al. to Sir Charles Brisbane, October 9, 1809, E. Cain, James Douglas, and Thomas Dickson to Brisbane, March 19, 1810, in Ebenezer Duncan, *A Brief History of Saint Vincent* (Kingstown, St. Vincent: E. Duncan, 1941), 27.

22. Dr. Earle Kirby, a retired veterinarian, and a longtime resident of St. Vincent, conducted me on a tour of the island in 1985. We climbed to the top of the Point Young promontory and had a magnificent view of the northern end of the island. "You see why they wanted to take it from the Caribs," said Dr. Kirby.

23. Lords Commissioners of the Treasury to Beckwith, October 3, 1806, PRO, CO 260/20.

24. Douglass's survey is in PRO, CO 441/10/3; a copy was given to me by Lester Browne of St. Vincent, a descendant of Thomas Brown.

25. Waddington Papers, 8:380, 383.

26. *Roach's London Pocket Pilot* (London, 1793), 49, in *DeCastro's Inns and Taverns of London*, MS 3110, 2 D-O, Guildhall Library, Gresham Street, London.

27. Abstract of Certain Deeds and Documents Recorded in the Office of the Registrar of Deeds St. Vincent relating to the Grand Sable Estate, October 15, 1872. Copy provided by Lester Browne of St. Vincent.

28. "Sir George Beckwith (1753–1823)," *DNB* 2:88–89.

29. E. Cain, James Douglas, and Thomas Dickson to Brisbane, March 19, 1810, Memorial of Ann Ross to Brisbane, August 4, 1809, Joseph Billinghurst and Thomas Dickson to Brisbane, May 11, 1809, PRO, CO 260/27.

30. Harrison to Edward Cooke, June 13, 1809, PRO, CO 260/26; Memorial of the Family of the Late Colonel Browne of the Island of St. Vincent, n.d., TAB.

31. Shephard, *Historical Account*, 183.

32. Extracts of letters from St. Vincent, May 11, 1810, PRO, CO 260/27; Memorial of the Family of the Late Colonel Browne, TAB.

33. Cecil Jenkinson to Brisbane, February 2, 1810, George Harrison to Brisbane, February 2, 1810, PRO, CO 260/27.

34. Extracts of letters from St. Vincent, May 11, 1810, Colquhoun to Harrison, July 10, 1810, PRO, CO 260/27.

35. Brown to Thomas A. M. Browne, March 16, 1810, TAB; Waddington Papers 8:221.

36. Brown to Liverpool, December 6, 1810, PRO, CO 23/57/100. J. Leitch Wright, Jr., inferred from this letter that Brown requested the governorship. There is nothing in the letter to indicate that Brown did more than relay the petition of his former acquaintances in the Bahamas (Wright, *Britain and the American Frontiers*, 157).

37. Extracts from Thomas Steele's day book, PRO, TS 11/657/2059.

38. Deposition of Thomas Brown, March 7, 1811, PRO, TS 11/1078.

39. Edward Foss, *Biographica Juridica* (London: J. Murray, 1870), 297.

40. Brown to Attorney General, n.d., PRO, TS 11/1078.

41. Deposition of Thomas Steele, February 26, 1811, PRO, TS 11/1078; Extracts from Thomas Steele's day book, PRO, TS 11/657/2059.

42. Foss, *Biographica*, 497; Brown to Attorney General (?), April 15, 1812, PRO, TS 11/657/2059; Moira's scribbled note and other documents relating to the trial are in PRO, TS 11/1078; *Annual Register*, 1812, 22–24.

43. The indictment against Brown is in PRO, KB 28/440, ro. 16; the account of the trial is in the *Annual Register*, 1812, 22–24.

44. *Annual Register*, 1812, 22–24.

45. PRO, KB 28/440, ro. 16.

46. *Augusta Chronicle*, May 8, 1812.

47. Documents initiated by V.G., March 27, 1812, and H.H., April 3, 1812, PRO, TS 11/657/2059.

48. Shephard, *Historical Account*, 182.

49. Report by the Committee appointed to enquire into the State of the King's Bench, Fleet and Marshalsea Prisons . . . , British Parliamentary Papers, Crime and Punishment Prisons, vol. 7, State and Management Sessions, 1809–15, Bodleian Library, Oxford, England.

50. Brown to Thomas A. M. Browne, n.d., TAB. While in prison, Brown put Grand Sable up for sale (*Royal Gazette*, Nassau, January 30, 1813). Evidently, there were no takers.

51. Waddington Papers, extra sheet attached to 8:383.

52. Shephard, *Historical Account*, Appendix XVII; printed account of the disaster, April 30, 1812, PRO, CO 260/29.

53. Brisbane to Bathurst, November 6, 1812, PRO, CO 260/29.

54. Memorial of Cayley and Weatherall, January 8, 1813, PRO, CO 260/29.

55. Brisbane to Bathurst, March 8, 1813, PRO, CO 260/29; Harrison to Edward Cooke, June 13, 1809, PRO, CO 260/26.

56. Memorial of the Family of the late Colonel Browne, TAB.

57. Thomas Brown to Liverpool, December 29, 1814, Additional Manuscripts, 38,260, f. 408, British Museum.

58. Brown's letter to the Duke of York was printed in the *London Morning Chronicle*, December 31, 1814.

59. Brown to "My dearest Puss," April 6, 1814, TAB.

60. Abstract of Certain Deeds and Documents Recorded in the Office of the Registrar of Deeds, St. Vincent, Relating to the Grand Sable Estate, October 15, 1872.

61. Brown to unknown, August 17, 1817, State Department Miscellaneous Collection, P. K. Yonge Library, University of Florida, Gainesville.

62. Andrew Clements, rector of Thornton Dale, Ellerburn, and Wilton, to Joan Leggett, September 13, 1982, courtesy of Joan Leggett.

63. For Moss's assuming ownership of Newton House, see Waddington Papers 8:221; see also Brian Pearce, "A Short History of Newton House" (Whitby, 1985), typescript at the Whitby Museum.

64. Brown to Daly, May 23, ?, TAB.

65. Duncan, *Brief History of Saint Vincent*.

66. Ibid.

67. Charles Day, *Five Years Residence in the West Indies* (London: Colburn and Company, 1852).

68. Shephard, *Historical Account*, Appendix VII.

69. Brown's will is in the document entitled "In the West India Estates Court (St. Vincent) Filed 17 October 1872, Re Browne Exparte Dobree, Supplemental Abstract of the Title of Thomas A. Browne and George McIntosh Browne to Grand Sable Estate in the Island of St. Vincent," St. Vincent Registry Office.

70. George Dundas, *St. Vincent, West Indies* (N.p.: N.p., 1880); Shephard, *Historical Account*, Appendix VII.

71. Brown to Jonas Brown, February 10, 1821, TAB. Although Thomas and his family had adopted the final "e" on their surname, Jonas maintained the original spelling.

72. Brown to Rev. Thomas Browne, February 7, [1821] TAB.

73. Brown to Daly, May 23, [1821], TAB.

74. Riley, *Homeward Bound*, 206, 212.

75. *Gentleman's Magazine*, August 8, 1825, cited in Waddington Papers, 8:221. William Wylly was in St. Vincent on July 5, 1825, during the last month of Brown's life (PRO, CO 714/140); document written by "son of Susan Harriett Browne" in possession of Joan Leggett, Oxford, England. Susan and her husband were buried in the same enclosed plot. When I visited the site in August 1985, only Allan McDowall's grave was marked.

12. The Legend and the Man

1. M'Call, *History of Georgia*, 2:380.

2. William Bacon Stevens, *A History of Georgia*, 2 vols. (Philadelphia: D. Appleton and Co., 1859), 2:251.

3. William Gilmore Simms, "Joscelyn: A Tale of the Revolution," *Old*

Guard: A Monthly Magazine Devoted to the Principles of 1776 and 1787 5 (January–December 1867): 409–10, 935.

4. Charles C. Jones, Jr., *The History of Georgia*, 2 vols. (Boston: Houghton Mifflin, 1883), 2:475–76.

5. Augusta Unit, Federal Writers Project in Georgia, Works Progress Administration, *Augusta* (Augusta: City Council of Augusta, 1938), 151.

6. Martha F. Norwood, "A History of the White House Tract, Richmond County, Georgia, 1756–1975," Georgia Department of Natural Resources, 1975.

7. Bob Harrell, "Tory's Revenge," *Atlanta Constitution*, March 11, 1984.

8. E. Merton Coulter, *Georgia, A Short History* (Chapel Hill: University of North Carolina Press, 1960), 144.

9. Coleman, *American Revolution in Georgia*, 134.

10. Gary D. Olson, "Loyalists and the American Revolution: Thomas Brown and the South Carolina Backcountry, 1775–1776," *SCHM*, 68 (October 1967): 201–19; 69 (January 1968): 44–56. Others who have studied the British "southern strategy" are Paul H. Smith, *Loyalists and Redcoats: A Study in British Revolutionary Policy* (Chapel Hill: University of North Carolina Press, 1964); Ira D. Gruber, "Britain's Southern Strategy," and Clyde R. Ferguson, "Functions of the Partisan-Militia in the South during the American Revolution: An Interpretation," in W. Robert Higgins, ed., *The Revolutionary War in the South: Power, Conflict and Leadership* (Durham: Duke University Press, 1979), 205–38, 239–58.

11. Searcy, "Thomas Browne: Loyalist," 84–94.

12. Searcy, *Georgia-Florida Contest*, 176–77.

13. Bailyn, *Voyagers to the West*, 556.

14. Lambert, *South Carolina Loyalists*, 307, 68.

Epilogue

1. Brown's will, dated March 8, 1821, is in a document entitled "In the West India Estates Court (St. Vincent) filed 17th October 1872". Lester A. Browne Papers.

2. Andrew Clements, rector of Thornton Dale, Ellerburn, and Wilton to Joan Leggett, September 13, 1982.

3. Copied by author during a visit to Trinity Church, Georgetown, St. Vincent, in August 1985.

4. The pamphlet is in the Bodleian Library, Oxford, England. Other information is in Waddington Papers, 8:221.

5. Day, *Five Years Residence in the West Indies*, 101.

6. Sir Bernard Burke, *A Genealogical History of the Dormant, Abeyant, Forfeited, and Extinct Peerages of the British Empire* (London: Harrison, 1866), 78–80. Brown's family charts are in TAB and in Waddington Papers, 3:221.

BIBLIOGRAPHY

Abbreviations

AO	Audit Office, British Public Record Office
CO	Colonial Office, British Public Record Office
CRG	*Colonial Records of Georgia*
Ms. CRG	Manuscript, Colonial Records of Georgia
GHQ	*Georgia Historical Quarterly*
GHS	
Collections	*Collections of the Georgia Historical Society*
HMC	Historical Manuscripts Commission
NYHS	
Collections	*Collections of the New-York Historical Society*
PRO	British Public Record Office
RRG	*Revolutionary Records of Georgia*
SCHGM	*South Carolina Historical and Genealogical Magazine*
	(Volumes 1 through 51 were so entitled)
SCHM	*South Carolina Historical Magazine*
	(Successor to *South Carolina Historical and Genealogical Magazine*, volumes from 52)
T	Treasury, British Public Record Office
TAB	Thomas Alexander Browne Collection in possession of Heather Lancaster, London, England
TS	Treasury Solicitor, British Public Record Office
WLCL	William L. Clements Library, University of Michigan, Ann Arbor

Primary Sources

Manuscript Collections

Archives of Ontario. Toronto, Canada.
  United Empire Loyalists: Enquiry into the Losses and Services in
  Consequence of Their Loyalty: Evidence in the Canadian Claims
  (microfiche, 1984)

Bodleian Library. Oxford, England.
British Parliamentary Papers, Crime and Punishment Prisons, Vol. 7,
State and Management Sessions, 1809–15
Rev. Thomas Alexander Browne, *Skeleton Lectures on the Catechism
with Analysis of the Confirmation Service*, in Theological Pamphlets
A–B
British Museum. London, England.
Additional Manuscripts
Liverpool Papers
Browne Family Papers. Private collection of Joan Leggett, Oxford,
England.
Thomas Alexander Browne Collection. Private collection of Heather
Lancaster, London, England. A microfilm copy of the collection is in the
Georgia Department of Archives and History, Atlanta.
Colonial Williamsburg Foundation. Williamsburg, Virginia.
Headquarters Papers of the British Army in America (microfilm)
Columbia County Courthouse. Appling, Georgia.
Deeds pertaining to Brownsborough
Duke University, Perkins Library. Durham, North Carolina.
Anthony Wayne Papers
Nathanael Greene Papers
Revolutionary War Collection
Georgia Department of Archives and History. Atlanta, Georgia.
Colonial Records of Georgia 1750–1802, Colonial Conveyences Book
CC1 1774–75 (microfilm)
Works Progress Administration typescripts edited by Mrs. J. E. Hays:
"Indian Letters, 1782–1839"
"Unpublished Letters of Timothy Barnard, 1784–1820"
"Creek Indian Letters, Talks, and Treaties, 1705–1839"
"Indian Treaties, Cessions of Land in Georgia, 1705–1837"
"Journal of the General Assembly of Georgia, January 2, 1787–
November 13, 1788"
Georgia Historical Society. Savannah, Georgia.
Antonio J. Waring Collection
John Adam Treutlen Papers
Margaret Davis Cate Collection
Guildhall Library. Gresham Street, London, England.
Local histories
Kingstown Courthouse, St. Vincent.
Documents pertaining to Grand Sable Estate
Lands and Surveys Department
Maps of Grand Sable Estate
Lester A. Browne Papers (private)

Kirkwall Public Library, Orkney Islands Archives. Kirkwall, Scotland.
    Balfour Papers
    Local histories
Library of Congress. Washington, D.C.
    East Florida Papers, copies of documents in PRO CO 5/556–57
    Hazard Pamphlets
    Papers of the Continental Congress, 1774–89
    Peter Force Papers
Massachusetts Historical Society. Boston, Massachusetts.
    Benjamin Lincoln Papers
National Archives. Washington, D.C.
    Georgia State Papers, 1777–88
    Papers of the Continental Congress, 1774–89
    Revolutionary War Claims
New-York Historical Society. New York, New York.
    Horatio Gates Papers
    Lachlan McIntosh Papers
New York Public Library. New York, New York.
    American Loyalists, Audit Office Transcripts, Vol. 28, Transcribed for
        the New York Public Library, 1900
    John Bowie Papers
    Thomas Addis Emmet Collection
North Carolina Department of Cultural Resources, Division of Archives
        and History, Raleigh, North Carolina.
    Records of Talks between Commissioners of the Continental Congress
        and the Southern Indians, Secretary of State, Continental Congress,
        1774–79
Public Record Office. Chancery Lane, London, England.
    Court of King's Bench
    Treasury Solicitor
Public Record Office. Kew, England.
    Audit Office
    Colonial Office
    Cornwallis Papers
    Treasury Papers
Richmond County Courthouse. Augusta, Georgia.
    Deeds, wills pertaining to revolutionary period
St. Augustine Historical Society, St. Augustine, Florida.
    Spanish Census of 1784.
    Map of St. Augustine and description of houses by Mariano de la
        Rocque, 1788
South Carolina Department of Archives. Columbia, South Carolina.
    Cornwallis Papers (microfilm)

Staffordshire Record Office. Stafford, England.
  Dartmouth Papers
State Historical Society of Wisconsin. Madison, Wisconsin.
  Lyman Draper Collection
University of Florida, P. K. Yonge Library. Gainesville, Florida.
  Joseph Byrne Lockey Collection
  Lydia Austin Parrish, "Records of some Southern Loyalists, being a
    collection of manuscripts about some 80 families, most of whom
    immigrated to the Bahamas during and after the American
    Revolution" (microfilm of typescript in Widener Library, Harvard
    University)
  State Department Miscellaneous Collection
University of Georgia Libraries, Special Collections. Athens, Georgia.
  DeRenne Collection
  Revolutionary Papers
  Telamon Cuyler Collection
  William Manson Papers
University of Michigan, William L. Clements Library, Ann Arbor,
    Michigan.
  Sir Henry Clinton Papers
  General Thomas Gage Papers
  Lord George Germain Papers
  Nathanael Greene Papers
  Earl of Shelburne Papers
  Miscellaneous Papers
University of North Carolina, Southern Historical Collection, Chapel Hill,
    North Carolina.
  Mackey-Stiles Papers
  Robert Howe Papers
University of South Carolina, South Caroliniana Library, Columbia,
    South Carolina.
  Andrew Pickens Papers
  John Rutledge Papers
  Revolutionary War Papers
University of Texas Library. Austin, Texas.
  British Empire Church Records, Society for the Propagation of the
    Gospel, Supplemental Letters and Papers, American Colonies II
    (1680–1850, Georgia and Virginia) (microfilm)
Western Carolina University, Hunter Library. Cullowhee, North
    Carolina.
  Cherokee Indian Collection (microfilm)
Whitby Literary and Philosophical Society Collections, Whitby Museum.
    Whitby, England.

Papers in possession of A. A. Berends (private)
Percy Burnett Papers
Waddington Papers

Published Collections

Burnett, Edmund C., ed. *Letters of Members of the Continental Congress*. 8 vols. Washington, D.C.: Carnegie Institute of Washington, 1921–36.

Candler, Allen D., ed. *The Revolutionary Records of the State of Georgia*. 3 vols. Atlanta: Franklin-Turner Co., 1908.

Candler, Allen D., Lucian L. Knight, Kenneth Coleman, and Milton Ready, eds. *The Colonial Records of the State of Georgia*. 28 vols. Atlanta: Various printers, 1904–16, 1979–82; vols. 29–39 are in manuscript at the Georgia Department of Archives and History, Atlanta.

Davies, K. G., ed. *Documents of the American Revolution, 1770–1783: Colonial Office Series*. 21 vols. Shannon: Irish University Press, 1972–81.

Egerton, Hugh Edward, ed. *The Royal Commission on Losses and Services of American Loyalists, 1783–1785*. Mass Violence in America Series. 1915. Reprint. New York: Arno Press and the New York Times, 1969.

Fitzpatrick, John C., ed. *The Writings of George Washington from the Original Manuscript Sources, 1745–1799*. 39 vols. Washington, D.C.: U.S. Government Printing Office, 1931–44.

Force, Peter, ed. *American Archives*. 4th ser. 6 vols. Washington, D.C.: M. St. Clair and Peter Force, 1837–46. 5th ser. 3 vols. Washington, D.C.: M. St. Clair and Peter Force, 1848–53.

Ford, Worthington Chauncey, ed. *Journals of the Continental Congress, 1774–1789*. 34 vols. Washington, D.C.: U.S. Government Printing Office, 1904–37.

Georgia Historical Society Collections. 20 vols. Savannah: Published by the Society, 1840–1980.

Hawes, Lilla Mills, ed. *Lachlan McIntosh Papers in the University of Georgia Libraries*. University of Georgia Libraries Miscellanea Publications, No. 7. Athens: University of Georgia Press, 1968.

———. "Minutes of the Executive Council, May 7 through October 14, 1777." *GHQ* 33 (December 1949): 318–30; 34 (March, June, September, December 1950): 19–35, 106–25, 203–26, 288–312; 35 (March, June, September 1951): 31–59, 126–51, 196–221.

———. "Some Papers of the Governor and Council of Georgia, 1780–1781." *GHQ* 46 (September 1962): 280–96, (December 1962): 395–417.

Historical Manuscripts Commission. *Report on American Manuscripts in the Royal Institution of Great Britain*. 4 vols. London: Various printers, 1904–9.

New York Historical Society Collections. Vol. 5. New York: Published by the Society, 1873. Volume 5 contains vol. 2 of the Charles Lee Papers, 1776–78.
"Official Letters of Governor John Martin, 1782–1783." *GHQ* 1 (December 1917): 281–346.
Stevens, B. F., ed. *Facsimiles of Manuscripts in European Archives Relating to America, 1773–1783, with Descriptions, Editorial Notes, Collations, References, and Translations.* 25 vols. London: Malby and Sons, 1889–98.

Contemporary Sources

Adair, James. *Adair's History of the American Indian.* 1775. Reprint. Edited by Samuel Cole Williams. Johnson City, Tenn.: Watagua Press, 1930.
Barnwell, Joseph W., ed. "Letters of John Rutledge." *SCHGM* 17 (October 1916): 142–45.
Barry, George. *History of the Orkney Islands.* London: Printed for Longman, Hurst, Rees and Orme, 1808.
Bartram, William. *Travels of William Bartram.* Edited by Mark Van Doren. New York: Dover, 1928.
Brown, Tarleton. *Memoirs.* Barnwell, S.C.: People Press, 1894.
Butler, Lewis, and Stewart Hare. *The Annals of the King's Royal Rifle Corps.* Vol. 1: Lewis Butler, *The Royal Americans.* London: Smith, Elder and Co., 1913. Includes Memoirs of Captain Patrick Murray.
Campbell, Colin, ed. *Journal of an Expedition against the Rebels of Georgia in North America under the Orders of Archibald Campbell Esquire Lieut. Colol. of His Majesty's 71st Regimt. 1778.* Darien, Ga.: Ashantilly Press, 1981.
Carman, Harry J., ed. *American Husbandry.* New York: Columbia University Press, 1939. Contains description of the Georgia backcountry by an anonymous planter.
The Case of the Inhabitants of East Florida. St. Augustine, East Florida: Printed by John Wells, 1784.
Charlton, Lionel. *History of Whitby.* York: Printed by A. Ward, 1779.
Coker, C. F. W., ed. "Journal of John Graham, South Carolina Militia, 1779." *Military Collector and Historian* 19 (Summer 1967): 35–47.
Corbitt, D. E., ed. "Papers Relating to the Georgia-Florida Frontier, 1784–1800." *GHQ* 19, 20 (December 1936)–25 (June 1941). Translations of Documents in Archivo Nacional de Cuba.
Davis, Robert S., Jr. *Quaker Records in Georgia, Wrightsborough, 1773–1793, Friendsborough, 1776–1777.* Roswell, Ga.: Augusta Genealogical Society, 1986.

Day, Charles. *Five Years Residence in the West Indies*. London: Colburn and Company, 1852.

Drayton, John. *Memoirs of the American Revolution*. 2 vols. 1821. Reprint. New York: New York Times and Arno Press, 1969.

Dundas, George. *St. Vincent, West Indies*, N.p., N.p., 1880.

Fanning, David. "Col. David Fanning's Narrative of His Exploits and Adventures as a Loyalist of North Carolina in the American Revolution." In Walter Clark and Stephen B. Weeks, eds., *The State Records of North Carolina*. Vol. 22. Goldsboro, N.C.: Nash Brothers, 1907.

Ford, Paul Leicester. *Proceedings of a Council of War Held at Burke Jail, Georgia, January 14, 1779, with a Narrative of the Subsequent Proceedings and the Proclamation Issued by Lieut. Col. James Ingram*. Brooklyn: Historical Printing Club, 1890.

Foss, Edward. *Biographica Juridica*. London: J. Murray, 1870.

Gibbes, Robert W. *Documentary History of the American Revolution*. 1853. Reprint. 3 vols. in 1. New York: New York *Times* and Arno Press, 1971.

Grimké, John Fauchereau. "Journal of the Campaign to the Southward, May 9th to July 14th, 1778." *SCHGM* 12 (April, July, October 1911): 60–69, 118–34, 190–206.

———. "Order Book of John Fauchereau Grimké." *SCHGM* 15 (January, April, July, October 1914): 51–59, 82–90, 124–32, 166–70.

Johnson, Joseph. *Traditions and Reminiscences Chiefly of the American Revolution in the South*. Charleston: Walker and James, 1851.

Johnson, William. *Sketches of the Life and Correspondence of Nathanael Greene*. Charleston: A. E. Miller, 1822.

Johnston, Elizabeth Lichtenstein. *Recollections of a Georgia Loyalist*. 1901. Reprint. Edited by Arthur Wentworth Eaton. Spartanburg, S.C.: Reprint Company, 1972.

Lee, Henry. *Memoirs of the War in the Southern Department of the United States*. New York: University Publishing Company, 1869.

"Letters of Patrick Carr, Terror to British Loyalists, to Governors John Martin and Lyman Hall, 1782 and 1783." *GHQ* 1 (December 1917): 337–44.

Moultrie, William. *Memoirs of the American Revolution. So Far as It Related to the States of North and South Caroline and Georgia*. 1802. Reprint. 2 vols. in 1. New York: Arno Press, 1968.

"Preston Papers." *Virginia Magazine of History and Biography* 27 (July and October 1919): 313–16.

Skeat, Walter. *Nine Specimens of English Dialects*. London: Published for the English Dialect Society by H. Frowde, Oxford University Press, 1896. Includes an article by George Newton Browne.

Tarleton, Banastre. *A History of the Campaigns of 1780 and 1781 in the Southern Provinces of North America.* London: T. Cadell, 1787.

Woodward, Thomas S. *Woodward: Reminiscences of the Creek or Muscogee Indians, Contained in Letters to Friends in Georgia and Alabama.* 1859. Reprint. Birmingham: Birmingham Book Exchange, 1939.

White, George. *Historical Collections of Georgia: Containing the Most Interesting Facts, Traditions, Biographical Sketches, Anecdotes, Etc. Relating to Its History and Antiquities, from Its First Settlement to the Present Time.* New York: Pudney and Russell, 1855.

Newspapers and Periodicals

Annual Register (London)
Bahamas Gazette
East Florida Gazette
Etherington's York Chronicle
Gazette of the State of Georgia
Georgia Gazette
Georgia State Gazette or Independent Register
London Gazette
London Morning Chronicle
Royal Gazette (South Carolina)
Royal Georgia Gazette
South Carolina and American General Gazette
South Carolina Gazette
Virginia Gazette
Yorkshire Journal

Secondary Works

Books

Abbot, W. W. *The Royal Governors of Georgia, 1754–1775.* Chapel Hill: University of North Carolina Press, 1959.

Alden, John Richard. *John Stuart and the Southern Colonial Frontier: A Study of Indian Relations, War, Trade, and Land Problems in the Southern Wilderness, 1754–1775.* 1944. Reprint. New York: Gordian Press, 1966.

Augusta Unit, Federal Writers Project in Georgia, Works Progress Administration. *Augusta.* Augusta: City Council of Augusta, 1938.

Bailyn, Bernard. *Voyagers to the West.* New York: Knopf, 1986.

Bell, Malcolm, Jr. *Major Butler's Legacy: Five Generations of a Slaveholding Family.* Athens: University of Georgia Press, 1987.

Bennett, Charles E. *Florida's "French" Revolution, 1793–1795*. Gainesville: University Presses of Florida, 1981.
———. *Southernmost Battlefields of the Revolution*. Bailey's Crossroads, Va.: Privately published, 1970.
Boatner, Mark Mayo III. *Encyclopedia of the American Revolution*. New York: David McKay, 1966.
Burke, Sir Bernard. *A Genealogical History of the Dormant, Abeyant, Forfeited, and Extinct Peerages of the British Empire*. London: Harrison, 1866.
Cameron, Viola Root. *Emigrants from Scotland to America, 1774–1775*. Baltimore: Genealogical Publishing Co., 1965.
Caughey, John Walton. *McGillivray of the Creeks*. Norman: University of Oklahoma Press, 1959.
Cashin, Edward J., ed. *Colonial Augusta: "Key of the Indian Countrey."* Macon, Ga.: Mercer University Press, 1986.
———, and Heard Robertson. *Augusta and the American Revolution*. Darien, Ga.: Ashantilly Press, 1975.
Chapman, John A. *History of Edgefield County from the Earliest Settlements to 1877*. 1897. Reprint. Spartanburg, S.C.: Reprint Company, 1980.
Clouston, J. Storer. *A History of Orkney*. Kirkwall: W. R. Mackintosh, 1932.
Coker, William S., and Thomas D. Watson. *Indian Traders of the Southeastern Spanish Borderlands: Panton, Leslie and Company and John Forbes and Company, 1783–1847*. Gainesville: University Presses of Florida, 1985.
Coleman, Kenneth. *The American Revolution in Georgia, 1763–1789*. Athens: University of Georgia Press, 1958.
———. *Colonial Georgia: A History*. New York: Charles Scribner's Sons, 1976.
Corkran, David H. *The Creek Frontier, 1540–1783*. The Civilization of the American Indian Series. Norman: University of Oklahoma Press, 1967.
Coulter, E. Merton. *Georgia, A Short History*. Chapel Hill: University of North Carolina Press, 1960.
Davis, Harold E. *The Fledgling Province: Social and Cultural Life in Colonial Georgia, 1733–1776*. Chapel Hill: University of North Carolina Press, 1976.
Davis, Robert S., Jr. *Encounters on a March through Georgia in 1779*. Sylvania, Ga.: Partridge Pond Press, 1986.
———. *Georgia Citizens and Soldiers of the American Revolution*. Easley, S.C.: Southern Historical Press, 1979.
———, ed. *The Wilkes County Papers, 1773–1833*. Easley, S.C.: Southern Historical Press, 1979.
DeVorsey, Louis, Jr. *The Indian Boundary in the Southern Colonies, 1763–1775*. Chapel Hill: University of North Carolina Press, 1966.

Duncan, Ebenezer. *A Brief History of Saint Vincent.* Kingstown, St. Vincent: E. Duncan, 1941.

Fenton, Alexander. *The Northern Isles, Orkney and Shetland.* Edinburgh: Donald, 1978.

Foster, William Omer. *James Jackson, Duelist and Militant Statesman, 1757–1806.* Athens: University of Georgia Press, 1960.

Gamble, Thomas. *Savannah Duels and Duellists, 1733–1877.* Savannah: Review Publishing Company, 1923.

Gemmett, Robert J. *William Beckford.* Boston: Twayne, 1977.

Graham, J. Geoffrey. *Captain James Cook, "Servant and Friend" of Captain John Walker.* Whitby: Abbey Press, 1986.

Hemperley, Marion R. *English Crown Grants in St. Paul Parish in Georgia, 1755–1775.* Atlanta: State Printing Office, 1974.

Higgins, W. Robert, ed. *The Revolutionary War in the South: Power, Conflict and Leadership.* Durham: Duke University Press, 1979.

Hoffman, Ronald, Thad W. Tate, and Peter J. Albert, eds. *An Uncivil War: The Southern Backcountry during the American Revolution.* Charlottesville: University Press of Virginia, 1985.

Hossack, B. H. *Kirkwall in the Orkneys.* Kirkwall: William Peace and Son, 1900.

Jackson, Harvey H. *Lachlan McIntosh and the Politics of Revolutionary Georgia.* Athens: University of Georgia Press, 1979.

Jackson, Harvey H., and Phinizy Spalding, eds. *Forty Years of Diversity: Essays on Colonial Georgia.* Athens: University of Georgia Press, 1984.

Jenkins, Charles F. *Button Gwinnett, Signer of the Declaration of Independence.* New York: Doubleday, Page, 1926.

Johnston, Edith Duncan. *The Houstouns of Georgia.* Athens: University of Georgia Press, 1950.

Jones, Charles C., Jr. *The History of Georgia.* 2 vols. Boston: Houghton Mifflin, 1883.

Jones, Dorothy, comp. *Wrightsborough, 1768, Wrightsboro, 1799, McDuffie County, Georgia, 1870.* Thomson, Ga.: Wrightsboro Quaker Community Foundation, 1982.

Kendall, Hugh P. *The Streets of Whitby and Their Associations.* Whitby: Whitby Literary and Philosophical Society, 1976.

Koenig, W. J., and S. L. Mayer. *European Sources of the American Revolution.* Epping, Eng.: Bowker, 1974.

Lambert, Robert Stansbury. *South Carolina Loyalists in the American Revolution.* Columbia: University of South Carolina Press, 1987.

Lawrence, Alexander A. *Storm over Savannah: The Story of Count D'Estaing and the Siege of the Town in 1779.* Athens: University of Georgia Press, 1951.

Lefferts, Charles M. *Uniforms of the American, British, French, and German*

Armies in the War of the American Revolution. Old Greeenwich, Conn.: We, Inc., 1971.

Lockey, Joseph Byrne. *East Florida, 1783–1785*. Edited by John Walton Caughey. Berkeley and Los Angeles: University of California Press, 1949.

Lumpkin, Henry. *From Savannah to Yorktown: The American Revolution in the South*. Columbia: University of South Carolina Press, 1981.

M'Call, Hugh. *The History of Georgia, Containing Brief Sketches of the Most Remarkable Events Up to the Present Day (1784)*. 2 vols. 1811–16. Reprint. 2 vols in 1. Atlanta: Cherokee Publishing Company, 1969.

McCrady, Edward. *The History of South Carolina in the Revolution, 1775–1780*. New York: Macmillan, 1901.

Moss, Bobby Gilmer. *Roster of South Carolina Patriots in the American Revolution*. Baltimore: Genealogical Publishing Co., 1983.

Mowat, Charles Loch. *East Florida as a British Province, 1763–1784*. 1943. Reprint. Gainesville: University Presses of Florida, 1964.

Nelson, Paul David. *Anthony Wayne, Soldier of the Early Republic*. Bloomington: Indiana University Press, 1985.

Norton, Mary Beth. *The British-Americans: The Loyalist Exiles in England, 1774–1789*. Boston: Little, Brown, 1972.

O'Donnell, James H. III. *Southern Indians in the American Revolution*. Knoxville: University of Tennessee Press, 1973.

Page, William, ed. *The Victoria History of the County of York North Riding*. 2 vols. London: Constable, 1914, 1923.

Palmer, Gregory, ed. *A Bibliography of Loyalist Source Material in the United States, Canada and Great Britain*. Westport and London: Meckler Publishing in association with the American Antiquarian Society, 1982.

Pancake, John S. *This Destructive War: The British Campaign in the Carolinas, 1780–1782*. University, Ala.: University of Alabama Press, 1985.

Preston, Clarence. *Captain William Scoresby, 1760–1829: Whitby's Most Successful Whaler*. 1964. Reprint. Whitby: Whitby Literary and Philosophical Society, 1972.

Proctor, Samuel ed. *Eighteenth Century Florida and the Revolutionary South*. Gainesville: University Presses of Florida, 1978.

Ramsay, David. *History of South Carolina from Its First Settlement in 1670 to the Year 1808*. 2 vols. 1858. Reprint. Spartanburg: Reprint Company, 1968.

Riley, Sandra. *Homeward Bound: A History of the Bahama Islands to 1850 with a Definitive Study of Abaco in the American Loyalist Plantation Period*. Miami: Island Research, 1983.

Searcy, Martha Condray. *The Georgia-Florida Contest in the American*

Revolution, 1776–1778. University, Ala.: University of Alabama Press, 1985.

Shephard, Charles. *An Historical Account of the Island of Saint Vincent.* 1831. Reprint. London: Frank Cass, 1971.

Siebert, Wilbur Henry. *Loyalists in East Florida, 1774 to 1783: The Most Important Documents Pertaining Thereto, Edited with an Accompanying Narrative.* 2 vols. Deland: Florida State Historical Society, 1929.

Stevens, William Bacon. *A History of Georgia.* 2 vols. Philadelphia: D. Appleton and Co., 1859.

Tanner, Helen Hornbeck. *Zespedes in East Florida, 1784–1790.* Coral Gables: University of Miami Press, 1963.

Tillman, Mamie Norris, and Hortense Woodson, eds. *The Hammond Family of Edgefield District.* Edgefield, S.C.: Advertiser Press, 1954.

Waterbury, Jean Parker, ed. *The Oldest City, St. Augustine: Saga of Survival.* St. Augustine: St. Augustine Historical Society, 1983.

Weir, Robert M. *Colonial South Carolina: A History.* Millwood, N.Y.: KTO Press, 1983.

Weston, William Jayns. *The North Riding of Yorkshire.* Cambridge, Eng.: University Press, 1919.

Willard, Margaret Wheeler, ed. *Letters on the American Revolution, 1774–1776.* Boston: Houghton Mifflin, 1925.

Wilson, Philip Whitwell. *William Pitt the Younger.* Garden City, N.Y.: Doubleday, Doran, 1930.

Wright, J. Leitch, Jr. *Britain and the American Frontier, 1783–1815.* Athens: University of Georgia Press, 1975.

———. *British St. Augustine.* St. Augustine: Historic St. Augustine Preservation Board, 1975.

———. *Florida in the American Revolution.* Gainesville: University Presses of Florida, 1975.

———. *William Augustus Bowles, Director General of the Creek Nation.* Athens: University of Georgia Press, 1967.

Articles

Ashmore, Otis, and C. H. Olmstead, "The Battles of Kettle Creek and Briar Creek," *GHQ* 10 (June 1926): 85–125.

Bast, Homer. "Creek Indian Affairs, 1775–1778." *GHQ* 33 (March 1949): 1–25.

Berends, A. A. "The Stone Horse Had Like to Been Down." *Whitby Literary and Philosophical Society Annual Report, 1982,* 16–19.

Cann, Marvin L. "War in the Backcountry: The Siege of Ninety-Six, May 22–June 19, 1781." *SCHM* 72 (January 1971): 1–14.

Cashin, Edward J. "'The Famous Colonel Wells': Factionalism in Revolutionary Georgia." *GHQ* 58, Suppl. (1974): 137–56.
————. "George Walton and the Forged Letter." *GHQ* 62 (Summer 1978): 133–45.
————. "Nathanael Greene's Campaign for Georgia in 1781." *GHQ* 61 (Spring 1977): 43–58.
————. "The Trembling Land: Covert Activity in the Georgia Backcountry during the American Revolution." *Proceedings and Papers of the Georgia Association of Historians 1982* (Marietta, Ga.: Georgia Association of Historians, 1983), 31–39.
Cole, Richard C. "The Siege of Savannah and the British Press, 1779–1780." *GHQ* 65 (Fall 1981): 189–202.
Coleman, Kenneth. "Restored Colonial Georgia, 1779–1782." *GHQ* 40 (March 1956): 1–20.
Davis, Robert S., Jr. "Captain Edward Barnard and the Ceded Lands Rangers." *Georgia Pioneers Genealogical Magazine* 15 (February 1978): 20–22.
————. "George Galphin and the Creek Congress of 1777." *Proceedings and Papers of the Georgia Association of Historians 1982* (Marietta, Ga.: Georgia Association of Historians, 1983), pp. 13–29.
————. "The Last Colonial Enthusiast: Captain William Manson in Revolutionary Georgia." *Atlanta Historical Journal* 28 (Spring 1984): 23–38.
Downes, Randolph C. "Creek-American Relations, 1782–1790." *GHQ* 21 (June 1937): 142–84.
Harris, Waldo P. III. "Locations Associated with Daniel Marshall and the Kiokee Church." *Viewpoints, Georgia Baptist History* 6 (1978): 25–44.
Heidler, David S. "The American Defeat at Briar Creek." *GHQ* 67 (Fall 1982): 317–31.
Hitz, Alex. "The Earliest Settlements in Wilkes County." *GHQ* 40 (September 1956): 260–80.
Jackson, Harvey H. "The Battle of the Riceboats: Georgia Joins the Revolution." *GHQ* 68 (Summer 1974): 229–43.
————. "Consensus and Conflict: Factional Politics in Revolutionary Georgia." *GHQ* 59 (Winter 1975): 388–401.
Jones, George Fenwick. "A Note on the Victor at Springhill Redoubt." *GHQ* 64 (Fall 1979): 377–79.
Lambert, Robert S. "The Confiscation of Loyalist Property in Georgia, 1782–1786." *William and Mary Quarterly* 20 (January 1963): 80–94.
Lawrence, Alexander A. "General Lachlan McIntosh and His Suspension from Continental Command during the Revolution." *GHQ* 38 (June 1954): 101–41.

———. "General Robert Howe and the British Capture of Savannah in 1778." *GHQ* 36 (December 1952): 303–27.

Miller, Randall M., ed. "A Backcountry Loyalist Plan to Retake Georgia and the Carolinas, 1778." *SCHM* 75 (1974): 207–14.

Mitchell, Robert G. "The Losses and Compensation of Georgia Loyalists." *GHQ* 68 (Summer 1984): 233–43.

Naisawald, L. Van Loan. "Major General Howe's Activities in South Carolina and Georgia, 1776–1779." *GHQ* 35 (March 1951): 23–30.

Nunis, Doyce B., Jr. "Colonel Archibald Campbell's March from Savannah to Augusta, 1779." *GHQ* 45 (September 1961): 275–86.

O'Donnell, James. "Alexander McGillivray: Training for Leadership, 1777–1783." *GHQ* 49 (June 1965): 172–86.

———. "A Loyalist View of the Drayton-Tennent-Hart Mission to the Upcountry." *SCHM* 67 (January 1966): 15–28.

Olson, Gary D. "David Ramsay and Lt. Colonel Thomas Brown: Patriot Historian and Loyalist Critic." *SCHM* 77 (October 1976): 257–67.

———. "Loyalists and the American Revolution: Thomas Brown and the South Carolina Backcountry, 1775–1776." *SCHM* 68 (October 1967): 201–19; 69 (January 1968): 44–56.

———. "Thomas Brown, Partisan, and the Revolutionary War in Georgia, 1777–1782." *GHQ* 44 (Spring 1970): 1–19; (Summer 1970):183–208.

Robertson, Heard. "Notes on the Muster Rolls of Lieutenant Colonel Thomas Brown's Battalion of Loyalist Provincial Rangers, 1776–1782." *Richmond County History* 4 (1972): 5–15.

———. "The Second British Occupation of Augusta." *GHQ* 58 (Winter 1974): 422–46.

Searcy, Martha Condray. "1779: The First Year of the British Occupation of Georgia." *GHQ* 67 (Summer 1983): 168–88.

Simms, William G. "Joscelyn: A Tale of the Revolution." *Old Guard: A Monthly Magazine Devoted to the Principles of 1776 and 1787* 5 (January–December 1867): 1–17, 91–103, 161–76, 241–60, 321–39, 401–21, 481–500, 561–76, 668–81, 731–45, 822–34, 897–935.

Wright, J. Leitch, Jr. "Creek-American Treaty of 1790: Alexander McGillivray and the Diplomacy of the Old Southwest." *GHQ* 51 (December 1967): 379–400.

Zimmer, Anne Y. "The Rhetoric of American Loyalism." *GHQ* 66 (Summer 1982): 145–58.

Dissertations and Theses

Braund, Kathryn E. "Mutual Convenience—Mutual Dependence: The Creeks, Augusta and the Deerskin Trade, 1733–1783." Ph.D. dissertation, Florida State University, 1986.

Mitchell, Robert Gary. "Loyalist Georgia." Ph.D. dissertation, Tulane University, 1964.

Peters, Thelma Peterson. "The American Loyalists and the Plantation Period in the Bahamas Islands." Ph.D. dissertation, University of Florida, 1960.

Searcy, Martha Condray. "Thomas Browne: Loyalist." Master's thesis, Louisiana State University, 1972. The author used the name Martha Condray Searcy Cohn at the time.

Sheftall, John McKay. "George Galphin and Indian-White Relations in the Georgia Backcountry during the American Revolution." M.A. thesis, University of Virginia, 1983.

Smith, W. Calvin. "Georgia Gentlemen: The Habershams of Eighteenth-Century Savannah." Ph.D. dissertation, University of North Carolina, 1971.

Wright, Homer E. "Diplomacy of Trade on the Southern Frontier: A Case Study of the Influence of William Panton and John Forbes, 1784–1817." Ph.D. dissertation, University of Georgia, 1971.

Moultrie, John, 168, 188
Moultrie, William, 96–97
Mount Young, 201
Mullryne, John, 24
Murray, Alexander, 179, 182
Murray, John (fourth earl of
  Dunmore), 178–86, 189, 227,
  325 (n. 9), 238
Murray, Patrick, 65, 78
Musgrove's Mill, Battle of, 113, 115

New Richmond, 20, 27, 53
Newton, Isaac, 4
Newton House, xi, 6, 190, 193–94,
  200, 202, 213–14, 296 (n. 14)
Ninety-Six: Treaty of, 31–33;
  Second Treaty of, 36; Loyalists
  of join Brown, 75; occupied by
  British, 105, 108–10, 112;
  increasing disaffection, 113, 121,
  128; Cruger relieves Brown,
  116–17, besieged by Greene, 131,
  138
Nootka Sound, 186
North, Frederick Lord, ix, 16, 39,
  152, 166

Obman, Jacob, 156
Oconee River, 10, 15–16, 49, 160
Ogeechee River, 10, 15, 46, 54, 67
Oglethorpe, James Edward, 20,
  107, 209
Okfuskees, 72
Old Town, 46, 67–68, 88
Oliver, Thomas, 7
Olson, Gary, 221
O'Neill, Arturo, 184
Opeitley Mico, 88
O'Reilly, Fr. Michael, 168, 187
Orkney Islands, xi, 8, 41, 296
  (n. 19)
Ottley, Drewry, 199–200

Pace, James, 320 (n. 7)
Panton, Leslie and Company, 185,
  187, 226
Panton, William, 175, 179, 185–86
Park, James Alan, 206
Parker, Hyde, 84
Parker, Sir Peter, 51
Paterson, James, 103, 105
Paul, Robert, 199
Pearis, Richard, 36, 108, 110, 133,
  165, 175, 181–82
Peirson, Ann Brown, 194
Pensacola, 54, 145
Perryman, 58, 81, 169, 184
Phillips, Robert, 50, 52, 58, 90
Philoutougi, 61
Pickens, Andrew, 30, 36, 92–94,
  108, 119, 128–29, 131, 136–37,
  150, 155, 243, 331 (n. 29)
Pinckney, Charles, 77
Pitt, William, 169, 175, 182,
  186–87, 196, 201
Porbeck, Fredrich von, 100, 130
Powell, James Edward, 175, 179
Pressick, George, 7
Prevost, Augustine, 243;
  disapproves of Rangers, 59,
  65–67, 74; opposes invasion,
  71–73; gains command of
  Rangers, 75–77, 79; invades
  Georgia, 81–82, 84–86; warns
  Indians, 92–93; recommends
  Brown, 95; invades South
  Carolina, 96–99; defense of
  Savannah, 100, 102–5; leaves
  Georgia, 105–6
Prevost, George, 101, 313 (n. 54)
Prevost, James Mark, 64–65, 74,
  78–80, 92, 94
Prince Frederick, 2
Provincial Congress, 21–22, 40
Pulaski, Count Casimir, 100
Pumpkin King, 15